Parliamentary History

Parliamentary History

A Yearbook

Volume 2
1983

ALAN SUTTON
ST. MARTIN'S PRESS

Alan Sutton Publishing Limited
17a Brunswick Road
Gloucester GL1 1HG

St Martin's Press
175 Fifth Avenue
New York, NY 10010

First Published in Great Britain in 1983
First Published in the United States of America in 1984

British Library Cataloguing in Publication Data

Parliamentary history. — Vol.2 —
   1. **Great Britain.** *Parliament* — **History** —
   Periodicals
   328.41'005   **JN500**

Alan Sutton edition
ISBN 0-86299-065-3
ISSN 0264-2824

St Martin's Press edition
ISBN 0-312-59721-5
ISSN 0264-2824

Typesetting and origination by
Alan Sutton Publishing Limited.
Photoset Bembo 10/11.
Printed in Great Britain

PARLIAMENTARY HISTORY

A Yearbook

Published by Alan Sutton Publishing Limited and St. Martin's Press for The Parliamentary History Yearbook Trust.

Grateful thanks are due to Shell U.K. Limited and the Twenty-Seven Foundation for their generous grants towards publication.

Cover illustration: 'Ready Mony the prevailing Candidate, or the Humours of an Election' [1727], reproduced by permission of the Trustees of the British Museum.

All contributions (which must not be longer than 10,000 words) should be typed on A4 paper (double spacing throughout), with footnotes typed separately. 'Notes for Authors' are available on request

Articles, notes and documents, and other material submitted for publication should be sent to the Editor, Eveline Cruickshanks, at the Institute of Historical Research, Annexe, 34 Tavistock Square, London WC1H 9EZ; or, in the U.S.A. and Canada, to Richard Davis (Chairman of the American Associate Committee) at the Department of History, Washington University, St Louis, Missouri 63130; books for review and completed reviews to the Reviews Editor, David Hayton, also at 34 Tavistock Square, London WC1H 9EZ.

CONTENTS

10 *Contents*

Parliamentary History, Volume 2 (1983)

THE MANAGEMENT OF THE ELIZABETHAN HOUSE OF COMMONS: THE COUNCIL'S 'MEN-OF-BUSINESS'

M.A.R. GRAVES

University of Auckland

Management was a subject which exercised the minds of Elizabethan Privy Councillors at the approach of each parliamentary session. It has also commanded the attention of Wallace Notestein and Sir John Neale, both of whom conceived of Parliament as a national political arena, rather than as a market-place of legislative business; as an occasion for friction, conflict, criticism of — and resistance to — royal policies, rather than as an exercise in co-operation.[1] Indeed Neale's specific purpose was 'to banish the old illusion that early-Stuart Parliaments had few roots in the sixteenth century'.[2] He found what he was looking for: a more independent, even obstreperous Commons, and frequent, if not persistent, opposition — particularly that novel phenomenon the 'Puritan choir', an *organized* opposition which was characterized by pre-session planning and a positive programme of its own. The 'choir', under the informal leadership of Thomas Norton, was active and disruptive in three successive sessions (1563, 1566–7, 1571). And it dominated Parliament with its campaigns for the Queen's marriage, settlement of the Succession, ecclesiastical reform, and punitive laws against the Catholics.[3]

In this increasingly disturbed parliamentary climate, management must have assumed a special significance for the government. Faced with the challenge of an organized Puritan opposition, the Council's specific managerial objective was to neutralize or defeat it and to push through official business despite it. Neale provided seemingly persuasive evidence of the existence of such an opposition. However, that evidence requires brief examination, if only to resolve the identity crisis which some of his opposition politicians must have suffered when they began to figure in successive drafts of this article as unofficial managers *on behalf of* the Privy Council. Neale's evidence is of three kinds. Most important, and indeed the very foundation of his thesis, is the famous 'Puritan choir' document, styled a 'lewde pasquyle' and dated 1566.[4] There is no longer any need to dwell on it at length.[5] It lists 43 Members, each one with accompanying descriptive tags. Some describe parliamentary episodes,[6] but nowhere is there a hint that these men were members of a Puritan party engaged in organized and rebellious courses against the Queen. The list excludes zealous Protestants and Marian exiles such as Nicholas and Clement Throckmorton, Anthony Cooke and James Morice; yet it includes moderate loyalists such as William Fleetwood, inveterate conservatives like Francis Alford, and such courtier-politicians as Robert Newdigate and Henry Goodere. Moreover, amongst the most prominent of this motley 'choir' were several lawyers and a City merchant who will shortly appear in a very different guise: Robert Bell, William Fleetwood, John Marshe, Thomas Norton and Christopher Yelverton.[7]

At the very end of the pasquil the anonymous author provides a vital clue as to its meaning:

> As for the reste
> theye be at Devotion
> and when theye be prest
> theye crye a good motion

He derides the majority, mindlessly following the bold and articulate who are described variously as 'orator, jangler, wrangler, glorious [i.e. boastful], merry, weary, pacifier, crier, earnest, hottest', and even 'drudger' — one remembers a bore as much as an orator. The pasquil is neither a party list nor a serious commentary on the politics and religion of those named, but a frivolous lampoon. 'Choir' does not mean collaboration, marching in unison to a Puritan battle hymn, but the fact that these men were vocal, not silent. The pasquil should be assigned to the world of political graffiti, not to that of organized parliamentary parties.

Neale's second form of evidence turns out, on closer inspection, to be a mere association of ideas. He built on to the pasquil a fabric of supposition and assertion, repeatedly referring to this 'troublesome forty-three' or 'our choir'.[8] So a Member agitating for a settled Succession was 'possibly one of our "choir"'; when Dean Nowell preached a radical sermon at the opening of Parliament in 1563, 'what an incitement [it] must have been to our troublesome forty-three'; a Commons' agitation 'undoubtedly included many of our "choir"'; and when an official proposal was forced to a division and only narrowly passed, 'our "choir", we may be sure, aided that hostile vote'.[9] Underlying all is the assumption that there did exist a clearly identifiable organized and radical opposition. And it is an assumption reinforced by Neale's insistence that to assume the contrary 'would be childish'.[10] However, when the lewd pasquil is exposed for what it is and the framework of his assumptions is dismantled, there remains only one piece of evidence to identify Norton, Bell, William Strickland and other 'choristers' as opposition Puritans: the religious campaign of 1571.

The object of that campaign was to enact the *Reformatio Legum*

Ecclesiasticarum,[11] six bills on religion,[12] and a revised version of the Book of Common Prayer. The technique adopted was for William Strickland to deliver an address on the *Reformatio* and, two days later, on the A, B, C Bills, and then for Norton to exhibit them to the House. There can be no doubt that these were rehearsed moves, but who organized them? There is no evidence to support Neale's insistence that there 'must have been party organization' behind them.[13] Furthermore Strickland and Norton publicly disagreed in the Commons over the authorship of the *Reformatio*.[14] It was hardly an encouraging start to a co-ordinated and rehearsed opposition campaign. Most important of all, the only genuinely radical proposal was Strickland's Prayer Book Bill, for which Norton demonstrated no support. The latter certainly advocated the *Reformatio*. His father-in-law, Thomas Cranmer, had bequeathed a copy to him, and he had recently lent it to John Foxe who had seen it through the press, with the approval of Archbishop Parker of Canterbury.[15] Norton also lent his support to the A, B, C Bills, which dealt with the condition of the Church and the quality of its clergy. He was rigorous in his insistence that the Church's defence against Catholicism depended upon the elimination of such abuses. As he told the Commons, 'hee was of [Mr Strickland's] mynde chiefelie for the avoiding and suppressing of Symoniacall ingrossementes'. Over a decade later, in 1582, his views had not changed. When he wrote a set of devices for the rooting out of papistry, in response to Sir Francis Walsingham's request, he could not resist a broadside against clerical abuses:

> [I] doe accompt non residence in state of sinne, and so damnable . . . [A]s bushoppe Cranmer sayd he might as well give his sister a benefice as to one that should serve it by a curate.

He then passed on to an attack on simony and corrupt presentations.[16] Norton's objectives did not vary, and they enjoyed continuous support from the no less consistent Council and episcopate. When the A, B, C Bills had been introduced for the first time, in the parliamentary session of 1566, 15 bishops had petitioned against the Queen's veto of Bill A.[17] Indeed Norton, bishops, Councillors, and Commons favoured both the A, B, C Bills and the *Reformatio*. In contrast Strickland's Prayer Book Bill was a radical proposal and a sole effort. It seems to have infuriated the Queen and it certainly angered the bishops, who realized that it jeopardized the success of all the other measures. Strickland was probably an anti-episcopalian Puritan. For once the 'lewde pasquyle' may have got it right with its legend: 'Josiah slew all the priests of the high places'.[18] But this does not apply to Norton, who was working in concert with men in high places. The whole episode looks very much like an official attempt to coerce the Queen — an attempt which came unstuck when the Council and its episcopal allies placed their trust not only in the reliable Norton but in Strickland, whose zeal outran his discretion.

Once the mythical nature of the 'Puritan choir' has been acknowledged, the official orchestration of the 1571 'campaign' has been divined, and the presbyterian campaigns in the Commons during the 1580s are recognized for what they were — damp squibs, engineered by a handful of Members and fizzling out under prompt conciliar action — Elizabethan parliamentary opposition begins to assume its right perspective. There *was* opposition: over Strickland's sequestration by the Council in 1571, the presbyterian Prayer Book Bills, and the monopolies debates in 1597 and 1601. Nor does this exhaust the catalogue of such occasions. Few of them, however, were *Puritan campaigns*, and in any case they were isolated episodes. In this respect parliamentary management was only an emergency function, to be called into play when contentious bills or issues threatened to obstruct the Council's business or frustrate its objectives. This was not the continuing and primary purpose of management.

In order to understand what was, it is necessary to descend from what has been called the 'champagne-headiness of high political drama' to 'the flat and often stale beer of parliamentary business'. Parliaments were summoned (occasionally) to give advice, (usually) to grant subsidies, and (invariably) to enact laws required by the Privy Council. These conciliar objectives were constantly threatened by too much business and too little time. An examination of acts alone gives no true indication of the volume of such business before Parliament. They constituted only the tip of the iceberg and must be combined with abortive bills in order to convey an accurate impression. The pattern seems clear enough: a sessional average of 93 bills in the Edwardian Parliaments, 48 in the Marian and 123 in the Elizabethan.[19] Moreover these may not constitute the sum totals of bills put into Parliament. In 1581 Norton, who had drafted or revised most of the acts in the session just ended, informed his dinner companions that he had also 'written many a bill of articles that the House did not see'. Were these bills which had been handed in to the Speaker but had not proceeded even to a first reading?[20]

There was also a consistent relationship between the number of bills before Parliament and the proportion which became acts: the greater the volume of business, the lower the success rate. Thus 36% of Edwardian bills became law, but when, in the Marian Parliaments, the number of bills was almost halved, 45% of them passed into law. To some extent this increase is apparent rather than real, because the Marian sessions were much shorter than those of the flanking reigns. On the other hand the workload was more equally distributed between the two Houses. The Elizabethan inundation of bills mainly affected the Commons, and it was then that the success rate dropped to 28%.[21] The figures illustrate the Privy Council's problem during Elizabeth's reign: a flood of bills in one House, many of which concerned personal, local or sectional interests — 56% of all measures in the Parliament of 1572–81 were of this kind.[22] An anonymous but obviously experienced Member understood the problem when he advised a Councillor in 1581:[23]

> Yf her Ma[jes]ties meaninge be to have the session shorte then it is good to abridge the thinges that lengthen the session w[hi]ch amongest others are these: The number of privat bills of singuler persons [and] 2. The bills of occupation, misteries and companies.

Thereby he touched on the Council's other problem: Elizabeth's preference for short sessions. There is ample evidence of conciliar concern to satisfy the near-incompatible conditions of brevity and productivity: Burghley monitoring the Commons' progress with periodic lists of bills and the stages which they had reached;[24] messages from the Lords to lay aside all private bills and give precedence to necessary commonwealth measures, especially in view of the approaching plague season;[25] a Commons committee to sort bills into an order of priority, with preference given to public business;[26] and the decision of the lower House to sit three afternoons a week, solely for the first readings of private measures — a practice shortly afterwards extended to every afternoon 'and then to proceed, as well to the second Readings of Bills'.[27] These were attempts to prevent private business from obstructing more urgent public matters during the normal morning sessions. The increasing use of committees to scrutinize bills may not have been a procedural device to improve efficiency but simply a way of removing business from the floor of the House.[28] Even then, as the backlog of bills mounted, the Commons had to appoint committees to meet during Sundays, recesses and even during the precious hours of the morning sittings.[29]

As if the pressure of business was not enough to contend with, there was always the Queen. She relentlessly drove Parliament on to finish as quickly as possible. Even in 1572, when the Bill against Mary Stuart — the very reason for which Parliament had been summoned — was before the Commons, Elizabeth harassed the House. She admonished it to lay apart 'all private Matters' in order to concentrate on that particular measure,[30] which she then required to be read on two consecutive days.[31] In this way Elizabeth sought to minimize the delays caused by rambling debate in an age when an hour-long sermon was a niggardly thing. On this occasion she came to the aid of her Council, but she also pinpointed yet another of its problems. Each man's desire to be heard, on private as well as public bills, led to lengthy and longwinded debate which could delay official business. Therefore it was the Council's concern to restrict opportunities for time-consuming discussion. Perhaps it prompted Speaker Popham who, in 1581, asked Members not to speak to bills on the first reading and to avoid 'unnecessary Motions or superfluous Arguments' in order to save time.[32] The Council in turn was advised by a Member who stressed the threat posed by 'Matters of Long Argument'. He recommended that the Speaker defer them until 'neere towarde the risinge of the howse', when time was short, thirsts long and hunger enlarged. He should not hastily reintroduce bills which had provoked lengthy debate already, whilst avoiding the impression that he was 'over-ruling or straineinge the liberties of the house'. The remedy advanced by this unknown adviser was 'the discreet interposinge of Committies', which would remove business from the Commons and tie it up indefinitely. He offered the same solution for contentious motions, for '[t]he more comitties that you make . . . the longer it wilbe ere the matter come in againe'.[33] In 1576 Speaker Bell had pre-empted this suggestion when he proposed that, in the interest of speed, any motion should be referred to a committee and discussion of it should be deferred until the committee had determined whether it warranted a bill.[34] Behind the particular advices of this Member lay a more general concern: an awareness that Members who needed time to secure the passage of their own bills knew that Parliament would only last until essential official business had been despatched. So 'such as woulde prolonge the session give as many delaies to that matter as they may'. To counter this he recommended the thorough preparation of government business before Parliament met — in particular that the subsidy bill should be 'readdie written both in paper and parchment'.[35]

In brief, speed and productivity required managerial efficiency. It was no fault of the Council that the Commons was less business-like than it might have been. Half of the Members in each new Parliament were novices.[36] They needed guidance and direction in the conduct of business. It was a point underlined by an experienced Member, William Fleetwood. In 1584 he described to Burghley the opening day in the Commons, with 'the knightes and burgeses out of all order, in troops standing upon the fflowre, making strange noises, there being not past [seven or eight] of the old parliamentes'. Committees may have been cursed with the same problem as Fleetwood reported when he was named to one chaired by Sir Walter Mildmay. It numbered 'lx at the least, all yonge gents . . . A[t] our metyng in the after noone [twenty] at ones did speak and there wee sate talking and dyd nothing untill night. So that mr Chaunc[ellor] was werie and then wee departed home'.[37] Another observant Member drew a contrast between new men, who were impetuous and 'gladdest of large parleamentes to learne and see fashiones' and the old hands who were more circumspect and attentive to business.[38]

Nor was this the sum of the Council's difficulties. It also had to combat absenteeism, which was the bane of Parliament. And yet it was understandable. Legislative business was technical, detailed and often tedious, a constant process of listening, discussing, scrutinizing and revising. First readings were literal recitals of the text: one subsidy bill took 'almost two hours' to read aloud. In one morning in 1584 Mildmay and Sir Christopher Hatton spoke for more than three hours between them.[39] Fleetwood too was no laggard in the art of bringing blissful relief to chronic insomniacs. A weary clerk noted his 'longe tedious talke nothing towching the matter in question. He tooke a theame *Res ipsa debit consilium* wherupon he replied still but to litle purpose'.[40] On one occasion he cheerfully admitted that 'you will say, I am out of the matter, but yet the best is, I will come in again'; on another he confidently informed the House, as he waded through a long speech larded with legal precedent and classical allusion (and largely irrelevant to the matter in hand), 'you would be content to hear me these two hours'; one address drifted off into a running commentary on what happened to the Bishop of Winchester's cook when someone mixed laxatives in his food; and twice he related the same lengthy tale about parliamentary bribery.[41] It is hardly surprising that parliamentary proceedings bred tedium and ennui, which, in turn, contributed to the prevalent absenteeism from the Elizabethan Commons.

Boredom was not the only enemy. Lawyers could be enticed away by the prospect of fat fees in the central law courts next door. In February 1585 Fleetwood moved that the serjeant bring back 'those of this House towards the Law, being the most part of them at the Bars in her Majesties Courts attending their Clients Causes, and neglecting the Service of this House'. The Commons concurred and they were recalled. Later that same morning Sir William Herbert drew the attention of the House to the fact that Fleetwood himself had departed and was 'presently pleading at the Common Pleas Bar, to the great abuse of this whole House'.[42] The absenteeism of lawyers, whose skills were vital to the legislative business of the Commons, could seriously impair efficiency. One Member perceived an advantage in this state of affairs when he cynically observed that, if contentious motions were referred to committees 'the longer it wilbe ere the matter come in againe, speciallie if you will appointe lawiers in terme time'.[43] However, this kind of advice was of little practical use to Councillors, who continually strove to muster sufficient expert, willing, active and experienced Members in order to overcome the problems posed by lack of time and a surfeit of business. The Privy Council's concern was inundation not confrontation, productivity not conflict.

Historians of Parliament in the Elizabethan period have not only neglected the real point and purpose of management. Frequently they have been seriously deficient in their accounts of managerial techniques, because they have confined themselves to formal, institutional and procedural devices: the Privy Council, the office of Speaker, committees, the Lords, and the royal veto.[44] What they have ignored is the socio-economic reality which filled out the formal, institutional structure of Queen, Lords and Commons. As Parliament was a meeting of the monarch and governing class, the network of connexions which interlaced that class and bonded it to the Crown were carried over into Parliament. That network also bridged the institutional gap between Lords and Commons, binding together individuals within each House *and* between the two chambers. The variety of connexions encompassed kinship, patron-client relationships, local and economic interests, political and religious loyalties, friendship, social deference and ambition. The Privy Council should not be excluded from this network. The obligation of Councillors to serve the Queen, and their special position around the chair of that royal nominee, the Speaker, formally and visibly marked them off from the rest of the House. But they were as much a part of that lattice of relationships as any other Members of Parliament.

Elizabethan politicking and the transaction of official business naturally operated through this network, not only at court and in the counties, but in Parliament too. Knights and burgesses willingly assisted the government in its pursuit of efficiency and productivity. Some did so out of loyalty to the state (Queen and Council) and the established religion, and others because of their connexion with individual Councillors. They were the Council's men-of-business, its advisers and informants, public relations officers, and even its attorneys. When that anonymous Member advised the Council to prepare its measures before Parliament assembled, he added that 'if it be not a matter too secret, it were well that some other privie of it afore'.[45] And the Council was prepared to make at least one man privy to some of its more confidential parliamentary intentions: Thomas Norton. Neale portrayed him as the leading light of an organized Puritan opposition. In fact he was the most impressive of all the Council's men-of-business. A practising lawyer in the City with an impeccable Protestant pedigree, he was admirably equipped to serve the government's turn.[46] His official duties as the first remembrancer (or secretary) to the lord mayor of London between 1571 and 1584, acting as middleman between royal and City government, drew him into the Council's service on a variety of commissions and other activities. His virulent anti-Catholicism made him even more valuable. So Norton became an 'establishment' man with friends and allies in high places, amongst them Buckhurst, Leicester, Archbishop Parker and Bishop Whitgift, the City's recorder, William Fleetwood, and the Lord Keeper, Nicholas Bacon.[47] At the very centre, the Privy Council, Mildmay was his long-time parliamentary collaborator, whilst his patrons included Hatton, Walsingham and above all Burghley. It was to them that he appealed when he fell foul of the Queen and was imprisoned in 1581–2 and 1583–4.[48] Even whilst Norton was in detention Walsingham requested from him a set of devices for rooting out papistry, and he produced for Burghley a draft justification (eventually published under the Lord Treasurer's name) of the government's treatment of Catholics.[49]

Norton's parliamentary record has been examined in detail elsewhere[50] and so need not be recited here. His record speaks for itself: that he was not transmuted from a loyalist into a Puritan opposition leader when he took his seat in the Commons but that, on the contrary, he consistently served the Council: in debate and committee and above all as a parliamentary draftsman. Although he was, in no sense, a Council 'employee', a paid agent, he frequently collaborated with Councillors: on the subjects of marriage and Succession in 1563–6/7, on the 'great cause' against Mary Stuart in 1572; against promoters in 1576; and in 1581, when he endorsed Mildmay's request for a subsidy and more biting laws against the Catholics, dominated the committee appointed to consider these, and ended up drafting the requisite bills.[51] This collaboration expressed not only Norton's personal connexion with individual Councillors, but also his political loyalty to the Council as a body. His devotion to the monarch was unquestionable, paraded in his writings and speeches. In practice, however, he consistently allied himself with the Council, not only to hurry the Commons along, but also to pressurize an obstinate, vacillating Queen for her own good. He once told friends at a dinner party that all he had done in Parliament was for the Privy Council, 'my chefest care', because, '[i]t is the wheeles of the councell that hould the chariott of England upright'.[52]

Norton was peerless, but he was not unique. The Commons always included men willing to serve. Whatever their motives, their role was to promote Council business. Inevitably their usefulness varied and at worst they could be an embarrassment. In 1571 Robert Newdigate moved for a subsidy, 'w[hi]ch speech was not liked of by the House'.[53] Irritated Members embarked instead on a wide-ranging criticism of administrative abuses. Henry Goodere compounded the Council's difficulties when he rose to argue that the House should cease its complaints and concentrate on the subsidy alone — as another Member caustically observed, 'sure hee showed a greate desire to winne favour'.[54] By flouting the convention that a Councillor should request supply, Newdigate and Goodere[55] simply piqued prickly Members into indignant defensive action. The anonymous adviser to the Council in 1581 pointed out that such conduct would cause 'some humerous bodie [to raise] some question of the liberties of the howse . . . and assuredlie w[i]th longe speeches to the troublesome prolonginge of the session'.[56] Nor were Newdigate and Goodere alone in their disconcerting demonstrations of ham-fisted loyalty. Sir Humphrey Gilbert's condemnation of the complaints against administrative abuses, and his warning that it was 'perilous' to debate the prerogative, was 'misliked' by many. Peter Wentworth was provoked to call him 'a flatterer, a lyer, and a naughtie man' and to compare him to the chameleon 'which can change himselfe into all coulours saveinge white . . . [and] to all fashions but honestie'.[57]

These men were politically naïve. They were no help but even a hindrance to the realization of conciliar designs. In contrast were those who abstained from brash declarations of loyalty — bound to be interpreted as obsequiousness — and instead busied themselves in the quiet, constructive service of the Privy Council. Their value depended on their recognition of two basic requirements of parliamentary service: not to ruffle the Commons' sensitivity about its privileges;[58] and to support the Council's policies, even when they were at variance with the Queen's, as they often were.[59] The Council's effective men-of-business were those who fulfilled these two conditions. It cannot be over-emphasized that these men did *not* constitute either a formal organized network of agents or a party. Membership of the group was fluid, constantly changing, often ephemeral, and the range of its ability considerable. At one end of the spectrum were those whose advice and assistance were occasional, albeit opportune. Thomas Dan(n)et(t), William Cecil's cousin and Member for a Seymour constituency (Marlborough), favoured the Grey claim to the Succession in the 1563–6/7 Parliament and, with Thomas Digges, spurred on the hunt for Norfolk and Mary Stuart in 1572.[60] William Humphrey, Cecil's business agent, kept him informed of the progress of the Battery and Mineral Works Bill in 1566,[61] whilst a Mr Melvyn reported on James Dalton's inflammatory speech against the Scottish queen,[62] and an unknown Member advised the Council on the choice of John Popham or George Bromley as Speaker in 1581.[63]

A second group of men-of-business were the professional lawyers, using Parliament as a stepping-stone to greater things. Typical examples were Richard Onslow, Robert Bell, John Popham and Christopher Yelverton (Speakers of the House of Commons in 1566/7, 1572–6, 1581 and 1597 respectively), Thomas Bromley and Thomas Wilbraham. The usual career progression was from borough service, *via* Parliament, to high office in the state. So Popham and Yelverton began as recorders of Bristol and North-ampton and ended as judges of Queen's Bench. Bromley, Onslow and Wilbraham rose from the recordership of London to become Lord Chancel-lor, Solicitor-General and attorney of the Court of Wards respectively.[64] This did not rob them of the capacity to take an independent stand in Parliament. So, in 1571, Bell insisted that the Queen's prerogative 'might and ought to be spoken yn that Howse', whilst Yelverton held forth on the Commons' liberties.[65] Their parliamentary services to the Council, however, more than compensated for their occasional lapses from grace.

These rising lawyers were connected by a professional affinity and 'old school' ties, not only with each other, but with members of the Privy Council. After all, during the 1570s two of their number, Bromley and Popham, became Councillors, whilst their fellows at the board included the Lord Keeper, Sir Nicholas Bacon, William Cecil, Walter Mildmay and Francis Walsingham (all of Gray's Inn). Their natural parliamentary alliance with the Queen's advisers can be no matter for surprise. Nevertheless they were not, for the most part, the Council's regular men-of-business in the Commons. Those who were constituted a separate, third group which, however, had significant connexions with Bell, Bromley and the other parliamentary lawyers. They were a motley crowd, including the Com-mons clerks who (if Fulk Onslow is any guide) may have kept Cecil informed of proceedings,[66] and the knights and burgesses of London. Prominent amongst the latter were Thomas Aldersey, Sir Rowland Hey-ward and John Marshe.[67] Paramount was Thomas Norton, but not far behind him was William Fleetwood, London's recorder between 1571 and 1592. The City's Members were amongst the most active Parliament-men. In 1581 Aldersey was appointed to 18 committees and three joint confer-ences, Fleetwood to 17 and five, Heyward to 12 and two, and Norton to 26 and five. Between 1571 and 1581 (and apart from Privy Councillors) Norton was first, Fleetwood fifth, Aldersey eighth and Heyward eighteenth in the frequency of their recorded appointments to committees — and this in a House which, in the same period, grew from 422 to 440 Members.[68]

Norton and Fleetwood constituted the axis of the London Members: both lawyers and, from 1571 on, both important City officials. In the sessions of 1571–81 the City's remembrancer delivered 40 recorded speeches and served on 107 committees, whilst the recorder's tally was 30 and 79. They were connected by marriage and friendship and acted together in the surveillance and interrogation of Catholics. They were also independent, hot and impetuous men, who were liable to overstep the mark.[69] Norton spent two spells in detention, whilst in 1576 Fleetwood was consigned to the Fleet for raiding the Portuguese embassy during the celebration of mass.[70] The recorder, like the remembrancer, was an intermediary between national and City government, consulting with Councillors about London affairs and acting on its behalf in the searching out of 'naughty' popish books and the examination of Catholic suspects. The Privy Council frequently resorted to him, not only to maintain order but also to supervise the book trade and the payment of mariners' wages, and to search out forged conveyances of land.[71] This frequent consultation was partly the inevitable consequence of his office — as recorder he was the City's legal counsel, a judge in its courts, and an *ex officio* justice of the peace, whereby he was also burdened with a wide range of administrative business. However, it was more than that, because the Council's confidence in him also derived from his energetic activity on its behalf. The value of his service by virtue of both his office and his personal reliability is clearly expressed in an urgent Council directive of September 1583. He was instructed 'hartely without delay to make your spedye repair hether that we may use your advise and help' and warned 'not to faile considering the confidence that of reason we must have of your redinesse in respect of your place'.[72] In 1576 even Elizabeth summoned him to her at Windsor for consultation.[73] Indeed her respect for him was such that her intention to appoint him one of the barons of the Exchequer was only stayed 'by an opynion she hathe that yt were not fyt to have him removed owt of the place he now supplyethe untyll another fytt man be fownde owt for that roome'.[74]

It was logical and natural for devout loyalists such as Fleetwood and Norton to co-operate with the Privy Council in Parliament too — and not just on matters of great moment. So, during a debate on a bill to dissolve Bristol's merchant corporation, Fleetwood defended the prerogative power to incorporate any town, concluding that failure to consult the Queen was 'perilous'.[75] Moreover it was Lord Burghley that the recorder (and Norton too) looked to as his parliamentary manager and to whom he addressed his advices and information on the City's affairs and Commons' proceedings.[76] As a *quid pro quo* Burghley had shielded Fleetwood from the consequences of his implication in the Succession campaign on behalf of the Greys in 1563[77] and he successfully interceded for Norton's release from detention in 1582.[78] However, although the remembrancer and recorder were pre-eminent in the duration and range of their services to their Queen, patron, and Privy Council, they were not alone. Sir Rowland Heyward, for example, joined with Fleetwood to discuss London's affairs with the Council, paired with him to confer with Lord Keeper Bacon about London's hospitals[79] and Ludgate[80] and to petition Councillors about the City's liberties.[81] And the intimacy and mutual benefit of City-Council relations are manifest in the royal service of ex-recorders. That relationship did not dissolve at the door of St Stephen's Chapel.

Yet the parliamentary relationship was an ambivalent one. Whilst London's Members collaborated with the Council in its designs,[82] they also constituted a lobby committed to the furtherance of the City's interests. Their own legislative programme and their politicking in opposition to rival vested interests consumed valuable time and could pose a threat to the Council's own objectives. This was inevitable, because the complex and often competing lobbies within London itself frequently sought the solution of their problems in parliamentary bills; so in 1587 the tallow chandlers spent money to promote a complaint against interlopers; and in 1597 the bakers endeavoured to suppress the baking of 'unlawfull' breads, revising an old bill for submission to the Commons and acquainting the Speaker with its contents.[83] The City's governors were not oblivious to the problem. They demonstrated their concern in a practical way when they endeavoured to regulate, canalize and diminish the flow of bills to the House of Commons. This was the objective of the court of aldermen when it required companies to submit their measures for its approval: in 1567 it summoned the promoters of three bills before it, ordered bills for meat and wines to be drawn, approved four others for the artificers and vintners and vetoed one presented by the brewers; in 1571 it scrutinized measures drafted by the clothworkers and wool-winders and gave the nod to four of them. The following year two others were referred for an extra-parliamentary solution — a novel sign. And in 1576 it submitted two bills to committees and allowed two more to proceed.[84] However, the system was not a watertight one and companies sometimes circumvented it.[85] Certainly enough bills got through, with (or without) the court's approval, to swell the volume of private business, and then it was frequently the duty of the City's Members to advance them. Thus the very men who served the Council also threatened the expedition of its business: when, for example, Wilbraham, Marshe, Heyward, Norton and Fleetwood were ordered to consider, draw or reform City bills, and when, in 1571 and 1581, London's Members were 'moved and spoken w[i]thall [by the court] for the furtheraunce' of several measures.[86]

London's governors were trapped in a dilemma: to care for City interests and yet to smooth the Council's path to parliamentary solutions. In 1566 the lord mayor appointed a special court to peruse proposed bills and, if appropriate, refer them for an extra-parliamentary solution: as in 1572 when the aldermen ordered the London artificers to forgo their bill and instead they would see 'good ordre therein taken to there quyetnes'.[87] A Member of the Commons, however, offered a more comprehensive solution: that whenever a London bill was introduced, its Members should 'be called and asked whether the matters be meete to be furthered, and also whether the same matter may not be suffitientlie amended by common counsell or otherwise amonge themselves, without troublinge of the parleament, and if it may, then to comend it to the Lorde maior and Aldermen to be considered at London, and soe to ridde the howse thereof '.[88] He added a warning that 'private billes ever be egerlie followed and make factions'.[89] Sound advice, which was particularly true of the City, with its multifarious interests, above all its measures for the preservation of timber and the suppression of iron mills. Norton, Fleetwood, Heyward and Marshe promoted them in 1563, 1571 and 1576, and the prolonged campaign culminated in the successful but time-consuming bill of 1581,[90] with Norton arguing tactically that '[n]owe [is the] best tyme to provide remedie. If we tary till xii mills be made, there wilbe mor cryers out and harder passadge'.[91] Even so there were criers out enough headed by Sir Henry Sidney, spokesman of the iron interest. Other boroughs too resisted City bills: thus its attempt to control the Kent cloth trade was foiled in 1571.[92] Conversely, London's Members acted, often under instructions, to obstruct or defeat measures harmful to its interests. In 1572 Heyward and Fleetwood were armed with information in order to offer more effective criticism of a bill for foreign artificers 'and to overthrowe [it] if they can'.[93] The recorder condemned the bill as slanderous and secured its committal, whilst another outburst, this time against a restrictive measure on apprenticeship, persuaded the House to reject it.[94] When, in 1572, a bill to prohibit the export of undyed cloth was exhibited, John Marshe marshalled arguments which foreshadowed criticisms of the Jacobean Cokayne project, and successfully demanded 'the whole bill to be overthrowne'. In 1587 the City was again active, instructing its representatives to engineer the repeal of a measure beneficial to Yarmouth's fishing industry.[95]

London's bills and its parliamentary lobby consumed time, the Council's most precious commodity. However, whilst the dual loyalties of those Members to City and Council could create competing priorities and obligations, they did not cause political conflict. Councillors and City representatives were mutually obligated in a constant two-way process.[96] Moreover there was an essential identity of interest, especially on such matters as national security, the 'right' religion, orderly administration, and economic regulation. Their political alliance was reinforced by a variety of personal connexions: Heyward was Burghley's mining associate, Dannet his cousin and Fleetwood his client, whilst Norton had a veritable network of conciliar contacts.[97] Their special relationship with the Queen's government was epitomized (and facilitated) by the fact that, as John Hooker records, apart from Privy Councillors who sat around the Speaker's chair, 'everyone sitteth as he cometh' except for the knights and burgesses of London and York who 'sit on the right side, next to the Councillors'.[98] That intimate relationship encompassed social fraternization and parliamentary collaboration: Norton taking supper at the Temple with Speaker Bell and the clerk Fulk Onslow during the Parliament-time, and passing on to the House the Lord Chancellor's advice on a Member's eligibility to sit there; or Rowland Heyward, protected by Speaker Popham from punishment for his indiscretion. Heyward was on the 1581 committee to scrutinize London's measure against iron mills. He exhibited to the House a new bill which the committee had not approved. However, when his punishment was called for, the Speaker brushed aside the demand, persuading the Commons that it was 'a thing of too small Moment for this House to . . . spend Time in'.[99] Was this an example of the *quid pro quo* — official favouritism — or simply prompt action to avoid time-consuming debate?

If it was the former it would accord well with the general picture which emerges: of the men-of-business receiving due recognition and protection for their services to the Council. After all, their assistance was vital. They supplied information on which successful parliamentary management, like efficient government, depended: Fulk Onslow reporting on the Mary Stuart debate, Bell keeping Burghley informed of the progress of the Rites and Ceremonies Bill, both in 1572;[100] and the reports of Fleetwood and an unknown correspondent in 1584.[101] They freely offered advice too: an unknown Member on the choice of Speaker in 1581 and ways of avoiding

'Matters of Longe Argument'; Norton against unnecessary legislation: Marshe and Fleetwood on bills concerning tanners and Newcastle's bid to annex Gateshead.[102] Most important, however, was the promotion of conciliar designs, especially when the Queen and Council were in disagreement. In the Succession 'campaign' of 1563, orchestrated by the Privy Council, Norton played the 'front man' for the petition committee (which was chaired by the Comptroller and included all the Councillors) when he read its draft to the House.[103] The voices of Dannet and Norton blended harmoniously with those of the Lord Keeper and Secretary; and in 1566–7 it was Cecil who wrote the Queen's promise to marry into the subsidy preamble.[104] Their efforts were thwarted by one person, the Queen. Similarly in 1571 the religious 'campaign' was a concerted effort by bishops, Councillors and their men-of-business. Norton, Bell, Dalton, Monson and Yelverton, all lawyers, pursued the Council's cause in the Commons, both in debate and in committee.[105] However, Strickland's rashness jeopardized the moderate programme of which they were advocates.[106] And in the end the Queen frustrated most of their efforts, even though they had enjoyed wide popularity, both in official circles and amongst the rank-and-file of the Commons.

Then in 1572 Parliament was summoned for action on Mary Stuart. The usual dilemma faced the Council: Elizabeth was prevaricating, this time over the Duke of Norfolk's execution and the limits to which she would go against Mary. So the dominant theme of the session was a drive for the duke's death and for the Scottish queen's attainder — or at least her exclusion from the Succession. That drive was once again stage-managed by the Privy Council. Robert Bell, a lawyer with Bacon connexions and an ardent protagonist of conciliar policies, was probably the Council's choice as Speaker for that very reason. In his disabling speech he identified a person in the land whom, many thought, 'no law can touch', whereas anyone of any condition should die for treason.[107] Lord Keeper Bacon's opening address had already hinted more obscurely at the Council's intention when he informed Parliament that it had been summoned[108]

> to devise lawes for the saftie of the Queen's Majestie, for sins the rebellious and traiterous conspiracies which of lat had ben reveled it was agreed both by the Queen's Privie Councell and by the wisest persons beside of her realme that it colde not stande with the saftie of her Majestie onlesse ther were mad some other provision by lawe than was at that present already mad.

The session which followed is perhaps the best documented example of collaboration between Councillors and their men-of-business. Persistent pressure was applied to the Queen. Norton, delivering 12 speeches against Norfolk and Mary, was actively supported by Thomas Digges (one of Bacon's clients), Thomas Dannett, Robert Newdigate, Thomas Wilbraham and others. They also seized the opportunity afforded by the Commons resolution of 24 May, that the Speaker should petition the Queen to execute the duke and that Members 'as shall think good to exhibit . . . any Reasons or Causes, to enforce [it], may, in the mean time of the next Session, deliver them in Writing, to Mr Speaker'. The House adjourned until the 28th to allow time for the compilation of such papers. The men-of-business were not idle. On 31 May Norton 'brought forth a paper in writing wherein he had written certaine reasons which should be delivered to the Speaker to be considered of, and collect the best for his purpose'.[109] Digges (supported by John Marshe) promptly followed this with a proposal that 'such causes as are put in writing might be committed to certaine to be allowed or disalowed of '. Not only he but also Thomas Dannet had already drafted arguments why Norfolk should die.[110] Digges's recommendation was given added strength by the Speaker's reluctance to approach the Queen without precise instructions. On the previous day he had 'willed the House to put him in writinge what thei wolde have him utter. For more than thei put him in writinge, he wolde not speake'. The Commons, in an attempt to overcome Bell's agitation, 'without further dealie beganne wholy to encline to have committes apointed, which shold consult upon and drawe out the fittest reasons to be uttered by the Speaker'.[111] The marshalling of arguments was yet another example of the Commons' constant pressure on the Queen to act, and it was sponsored and led by the men-of-business. But they could not have proceeded far when, two days later, Norfolk was executed.

Meanwhile the lower House had not neglected Mary Stuart. Nor were the men-of-business negligent of their duty. When, on 12 May, the Commons named 44 Members to confer with a Lords committee and the Queen's learned counsel on 'the great matter' of the Scottish queen, they included Heyward, Wilbraham, Fleetwood, Popham, Yelverton, Norton and Dalton. Two days later Sir Francis Knollys introduced Wilbraham, who reported to the House at length on the proceedings of the joint committee. On 15 May the morning was consumed in debate. Norton led the way, combining a characteristically relentless prosecution of the cause with a disarming call 'to procede with reverence towarde the Queen's Majestie'. On the 19th it was Wilbraham who once again reported to the House on the further proceedings of the joint committee. It had devised two bills. One rehearsed Mary's treasons and included a petition 'that she might be attainted and disabled to take any dignitie of this realme upon her'. The alternative simply adjudged her 'unable to enioye the crowne of this realme after the Queen's time', with attainder as the penalty 'yf she did procede to any attempt herafter'. However, Wilbraham's information was accompanied by a bombshell: that Elizabeth had opted for the second bill and deferred further 'procedinge in the first untill a more convenient time were offered'.[112] Both Houses protested that the first bill was the only sure guarantee of the Queen's safety, whereupon, on the 23rd, she repeated her decision in messages conveyed to them by Privy Councillors.[113]

Sir James Croft, the Comptroller, gave the Council's lead to the men-of-business in the Commons. He lamented that 'it was his chaunce to be the bringer of so uncomfortable a messadge. He would be glade if he could take away the cause of dispaier. He wisheth the order purposed [i.e. the adoption of the first bill] might be proceeded in to gather the reasons of

our refusall into writing. The same he hopeth will move her Majestie'.[114]
Croft had proposed a procedure to which the Commons was to resort again
the very next day, in the matter of the duke's execution. He must have
known that he was giving the Council's devoted followers their head. The
news of the Queen's decision had given Norton the excuse to call, yet again,
for Norfolk's death, whilst Newdigate had been appalled at the report and
had 'looketh nowe for no good'.[115] The Treasurer of the Household and
senior Councillor, Sir Francis Knollys, added the weight of his respected
opinion to the words of Croft and set forth guide-lines of action: to petition
the Queen in favour of the first bill, either by the Speaker or (preferably) by
a joint motion with the Lords. In the meantime the 'reasons of our
resolucions he wisheth to be made in readinesse that the same may bee
presented'. Speaker Bell took his cue from the Council, acknowledging that
the House misliked the Queen's decision and recommending joint action
with the upper House.[116] The Commons followed the official lead and
approached the Lords which, on 24 May, gave a favourable reply.[117] At the
resultant joint committee 'it was by them agreed that every man sholde set
downe in writinge sutch reasons as he thought were best able to move the
Queen herin, and that first the bisshoppes sholde set downe reasons
movinge the conscience, and next reasons for pollicie, in which *tacite* sholde
be aunswered sutch obiections as the Queen were able to make for the not
procedinge in the first bill. The civilians drewe reasons *ora et contra*'. The
fact that this voluminous written case was presented to the Queen probably
within two days (and certainly by 28 May when she made her reply)[118]
conjures up a picture of many midnight candles burning around Westminster and Whitehall. It also suggests that the work was already in hand when
the joint committee met, because it is difficult to believe that the 'formidable dossier',[119] with the bishops' arguments heavily larded with biblical
references, was drafted, revised and written in fair copy between Saturday
and Monday. There survive 'ffragmentes in papers to induce thexecution of
the Scott[ish] Q[ueen]', two drafts of 'reasons' and a petition which appear
to be earlier copies of the civilians' arguments, and a draft of the bishops'
arguments which may be an intermediate version.[120] The Saturday afternoon joint committee meeting, in which many of the 66 Members would
have wanted their say, must have been a lengthy one. The surviving bits
and pieces indicate that the drafting process went through several stages — a
near impossibility to conceive and bring to birth such a weighty document
in little more than 36 hours. In that case one must seek to explain how such
a weighty exercise in political persuasion was ready to be presented on
Monday morning. And there is only one feasible explanation: that the
whole exercise was stage-managed by a Privy Council anxious to coerce the
Queen into acceptance of the first and more punitive bill. Knollys and Croft
had guided the House to adoption of a joint petition. They and other
Councillors, including Sir Walter Mildmay, were amongst the Commons'
membership of the joint committee, whilst some of their colleagues at the
Council board — in particular Burghley, Bedford, Leicester, Sussex and
Howard of Effingham — came from the Lords.[121]

Burghley was the key. If the Council orchestrated these moves, then he was their conductor. On 21 May he had lamented that 'there can be found no more soundness than in the Common House, and no lack appearing in the Higher House; but in the highest person such slowness in the offers of surety and such stay in resolution as it seemeth God is not pleased that the surety shall succeed'. And when the fruitless session was over, with neither bill accomplished, he expressed at the same time both his frustration and that of the Council:

> All that we have laboured for and had with full consent brought to fashion — I mean a law to make the Scottish Queen unable and unworthy of succession of the crown — was by her Majesty neither assented to nor rejected, but deferred.

He stressed that the fault lay not in 'us that are accounted inward counsellors',[122] and the evidence confirms this. Burghley in particular did all that he could. He monitored the Commons' progress with the aid of reports drafted by its clerk, Fulk Onslow, a Council appointee.[123] He assisted in the deliberations of the joint committee on 24 May and endorsed a draft of the bishops' arguments.[124] Perhaps he it was who prompted the Commons, in the Queen's name, to concentrate on the Bill against Mary Stuart, 'laying apart all private Matters'[125] — one can only speculate — but he certainly intervened to cut short the time-consuming Bill for the Earl of Kent which spawned a conflict with Lord Compton, resulted in successive representations by both parties at the bar of the House, and occupied precious hours of Parliament's time in ten daily sittings. Finally, on 25 June, 'letters from the Lord Burghley, directed unto Mr. Speaker', deferred the bill.[126] Above all he looked to his men-of-business to stir up the House, guide it to the 'right actions' and coerce the Queen into judicial proceedings against Mary. Norton, as usual, was to the fore. From the very beginning of the session he had been an outspoken advocate of harsh measures and he was duly appointed to the joint committee on 'the great Cause'. On 15 May it directed 'a Platte to be devised for their Manner of Proceeding in the Matter concerning the Queen of Scots'. That 'platte' (or list of headings or articles on which the bill was to be structured) ended up in Norton's personal papers — a sure sign that he was either active in its devising or the sole author.[127]

Norton (together with Sir Rowland Heyward, Dalton, Fleetwood, Popham, Yelverton and other men-of-business) was also present with his patron, Burghley, on the joint committee which met in Star Chamber on 24 May. Once again there is evidence that he was active. His possession of those 'ffragmentes in papers to induce thexecution' of Mary, copies or drafts of arguments to persuade the Queen 'to proceede iudiciallie' against her, and two joint petitions directed to the same end; all testify to his involvement.[128] On the floor of the House too he played the Council's game and maintained parliamentary pressure on Elizabeth. Amongst his papers which were seized and inventoried by Thomas Wilkes (clerk of the Council) after his death, were notes for a speech. Wilkes calendared them as 'Reasons to induce her Ma[jes]tie to proceed against the Scott[ish] Q[ueen] according to the firste motion in parlament. Thexecution of the duke of Norff[olk]'. The terse description adequately identifies the twin obsessions of Norton in this session. It also locates the delivery of his speech at some point between 15 May ('the firste motion') and 2 June (Norfolk's execution).[129] On 25 June, near the end of the session, Norton also publicly reaffirmed his support for 'the great Cause' in general and for the proceedings of the two Houses on 24–26 May in particular: 'The matter hath beene considered by the bishoppes according to the word of God, by the civilians and by the iudges of the common lawe, and all have agreed that it is iust and lawfull.'[130]

Nevertheless the campaign of Councillors and men-of-business ground to a standstill because of Elizabeth's obstinacy. She informed both Houses that she intended to proceed by the second bill which was to be drawn by her learned counsel, and that, in the meantime, further discussion on the subject should be suspended.[131] The Council was in a dilemma. It regarded the second bill as inadequate, although it was better than nothing. However, there was urgent need for haste. The new bill was only entered into the Lords on 31 May and it did not reach the Commons until 5 June.[132] Already it was early summer and the approach of the plague season, and the Queen was anxious to clear the overcrowded metropolis. As early as 21 April the previous year the Lords had desired that the lower House 'would spend the Time in proceeding with necessary Bills for the Commonwealth, and lay aside all private Bills in the mean time', because 'the Season of the Year waxed very hot, and dangerous for Sickness'.[133] Therefore it is understandable that, when the bill came down to the Commons on 5 June 1572, it was accompanied by a message from the Lords that 'the Time of the Year considered, the Queen's Majesty's Pleasure is, that this House do proceed in that . . . laying apart all private Matters'.[134] It is not clear whether this was the Queen's express wish or that the Council simply acted in her name. Whatever the true source of this message was, the Council knew that speed was of the essence because Parliament could not be prolonged much longer into summer. Moreover they must have known of the impending visit of the French ambassador, the Duc de Montmorenci, during which both Houses were to be adjourned from 11 to 24 June.[135]

Burghley in the Lords and his conciliar colleagues in the nether House had to contend with three problems in order to get the bill through the Commons in time: the competition of private bills, the size of the bill and the desire of many Members to speak at length on the measure. Their worst fears must have been realized because the House did not lay aside all private matters. The Councillors had no more success than Canute in stemming the tide. In the remaining 11 morning sessions it considered 33 private bills, the Bill for Continuance of Acts, and a privilege case; there were two joint conferences with the Lords on the Continuation Bill and private measures, and quasi-judicial proceedings on the Earl of Kent's Bill and the misconduct of one Andrew Fisher.[136] Competing with these petty measures (the Continuation Bill apart) was the Bill against Mary Stuart. It was of prodigious size, its preamble alone running to 2,000–2,500 words.[137] How could the Council hope to engineer its passage through the House in time when so many Members sympathized with Mr Colby, 'that every man may speake his fill: Corne, the more it is grouned, the meale wilbe the finer'.[138] Norton retorted: 'Corne to long grouned makes burnte meal.'[139] Norton again. Burghley had turned to his men-of-business (including the Speaker) to achieve the passage of at least the less satisfactory bill. Someone (and it may have been a parochially orientated Member rather than a devotee of the Council) persuaded the House 'to sit at Afternoons from Three of the Clock till Six; and to proceed but only in private Bills'[140] — whoever was the inspiration for such a move, it resulted in 24 readings of bills on seven afternoons.[141] On the length of *the* bill and Members' proclivity to debate it, however, we can be more sure. Yelverton and Norton deplored the inadequacy of the bill but protested their loyalty.[142] Norton wanted a proviso declaring that the Commons' meaning was not to affirm any title in Mary Stuart.[143] He was dealing the Council's complex hand: to get the bill through the Commons, with its competing priorities, to reinforce the bill against Mary, and at the same time fend off Elizabeth for a few more precious days.

The Council's hand was also evident: the message (probably Burghley's) which accompanied the bill down to the Commons on 5 June; Hatton persuading the Speaker with 'it was guessed . . . a message from the Quene for the readinge againe of the Scottish Queen's bill' on the sixth — which 'ther was mutch stickinge' at, because it was so hasty, but which was read 'through the meanes of the Speaker especially'.[144] The bill was then ordered to 'be drawen into articles because it was so longe, and that every man might speak to every article . . . For otherwise the length of the bill was sutch, and the occasions of speach therin so many, as two or three men speakinge might spende a whole foornowne. It seemed herupon good that certaine of the ripest wittes within the House sholde be apointed to have conference upon every point in the bill, and after upon the readinge of it by articles thei sholde utter ther opinions, as in shewinge what thei thought amisse. . . . This resolution eased the House of mutch labor, and saved the expence of mutch time'[145] — the Council's consistent objective. And who were 'the ripest wittes'? Two Privy Councillors (Sir Walter Mildmay and Sir Ralph Sadler), two royal officials (Sir George Bromley and Thomas Wilbraham, respectively attorneys of the Duchy of Lancaster and the Court of Wards), and five lawyers (Roger Manwood, Robert Monson, Norton, Popham and Yelverton).[146] Once again the Councillors and their men-of-business were in harness together. Their attempts to cut corners and save time achieved the desired result: on 25 June the bill passed the Commons.[147] However, at the end their efforts came to nought because the Queen, in effect, vetoed the bill. Norton's papers, which included draft bills, petitions, plattes, and 'sondrie loose papers' of notes all testify to his considerable but abortive labours.[148] Yet what comes through most forcibly, and not just in 1572, is the practical assistance which not only Norton but a considerable number of Members lent to the Council in the pursuit of its objectives.

Furthermore the collective significance of these men-of-business appears to have risen sharply in 1571. Of course this impression may be illusory, because of the dramatic increase in surviving materials from that date: for example journals, reports, and parliamentary collections compiled by Thomas Cromwell, William Fitzwilliam, Fleetwood, Hooker, Onslow and other, anonymous, Members. On the other hand several events in 1571-2 are probably more than coincidental: Cecil's elevation to the Lords, the appointments of Norton, Fleetwood and Onslow, as remembrancer, recorder and Commons clerk, all in 1571, and Bell's election as Speaker in 1572.[149] Burghley, now absent from the lower House, yet still overseeing parliamentary business, needed eyes and ears there. It is from 1571 onwards that the parliamentary diaries, unofficial journals, reports and advices survive. Some of them may have been written to satisfy personal interest. But Onslow's descriptions of proceedings in 1572, 1581 and 1586-7[150] and the parliamentary 'information' of 1584[151] were probably intended for Burghley's eyes. Fleetwood's reports certainly were,[152] whilst the anonymous advices of 1581 were also destined to land on a Privy Councillor's desk.[153]

From 1571 onwards, pressure to prefer public business to private, and to hurry it through, came from the Lords. There Burghley brooded, schemed, guided and regulated: directly through messages, advices and instructions to speed up business and to sort bills into priority,[154] and indirectly, through the men-of-business. So Norton was fertile in devices to save time, the Speaker supplied the Lord Treasurer with lists of bills and the stages which they had reached, and others kept him informed of proceedings.[155] It was from that year too that the Speaker called for Members 'to spend little Time in Motions, and to avoid long Speeches',[156] or that (as in 1581) he delivered a stricture on the need to speak briefly to the point, advising them not to waste time in unnecessary motions or superfluous arguments because 'the Parliament was like to be very short'.[157] The most effective instruments for the attainment of Burghley's objective of short, productive sessions were the unofficial men-of-business. First, because, in the furtherance of conciliar policies which were at variance with the Queen's, they dared to act where the Councillors would not or could not. Inevitably they risked Elizabeth's displeasure and even that of the Council if they went too far. At the end of the 1571 Parliament, during which Norton had tacked on to the Treasons Bill an extreme penal and retrospective amendment, he was publicly censured and all but named by the Queen for his action.[158] On one occasion Fleetwood was reprimanded 'for hastie speech';[159] and Bell was so hardly dealt with by the Council for a rash pronouncement that he returned to the House with 'amazed countenance'.[160] Norton once told the Commons, 'I confesse that no man in this companie hath more cause to feare mistakinge than myself. For I am suer that no man's speach hath ben oftener mistaken than myne'.[161] Yet it was precisely this boldness which made them invaluable to the Council. Secondly, the Commons displayed a prickly sensitivity if it felt the heavy hand of officialdom constraining its liberties. For this reason an experienced Member questioned the advisability of open parliamentary guidance and direction by Councillors.[162] Popular and respected knights and burgesses could secure the transaction of official business without arousing the suspicion or incurring the odium of the Commons, 'leavinge the house to theire fulle libertie, who in theire greatest libertie wilbe most frankelie obsequious'.[163]

Not that Norton, Fleetwood and the rest were obsequious to the Council. They were not always in agreement amongst themselves.[164] They could pursue objectives tangential to the Council's parliamentary interests: so Bell and Popham joined in the clamour against administrative abuses in 1571 (although they then drew back and joined with Norton and the Councillors in recommending no more than a humble suit to the Queen for reformation).[165] Furthermore it was not uncommon for them to be the object of criticism from Councillors. When 'Norton the Bold' (as the lewd pasquil describes him) put his controversial addition to the Treasons Bill of 1571, Crofts described it as 'but the devise of a private Man' — though he added 'it iustlie deserved commendation'.[166] And when, in the following year, he criticized the classification of minstrels as rogues 'though they goe not aboute', Sir Francis Knollys in his grandest censorious manner reprimanded him that 'so good a bill [against vagabondage] be not hindered for smale scruples'.[167] However, such verbal clashes should not be misread. Sometimes they reflected divisions within the Council, rather than between it and its men-of-business. And frequently they represented no more than the cut and thrust of debate. Norton himself acknowledged 'that where manie men be, there must be manie myndes, and, in consultations, convenient it is to have contrary opinions . . . thereby the rather to wrest out the best'.[168] These men were not courtier-chameleons but men of independent temper retaining, within the framework of their loyalties, room to manoeuvre and to disagree with the Queen's government. Nevertheless they generally conformed in action to the example set by Thomas Norton:[169]

> All that I have done I did by comaundement of the House, and specially of the Quenes Counsell there, and my chefest care was in all thinges to be directed by the Counsell.

Norton had no equal in his professionalism, skill as a draftsman, and energy. His death on 10 March 1584 must have been a serious blow to the Council's managerial system. However, although he had no obvious successor, the parliamentary type which he represented — the men-of-business — continued to serve. John Popham was criticized for his blatantly partisan conduct as Speaker in 1581.[170] There was the clock-watching Thomas Digges, hurrying things along — according to one Member he frequently intervened when a debate proved lengthy, saying 'every matter must have an end' and drew it to a conclusion;[171] or he would cut short prolonged discussion by proposing that the bill before them be put to the question.[172] In 1597 the Speaker, Yelverton, apologized for his failure to secure the passage of a bill for Sir Robert Cecil, despite putting the question twice.[173] Thirteen years before, William Fleetwood assisted the Councillors in an embarrassing parliamentary situation. He informed Burghley that, when Sir Francis Knollys moved the House to elect a Speaker and proposed Sir John Puckering for the place, the Commons fell silent and no one responded. So 'I said to my companions about me "crie puckering" and then they and I begynnynge, the rest did the same'.[174] Such examples of the men-of-business at work can be multiplied many times over. And no session was without them: for example, in the Parliament which met shortly after Norton's death in 1584, Thomas Cromwell, James Dalton and Sir Walter Mildmay's son-in-law, William Fitzwilliam, were active. And Cromwell, Digges, Fitzwilliam and an unknown Member compiled accounts which, like Fleetwood's, may have been meant for Burghley's attention.

The 'post-Norton' sessions (1584–1601) await a detailed investigation. Only then can we decide whether the diminishing number of Councillors in the late Elizabethan Commons signified a decline in effective parliamentary management — or whether they continued to be assisted by loyal and energetic Members who did much of their work for them. However, until (and including) 1581, which was Norton's swansong, the outlines are clear: that the Privy Council had to secure its objectives in the teeth of too much business, too little time, an inefficient House of Commons and an obstinate Queen; and that its men-of-business were crucial to its success.

Notes

1   W. Notestein, 'The Winning of the Initiative by the House of Commons', *Proceedings of the British Academy*, XI (1924–5), 125–75; Sir John Neale, *Elizabeth I and Her Parliaments* (2 vols., 1953–7).

2   Neale, *Elizabeth I and Her Parliaments*, I, 11.

3   *Ibid.*, 91–240.

4   Cambridge U.L., MS. Ff. V, 14.

5   G.R. Elton, 'Parliament in the Sixteenth Century: Functions and Fortunes', *Historical Journal*, XXII (1979), 272–3.

6   E.g. John Molyneux — 'Molyneux the mover' — put a motion for the Commons to renew its suit to the Queen for settlement of the Succession: Camb. U.L., MS. Ff. V, 10; Neale, *Elizabeth I and Her Parliaments*, I, 137, 158–9.

7   Bell and Fleetwood attended the Middle Temple, Norton the Inner Temple and Yelverton Gray's Inn. Bell and Yelverton eventually became judges, whilst Fleetwood and Norton were practising lawyers. John Marshe was a mercer and Merchant Adventurer: *D.N.B.* (Bell, Fleetwood, Norton and Yelverton); F.F. Foster, *The Politics of Stability: A Portrait of the Rulers in Elizabethan London* (1977), p. 107, n.2.

8   E.g. Neale, *Elizabeth I and Her Parliaments*, I, 95, 101, 104–5, 115–16, 134, 137, 139–40, 142, 145, 152, 162, 176, *etc.*; Camb. U.L., MS. Ff. V, 14.

9   Neale, *Elizabeth I and Her Parliaments*, I, 95, 101, 109, 134.

10 In another place we are intimidated by the stricture that '[i]t would take a simpleton not to suspect a planned drive': *ibid.*, 166, 195.

11 A draft revision of canon law, effected by an Edwardian commission under Thomas Cranmer but which had not received statutory confirmation.

12 The famous 'alphabetical bills': Bill A was designed as a statutory confirmation of the Articles of Religion as approved in the Convocation of 1562–3: the rest (B–F) dealt with

the quality of the clergy, absenteeism, corrupt presentations, the buying and selling of benefices and pensions paid from them. During the session Bill F was incorporated into Bill E and so disappeared, but Bill G, concerning the commutation of penance, was added to the list: Neale, *Elizabeth I and Her Parliaments*, I, 166, 209; *C.J.*, I, 83.

[13] Neale, *Elizabeth I and Her Parliaments*, I, 195. W.H. Frere wrote that the *Reformatio* 'was not a code to command the support of the puritan party, though there were details in it, especially as regards discipline, which might have evoked its sympathy': *The English Church in the Reigns of Elizabeth and James I . . .* (1924), p. 165.

[14] Strickland attributed it to 'Peter Martir, Paulus Fagius, and other[s]', but Norton informed the House that it had been 'drawne by that learned man Mr. Doctor Haddon, and penned by that excellent learned man Mr. Cheeke': *Proceedings in the Parliaments of Elizabeth I. Volume I: 1558–1581*, ed. T.E. Hartley (Leicester, 1981), pp. 200–1.

[15] Neale, *Elizabeth I and Her Parliaments*, I, 194; J.C. Spalding, 'The Reformatio Legum Ecclesiasticarum of 1552 and the Furthering of Discipline in England', *Church History*, XXXIX (1970), 167; Trinity College, Dublin, MS.535 (anonymous journal) [hereafter cited as 'anon. jnl.'].

[16] P.R.O., S.P. 12/177, ff. 35, 46, 50, Norton's 'Devices'; B.L., Cotton MS. Titus F.I, ff. 136–136v.

[17] *Correspondence of Matthew Parker . . . 1535 to . . . 1575*, eds. J. Bruce and T.T. Perowne (Parker Soc., Cambridge, 1853), pp. 292–4. In 1571 even the Queen saw the virtues of two of the alphabetical bills — B (on the quality of the clergy) and E (on simony) — and gave the royal assent to them: *C.S.P. Dom.*, 1547–80, p. 285.

[18] Camb. U.L., MS. Ff. V, 14.

[19] Based on calculations from *L.J.* and *C.J.* until (and including) 1581.

[20] W.D. Cooper, 'Further Particulars of Thomas Norton, and of State Proceedings in Matters of Religion in the Years 1581 and 1582', *Archaeologia*, XXXVI (1855), 110.

[21] These figures are calculated from *C.J.*, I–II and *L.J.*, II–V.

[22] I am indebted to David Dean for this information.

[23] B.L., Harl. MS. 253, ff. 32–6.

[24] E.g. P.R.O., S.P. 12/77/54; 12/78/11, 17, 35 (1571); 12/86/47, 53 (1572); 12/107/45–6, 58, 77–80 (1576).

[25] 21 Apr. 1571: *C.J.*, I, 85.

[26] 26 Apr. 1571: *ibid.*, 86.

[27] *Ibid.*, 88, 91.

[28] Cf. Sir John Neale, *The Elizabethan House of Commons* (1961), pp. 376–7.

[29] T.C.D., MS. 1045 (Thomas Cromwell's journal for the parliamentary sessions of 1572–84) [hereafter cited as 'Cromwell'], ff. 46v, 61, 122v.

[30] 5 June: *C.J.*, I, 100.

[31] Bodl., Tanner MS. 393 (anonymous private journal of proceedings in 1572) [hereafter cited as 'Tanner'], f. 62.

[32] 21 Jan. 1581: *C.J.*, I, 118. In 1587 William Lambarde concurred with the practice of avoiding debate at the first reading 'which is a means . . . to save a great deal of time': *The Harleian Miscellany . . .*, ed. Thomas Park (10 vols., 1808–13), V, 260.

[33] B.L., Harl. MS. 253, ff. 34v–35.

[34] Cromwell, f. 116.

[35] B.L., Harl. MS. 253, ff. 35–35v. The significance of this advice should not be overlooked. It is a commonplace that the Commons had the authority to initiate lay taxation: a Privy Councillor would request a subsidy in a justificatory address to the House, which determined the size of the grant and appointed a committee to work out the details and draft the bill. Yet this Member's advice must give us pause to think. Paper bills were only engrossed on parchment after the second reading in the House of origin — in other words when, barring strong objections in the other chamber, they seemed likely to pass into law. If the Council's anonymous adviser was not recommending a radical departure from accepted practice, then the granting of supply may have been more of a formality than has been recognized in the past. After all he was proposing that both the initial and final drafts of the subsidy bill should be drawn up by the Council even before a grant had been requested.

36   Neale, *Elizabethan Commons*, p. 309.

37   B.L., Lansdowne MS. 41, f.45, Fleetwood to Burghley, 29 Nov. 1584.

38   B.L., Harl. MS. 253, f. 32.

39   B.L., Lansd. MS. 41, f. 45; Neale, *Elizabethan Commons*, pp. 370, 408.

40   House of Lords R.O., Braye MS. 3186 (Fulk Onslow's journal, 24–31 May, 25 June) [hereafter cited as 'Onslow'], f. 2v.

41   B.L., Lansd. MS. 43, f. 164 *et seq.*; Neale, *Elizabethan Commons*, pp. 375, 410.

42   *The Journals of All the Parliaments during the Reign of Queen Elizabeth . . .*, ed. Sir Symonds D'Ewes (1682; repr. Shannon, 1973), p. 347.

43   B.L., Harl. MS. 253, f. 35.

44   This criticism is equally applicable to both Sir John Neale and Wallace Notestein.

45   B.L., Harl. MS. 253, f. 35v.

46   For details of his life and career see *D.N.B.* and M.A.R. Graves, 'Thomas Norton the Parliament Man: An Elizabethan M.P., 1559–1581', *Historical Jnl.*, XXIII (1980), 17–19.

47   Graves, 'Norton', pp. 18–19, 26–7, 29–33; Marie Axton, *The Queen's Two Bodies: Drama and the Elizabethan Succession* (1977), pp. 39–41; John Strype, *The Life and Acts of Matthew Parker . . .* (3 vols., Oxford, 1821), II, 143; *idem*, *The Life and Acts of John Whitgift . . .* (3 vols., Oxford, 1822), I, 57–61; Inner Temple, Petyt MS. 538/38, f. 65; 538/47, f. 461; B.L., Add. MS. 33271, f. 42, Norton to Anthony Bacon, 20 Feb. 1579.

48   Graves, 'Norton', pp. 18, 19, 23, 31–3. Also e.g. B.L., Lansd. MS. 33, f. 61, Norton to Burghley, 30 Sept. 1581; Add. MS. 48023, same to same, 13 Jan. 1582; Add. MS. 15891, ff. 81d–82, Norton to Hatton, 28 Feb. 1582. When under house arrest in 1582 Norton penned a letter to Walsingham in which he referred to Mildmay's 'olde charitable thinkinges of me'. He went on to describe Hatton as 'that noble natural true gentleman who knoweth that I know I am bound to him', but added, 'my good L[ord] Tresorer is the only man in whome I have and do lay the course of my relefe': P.R.O., S.P. 12/152, f. 72 (27 Mar. 1582).

49   P.R.O., S.P. 12/177/59, ff. 145–66; 12/152, f. 72.

50   Graves, 'Norton', pp. 17–35.

51   *Ibid.*, pp. 23, 29–32.

52   Cooper, 'Further Particulars of Thomas Norton', p. 110; P.R.O., S.P. 12/177, f. 28, Norton's 'Devices'.

53   Anon. jnl., f. 7.

54   *Ibid.*, f. 8.

55   Newdigate, a Bedfordshire gentleman, was admitted to Lincoln's Inn in 1550 and sat for Buckingham in 1563–6/7 and 1571 and Berwick in 1572–81. Goodere, a member of the Warwickshire gentry, educated at Gray's Inn, and representing Stafford (1563–6/7) and Coventry (1571), had a chequered history. In 1564 he advised the Bishop of Coventry and Lichfield on the religious loyalty of Warwickshire j.p.s, and was himself designated one of the 'Good men and miet to continew in office'. However, later he was in disgrace for his association with the projected marriage between Mary Stuart and the Duke of Norfolk and even earned a spell in the Tower. Gradually he worked his way back into royal favour and served under Leicester in the Low Countries. The details in these and the following biographical sketches have been supplied from *D.N.B.*; Christina H. Garrett, *The Marian Exiles: A Study in the Origins of Elizabethan Puritanism* (Cambridge, 1938; repr. 1966); Foster, *Politics of Stability*; History of Parliament Trust biographies (since published in P.W. Hasler, *The House of Commons 1558–1603* [3 vols., 1981]), to which I was given generous access in the late 1960s and early '70s; 'A Collection of Original Letters from the Bishops to the Privy Council 1564', ed. Mary Bateson, *Camden Miscellany IX* (Cam. Soc., new ser., LIII, 1895), 46; and a variety of other sources which are specified where relevant.

56   B.L., Harl. MS. 253, f. 34.

57   Anon. jnl., ff. 24, 33v; Hartley, *Proceedings*, pp. 247–8.

58   An experienced Member recommended 'leaving the house to their fulle libertie, who in theire greatest libertie wilbe most frankelie obsequious': B.L., Harl. MS. 253, f.32v.

59   E.g. over marriage and Succession (1563–6/7), Norfolk's execution and Mary Stuart's punishment (1572), ecclesiastical reform (1566/7 and 1571), and punitive anti-Catholic laws (1571 and 1581).

[60] Dannett passed Robert Beale's discourse on the Earl of Hertford's clandestine marriage to Lady Catherine Grey to the earl's lawyers: M. Levine, *The Early Elizabethan Succession Question 1558–1568* (Stanford, 1966), pp. 65, 72; C. Read, *Mr Secretary Cecil and Queen Elizabeth* (1955), p. 279; Neale, *Elizabeth I and Her Parliaments*, I, 278–80; Cromwell, f. 55; Hartley, *Proceedings*, pp. 295–8. Dannett had been implicated in the rising of the Duke of Suffolk (Catherine Grey's father) in 1554, for which he was imprisoned and indicted, but released after a month and later pardoned. He enjoyed Elizabeth's favour which in 1561 expressed itself gratuitously in the form of an annuity of £150: D.M. Loades, *Two Tudor Conspiracies* (Cambridge, 1965), pp. 33–4, 101–2, 117–18. Thomas Digges, a mathematician educated at Cambridge, was Lord Keeper Nicholas Bacon's protégé. After his patron's death in 1579 he became a client of the Earl of Leicester: R. Tittler, *Nicholas Bacon: The Making of a Tudor Statesman* (1976), pp. 58, 145; Neale, *Elizabethan Commons*, pp. 212, n.2 and 411.

[61] Nov.–Dec. 1566: *C.S.P. Dom.*, 1547–80, pp. 283–4.

[62] 24 Nov. 1566: *ibid.*, p. 283.

[63] B.L., Harl. MS. 253, ff. 33–33v.

[64] Robert Bell (Cambridge and Middle Temple) was appointed Chief Baron of the Exchequer in 1577. Thomas Bromley (Oxford and Inner Temple) was recorder of the City (1566–9), Solicitor-General (appointed 1569) and Privy Councillor and Lord Chancellor (1579–87). Richard Onslow (I. Temple) advanced smoothly from London's recordership (1563–6) to the office of Solicitor-General (1566–71). Popham (Oxford and M. Temple) was not only Bristol's recorder but also one of its M.P.s (1571–81). From the time he was sworn of the Privy Council in 1571 his distinguished career was characterized by a steady, undramatic rise, becoming successively Solicitor-General (1579), Attorney-General (1581), and Chief Justice of Queen's Bench (1592). Christopher Yelverton's career too was grounded upon a local power base. Educated at Gray's Inn, he was not only recorder of Northampton but also represented local constituencies in the Commons: Brackley (1563–6/7), Northampton (1572–81) and one of the shire seats in 1593 and 1597. As the Queen's reign drew to a close (1602) he was named a justice of Queen's Bench. For Thomas Wilbraham the rewards of service were more modest (perhaps because of an early death, 1573), but his career followed a standard pattern: recorder of London (1569–71), parliamentary service (London 1571 and Westminster 1572), and an attorney of the Court of Wards. In 1572 he played a prominent part in Parliament when he was introduced by a Councillor, Sir Francis Knollys, and delivered a report, distinguished by its cogency and length, on the charges against Mary. However, his service to the Council was largely confined to this one episode: Tanner, ff. 46v–51; *D.N.B.*; Cromwell, f.7v.

[65] Anon. jnl., f. 35; Foster, *Politics of Stability*, pp. 141, 142, n., 188; Hartley, *Proceedings*, pp. 248–9.

[66] Elton, 'Parliament in the Sixteenth Century', pp. 266–7.

[67] Thomas Aldersey, a haberdasher who sat on the City's common council between 1571 and 1599 (and in the Commons 1581–7) rendered important financial services to the Crown and enjoyed a characteristic variety of links with royal government. In 1575 he was one of a group of merchants who helped in 'soliciting, collecting and carrying foreign loans'; in 1582 he investigated the illegal exportation of gold; and in 1587 he was one of the mortgagees of the Earl of Leicester, holding (with others) lands worth £7,000 for a loan of £2,000: Foster, *Politics of Stability*, pp. 138, n.7, 140, 145, 165. Rowland Heyward, described by Foster as the 'most remarkable alderman of this time', brought the prestige of his wealth and civic activity with him into the Commons. He served twice as mayor, for 33 years in the court of aldermen (1560–93) and in three parliamentary sessions (1572–81), amassed a fortune, and received a knighthood. As an honorary member of the Inner Temple from 1561 he must have had contact with two of its members, Thomas Norton and Thomas Sackville (the Queen's cousin and later Lord Buckhurst) who, in the following January, staged their dramatic succession tract, 'Gorboduc', before the Queen. Perhaps it also introduced him to Richard Onslow, one of the governors of the Inner Temple, and Robert Dudley, who was created 'Prince Pallaphilos' in the inn's Christmas revels of 1561–2: Marie Axton, 'Robert Dudley and the Inner Temple Revels', *Historical Jnl.*, XIII (1970), 365–7, 374. He must have established a financial relationship with the

Queen's favourite, and with William Cecil too, when he became governor of the
Company of Mineral and Battery Works, which was chartered in 1568. He retained the
governorship for many years, during which Leicester and Cecil were prominent sharehol-
ders: M.B. Donald, *Elizabethan Monopolies: The History of the Company of Mineral and
Battery Works . . . 1565 to 1604* (1961), pp. 21, 35–9, 71, 74; Foster, *Politics of Stability*, pp.
73–4, 83, 111, 147, 164. John Marshe was another pillar of the City community: a mercer,
governor of the Merchant Adventurers' Company, member of the Muscovy and Spanish
Companies, common serjeant, City solicitor (1563–79), member of the common council
and under-sheriff of London. He represented the City in every Elizabethan Parliament
until his death before the 1581 session: *ibid.*, pp. 107, 171, 188.

68   Neale, *Elizabethan Commons*, p. 146. Individual performances have been calculated from
Lords R.O., Journals of the House of Commons, I–II; D'Ewes, *Jnls.*; anon. jnl.; Tanner;
Cromwell; Hooker's journal in Hartley, *Proceedings*, pp. 243–58; Onslow. Other active
Members included Sir Thomas Sampole, Thomas Cromwell, Sir William More, Sir
Thomas Scot, Serjeant Flowerdew, Edward Lewkenor, Sir Thomas Browne, James
Dalton and Francis Alford.

69   B.L., Lansd. MS. 23, ff. 53–8; Cromwell, f. 58.

70   Fleetwood's object was to arrest any Englishmen who were present. This was not
surprising, because the embassy was a common resort for English recusants, but the result
was a fiasco. The bewildered Recorder was hurried away to the Fleet prison where,
however, he assumed a hairshirt of resignation, informing Burghley that there 'a man may
quietly be acquainted with God': B.L., Lansd. MS. 23, ff. 51, 54–5, 58; T. Wright, *Queen
Elizabeth and Her Times . . .* (2 vols., 1838), II, 37–41, 62–4.

71   E.g. *Acts of the Privy Council*, XIII, 19–20, 68, 135, 164, 298, 305, 331–2, 360; Corp[oration
of] London R[ecords] O[ffice], Rep[ertories of the court of aldermen] 16, f. 145v; W.H.
and H.C. Overall, *Analytical Index to . . . the Remembrancia . . .* (1878), pp. 206, 295, 384,
537, 570; Wright, *Elizabeth*, II, 17–21, 37–41, 62–4; P.R. Harris, 'William Fleetwood,
Recorder of the City, and Catholicism in Elizabethan London', *Recusant History*, VII
(1963–4), 107–19.

72   Overall, *Remembrancia*, p. 537.

73   Bodl., Tanner MS. 84, f. 202.

74   Harris, 'Fleetwood', pp. 118–19.

75   Anon. jnl., f. 13.

76   Wright, *Elizabeth*, II, 66–74, 86–9, 97–8, 159–61, 164–7, 169–74, 240–7, 291–3, 308–9;
B.L., Lansd. MS. 41, ff. 15–16; 43, ff. 164–75.

77   Tittler, *Bacon*, p. 123.

78   Wright, *Elizabeth*, II, 167–8.

79   Corp. London R.O., Rep. 17, f. 342; 18, f. 179.

80   *Ibid.*, 20, f. 155.

81   *Ibid.*, 18, f. 179.

82   Anon jnl., ff. 12v, 35–35v; Hartley, *Proceedings*, pp. 245–6.

83   Corp. London R.O., L.A.B., 2 (tallow chandlers); A.B.3, 86 (bakers). I am grateful to
Mark Benbow for this information.

84   Corp. London R.O., Rep. 16, ff. 118v–119, 128–128v, 134, 139v–141, 275v; 17, ff.
129v–130, 134v, 141v, 144, 152v, 311v, 335, 337, 343v; 18, f. 130; 19, ff. 35, 43, 45v.

85   E.g. *ibid*, 16, f. 275v.

86   *Ibid.*, 17, f. 152v; 19, f. 499. In 1593 and 1597 the court appointed a legislative committee
to devise bills and it sought the Speaker's favour in the advancement of two measures:
both practices are evidence of a more systematic attempt to use Parliament in order to
promote City interests. Neale, *Elizabethan Commons*, p. 386.

87   Corp. London R.O., Rep. 17, f. 337. See also Rep. 16, ff. 262–262v, 277.

88   B.L., Harl. MS. 253, f. 34.

89   *Ibid.*

90   *C.J.*, I, 69, 85, 110, 120, 125, 129, 131–3, 136.

91   Cromwell, f. 33.

92   *Ibid.*; Hartley, *Proceedings*, pp. 247–8.

93   Corp. London R.O., Rep. 17, f. 335.

94 Cromwell, ff. 43, 47.
95 Corp. London R.O., Rep. 21, f. 393. See also Neale, *Elizabethan Commons*, pp. 385–6.
96 Corp. London R.O., Rep. 16, f. 145v; 17, f. 342; 18, ff. 175, 179.
97 Also Digges owed his nomination for Southampton in 1584 to Leicester; Bell (when Member for King's Lynn) nominated the earl as high steward; and in the mid-1580s Aldersey was one of the mortgagees of his lands worth £7,000: Foster, *Politics of Stability*, p. 145; Neale, *Elizabethan Commons*, pp. 209, 212. Fleetwood acknowledged a special allegiance to Lord Keeper Bacon too: B.L., Lansd. MS. 24, f. 10.
98 Neale, *Elizabethan Commons*, p. 365. In a subtle way this physical juxtaposition may have encouraged collaboration or, at least, inhibited public disagreement. In the modern Parliament government and opposition sit on opposite sides of the chamber, facing each other — a confrontational position. Members who sat in physical intimacy, rubbing shoulders and facing the same way, were deprived of this psychological stimulus to opposition. Furthermore men who worked together tended to sit together — so there developed 'the rebellious corner in the right hand of the House' in 1597: Hayward Townshend, *Historical Collections . . .* (1680), pp. 199, 298.
99 Neale, *Elizabeth I and Her Parliaments*, I, 337; D'Ewes, *Jnls.*, p. 283; *C.J.*, I, 127.
100 Onslow, ff. 1v–6v; Elton, 'Parliament in the Sixteenth Century', pp. 265–7; P.R.O., S.P. 12/86/47.
101 B.L., Lansd. MS. 41, f. 15; 43, ff. 164–75. Fulk Onslow's notes in 1581 and 1586–7 may have been destined for the Lord Treasurer's desk: Elton, 'Parliament in the Sixteenth Century', pp. 265–7.
102 B.L., Harl. MS. 253, ff. 33–33v, 35; P.R.O., S.P. 12/177, ff. 144, 147v; B.L., Lansd. MS. 20, ff. 4, 6.
103 *C.J.*, I, 63; B.L., Cotton MS. Titus F.I, f. 76v.
104 Neale, *Elizabeth I and Her Parliaments*, I, 162–3.
105 *C.J.*, I, 83–7, 91; anon. jnl., ff. 5v–7, 11v–12.
106 See above, pp. 12–13.
107 Cromwell, ff. 1–4.
108 Tanner, f. 45.
109 Hartley, *Proceedings*, pp. 313, 299–301.
110 *Ibid.*, p. 313. They were designed to be exhibited in the Commons, although it is not known whether they were. Nevertheless it is revealing that three men-of-business, all connected with Bacon or Burghley, had come armed with papers designed to give added weight to a parliamentary petition to the Queen: *ibid.*, pp. 294–8.
111 Tanner, f. 60v.
112 *L.J.*, I, 706; *C.J.*, I, 94–5, 97; Tanner, ff. 46–51v, 53–55v; Cromwell, ff. 7v–15v, 25–25v.
113 Tanner, f. 59; Cromwell, ff. 25v–27v, 36–40v; *C.J.*, I, 97.
114 Cromwell, f. 40v.
115 *Ibid.*, ff. 36v–37, 39.
116 *Ibid.*, ff. 40v–41.
117 *C.J.*, I, 98.
118 Tanner, f. 59v; Onslow, f.1.
119 As Neale rightly calls it: *Elizabeth I and Her Parliaments*, I, 269; B.L., Cotton MS. Titus F.I, ff. 172–186v.
120 Salisbury MSS. (the Marquess of Salisbury, Hatfield House, Hertfordshire), Cecil MS. 140/5, list of Thomas Norton's papers; Neale, *Elizabeth I and Her Parliaments*, I, 269.
121 *C.J.*, I, 95, 98; *L.J.*, I, 706.
122 Sir Dudley Digges, *The Compleat Ambassador . . .* (1655), pp. 219, 203.
123 Elton, 'Parliament in the Sixteenth Century', pp. 265–7.
124 Neale, *Elizabeth I and Her Parliaments*, I, 269.
125 *C.J.*, I, 100.
126 *Ibid.*, 96, 98–102.
127 *Ibid.*, 95; Cecil MS. 140/5.
128 Cecil MS. 140/5; *C.J.*, I, 95, 98–9.
129 Cecil MS. 140/5.
130 Cromwell, ff. 65–65v.

[131] Tanner, f. 60; Cromwell, ff. 44v–45.
[132] *L.J.*, I, 715, 717; *C.J.*, I, 100.
[133] *C.J.*, I, 85.
[134] *Ibid.*, 100.
[135] *Ibid.*, 102; Tanner, f. 62v.
[136] *C.J.*, I, 100–3.
[137] Neale, *Elizabeth I and Her Parliaments*, I, 281–3; B.L., Cotton MS. Caligula B. VIII, ff. 240–246v; Onslow, ff. 4–6.
[138] Cromwell, f. 58.
[139] *Ibid.*
[140] *C.J.*, I, 101.
[141] *Ibid.*, 101–3.
[142] Cromwell, ff. 52v–53v.
[143] *Ibid.*, f. 53v.
[144] Tanner, f. 62.
[145] *Ibid.*; ff. 62–62v.
[146] *C.J.*, I, 101.
[147] *Ibid.*, 102.
[148] Cecil MS. 140/5.
[149] *D.N.B.* (Cecil, William); Corp. London R.O., Rep. 17, ff. 90, 101v–102; *C.J.*, I, 94.
[150] Elton, 'Parliament in the Sixteenth Century', pp. 265–7.
[151] B.L., Lansd. MS. 43, ff. 164–75.
[152] E.g. *ibid.*, 41, f. 45.
[153] B.L., Harl. MS. 253, ff. 32–6.
[154] E.g. *C.J.*, I, 85–6, 96, 100, 102; Hartley, *Proceedings*, p. 248.
[155] Graves, 'Norton', pp. 24–5; P.R.O., S.P. 12/77/54; 12/86/47; 12/107/45–6, 58, 63, 77–80.
[156] *C.J.*, I, 83.
[157] *Ibid.*, 118. Three days later he reiterated the point.
[158] The Queen made reference to 'someone learned man [who] dyd put to the same one other byll additionall, which stretched so farre . . . full miche agayst our good will and pleasure [and] we mislyked it verie mich': Hartley, *Proceedings*, pp. 256–7.
[159] B.L., Cotton MS. Titus F.I, ff. 142v–3.
[160] Inner Temple, Petyt MS. 538/17, f. 252b.
[161] Tanner, f. 63v.
[162] B.L., Harl. MS. 253, ff. 32v, 34.
[163] *Ibid.*, f. 32v.
[164] E.g. B.L., Cotton MS. Titus F.I, ff. 142v–143.
[165] Hartley, *Proceedings*, pp. 245–6; B.L., Cotton MS. Titus F.I, ff. 137v–138.
[166] *Ibid.*, ff. 148v–149.
[167] Cromwell, f. 29.
[168] B.L., Cotton MS. Titus F.I, f. 170.
[169] Cooper, 'Further Particulars of Thomas Norton', pp. 109–10.
[170] *C.J.*, I, 134.
[171] B.L., Lansd. MS. 43, f. 169v.
[172] *Ibid.*, f. 178v.
[173] H.M.C., *Salisbury MSS.*, VII, 482–3.
[174] B.L., Lansd. MS. 41, f. 45.

Parliamentary History, Volume 2 (1983)

WARDSHIP IN THE PARLIAMENT OF 1604

PAULINE CROFT

Royal Holloway College, University of London

The debates on a scheme of composition to buy out wardship, which took place in the opening session of James I's first Parliament, have often attracted the attention of historians. As is well known, the main outlines of the scheme and many of the points raised in discussion prefigure in some detail the more famous plan for a 'Great Contract' which Robert Cecil, Earl of Salisbury, presented to the House of Commons in February 1610. In an important recent article, examining these debates along with the other issues discussed in 1604, R. C. Munden has argued that the rapid 'growth of mutual distrust' which was so marked a feature of this Parliament should be attributed less to the ineptitude and personal defects of the King himself than to the existence of policy disagreements and faction fighting among the King's principal advisers, the great lords at court and in the Privy Council. Similarly A.G.R. Smith, writing on the Great Contract, has noted in passing a change of mind apparently shown by Salisbury himself in 1604 which caused the earlier plan to collapse.[1] It will be the purpose of this short article to put forward new reasons for that breakdown in negotiations and to throw fresh light on the tangled course of events in 1604. To do so a brief chronological account is first needed.

Opposition to the whole system of wardship had been manifest in the House of Commons for many years. A heated debate had taken place in 1585, when Burghley as Master of the Wards had put forward two bills to end current devices for defrauding the Queen of her due revenue from wardship. It was on this issue that the young Francis Bacon, by 1604 one of the most experienced Members of the House, made his first parliamentary speech.[2] On Burghley's death in 1598, it had been suggested that the unpopular Court of Wards might be abolished in return for a fixed annual payment to the Crown; but the scheme was not discussed in any detail and in due course, after a short interregnum, Robert Cecil succeeded his father as Master of the Wards, thereby apparently ensuring the stability and continuity of the old system. However, shortly after the accession of James I, Cecil himself took the idea of abolition a step further. In the summer of 1603 Dorset, the Lord Treasurer, was casting around for methods of increasing the royal revenue, already under pressure from James's lavish generosity. Dorset proposed to sell all royal copyholders their freehold, to grant 60-year leases of Crown lands and fee farms in return for small entry fines but with a greatly increased rent, and to accept composition for respite of homage. Like wardship, respite of homage resulted from the anachronistic survival of feudal tenure, although it brought in far less revenue. Salisbury then broadened this tentative attack on fiscal feudalism by proposing in addition the far more radical plan 'to have wards turned to a certain annual rent to be propounded in parliament'.[3]

Further evidence that Salisbury would support such a major change came at the opening of the parliamentary session in 1604. On 23 March, the first day of business, the veteran Sir Robert Wroth rose to move 'that matters of most importance might first be handled'. After requesting a confirmation of the Book of Common Prayer, he asked 'for wardship, that the king might have a composition, and the subjects freed from that tenure', and instanced several other long-standing grievances for discussion, such as monopolies and purveyance. Wroth's initiative was for many years adduced as evidence of the rising independence of speakers in the Commons, but more recently it has been shown that he regarded himself as a client of Salisbury, and therefore his speech was probably pre-arranged, a reflection of government thinking rather than of independent views.[4] After a discussion of Wroth's motion, the Commons resolved to ask the Lords for a conference on wardship, in particular to discuss the framing of a joint petition to James I for leave 'to enter into consideration of some project of recompense to be given to his highness'. The royal permission was of course necessary before any debate on a matter of royal prerogative could take place. The conference duly convened on 27 March, and touched on several of the grievances that Wroth had raised, but as it was hinted that reforms were already on the way as regards purveyance, it was agreed to petition to treat of wardship and respite of homage only. However, after agreeing so far, the conference broke up abruptly when Salisbury also raised the issue of the controversial election case concerning Sir Francis Goodwin. The Commons committee refused to discuss the matter, on the grounds that it had already been decided, and returned to the lower House.[5]

The project for wardship rested there for nearly seven weeks while other issues such as the Buckinghamshire election and the royal plan for the Union dominated parliamentary business. Discussion on purveyance, however, continued, and on 8 May the Lords 'for remedy propounded composition by the subject, £50,000 per annum'. This re-awakened interest in the possibility of a similar remedy by composition for wardship, and vigorous attempts were made by at least two Members of the lower House to join the two schemes together. The Commons nevertheless resolved after considerable debate that composition for wardship should 'go single' and decided to resume negotiations by asking the Lords to join in a petition to abolish feudal tenures.[6] Such a move would bring to an end primer seizin, respite of homage and licenses of alienation, as well as wardship, so any composition would have to recompense the Crown for the revenue lost from all of them.

The Commons continued to receive the support of the Lords for their project, for on 21 May the committee-members from the upper House requested that at their next meeting the Commons committee would 'come furnished with the grounds and reasons to induce the king as they [the Lords] also mean to do'.[7] The next day the Commons committee met again on its own for a further discussion of their scheme, but on 24 May there came what may in retrospect be construed as the first sign of government hesitation. The Lords sent word that they wished to postpone the conference arranged for the following day, with the vague excuse that some of the peers designated to meet the Commons could not be present since they were 'commanded to attend the king's majesty at that time for some other occasion'. With no sign of disquiet over the delay, on 25 May Sir Edwin Sandys read out to the lower House the 'heads of such course as was thought meet to be proceeded in by the committee, touching the matter of wardship'. There was no time for discussion that day so on the morning of Saturday 26 May, the day now appointed for the deferred conference with the Lords, the committee's 'heads' were once again read out in the House, this time by the clerk. The heads reveal that the Commons committee had done a great deal of hard thinking on the issues under scrutiny. In addition to putting forward strong arguments in principle for the abolition of wardship, they had also anticipated a number of problems, such as the need to compensate the redundant officers of the Court of Wards. Central to their proposal was the outline of a scheme for the assessment, by a commission, of the amount of land held by tenure-in-chief, and the setting by the commissioners of a 'proportionable rate', since it was tenants-in-chief who would be the chief beneficiaries of the abolition of wardship. The committee intended that the next session of Parliament would finalize the project, thereby allowing a calculation of the total compensation which would accrue to the Crown. They promised that the as yet unspecified amount of composition would be 'not only proportionable to the utmost benefit that any of [James I's] progenitors ever reaped hereby, but also with such an overplus and large addition as in great part to supply his majesty's other necessities'.[8]

No sooner had the clerk finished reading the heads than Sir Robert Wroth rose to speak. In a staggering change of tack, he opposed all the conclusions of the committee on wardship, of which he was a member, and which had been set up to implement his original motion of 23 March. 'Impossible that any good should come of this course in the matter of wardship etc.: he foresaw it, he knew it.' Instead of supporting the committee's project for composition, Wroth now had an entirely new suggestion to put forward. 'Moved therefore that every man by his last will and testament might dispose of his child, paying the like fine etc. And that some bill to that purpose might be thought on.'[9] Wroth's backtracking was at once followed by similar action in the Lords. That very afternoon, 26 May, at their conference with the lower House, the Lords, far from bringing further reasons to persuade the King to consent to composition for wardship, as they had promised to do, instead told the Commons' representatives to drop the whole idea of buying out feudal tenures. Sandys reported back to a startled lower House that 'instead of acceptation and assent to join in petition to his majesty', he could deliver 'from their lordships no other than matter of expostulation, opposition of reason to reason, admonition, or precise caution'. It can scarcely be a coincidence that Wroth's change of mind in the Commons immediately preceded such a change on the part of the Lords. Dr Tyacke, who confined himself to a consideration of Wroth's actions in proposing his original motion on 23 March, was very cautious in assessing the degree of direction behind his moves, warning that 'nothing . . . allows us to assert positively that Wroth spoke with the approval of Robert Cecil, although it is likely that he did. His proposed programme seemingly mirrors recent thinking in government circles'. But the identical change of direction, first by Wroth and then by the Lords committee on the very same day, surely proves beyond doubt that not only during the opening debate in Parliament, but throughout the session, Wroth was acting as the faithful and regularly briefed spokesman for Salisbury's plans for wardship.[10] The nature of Wroth's alternative suggestion, which will be examined below, is further evidence for this firm conclusion.

Between 22 May and 26 May, then, something had persuaded Salisbury to change his mind in the middle of the negotiations, abandoning the course of action that he had favoured since 1603 and had, through Wroth, placed before the Commons in March 1604. What was it? It has been suggested that by 26 May Salisbury had realized that he was not going to get his way in the parallel discussions on purveyance, and had decided that a deal on wardship alone was not worth pursuing.[11] It is true that by 26 May the debates on purveyance were proving unfruitful, but as late as 2 June courtier spokesmen such as Sir George More were still encouraging the House to continue with them. In any case, already on 16 May the Commons had firmly decided that wardship should 'go single', so it seems unlikely that Salisbury clung to a double solution until 26 May then precipitately abandoned both. More plausible is the suggestion that he withdrew his plans for wardship after sensing the King's lack of support for the scheme, or even perhaps after an order to drop it.[12] But again, James's overriding preoccupation with the Union and absence of interest in wardship were well known before 26 May. Above all, such an interpretation, which emphasizes the role of the King, fails to take sufficiently into account the Commons' animus against the Lords over the collapse of the scheme and their clear feeling that they had been misled. 'We had entered into this labyrinth hoping your lordships would have been an Ariadne to us', wrote Sir John Holles, and it is apparent from the rest of his letter that he and many others resented what they saw as duplicity on the part of the Lords, not the King.[13] Although the lack of progress on purveyance and the unenthusiastic attitude of James I may well already have been worrying Salisbury, these factors on their own do not explain the suddenness of his change of mind. A more convincing explanation is needed, and one can be put forward which accords much better with Mr Munden's general stress on the role of faction.

On 16 May the Commons had named a committee for the forthcoming conferences with the Lords on wardship. Included among its members were John Hare, energetic and long serving clerk to the Court of Wards, who sat for Morpeth, and Sir Edward Lewkenor, Member for Maldon and a lawyer who practised a great deal in the court.[14] As the committee embarked on its series of meetings, views embodying the most forceful opposition to wardship were put forward by the other Members. By 25 May these hostile views had been marshalled into the heads of a petition which the lower House was still hoping would be jointly presented to the King by the Lords and Commons. Many of the accusations against wardship made at the committee and set out in the petition were presumably carried back to their colleagues in the Court of Wards by Hare and Lewkenor. These accusations were regarded by the officers of the court as malicious and slanderous lies. Stung by the force of the allegations, and unmoved by the offers of a pension for themselves — offers which may of course only have been made after rumours of their counter-offensive began to circulate — the officers moved to defend their jobs and their honour. One of them, probably Hare himself, still smarting from his experience in the committee, drew up a vigorous reply to the charges contained in the petition and presented it directly to Salisbury.[15]

The document, headed 'the petition pretended to be made unto the king for composition for his tenures upon these points', took up the Commons' arguments one by one. It stated that wardship was not unique to England, as the Commons alleged: more onerous versions existed in France, Spain and Italy. Where the Commons argued that feudal tenure had originated in the need to raise forces for border defence against Scotland, a need now rendered obsolete by the union of the two crowns, the officers of the Wards had a very different view of the origins of feudalism. Tenures were 'by prescription long before the conquest', so the change in the situation brought about by James's accession was irrelevant. In particular the author energetically denied the allegation that the court took young children away from their mothers, and with some factual support stated that on the contrary the long-term interests of the ward were better served by 'the good government of the court' than by the intervention of possible stepfathers and family friends. As for offers of compensation, they would have to be very substantial indeed to be worthwhile; £30,000 would barely cover the basics. A more reasonable sum would be £60,000 with a further £20,000 *p.a.* to compound for the King's loss of 'honour and strength'. The King's aids, licences of alienation and fines for respite of homage, together with the savings to the subject of fees at present paid to the sheriffs, officers and clerks of the court, were worth another £40,000, coming to £120,000 *p.a.* in all. Even allowing for a considerable element of exaggeration in these figures, the message was clear; the King's losses were likely to be far greater than any conceivable composition offered by the Commons.

The riposte on behalf of the officers of the court, Salisbury's direct subordinates, can only have been drawn up when the discussions on the possible form of the committee's petition were well advanced, for it follows in some detail the arguments finally read out in the House by Sandys on 26 May.[16] A likely time for its composition and presentation to Salisbury would therefore be around 24 May — the very day the Lords postponed the conference previously arranged with the Commons. There can be no doubt that Salisbury had studied the document with the greatest attention, for the back page is covered with jottings in his own distinctive hand, summarizing the main points of the argument and concluding with the words 'difficulty . . . impossibility for any time'. Salisbury also made use of a number of the points in the document in his own speech to the joint conference of the Lords and Commons committees on the afternoon of 26 May, although not surprisingly he scaled down the officers' financial calculations.[17] The circumstantial evidence, then, all indicates that it was this document, presented to Salisbury just as the Commons were concluding their discussions, that persuaded him to change his mind. The officers of the Court of Wards, led by Hare, had taken the issue out of the Commons and acted as an independent pressure group to lobby the Master of the Wards himself.[18]

The document drafted by the officers contained little that can have come as a surprise to Salisbury. Not one of their points was novel, nor can he ever have expected those who looked to the court for their livelihood to have much enthusiasm for his proposal to abolish it. But their attack brought home the highly embarrassing probability of a public demonstration of the wide difference of opinion over the potential advantages of the scheme between the Master and his experienced and influential subordinates. This could not fail to undercut even further both royal and conciliar support for the project, once it became known. The petition may also have caused him to reflect that the plan for composition was alienating his own supporters while not bringing him any compensation in the form of additional patronage or income. Nor would its success necessarily increase his standing with James I. Salisbury was not yet Lord Treasurer; it would be Dorset who would reap the political benefits of an improvement in the King's financial position. By their action in lobbying him, the officers of the Wards had added to, and crystallized, all those doubts and uncertainties already evident in the situation. Their document was the last straw, the final consideration which decided him to drop the plan in the middle of negotiations with the Commons. The Lords' reply to the Commons committee, opposing the scheme of composition as potentially offensive and disparaging to the Crown, was, and was seen to be, a smokescreen for this sudden change of mind on the part of Salisbury himself.[19]

A further clue to the development of Salisbury's thinking over those vital last few days can be found by examining the content of the alternative motion put forward by Sir Robert Wroth — 'moved therefore that every man by his last will and testament might dispose of his child, paying the like fine etc. And that some bill to that purpose might be thought on'. This was a direct reference to the recently implemented reform in the Court of Wards by which Salisbury had made it possible for all tenants-in-chief to buy out the wardship of their heirs during their own lifetimes. This 'revolutionary'[20] measure allowed the tenants-in-chief to vest the care of their children in guardians of their own choice, instead of being forced to leave the matter in the hands of the court after their death. Such a personal arrangement had been known before but hitherto it had been the jealously guarded privilege of a few Crown servants. If in future all tenants-in-chief availed themselves of the new offer — or if, as Wroth now suggested, they were obliged by law to do so — the reform would undercut much of the opposition to the court. Parents would be granted control over the future welfare of their children and the oversight of their estates, but the royal revenues from wardship would not be lost; indeed they might well increase.

Wroth's suggestion that an element of compulsion might be necessary to achieve this apparently desirable improvement is in itself illuminating. The Commons were aware of the recent reform in the practice of the court but seem to have failed to appreciate its long-term significance.[21] They were not alone in this, for unexpectedly as yet the Court of Wards had received little response to its new offer. Tenants-in-chief were proving disappointingly slow in taking up the new privilege thrown open to them, and had not grasped the full advantages of it. Salisbury had been compelled to write at length to the feodaries of the court, who had been charged with the task of making known the new offer in the counties, setting out the answers to a number of points that had been raised. Among them was an inquiry made apparently by several tenants-in-chief, asking for clarification of the position if a landowner were to invest money in buying out the wardship of his eldest son only to have the child predecease him. Salisbury replied that the money paid to the court applied to the wardship of the heir, whoever he or she might be, and not to an individual child.[22] The need to allay such apprehensions was holding up applications to make composition. Salisbury might therefore reasonably expect that if tenants-in-chief were compelled by statute to take advantage of his new offer, they would at last appreciate its genuine benefits. Opposition to wardship would then fade away, for no one in future could justly accuse the court of treating children as saleable commodities; the arrangements for their care and upbringing would have been made by their parents, with the court merely acting in effect as an executor. After reading the document submitted by the officers of the court, Salisbury must have turned his thoughts to examining alternatives to composition. Here, in his own recent reform of the practice of the court, was a way forward. Wroth could withdraw his earlier motion and substitute one which, it was hoped, would defuse the political opposition to wardship while leaving the court and its revenue intact.

The move was a miscalculation, which succeeded only in creating a more serious political problem. Salisbury's *volte-face* caused turmoil in the Commons. The dismay and indignation of Members of the lower House can be seen in their decision, immediately on receiving Sandys's report of the abortive conference with the Lords, to justify their proceedings on wardship directly to the King himself, a decision which gave birth to the Commons Apology. As Sir Thomas Ridgeway tellingly pointed out, they wished particularly that the matter of wardship, 'so advisedly and gravely undertaken and proceeded in, might not die, or be buried in the hands of those that first bred it'. Sir John Holles was embittered by fears that the Lords would deliberately misreport the Commons' proceedings to the King: 'So they have the sunshine and we the shade, they are the grave and wise aristocracy, we the giddy populace.' He went on to conclude despondently, 'it is bootless to endeavour good for the public when the ablest operators disavow us'.[23] Moreover, hopes that opposition to wardship would fade away as a result of the manoeuvre were to be disappointed. During the next round of debates on the Union, in December 1606, the question of escuage provided an opening for Fuller to raise once more the matter of wardship. At once, the lower House clamoured for its complete removal.[24] It was even rumoured in the Commons that Salisbury himself might once again favour the dissolution of the Court of Wards, but this seems either to have been a deliberate attempt by the speakers opposing wardship to encourage the more timid to join them, or possibly even a lingering memory of his initial attitude at the opening of the 1604 session. In 1606 Salisbury gave the idea no encouragement and in the event the Commons did not pursue any scheme of composition. Flexible, fairminded and open to innovation as he was, the words and actions of the Master of the Wards between 1604 and 1610 all indicate that he saw no fundamental objection to wardship as such. Rather, his aim was to achieve a humane system that would still be efficient in generating revenue for the Crown.[25] In this pragmatic attitude he differed with increasing sharpness from leading Members of the lower House such as Fuller, who in 1606 flatly described wardship as 'against the laws of God and nature'. Public opinion favoured Fuller rather than Salisbury, as can be seen in contemporary plays such as *The Miseries of Inforst Marriage* by Wilkins, reprinted four times between 1607 and 1637, and the melodrama *A Yorkshire Tragedy*, printed in 1608 and 1619 and once attributed to Shakespeare, which showed how the emotional pressures engendered by the system of wardship could in extreme cases lead to multiple murder.[26]

In February 1610 Salisbury offered further reforms in wardship as part of his initial ten-point offer which opened negotiations for the Great Contract. Once again the Commons showed that they were interested only in abolition, not amelioration; it was the same difference of approach that had become visible in the breakdown of the conference between the Lords and Commons in May 1604.[27] But in 1610, Salisbury had to contend not only with a major difference of attitude, but also with the aftermath of suspicion and disquiet caused by memories of his own sudden backtracking on the previous occasion. For sending out such conflicting signals, and treating the Commons in so cavalier a fashion on such a sensitive issue, Salisbury must bear a considerable part of the blame for that 'growth of mutual distrust' which brought the first session of James's first Parliament to so negative an end. The consequences of his earlier actions were to bedevil his efforts to complete the Great Contract in the more urgent circumstances of 1610.

Notes

1 R.C. Munden, 'James I and "The Growth of Mutual Distrust": King, Commons and Reform, 1603–1604', *Faction and Parliament: Essays on Early Stuart History*, ed. K. Sharpe (Oxford, 1978); A.G.R. Smith, 'The Great Contract of 1610', *The English Commonwealth 1547–1640: Essays in Politics and Society Presented to Joel Hurstfield*, eds. P. Clark, A.G.R. Smith and N. Tyacke (Leicester, 1979), p. 117.

2 *The Journals of All the Parliaments during the Reign of Queen Elizabeth . . .*, ed. Sir Symonds D'Ewes (1682; repr. Shannon, 1973), p. 315; Sir John Neale, *Elizabeth I and Her Parliaments* (2 vols., 1953–7), II, 91–3.

3 *C.S.P.Dom.*, 1598–1601, p. 110; 'The Journal of Sir Roger Wilbraham . . .', ed. H.S. Scott, *Camden Miscellany X* (Cam. Soc., 3rd ser., IV, 1902), pp. 62–3.

4 N.R.N. Tyacke, 'Wroth, Cecil and the Parliamentary Session of 1604', *B.I.H.R.*, L (1977). Accounts of Wroth's motion vary slightly. *C.J.*, I, 151 omits any mention of composition and does not list licences of alienation, but these details are added by Sir Edward Montague in his 'Journal': H.M.C., *Buccleuch (Montagu) MSS.*, III, 80.

5 H.M.C., *Salisbury MSS.*, XXIII, 130–4; *Buccleuch (Montagu) MSS.*, III, 83.

6 *C.J.*, I, 207, 211; H.M.C., *Salisbury MSS.*, XXIII, 134–5.

7 *L.J.*, I, 303; *C.J.*, I, 221.

8 *L.J.*, I, 305; *C.J.*, I, 227–8; H.M.C., *Salisbury MSS.*, XXIII, 136–8.

9 *C.J.*, I, 228.

10 *C.J.*, I, 230; Tyacke, 'Wroth, Cecil and the Parliamentary Session of 1604', p. 122; H.M.C., *Salisbury MSS.*, XXIII, 138–9.

11 Smith, 'Great Contract', p. 117.

12 *Ibid.*; *C.J.*, I, 231.

13 H.M.C., *Portland MSS.*, IX, 12.

14 H.M.C., *Salisbury MSS.*, XXIII, 135; H.E. Bell, *An Introduction to the History and Records of the Court of Wards and Liveries* (Cambridge, 1953), pp. 26–8, 158.

15 The heads of the Commons petition are listed in *C.J.*, I, 227: the reply of the officers is P.R.O., S.P. 14/52/88, entitled 'The petition pretended to be made unto the king for composition for his tenures upon these points'. The document is wrongly dated to 1610 in *C.S.P. Dom.*, 1603–10, although its reference to 'this last year since his majesty came to the throne' proves that it refers to 1604 and is, as its title indicates, a reply to the Commons petition of that year. It is correctly dated to 1604, but without any explanation, by Bell, *Court of Wards*, p. 139, n. Much of the document is in the first person and sounds like the usually assertive style of John Hare, but as it is a fair copy and not in his own handwriting it cannot be attributed to him directly. However, the circumstantial evidence is strong: Hare was by far the most politically active of the officers of the court and drafted similar responses on other occasions when the court was threatened (cf. P.R.O., S.P. 14/55/60, written in 1610). Moreover the writer distinguishes between the need for composition for purveyance and the scheme for composition for wardship, as Hare did by his vote in the Commons debate of 16 May 1604 (*C.J.*, I, 211). He is careful to pay due tribute to the disinterestedness of the Master of the Wards in being willing to surrender his office if composition proved profitable to the Crown; as a client of Salisbury Hare would be well aware of the need to avoid giving any offence by misrepresenting the Master's position.

16 Parts of the document sound as if they were replying, not to the final version of the heads, but to a penultimate draft couched in even blunter language. There is a small piece of indirect evidence to support this surmise. The Commons Apology of June 1604 (H.M.C.,

Salisbury MSS., XXIII, 151) denied as 'an untrue and calumnious report' that any Member had ever said that wardship was 'a slavery under your majesty more than under our former princes', and this charge certainly does not appear in the Commons petition. However, the officers' refutation contains several rebuttals of this same accusation of slavery, so it seems likely, despite the Commons' denial, that such language had been used in the committee, although for obvious reasons it was not included in the petition itself.

[17]   *C.J.*, I, 230.

[18]   It is clear from other evidence that Hare was accustomed to lobbying Salisbury on matters of importance. A sharp rebuke to him, noted in H.M.C., *Salisbury MSS.*, XVI, 128, refers to his activities sometime before 9 June 1604 and may well be related to his role as leader of the officers of the Wards.

[19]   *C.J.*, I, 230–1; H.M.C., *Portland MSS.*, IX, 12.

[20]   It is thus described by Bell, *Court of Wards*, pp. 117, 136–7.

[21]   *C.J.*, I, 227.

[22]   P.R.O., S.P. 46/61/41, Salisbury to Sir Henry Wallop *et al.* [damaged, but 1604]. Letters to the county feodaries urging them to encourage tenants-in-chief to compound had been sent out on 3 Sept. 1603: H.M.C., *Salisbury MSS.*, XV, 267, 276; E. Lodge, *Illustrations of British History . . .* (3 vols., 1791), III, 189.

[23]   *C.J.*, I, 230–1; H.M.C., *Portland MSS.*, IX, 12.

[24]   P.R.O., S.P. 14/24/13, Wilson to Salisbury.

[25]   Salisbury defended the system in February 1610 with the remark, 'I know of no other fault in the court of Wards but that the subjects pay too little and that the king hath not all': *Proceedings in Parliament 1610*, ed. Elizabeth Read Foster (2 vols., 1966), I, 16.

[26]   P.R.O., S.P. 14/24/13; *A Short-Title Catalogue of Books Printed in England, Scotland, and Ireland . . . 1475–1640*, comp. A.W. Pollard and G.R. Redgrave (1926), Nos. 22340, 25636.

[27]   S.R. Gardiner, *Parliamentary Debates in 1610 . . .* (Cam. Soc., LXXXI, 1862), pp. 16, 30 ; *Proceedings in Parliament 1610*, ed. Foster, II, 66–9.

Parliamentary History, Volume 2 (1983)

THE HOUSE OF LORDS AND THE APPELLATE JURISDICTION IN EQUITY 1640–1643*

JAMES S. HART

Sidney Sussex College, Cambridge

The history of the Cavalier Parliament of Charles II is marked by a continuing, if intermittent, struggle between the two Houses of Parliament over claims advanced by the House of Lords to exclusive jurisdiction as a court of law. One of the central episodes in that struggle arose in 1675 over the House of Lords' claim to an independent appellate jurisdiction in equity. During the spring of that year, the Lords had begun proceedings on three separate appeals from the court of Chancery; the well known case of Shirley v. Fagg, and two additional appeals brought, respectively, by Sir Nicholas Crispe and Sir Nicholas Stoughton. In all three cases, the proceedings begun in the upper House had been violently opposed by the House of Commons, initially, and importantly, on grounds of parliamentary privilege (the presumptive defendants in the Lords, in each case, being Members of the lower House) and subsequently, on grounds that the House of Lords had greatly overstated the extent of its judicial authority. The differences between the two Houses had quickly become irreconcilable and ultimately compelled Charles II to prorogue Parliament on two successive occasions, in June and November of 1675. When Parliament was recalled 17 months later, in February 1677, the House of Commons declined to challenge the Lords' continuing claim to act as a court of last resort. The failure of the lower House to revive the dispute allowed the House of Lords to establish its independent appellate jurisdiction in equity, which it continued to exercise, without impairment, from that point forward.

* I would like to thank Dr J.S. Morrill and Dr Sheila Lambert for their valuable suggestions and corrections to an earlier draft of this article. The responsibility for any remaining or additional mistakes in this final draft is entirely my own.

Despite the lasting effects of the concession made by the House of Commons, Restoration lawyers and legal scholars found the resolution of the dispute of 1675 altogether too inconclusive to stand unchallenged. The Lords had essentially won their point by default. The jurisdiction had been established *de facto*, but not *de jure*, and on that basis it invited dispute. The dispute, not surprisingly, turned on the question of precedent. The Lords had argued in 1675 that the authority to hear appeals in equity, as with common law writs of error, had been 'undoubtedly fixed and permanently lodged' in the upper House.[1] Lacking a specific statutory authority, their case had come to rest on a general assertion that their appellate jurisdiction had evolved as a matter of long standing practice. The argument advanced by the Lords in 1675, in fact, had its origins in proceedings six years earlier, in the case of Slingsby *v*. Hale. On that occasion, the Lords had accepted an appeal from the court of Chancery brought by one Henry Slingsby. The defendant, Hale, was once again a Member of the lower House, and the Lords' proceedings on the case elicited a similar protest from the House of Commons. In this case, however, the Lords referred their proceedings to their own committee for privileges with instructions that they were to 'report not onely the state of the case, but the rationality of it'.[2] The committee's report declared that 'in the case depending in the House upon appeal, the proceedings have been according to the course of Parliament, and former precedents'.[3] In the event, the appellant, Slingsby, withdrew his suit, and the matter went no further. But the committee's report of 1669 was, in fact, resurrected by the committee for privileges in 1675, and on their recommendation became the basis for the Lords' claim, in Shirley *v*. Fagg, that 'it was the undoubted right of the Lords in judicature to determine, in time of Parliament, appeals from inferior courts'.[4] Perhaps for that reason, the Lords declined to debate the origins of the jurisdiction itself, and the specific precedents supporting their claim were never elucidated, at least in the resolutions of the House which emerged from the debate.

At face value, the claim to precedent was undoubtedly based on the fact that the House had been accepting Chancery decrees for review as a matter of course and without opposition from the very first month of the Restoration. But there is also some indication that the Lords had in mind precedents which derived, not only from the Restoration Parliaments, but from the Long Parliament of Charles I. The House of Lords had been actively engaged, throughout the Long Parliament, in the review of equity decrees in general, and Chancery decrees in particular, and those proceedings were in fact mentioned repeatedly by Members of the House of Commons during the debates on the Lords' appellate jurisdiction in 1675. Henry Powle, as an example, claimed that the jurisdiction was 'no ancient thing', but admitted that 'there are precedents of their taking appeals in the time of the Long Parliament, in irregular times'.[5] Mr Serjeant Jones offered that there were precedents to be derived of that Parliament, but claimed that they were 'of no great weight'.[6] Sir Edward Dering and Sir Leoline Jenkins offered extended opinions on the 1640s as well, the latter going so far as to suggest that 'by voting that the Lords had no power of judging appeals, we did take away and avoid all the judgements that they made', which, he said 'might be of dangerous consequence'.[7]

While it cannot be argued on the basis of concrete evidence that the Lords deliberately advanced the precedents derived of the Long Parliament in support of their claim to long standing practice, the Commons debates clearly suggest that the issue had been raised at some point in the proceedings. Their importance is also suggested by the fact that they are cited in detail by Denzil, Baron Holles in his treatise on the appellate jurisdiction of the House of Lords. Holles, a member of the Lords' committee for privileges in both 1669 and 1675, wrote the treatise in 1675, in the wake of the dispute over Shirley *v.* Fagg. He responds to the negative aspersions cast on the proceedings of the 1640s by the House of Commons, and argues that[8]

> in latter times, that is . . . in all the last King's reigne and so much as is past of the King's reigne that now is, presidents are frequent of appeals in Parliament from the Court of Chancery. . . . And it hath formerly been the opinion of the House of Commons that Moderne presidents are best; and strongly was it urged by them in the case of the Earle of Clarendon, to induce the Lords to commit him to prison upon a general impeachment without special matter shewn, from one single president of that being done, in the case of the Earle of Strafford. But now they are of another mind.

Holles clearly felt that those 'moderne' precedents were both valid and important. In that treatise, he paints a picture of the House of Lords in the 1640s acting 'as the supreme Court to which all persons aggrieved did apply themselves for relief'.[9] He cites cases appealed to the House from Star Chamber, High Commission, the Privy Council, and the court of Chancery. He states, finally, 'multitudes of such presidents may be produced . . . but these are sufficient to show that, upon complaint, the Peers hath still given redress to whatever hath been done amiss by any other court, Ecclesiastical or Civil, Court of Equity or Court of Law, and was never found fault with till now'.[10] Holles's description of House of Lords' judicature during the 1640s is an accurate one, but the importance which he attached to those proceedings was a matter of considerable dispute. Between 1675 and 1700 Sir Robert Atkyns, William Petyt and Sir Matthew Hale offered challenges to the Lords' authority to act as a court of last resort in equity, and each of them, in turn, focused directly on the claims of precedent implied from the proceedings of the Long Parliament.[11] Hale's treatise, written, though not published, contemporaneously, is perhaps the most comprehensive disclaimer. His argument against the appellate jurisdiction is typically wide-ranging, but it quickly comes to terms with the issue of modern precedent, and specifically with the presumptive importance attached to those cases heard and reviewed by the Lords in the 1640s. Hale's position is unequivocal. He begins his discussion by saying:[12]

> If the Lords could give us good evidence of record of their ancient and common practice of reversal of decrees in Chancery by an inherent jurisdiction residing without commission or delegation from the King, it would be of great moment

for the asserting of their jurisdiction in this particular. But upon strict search and inquiry we shall find a great defect in the proof of that fact . . . I could never find any precedent of any greater antiquity than 3 Charles I, nay scarce before 16 Charles I, of any such proceedings in the Lords' House.

Having then narrowed the scope of the dispute to the proceedings of the Long Parliament, Hale proceeds to isolate those proceedings from the canon of acceptable parliamentary precedent:[13]

When the Long Parliament came . . . such a throng of complainants poured into Parliament, and especially into the Lords' House, as transported proceedings in that House beyond the known, ancient, and regular bounds thereof. Complaints of decrees, sentences, and judgements came in apace, and were promiscuously heard. And indeed, it would be too hard a task for any person to justify all of the proceedings of that time to be consonant with the ancient and regular proceedings of Parliament.

As a whole, Hale's argument makes clear that his purpose was not simply to discredit the judicial proceedings of the Long Parliament on the readily available grounds of political and constitutional instability. His intention was to suggest that the Lords' assumption of an appellate jurisdiction in equity had been part and parcel of what he saw as the singular political thrust characterizing parliamentary activity in the period. The claim to jurisdiction, in and of itself, suggested to Hale a certain wilful disregard of established legal prerogatives. The Lord Keeper was, after all, as James I had reminded his Star Chamber audience in 1616, both in theory and practice, the dispenser of the King's conscience.[14] By claiming the right to review and reverse the Lord Keeper, the Lords, in Hale's view, were, by extension, calling into question the pre-eminent authority of royal justice, or, at the very least, were presupposing that it was susceptible to a process of parliamentary review.

Hale's sense of a wilful disregard of prerogatives was then only reinforced when the proceedings of the Long Parliament were measured against the attitude demonstrated by the House in two equity appeals brought during the 1620s. In both Bouchier's case, in 1621, and Mathew's case, in 1624, the Lords, for different reasons, appeared to decline the exercise of the appellate authority. In Mathew's case, the Lords had, on the basis of an Elizabethan precedent, requested that the King appoint a commission for review of the original decree.[15] The failure of the House to exercise similar restraint in the 1640s suggested to Hale an important change in the Lords' attitude towards established legal proceedings. His perception was also clearly influenced by the impeachment of Lord Keeper Finch in the opening months of the Long Parliament, and by what he saw as a direct cause and effect relationship between the general indictment of the judge and the subsequent rush to review his individual decisions. Hale drew the corollary with reference to Bacon, and by way of comparison, suggests that Finch's impeachment and the Lords' assumption of an appellate jurisdiction over his court were nothing so much as variations on the same political theme.

For Hale then, as for Atkyns and Petyt, judicial review of equity, as it was exercised in the Long Parliament, was invalid, at least for use as precedent, because it had been principally motivated by political, rather than by purely judicial, considerations. Hale's use of the word promiscuous was not accidental. It was a useful and appropriate adjective to register his conviction that the review and reversal of Chancery decrees had been, in the first instance, indiscriminatory, ill-conceived, and arbitrary; in modern parlance, an unwarranted 'winning of the initiative' in point of judicature.

Interestingly, Hale's condemnation of judicial review in the Long Parliament has, in fact, been adopted more or less uncritically by every historian who has since taken note of those proceedings. Francis Hargrave, Hale's eighteenth-century editor, perhaps not surprisingly, characterized the Lords in the 1640s as 'arbitrarily encroaching upon and controlling the ordinary jurisdictions of the Kingdom and invading the functions both of judges and juries'.[16] C.P. Cooper, the nineteenth-century legal antiquarian, simply paraphrased Hale, and then Hargrave, and dismissed the appellate jurisdiction as an 'usurpation'.[17] Somewhat more recently, Thomas Bevan described the exercise of the jurisdiction as 'one of the Peers' aggressions in judicature'.[18] Clearly then Hale established something of a tradition, and subsequent historians have been predisposed to condemn the judicial proceedings of the Long Parliament, and particularly the appellate jurisdiction in equity, because of the very strongly implied association between those proceedings and the general political direction taken by the Long Parliament as a whole.

But is that association a fair one? Hale's study, on which this orthodoxy effectively rests, was, in its political terms, a very brief, generalized and superficial account. More importantly, Hale's account does not provide, nor has any account since provided, a detailed examination of the process of judicial review itself, of the procedures used by the House of Lords in that process during the 1640s, or significantly, of the substantive issues expressed, individually and collectively, by the cases under review.[19] On both counts, the interpretation invites a re-examination.

In fairness, it must be said that Hale's treatise was not, in any sense, meant to be a history of the Long Parliament, or any other. It was only meant to define the limits of the legal jurisdiction of the House of Lords, and its political assumptions, however important, are necessarily generalized. The fundamental weakness of Hale's argument is therefore its political simplicity, its reliance on broad symbols of conflict, and consequently, its failure to distinguish between real and imaginary political divisions and arguments.

To begin with, Hale's understanding of the judicial activities of the House in appellate proceedings during the 1620s is only partially accurate. In Bouchier's case in 1621 the plaintiff appealed to the House on grounds that the Lord Keeper had not properly heard the case and that, accordingly, the decree had been issued 'precipitately'.[20] His appeal was, in effect, nothing more than an attack on the judicial conduct of the Lord Keeper, and the Lords accepted and reviewed the case within that very narrow context. The substance of the decree, and the relative merits of Bouchier's case in law, were never discussed. Hale claimed that the House, understanding the limits of its jurisdiction, 'would never proceed to rehear the case on the merits thereof, as desired by the petitioner'.[21] However, as J.F. Macqueen pointed out in his study of the appellate jurisdiction, the House was never required to do so. The plaintiff ultimately confessed to the unfairness of the accusation, and the House acquitted the Lord Keeper of the charge. There is no evidence to indicate that, had the occasion arisen, the Lords would have evaded or declined their responsibility to review the decree itself.[22] Hale also set great store by the fact that the committee for privileges, which had initially reviewed Bouchier's petition, had found his use of the word appeal 'unusual', but he fails to explain further that, having said that, the committee left the form of the petition to the consideration of the House as a whole, and went on to recommend that the case be heard expeditiously.[23] In short, the evidence produced by this case, in so far as it reflects the attitude of the House towards its appellate jurisdiction, is singularly inconclusive.

Hale's interpretation of Mathew's case, heard in 1624, is equally misguided. In the course of proceedings on that case, the Lords did in fact order the Lord Keeper to solicit the King's approval for a commission of review. But that commission was to include eight members of the House of Lords, and they were to be nominated, not by the King, but by the House itself. It is also arguable that that decision to request a commission from the King was based, not on an inherent insecurity about their jurisdiction, but on a recognition that the case had already been heard and determined by the King himself. Hale fails to mention the fact that William Mathew had initially appealed against the Lord Keeper's decree to the King. James I had reviewed the case, but had, in the end, supported the original Chancery judgment. It was only then that Mathew appealed to the House of Lords. The Lords clearly felt that the decree was erroneous and ought to be reviewed. They proceeded with the case in spite of a previous determination by the Crown, but chose, in Macqueen's words, 'a course of proceeding respectful of the Crown, and appropriate to the object in view'.[24] Their request for a commission should then be seen, not as a denial of their appellate authority, but as a bold, if very careful and diplomatic, affirmation of it. In the event no commission issued, and in 1625 Lord Keeper Williams was summoned to the House to account for the fact that no action had been taken on Mathew's case, and on one other. Williams claimed that the King had refused the commission on the grounds that it had not issued by his own mandate. The House was unmoved, and the Lord Keeper was subsequently brought to acknowledge the right of the House to issue the commission, and to seek the pardon of the House for failing to effect a resolution of the case.[25] The later proceedings indicate that, far from abandoning their interest in deference to an independent royal commission, as Hale would have it, the Lords exercised a continuing and active interest in the case, according to what they saw was their right and their responsibility.

The conclusion drawn by Hale from the absence of commissions in the 1640s is also somewhat less tenable if one realizes that the House was actively engaged in the review of at least three Chancery decrees, including the still unresolved Mathew's case, in the Parliament of 1628.[26] Those proceedings were conducted without any commission being suggested or pursued, and furthermore, without any resistance being offered by either the Crown or the then Lord Keeper Coventry. In that sense, the Crown's resistance to the proceedings in Mathew's case appears to be something of a temporary aberration. Given the continuation of appeals, the absence of any attempt on the part of the Crown to interfere, either in 1628, or more importantly, in 1640, suggests that the Crown and the House of Lords may have come to realize that the issue, if indeed it was an issue at all, was one of form rather than substance. Pike's conclusion on the subject of commissions seems appropriate:[27]

> The Parliament, in the sense of the King, Lords, judges, and high officers of State, was the original fountain of justice from which flowed remedies not to be obtained elsewhere. It may have been technically incorrect to address a petition in the nature of an appeal, to the Lords alone, but hardly more incorrect than to address a petition, in the first instance to the Chancellor alone. The Chancellor was the King's Chancellor and the Parliament was the King's Parliament. It does not appear that the King's prerogative suffered more by a petition to the Lords in Parliament than by a petition to the Chancellor in Chancery.

Indeed, in so far as the King was aware of the civil litigation proceedings as a whole, he appears to have been more interested in aiding and abetting the process, than in resisting it. He did so on a number of occasions; in one case, for example, by denying royal protection where it had been claimed by a recalcitrant defendant, and in another, by directly referring a suit, initially appealed to King and Council, to the House of Lords for trial.[28] The King's response in the latter case is of some interest. The suit in question was not in fact an appeal from a Chancery decree, but instead involved a case of contested patents, granted by the King, to the officers of that court. The notation of referral on the original petition reads simply: 'His majesty is pleased to recommend this petition to the Lord Privy Seal and the Viscount Say and Sele . . . to acquaint the Lords of the House of Parliament therewith, that this cause may receive a hearing in such convenient time as their Lordships shall think fit.'[29] The King's willingness to allow the Lords to adjudicate this case, in which both he, as author of the patents, and the Lord Keeper, as titular administrator of the court, were indirectly parties, would seem to belie any notions that he possessed an overwrought sensitivity about his judicial prerogatives, at least in so far as they may have been involved in the proceedings of the House of Lords. It is possibly unfair to draw too many conclusions from a case that did not specifically entail the review of a Chancery decree. But the singular informality of the King's reference in this case, to say nothing of the lack of any sign of opposition to the proceedings as a whole, suggests that, for the purposes of civil litigation at least, the relationship between the King and his 'Council in Parliament' was perhaps more symbiotic than Hale, for one, may have imagined.

Likewise, it must be said that the causal relationship, suggested by Hale, between impeachment and judicial review, is largely an illusory one. Hale seems to have imagined that the members of the Long Parliament were, in their proceedings, incapable of viewing the Lord Keeper as anything other than a symbol of arbitrary, prerogative government, and that, accordingly, they embarked with singular vision on a campaign to circumscribe the authority of the office, through impeachment on the one hand, and judicial review on the other. In Hale's view, the two proceedings were similar in motivation and execution. However plausible that interpretation may have been for those writing with the necessarily limited perspective of Restoration hindsight, it does not accord well with the facts. It is clearly a mistake to assume that the House of Lords deliberately failed to distinguish between the Lord Keeper's authority as it had been exercised at court, in his capacity as senior Privy Councillor, and his authority as it had been exercised in court, in his role as chief judge of equity in civil litigation. It is possible, as Hale recognized, that the effect of Finch's impeachment on the public at large may have been to suggest, in a general way, that Finch's decrees were eminently worthy of review. But it is an altogether different proposition to conclude that the House of Lords would necessarily have made the same assumption, and then have proceeded directly from impeachment to a wholesale review of Finch's Chancery decrees. The two sets of proceedings were altogether different in character and origin. As Hale had seen, the impeachment against Finch had been a punitive measure, and in a sense, a preventative one. But it was designed to remove a specific evil counsellor from his influence over Crown policy. It was directed, not against the office of lord keeper, but against the man who happened to hold that office.

Judicial review, on the other hand, was a reactive process, or more accurately, a responsive one, in the sense that it developed slowly and progressively as a result of pressure exerted from outside Parliament by disgruntled litigants in search of judicial remedy. There is no evidence to indicate that the assumption of the appellate jurisdiction was, in any way, premeditated, and even less evidence to suggest that it had any real connexion with Finch's impeachment. The indictment against Finch, brought up by the House of Commons, was, in any case, predominantly an attack on his performance as Chief Justice of Common Pleas, not as Lord Keeper, and the only substantive legal issues cited in the indictment concerned the undue pressure which he was alleged to have exerted on the puisne judges to conform to the Crown's argument in the ship money case. The indictment had precious little bearing on his responsibilities as they may have been used or abused in the course of civil litigation in Chancery, and his impeachment would not therefore have led logically or inevitably to a re-evaluation of his decisions in that court. In point of fact, the appellate jurisdiction began as a result of a series of appeals accepted for review in January and February 1641, none of which were appeals from Finch's decrees. They were, by and large, appeals from the decrees of Finch's immediate predecessor, Lord Keeper Thomas Coventry. Finch's decrees represent less than half of all of the judgments accepted for review in the first two years of the Parliament, and the first action taken on one of Finch's decrees does not occur until mid-May 1641, some six months after his impeachment.[30]

Hale's interpretation also fails because it does not take into account the ongoing position of the Lord Keeper vis-à-vis his responsibilities to, and his relationship with, the House of Lords. Littleton, who succeeded Finch as Lord Keeper in January 1641, remained active, during the first crucial year of this Parliament, as a legal adviser and assistant to the Lords. His attendance and assistance were not compulsory, but when he did attend, he served as Speaker and presiding officer of the House, and presumably would have been able to exercise some measure of control over the order of business. It would seem unlikely therefore, at least in theory, that he would have presided over, much less assisted, the House in the abrogation of his own judicial authority, if in fact he had viewed the appellate jurisdiction in those terms. Littleton was clearly aware of the jurisdiction being exercised, and offered no apparent resistance to the appellate proceedings, or to the orders to him in the court of Chancery which they often produced. On the contrary, Littleton appears to have viewed the relationship between the court of Chancery and the court of Parliament, not in terms of jurisdictional rivalry, but in terms of co-operation. As late as February 1642, Littleton, with the assistance of Mr Justice Reeve, Mr Justice Crawley and Baron Hendon, recommended that a case over which he was presiding in Chancery be removed, by the plaintiffs, into the House of Lords for final resolution. That particular case involved a disputed assignment of the profits of a Fine office, and the order removing the case suggests that the Chancery bench saw the House of Lords as the most appropriate venue for the dispute. It reads:[31]

> Upon mature and solemn consideration of the matter, his Lopp and the said Lords the Judges assisting, finding the matter to concerne an Office of Publique Administration of Justice, and the variance between the Plaintiff and the Defendant of great weight and consequence, held the matter to be most apt and proper for the directions of the high Corte of Pliament, and doth therefore leave the parties to apply themselves accordingly.

If the advent of judicial review had dire consequences for the court of Chancery, or for the judicial prerogatives of the Crown, they appear to have been lost on Littleton and his colleagues on the bench.

All of this is meant to suggest that, contrary to the imaginations of Restoration and post-Restoration historians, the advent of the appellate jurisdiction over the court of Chancery in 1640–1 was not, in any identifiable way, related to the political aims and ambitions of the members of the House of Lords, and to suggest further that it was neither an important, nor a symbolic, issue of constitutional conflict between Crown and Parliament. I would like to argue, alternatively, that the decision to accept and adjudicate Chancery appeals (in so far as a conscious decision was ever made) was motivated not by political ambition, but by a recognition, made on a case by case basis, of the need to address a number of clearly articulated problems inherent in the procedural and substantive law administered in that court. The evidence for that argument lies partially in the procedures used by the House of Lords in the course of appellate proceedings, and partially in the important legal issues presented by the case under review.

The process of judicial review began effectively with the presentation of an initiating petition by the appellant, which set forth the facts of the case and made the request for review of the Chancery decree. The petition was then delivered to the committee for petitions, read in committee, and then either accepted or rejected on what appeared to be the relative merits of the case. If the petition was accepted, it would then be taken before the whole House, read, and then formally referred back to the committee for petitions.[32] The same day, or very shortly thereafter, a day would be appointed for the hearing, and notification given to all parties and their counsel. The petition would then be numbered by the clerk in order to establish its precedence among the other cases being heard concurrently, and a copy of the decree, and any other material germane to the case, requested of the court.[33] Any written testimony was to be copied and the deposition provided the opposing party before the hearing. Witnesses, if any, were summoned by warrant of the House and sworn by the clerk. The hearing itself was conducted by a committee nominally consisting of 50 or more members of the House, assisted by two or more justices. (Daily attendance can be assumed to have varied to some degree, but the House initially established a minimum of seven members as an operating quorum.) During the course of the hearing arguments were heard at length by counsel on both sides and, if need be, specific points of law were referred for consideration and report by the judges. If in fact the complaint against the decree proved unjustified, the committee was empowered to levy a fine against the plaintiff and award costs for the defendant's charges in the suit.[34] Alternatively, if the committee found the complaint to be just, for whatever reasons, an appropriate order or recommendation would then be forwarded, in a formal report, to the full House for review and ratification.

The proceedings at each stage were conducted in a careful, orderly, and responsible fashion which generally followed established rules of judicial fairness. The procedures guaranteed the widest possible scope for the presentation of argument and accompanying evidence on both sides, and, accordingly, provided ample opportunity for a full and effective discussion of the issues. Any judgment, either at the initial review of the case or at the conclusion of the hearings, was made by a large and widely representative committee, and was reviewed in both instances by the whole House before any action was taken. There was, in short, very little about the process that could fairly be called arbitrary or indiscriminatory.

The formal commission given to the committee for petitions at its inception in November 1640 directed that the committee 'meet, read, and peruse petitions, reject those that are fit to be relieved at the Common Law or Courts of Equity, and retain only those that are fit for their Lordships' consideration'.[35] The directive was clearly intended to discourage, rather than precipitate, unwarranted appeals. However, even that commission was sufficiently vague, in its definition of what was fit to be retained by the Lords, to require a more precise order. The original commission was then amended in June 1641, and the committee was ordered to retain only those petitions 'that are without any other remedy but in Parliament'.[36] The intent was the same, but the strictures were made even tighter. Parliamentary review was meant to be an extraordinary means that was only to be used when ordinary means of judicial remedy had been exhausted. I would like to suggest that, for a number of reasons, appeals from decrees in the court of Chancery represented a special class of litigation for which that remedy in Parliament was not only necessary, but appropriate.

The central problem facing Chancery litigants in the first half of the seventeenth century was the very absence of any effective appellate recourse from decrees in that court. Hale in fact made note of the problem in the aforementioned treatise. He claimed that there were only three conceivable ways of subjecting a Chancery decree to review and possible reversal, none of which were particularly efficacious. The first of these was to petition the Lord Keeper for a rehearing of the case, before the decree, which he had just issued, had been enrolled. Since the rehearing would, in most cases, be conducted by the same Lord Keeper, some extraordinary means would have to be shown to convince him to reverse himself. The second was the formal bill of review, brought after enrolment of the disputed decree. This process is appropriately described by Hale as 'a somewhat strait-laced method'.[37] The disgruntled litigant was required, under bill of review procedure, to perform all points of the decree in question before any review would be entertained — a requirement that could and often did impose extraordinary hardships on the complainant. In addition, the bill of review had to allege some technical irregularity, either in the way the decree had been drawn, or in the proceedings themselves. It was not designed to address substantive legal issues or matters of interpretation that may have been in dispute. The third and final method mentioned by Hale was appeal by petition to the King, a procedure by which the petitioner sought an entirely new hearing by the King, or by special commissioners appointed under the great seal. Hale claimed that this was 'the regular and legal way of proceeding', but acknowledged at the same time that 'the reason they have not issued oftener is in respect of the great charge and delay in such commissions'.[38] The procedure was singularly unpopular, and appears to have been used only twice before 1640; in Moyle Finch's case in 1598,[39] and, after a fashion, in the aforementioned Mathew's case in 1624. The only other conceivable avenue of redress was to proceed by private bill and reverse the decree by Act of Parliament. The procedure was tried on a number of occasions in the 1620s, in attempts to reverse decrees in Chancery and in the Court of Requests.[40] All attempts appear to have been unsuccessful, as was the single attempt made in the 1640s.[41]

The relative inviolability of the Lord Keeper's decrees was a long standing and serious issue of contention in the early Stuart period. Coke certainly recognized the problem when arguing, albeit from a rather different perspective, in favour of common law prohibitions over equity courts. He advocated the use of prohibitions, in part, because there were no other controls available. 'Their rule and judgements', said Coke, 'are as binding as the laws of the Medes and Persians, not to be altered.'[42] There was in fact an attempt in the Parliament of 1624 to establish an independent appellate court from decrees in Chancery, along the lines of the existing 'court' of Exchequer Chamber, but the effort was unsuccessful, and by 1640 disgruntled litigants still faced a legal *cul-de-sac* in terms of appellate remedy from Chancery.[43]

That in itself explains in part the pressure brought to bear on the House of Lords to assume responsibility for review, and there are any number of litigants who cite that specific problem in an attempt to compel the House to accept their case. As an example, in June 1641, Sir Conyers Darcy appealed to the House against a decree which had been issued against him two years earlier, in June 1639. On that occasion Lord Keeper Coventry, with Justices Bramston, Jones and Berkeley assisting, had abrogated a property agreement between Darcy and his great-aunt Ann Saville. In that agreement Saville had released all claims to a property called Rothwell Haigh Park, in return for two annuities for her and her children. The court had declared that the agreement had been fraudulently obtained, and accordingly awarded possession of the property to the plaintiff and ordered Darcy to repay the mean profits of the land for the preceding three years during which he had held the property, a sum of almost £1,500. Darcy had delayed payment of the award until, as he says, 'he might question the unjustness of the decree in Parliament'.[44] However, on the advice of his counsel, he had in the meantime attempted to bring a bill of review, but had found the way blocked. A process of contempt had issued out against him and his complaint to the House of Lords clearly illustrates his predicament: 'by the precise rules of that court, yor petr cannot be admitted to any reversal of the said decree upon a Bill of Review, without payment first made of the sum decreed, which yor petr can no ways perform.'[45] Almost a year later, in May 1642, Sir William Russell addressed a petition to the House with an almost identical complaint. The defendants, said Russell, 'have no remedy in Chancery but by Bill of Review, which in the formalities thereof will spend too much time and charge, and yet the merits of the cause, at the end of that way, will be no riper for a determinant hearing than now'.[46]

Both petitioners point to the same problem. But the absence of a viable appellate recourse was really only part of the story. Darcy's complaint about the inherent limitations of bill of review procedure, while illustrative, was really incidental to his case. He had, as he said, intended to bring his case before Parliament at the earliest available opportunity. His argument for doing so rested in part on his general reservations about Chancery's internally conducted review procedures, but more directly on his exceptions to the nature and substance of the original decree. His case, as a whole, is in fact illustrative of the kind of complaint about the substantive law administered in Chancery which compelled litigants to look to the House of Lords for remedy.

As indicated earlier, the plaintiff, Ann Saville, had brought her bill in Chancery to be relieved against the articles of agreement executed between herself and Conyers Darcy. She argued that she had signed the original release agreement without a full understanding of her right and title to the property in question, and that she had remained ignorant of her title because of a deliberate deception perpetrated by Darcy. The responsibility of the court was then to determine whether fraud had actually been committed; whether or not the articles of agreement had been obtained, as the plaintiff claimed, 'by surprize and practice'.[47] However, in the course of proceedings the plaintiff moved the court for a process of discovery, a procedure which required the defendant to produce for the plaintiff's examination all relevant deeds, evidence and records relating to the property in dispute. Normally, the process of discovery was the object of an initiating bill and was meant, in most cases, to be an end in itself; that is, it was meant to produce the documents for the plaintiff's use, ostensibly in a subsequent trial at law. When moved in the course of proceedings, the object was to bring the deeds and evidence before the court itself, in the hope of influencing the opinion of the bench on the intrinsic merits of the plaintiff's case, in both law and equity. Even so, the process of discovery did not allow the court to impose judgment, as part of those proceedings, on the validity of the deeds themselves, or on the principal question of title. That was a matter wholly within the cognizance of the common law. In Darcy's case, however, the court not only compelled the defendant to surrender his deeds and evidences to the court, but then proceeded to examine the documents and render judgment on their validity to prove title. Consequently the decree issued by the court declared initially, that the articles and agreement had indeed been obtained 'upon a surprizal, and ought not to stand in equity'.[48] It then went on to say that 'the defendant, Sir Conyers Darcy, if the Articles and Release had not been made, had no title either in law or equity', to the lands in question.[49] On that assumption, the court then awarded possession of the property to Ann Saville, 'and her heirs', and ordered Darcy to make restitution for what it considered to be the lost profits due to the plaintiff.

The principal issue, as the defendant saw it, was that the court had exceeded its jurisdiction by proceeding from a declaration of the question of fraud to a declaration on the question of title. 'By means whereof, all other titles of yor petr are bound up, though not comprised in the bill, answer, and proceedings.'[50] The pronouncement on title (issued, it must be remembered, with the concurrence of three common law justices) combined with the injunction for possession, and the order cancelling the original release agreement, was effective, as it was surely meant to be, in discouraging the defendant Darcy from pursuing his case any further. And in fact, in the defendant's view, the court's decree had effectively settled the property on Ann Saville and in the process severely compromised any chance which he might have subsequently had to establish his title and recover possession at common law.

In its outlines, Darcy's case is not unusual among those appealed to the House of Lords. In November 1641, Nicholas Bourlacy petitioned the

Lords for a reversal of a decree issued against him, as a defendant, three years earlier, in November 1638. He prefaced his case by saying, 'by the laws and statutes of this Realm, all titles for land that depend on a point of law, ought to receive tryall at the Common Law, as not decreeable in a court of Equity, unless it be by consent of the parties'.[51] Having established that as an operating premise, he went on to describe the hearing in Chancery:[52]

> A suit being joined and witnesses examined and yor petitioners served with process, on 27 November 14 Caroli, Richard Berry's counsel stated the cause to be a point in law not pleaded in the Bill nor answer; and thereupon the then Lord Keeper bade yor petitioner's counsel to answer that matter in lawe. Whereupon, Mr Sgt Glanville replied that he came not hither to argue a point in law, but to defend the Equity of his client's cause, and pray'd the Lord Keeper to hear it. And that if Berry would depend on his title at law, that it might be dismissed to the lawe. But the Lord Keeper would neither hear the Equity nor dismiss it . . . Four days after an order was entered, whereby the land was decreed to Berry, both in law and equity, and thereby taken out of your petitioner's hands and settled on Berry.

The decree itself confirms Bourlacy's complaint in all points. The court had referred consideration of the principal deed supporting the plaintiff's case to Justices Bramston, Jones and Berkeley. Ostensibly on their opinion, the court had declared that the plaintiff 'hath good title to the said lands, both in law and equity'.[53] Accordingly, the defendants were ordered to deliver up all deeds and records in their custody relating to the property, and possession was awarded to the plaintiff, 'against the defendants, their executors, administrators, and assigns'.[54] As in Darcy's case, a commission was awarded to determine the value of the mean profits acquired during the defendant's unlawful possession, and the defendants ordered to make appropriate restitution.

A similar complaint was lodged in February 1641, by one Thomas Leveson, appealing a decree issued against his father by Lord Keeper Ellesmere in 1615. Leveson, appealing as heir to the property in question, argued for appeal on grounds of jurisdiction:[55]

> Whereas by the ancient and fundamental laws of this Kingdom, Courts of Equity were established for the mitigation of the rigor of the Common Law and for the redress of frauds, trusts, and matters not relievable by the rules of ordinary judicature. . . For matters of fact tryable by jury and matters determinable in law by the judges, the same are properly tryable in the ordinary courts of Justice according to the Common Law.

The case appears to have originated in Chancery on the plaintiff's bill of discovery, the plaintiff attempting to force Leveson's father to produce his deeds and records of title. The deeds were duly surrendered up, but the court then proceeded to consider the deeds as the principal issue in dispute, and to issue judgment on the question of title, without, as Leveson claimed, 'any ground in Equity or cause to give the Corte of Chancery jurisdiction'.[56] The decree is not unlike the two preceding examples:[57]

His lopp finding the defendant's title to the said prebends to be wrongful as aforesaid; do order and decree that the complainant be restored to the absolute possession of the said prebends in question, and that the plaintiffs and their successors shall and may have and hold and enjoy the said prebends forever hereafter . . . against the defendant, his heirs and assigns, and all claiming under him.

In this case, however, the court added, almost as an afterthought, that the defendant, Leveson, had the right to attempt to recover the property at common law. Even so, the court had examined the principal deeds on which a subsequent trial might be based, declared them insufficient to prove title, and awarded possession 'absolutely' to the plaintiffs and their 'successors'. It is not surprising therefore that Leveson felt that his opportunities to prove his right had been somewhat abridged. His argument in support of appeal in the House of Lords was based on his belief that a judgment on title was simply not within the purview of the court of Chancery at all, but could only be properly and fairly made in a trial by judge and jury at the common law.

That argument also forms the centrepiece of a document in the State Papers Domestic ascribed by the archivists as dating from December 1640 and probably belonging to the committee for courts of justice. It is entitled 'the grievances that grow by the absoluteness of the Lord Chancellor'.[58] The document contains a list of grievances and a proposed list of remedies, and the phrasing suggests that its author had in mind a bill to reform Chancery practice. It must be said parenthetically, however, that the document itself does not provide any definitive evidence to verify either the date given to it, or its relationship to a committee of either House. The list of grievances contains nothing that would indicate that they were necessarily indigenous to 1640, rather than say to 1621 or 1624, when extended discussions on the nature of Chancery jurisdiction took place. Having said that, however, it is possible to suggest that there is a striking similarity between the points raised in these cases and the complaints outlined in the document.

There are three central grievances presented. The Chancellor is accused of 'decreeing matters upon a collateral matter grown upon motion, neither contained in Bill nor Answer', of 'awarding possession by injunction as if recovery were at Common Law', and of 'deciding titles of law in the Chancery upon English Bills calling one or two justices to assist him'. The author then desires that it be enacted that 'no cause be heard and ordered by him but upon Bill and Answer, and nothing decreed which is not expressly in the Bill', and finally, that 'all bills that contain matters of Law be referred to the Common Law'.

The distinction implied in this list of grievances and remedies, as in the cases above, is an important one. Matters of law were clearly outside Chancery's jurisdiction, and Ellesmere himself had, on one occasion, agreed that matters determinable at law which had arisen incidentally in Chancery, as for instance in the process of discovery, should be referred to the courts of common law, once the points in equity had been settled.[59] The Lord Keeper's decree in the aforementioned Moyle Finch's case, in 1598, had been reversed precisely because that rule had not been observed. It was meant to be a standard rule of Chancery practice, but as these cases indicate, there was no guarantee that the principle would be adhered to unfailingly, especially given the pressures, both internal and external, on the court to accommodate and maintain an increasing amount of real property litigation. And, on the face of it, the procedures were logical; a declaration on title, in a sense, followed naturally from the legitimate process of discovery, and the recovery of possession was a natural consequence after judgment on title. But the responsibility for establishing title fell to the common law, and the combined effect of these procedures was to pre-empt that responsibility, and in a way that, as W.J. Jones has illustrated, could make it difficult, if not impossible, for parties to continue at common law at all.[60] The procedures could work to a fair advantage. Jones points out in fact that 'by controlling the further development of litigation, Chancery was fulfilling its professed intention of preventing unnecessary and vexatious suits at law'.[61] But the procedures could present a danger, as well as an advantage, and in those cases where important issues of proprietary right were at stake, the breakdown, as litigants saw it, in the traditional distinction between equitable and common law remedies, between the remedy offered by judge and jury, and that offered by the Chancellor, was conceived as a major grievance. The theme is expressed time and again in the petitions to the House of Lords.

The cases mentioned above represent only one type of complaint about Chancery proceedings. There are others which reflect altogether different problems. The most frequent source of complaint lay in what litigants perceived as technical errors or irregularities in the court's proceedings. There is a case, for instance, in which the plaintiff alleges that the court failed to provide an adequate hearing for the party and his counsel before the final decree was issued; another in which the appellant complains that the Lord Keeper proceeded to judgment on the bill and answer only, without allowing for the examination and testimony of witnesses; and any number which complain of interlocutory orders and final decrees being issued by the Masters in Chancery without a hearing of the case or the point at issue, by the Lord Keeper. These complaints are, incidentally, enumerated in the list of grievances mentioned above.[62]

The transition from Lord Keeper Coventry to Lord Keeper Finch, in January 1640, appears to have created a number of problems as well. The case of Lady Elizabeth Cope, for example, was allowed, under Lord Keeper Coventry, to proceed in Chancery as far as examination and publication, the last stage before hearing, but was then dismissed without hearing, by Lord Keeper Finch, on grounds that her original bill, which had initiated the proceedings, had not contained sufficient matter in equity.[63] Similarly, there is a case in which the court, under Coventry, had, as an interim measure, referred the parties to a trial at common law for a determination on the question of title. When the suit returned to Chancery, now under Finch, the Lord Keeper declared that the original reference had been unnecessary and 'vexatious' and promptly awarded possession to the defendant, in direct contradiction to the plaintiff's verdict for title at the common law.[64] On such occasions Selden's famous aphorism associating equity and conscience with the length of the Chancellor's foot, might have sprung quickly to mind.

Even so, I do not want to suggest that the cases appealed to the House of Lords represent an incipient rebellion against the court of Chancery during this period, or that the court itself had become, in its proceedings, consistently arbitrary or unjust. The number of appeals to the House is, in fact, very small compared to the amount of litigation which passed successfully through that court in any given term. Between January 1641 and January 1643 the House accepted only 68 appeals from that court, and while this is a striking departure from the records of previous Parliaments, it is insignificant when compared to the thousands of cases adjudicated in Chancery every year. What I would like to suggest is that, on occasion, the procedures of the court could be abused, subtly manipulated, or in fact neglected altogether, in a way that could severely compromise the interests of individual litigants. In those cases, appeal to the House of Lords was a reflection of genuine need.

The Lords' response to all of these cases was, as suggested earlier, carefully considered, and in most cases specifically tailored to meet the needs of the individual case. The grounds for appeal advanced by Sir Conyers Darcy and Thomas Leveson, for example, were at face value very similar. But their cases were in fact very different in an important way. Leveson claimed that his case had no business being brought to Chancery in the first instance, that the only issue before the court had been the question of title, and that belonged within the cognizance of the common law. Darcy, on the other hand, did not dispute the appropriateness of the court of Chancery as a venue for his opponent's original complaint, only the decree which had proceeded from it. The Lords clearly felt that both decrees should be 'set aside', but they recognized that, despite the similarities of the decrees, there was a fundamental difference in the legal requirements of either case, and chose remedial measures appropriate to each. Leveson's case was, with the consent of both parties, referred to a trial at common law, and the defendant was ordered to plead to the plaintiff's suit without delay, so that the 'right of the prebend might be speedily determined'.[65] Conversely, Darcy's case was referred back to Chancery with specific instructions that the Lord Keeper was 'upon a new Bill . . . to hear the cause upon the whole matter and merits of the cause and the Articles and Agreement . . . without any respect paid to the former decree'.[66] For his part, Darcy was ordered to put in sufficient security in Chancery to cover the £1,500, 'in case the cause shall be decreed against him'.[67]

On balance, the majority of actions taken by the House followed that taken in Darcy's case; that is, the case was referred to the Lord Keeper with an order or recommendation that the case be reheard. In that sense, the Lords exercised the jurisdiction with considerable restraint. The Lords were principally concerned that a rehearing be made available in those cases where it appeared to be warranted. They could, and did on occasion, specify the procedures to be used; that is, they could instruct the Lord

Keeper to admit a bill of review without requiring performance of the original decree, or they could direct that a new bill be brought by one of the parties, so that the case could be heard on its merits. But beyond that, there was no attempt to pre-empt any judgment which the Lord Keeper might ultimately make. The specific wording of the orders could and did vary to some degree in each case, but the general substance altered very little. The Lord Keeper was to rehear the case and 'do as in his wisdom he shall think fit'.

The wording of the judgments on the original decrees, such as exist, reflects much the same attitude. The Lords set aside decrees, they did not reverse them. The distinction is an important one. Setting aside a decree simply cancelled its effects; it was a half-way measure which made possible a rehearing of the case, on its merits, or in a more appropriate venue. Reversing a decree implies a qualitative judgment on the substantive legal issues originally in dispute between the parties. The Lords frequently did the former, but rarely, if ever, the latter. The responsibility of the House, as it appears to have been perceived by its members, was to review these cases only in the context of their lower court proceedings, and to establish whether those proceedings had been conducted according to what they saw as the proper rules of judicial process. The House did not see itself as a forum for the retrial and final judgment of any of these cases on their intrinsic merits. Only twice, very early in the proceedings, did the House venture to impose its own judgment on a case, and in one of those instances did so with the understanding that its order would be executed in Chancery, according to established Chancery procedures.

And, it must be remembered, the Lords could and did exercise their authority in favour of the Lord Keeper's decree. Unfortunately, the records of the cases dismissed usually disappeared with the cases themselves. There are, however, a few instances in which the suit proceeded to a full hearing before being dismissed, and in those cases it is clear that the appellant had been unable to substantiate any charge of judicial malfeasance on the part of the Lord Keeper or his court. As an example, in May 1641, Edmund Harrington, Giles Johnson and Thomas Marshall petitioned the House, on behalf of their wives, asking review of a decree issued by Lord Keeper Coventry in February 1627. The plaintiffs had originally exhibited their bill in Chancery to be relieved against what they claimed was a fraudulent mortgage and redemption. The plaintiff's father, one Richard Cole, had, in 1598, mortgaged a manor house and accompanying tenements to one Richard Ingram for £100, on condition of redemption after one year, for the repayment of £110. Richard Cole then died, and the plaintiffs claimed that their mother, his widow, had deliberately failed to repay the debt on the day of redemption, thereby allowing the property to be forfeited. The widow then repurchased the property in her own right from the mortgagee, subsequently remarried, and then sold the property to one Robert Talcott. The plaintiffs claimed that the forfeiture and repurchase had been pre-arranged in order to deny them their rightful inheritance. They also alleged that Robert Talcott had been aware of the fraud when he purchased the property in the final transaction. Their suit had proceeded in Chancery to publication and hearing, but had been dismissed by Lord Keeper Coventry on grounds that the day of redemption had passed two months before Richard Cole's death, not after it, and that his widow could not then be held responsible for the forfeiture of the property. Furthermore, she had repurchased the property by valid deed and bargain, and had in fact held the property for five years, while offering it to a number of prospective buyers, before finally selling it to Robert Talcott. The Lords, in reviewing the case, issued a commission to two Essex j.p.s to examine witnesses and establish the facts of the case. Their report corresponded to the facts outlined by Coventry in the Chancery proceedings, and accordingly his decree was confirmed and the case dismissed from the House.[68]

It is also worth noting that the Lords were asked on a number of occasions to enforce previous Chancery decrees. As an example, Samuel Hopkins, a vicar, petitioned the House in 1641 claiming that he had previously obtained two orders in Chancery, in 1638, awarding him one third of the tithes of his parish, according to an agreement which he had made with the impropriator of his living. The agreement had not been performed according to the Chancery orders. The Lords reviewed the case, and ordered that the case be 'specially recommended to the Lord Keeper, and that his Lordship would be pleased to put the said orders into speedy execution, by sequestration or otherwise, according to the justice of that court'.[69]

What I would like to suggest is that the House of Lords functioned in these cases less as a court offering substantive legal judgments, and more as a kind of administrative tribunal whose responsibility it was to remedy the effects of irregularities in judicial procedure. It exercised judicial review over the court of Chancery in order to guarantee the proper administration of equity, and to retain and reinforce what it saw as the necessary and appropriate limits of equity jurisdiction. The House did not set out to retard or reform the court of Chancery as a court of real property litigation. The Lords fully recognized the importance and utility of Chancery, and dealt with the court in these proceedings with considerable circumspection and care. What the House did offer was protection and remedy in those cases where the legal interests of individual litigants had been compromised by irregular proceedings and judgments in that court.

That, in itself, should suggest that the appellate proceedings of the House of Lords were not, as Hale and others imagined, the reflection of an inherent antithesis either between Crown and Parliament, or between Parliament and the court of Chancery. The proceedings were neither arbitrary nor ill-conceived, but were instead orderly and responsible; an important and very necessary response to the clearly articulated problems and needs of individual litigants. They were, as Sir Edward Dering suggested during the Commons debates of 1675, 'too much to be blown away with a breath in an hour's discourse'.[70]

Notes

[1] *C.J.*, IX, 352.
[2] H[ouse of] [Lords] R.O., minutes of the committee for privileges, old ser., Vol. II, ff. 66–8.
[3] *Ibid.*
[4] *Ibid.*, ff. 116–17.
[5] A. Grey, *Debates of the House of Commons . . .* (10 vols., 1769), III, 142.
[6] *Ibid.*, 206.
[7] *The Diaries and Papers of Sir Edward Dering . . .*, ed. M. Bond (House of Lords R.O., Occasional Publication No. 1, 1976) p.74.
[8] Denzil, Baron Holles, *The Case Stated Concerning the Judicature of the House of Lords in Point of Appeal* (1675), p. 65. Holles's first treatise on House of Lords judicature, *The Grand Question Concerning the Judicature of the House of Peers* (1669), makes very clear that the Lords did advance precedents from the Long Parliament to demonstrate their authority to hear cases in the first instance, in the case of Skinner *v.* East India Company in 1668. The treatise in fact outlines, in some detail, the arguments presented by members of both Houses in conferences on that case. According to Holles, the Lords were 'copious in the enumeration of these later precedents' (p. 174).
[9] *Ibid.*, p. 45.
[10] *Ibid.*
[11] Sir Robert Atkyns, *A Treatise of the True and Ancient Jurisdiction of the House of Peers* (1699); B.L., Hargrave MS. 115, William Petyt, 'A Discourse Concerning the Judicature in Parliament . . .'; Sir Matthew Hale, *The Jurisdiction of the Lords' House . . .* (1796).
[12] Hale, *Jurisdiction*, p. 184.
[13] *Ibid.*, 194.
[14] *The Political Works of James I*, ed. C.H. McIlwain (Cambridge, Massachusetts, 1918), p. 331. See also G.W. Thomas, 'James I, Equity and Lord Keeper John Williams', *E.H.R.*, XCI (1976), 506–28.
[15] *L.J.*, III, 421.
[16] Hale, *Jurisdiction*, Introd., p. lx.
[17] C.P. Cooper, *The House of Lords as a Court of Appeal* (1828), p. 14.
[18] Thomas Beven, 'The Appellate Jurisdiction of the House of Lords,' *Law Quarterly Review*, XVII (1901), 167.
[19] A full study of House of Lords procedure in the early Stuart period is anticipated in a forthcoming book by Professor Elizabeth Read Foster.
[20] *L.J.*, III, 179.
[21] Hale, *Jurisdiction*, p. 195.
[22] J.F. Macqueen, *A Practical Treatise on the Appellate Jurisdiction of the House of Lords and the Privy Council* (1842), p. 74. Despite the narrow context in which the case was considered, a number of lords in fact expressed the view, in the course of the debates, that the Lords had the authority to review the decree itself, and any other Chancery decree, on the basis of its intrinsic merits in law. Lord Saye and Sele argued strongly that the case ought to be taken, because 'there is no appeale from the Chauncery but hither'. Lord Houghton claimed that appeals against Chancery decrees belonged to the House of Lords alone, 'this being the Supreme Court'. Even Lord Keeper Williams, whose decree was under review, agreed that the House of Lords was the most appropriate forum for appeals against Chancery decrees, provided that the King's permission had been obtained beforehand: S.R. Gardiner, *Notes of the Debates in the House of Lords Taken by Henry Elsyng in 1621* (Camden Soc., CIII, 1870), pp. 107–8.
[23] *L.J.*, III, 189.
[24] Macqueen, *Practical Treatise*, p. 76.
[25] *L.J.*, III, 530.
[26] H.L.R.O., Main Papers, 3 Apr. 1628 (Ralph Starkey's case, Lane *v.* Baude), 8 Apr. 1628 (Anthony Lamplaugh's case), 25 May 1628 (Mathew's case).
[27] L.O. Pike, *A Constitutional History of the House of Lords* (1894), pp. 297–8.

[28] *L.J.*, IV, 111 (James *v.* Sawyer); H.L.R.O., Main Papers, 8 Feb. 1641 (Burgh *v.* Morley).

[29] H.L.R.O., Main Papers, *loc. cit.*

[30] *Ibid.*, 24 May 1641 (Dawes *v.* Hopton).

[31] P.R.O., C.33/182, f. 329 (Blake *v.* Rolfe).

[32] The procedure could, on occasion, vary. Petitions, in some cases, were brought directly into the House (more often than not by individual members), and given a first reading there, before being referred to the committee for petitions.

[33] H.L.R.O., Main Papers, 23 Dec. 1640, book of orders (Bourlacy *v.* Berry, Smith *v.* Harris).

[34] *L.J.*, IV, 263, 268.

[35] *Ibid.*, 255.

[36] *Ibid.*, 263.

[37] Hale, *Jurisdiction*, p.185.

[38] *Ibid.*

[39] Sir Edward Coke, *The Fourth Part of the Institutes of the Laws of England . . .* (4th edn., 1669), p. 85.

[40] See, for example, H.M.C., *3rd Rept.*, App., pp. 22, 30, 34.

[41] H.L.R.O., Main Papers, 25 June 1641; *L.J.*, IV, 289 (Griffin *v.* Griffin).

[42] Charles M. Gray, 'The Boundaries of the Equitable Function', *American Journal of Legal History*, XX (1976), 199.

[43] H.M.C., *3rd Rept.*, App., p. 29. The issue was later taken up by the Hale Commission on law reform in 1652. The commission's report, issued in March 1653, recommended the abolition of the bill of review procedure in Chancery (as well as writ of error procedure at common law,) and the creation of a single appellate court designed to handle all appeals from both common law and equity courts. The new court was to be composed entirely of laymen, appointed to the bench by Parliament. Judges, attorneys and court officers were specifically excluded as candidates in the wording of the proposed legislation. Hale's endorsement of a lay appellate court in 1653 is strikingly at odds with his subsequent conclusions on the matter, as they emerge in *The Jurisdiction of the Lords' House*. By 1675, when the treatise was written, Hale, perhaps not surprisingly, reverted to a far more conservative position, evincing a strong disinclination to allow the House of Lords even the right of review over the Chancellor's decrees without a special commission from the King. On the Hale Commission, see Mary Cotterell, 'Interregnum Law Reform: The Hale Commission of 1652', *E.H.R.*, LXXXIII (1968), 689–704. For the commission's report see *A Collection of Scarce and Valuable Tracts . . . of the late Lord Somers*, ed. Sir Walter Scott (2nd edn., 13 vols., 1809–15), VI, 191–245.

[44] H.L.R.O., Main Papers, 23 June 1641.

[45] *Ibid.*

[46] *Ibid.*, 16 May 1642.

[47] *Ibid.*, 23 June 1641.

[48] P.R.O., C.33/176, f. 656.

[49] *Ibid.*

[50] H.L.R.O., Main Papers, 23 June 1641.

[51] *Ibid.*, 27 Nov. 1641.

[52] *Ibid.*

[53] P.R.O., C.33/175, f.266.

[54] *Ibid.*

[55] H.L.R.O., Main Papers, 10 Feb. 1641.

[56] *Ibid.*

[57] *Ibid.*

[58] P.R.O., S.P. 16/473, f.106.

[59] W.J. Jones, *The Elizabethan Court of Chancery* (Oxford, 1967), p. 456. See also G. Spence, *The Equitable Jurisdiction of the Court of Chancery* (2 vols., 1846–8), II, 678.

[60] Jones, *Elizabethan Court of Chancery*, p. 465.

[61] *Ibid.*, p. 456.

[62] These problems were in fact specifically addressed by the Hale Commission of 1652. The commission proposed a number of internal administrative reforms for the court. Notifica-

tion procedures were to be tightened, guidelines were to be imposed to ensure the proper examination of witnesses before hearing, intermediate references to the Masters in Chancery were to be strictly controlled, and a full hearing of both parties was to be guaranteed before the issue of any interlocutory order or final judgment. See *Somers's Tracts*, VI, 191–245.

63   H.L.R.O., Main Papers, 23 Jan. 1641.
64   *Ibid.*, 16 May 1642 (Russell *v.* Hanford); P.R.O., C.33/179, f.159.
65   *L.J.*, IV, 158.
66   *Ibid.*, 284.
67   *Ibid.*
68   H.L.R.O., Main Papers, 3 June 1643; *L.J.*, VI, 79.
69   *L.J.*, IV, 372.
70   *Diaries . . . of Sir Edward Dering*, p. 92.

Parliamentary History, Volume 2 (1983)

THE ELECTIONEERING OF SARAH, DUCHESS OF MARLBOROUGH*

FRANCES HARRIS

British Library

'I am confydent I should have been the greatest Hero that ever was known in the Parliament Hous', Sarah, Duchess of Marlborough, announced in 1714, 'if I had been so happy as to have been a Man.'[1] But if her sex condemned her always to be an observer of activities inside the Houses of Parliament, it did not debar her from electioneering. Indeed her opportunities for this were exceptional. As she remarked herself in another connexion, 'my case is in many things different from other wemens'.[2] The Duke of Marlborough's long absences on campaign between 1702 and 1711 gave her more scope for independent political action than she would otherwise have had, and when he was incapacitated by a stroke in 1716, the management of their affairs fell largely into her hands. From the time of his death in 1722 until her own in 1744, she acted as administrator of the family estates, and as self-appointed invigilator of the political activities of her grandsons. Although there were some personal confrontations with voters, her sex, and in later years her increasing infirmities, meant that much of her electioneering was conducted by delegation to male agents, and above all by letter. She kept up a vast correspondence throughout her life, much of it political, and a great deal of it, particularly of the Queen Anne period, destroyed in her own lifetime. But enough survives among her papers in the Blenheim archive (now British Library, Additional MSS. 61414–80) and elsewhere, to illuminate at least some of the episodes in her 40 years of electoral involvement.

* I am grateful to the following for allowing me to consult and quote from manuscripts in their possession: the Marquess of Tavistock, the Trustees of the Bedford Estates and their archivist, Mrs M. Draper; the Head of Record Services, Devon Record Office; the Director of the Pierpont Morgan Library; Mrs Ann Cooper, Clerk to the Woodstock Town Council.

Her family's extensive property in St Albans and at Sandridge nearby provided the foundation of her electoral interest. Her grandfather, Sir John Jenyns, and her father, Richard Jenyns, who had both sided with Parliament during the Civil War, represented the borough successively in the House of Commons between 1640 and 1668.[3] By 1684 Sarah and her husband had acquired sole possession of the family estates, and had made St Albans their chief place of residence. Initially, as might be expected, it was John Churchill rather than his wife who managed the electoral interest which they had inherited there. He had been a Member of the brief first Exclusion Parliament in 1679, and before he was raised to the English peerage in 1685, had intended to stand as a candidate for St Albans himself.[4] Once in the House of Lords he set up his brother George, and ensured that he was returned for the borough at every general election for the next 20 years. This cannot have been entirely to Sarah's liking. A Whig by temperament and family inheritance ('the true born Whig', as Marlborough called her),[5] she was never on easy terms with her high Tory brother-in-law. The Whiggism of Charles, Lord Spencer, who had married her second daughter in 1700 and was soon to become the third Earl of Sunderland, was far more congenial to her, and in the first election of Queen Anne's reign she involved herself readily in his unsuccessful bid for the county seat of Northamptonshire. Her intervention in elections at this period carried more weight and attracted more attention than it might otherwise have done, because of her long standing intimacy with the Queen.[6]

During these very early years of Queen Anne's reign the Duchess had also formed a close friendship with Elizabeth Burnet, wife of the Bishop of Salisbury. A staunch Whig herself, Mrs Burnet had first-hand contacts with a number of Whig M.P.s through her brother-in-law Robert Dormer, Justice of Common Pleas and Member for Northallerton.[7] Her letters to Sarah in 1704 and 1705 are much concerned with parliamentary affairs, particularly with the Tory attempt to tack the Occasional Conformity Bill to the land tax, and from them it is clear that some of the Whig Members were taking advantage of Mrs Burnet's friendship with Sarah to bring pressure to bear on the Marlborough-Godolphin ministry, as the general election of 1705 approached. In November 1704 Mrs Burnet reported that 'a very considerable man in the House of Commons' had come to the bishop with the intention that what he said should be reported to Sarah or Godolphin. His message was that the Whigs

> were very desirous to have some assurance that the approching desolution & folowing Elections (this being the last Session) might be so taken care of . . . that the enemies to the establishment might have no advantage; but that the Lieutenancy & Justices of the Peace, may be so impartially regulated, & put into the hands of Men of Estates & honesty that all just cause of complaint may be taken away.

If Godolphin would give them this assurance, they would rely on his word. Otherwise, 'they must think themselves obliged . . . to endeavour what they can to recommend themselves to the nation before a new Election'.

There were more thinly veiled threats ('had they not a sincere regard for the Government they know how to be uneasy as well as others'), and in February 1705 the further hint that 'few things will oblige more than oposing, at least giveing no assistance to tackers or their avowed friends'. Discreetly prompting the duchess, Mrs Burnet added, 'you are the best judg if it is proper to be spoak on farther'.[8]

The duchess, of course, was only too glad of the excuse to urge these points on Marlborough and Godolphin, whom she had always regarded as too sympathetic to the Tories. She had already accused Godolphin, who discussed his parliamentary strategy with her, of being 'unactive' against the Tackers.[9] Her intense interest in this issue, stimulated by her contacts with Mrs Burnet, prompted her to take a more personal share in the forthcoming elections. For John Gape, George Churchill's fellow Member at St Albans, was not only a Tory but a Tacker. The candidate set up against him by the government in 1705 was Admiral Henry Killigrew, who had owned property nearby for some years.[10]

On 17 April 1705 the duchess wrote to one of her agents at St Albans in Killigrew's favour. The letter, in keeping with the government's policy of making a distinction between Tackers and moderate Tories, was discreet enough:

> Having heard that Mr John Tombes who keeps my lord Marlboroughs courts at Sandridge has an interest in the town of St Albans I give you the trouble of this to desire you will speke to him from me, to use it in promoteing Mr Killigrew's Election as well as my brothers . . . the admerall & all his family having been allways in the true interest of the church, very zealous upon all occasions . . .

She was later to claim that this letter was the cause of 'a great noise the torys made against me in the hous of commons', when the election came to be considered there.[11] In fact her involvement was far more extensive than this. She had not only sent her agents to all the freemen in the borough, but had also gone to St Albans herself to canvass a number of them personally. Well primed for her task, she was able to read or quote to them from 'King Charles 2d's Speech against Tacking'. Her main argument was that Tackers 'would be injurious to the Government, and were for the French Interest'; but to one voter she added that 'it was the Queen's desire, that no such Men should be chose'. This use of the Queen's name was particularly calculated to arouse Tory anger. Nevertheless, for all her efforts, the duchess did not have much success. A number of freemen evidently considered that they had discharged their obligations to her family by giving one vote to George Churchill, and put her off with the flat statement that they were already engaged for the other to Gape. A local clergyman, Dr John Coatsworth, even ventured to bandy words with the duchess, '*pro* and *con*, as to several Points of State'.[12]

Killigrew was defeated, but petitioned against Gape on the grounds that the mayor and returning officer had shown partiality in determining the validity of some freemen's votes. The Whig leader Lord Halifax, one of

Sarah's most assiduous and optimistic correspondents during the election, condoled with her about the 'foul play' she had met with at St Albans, and promised her that a Whig majority in the new Parliament would make 'Gape and his Mayor . . . repent their Return'.[13] There was a good prospect of this, for a Whig told Mrs Burnet, who in turn told Sarah, that 'he would consider the merits of the cause when it was only a Torry, but if he was a Tacker he cared not what his cause was, he lookt on him as a frenchman, a Common enemie'.[14]

Sarah, maintaining that she had done 'no one thing but what was very reasonable & cautious' in her support of Killigrew, was privately dismissive about Tory rumours of her unwarrantable interference in the election. Nevertheless she realized that she could expect to be roughly handled by the Tories when the case came to be heard, and was nervous about the result,[15] particularly as their losses in the election had not been as great as Halifax had predicted. Tory accusations of bribery against her did not amount to much. The best evidence they could muster was a present of 20 guineas given to one of the freemen, Thomas Crosfield, who was also an old servant of the duchess's mother, to free him from gaol.[16] But both Whigs and Tories at this period greatly overestimated the extent of Sarah's political influence with the Queen, and she had encouraged their misconceptions by her use of the Queen's name at the election. It was in reference to this that William Bromley, in the course of the hearing, compared her to Alice Perrers, favourite of Edward III ('some strang woman in a history I have forgot', was Sarah's version of this allusion); 'for indeed', Bishop Burnet added, 'she was looked upon by the whole party, as the person who had reconciled the whigs to the queen, from whom she was naturally very averse'.[17] And it was not only the Tory party which took this view. The duchess had made a more successful contribution to the Whig electoral cause in 1705, when she persuaded her young son-in-law, Lord Bridgwater, to nominate Harry Mordaunt for Brackley in Northamptonshire, a borough controlled by his family. Sunderland wrote to her in warm approval, 'I dare say it will have the good effect of uniting him, & Lord Wharton [Mordaunt's cousin and the leading Whig electioneer] which will make all things easy hereafter in that Country'. And he added, 'I must say one thing in generall upon all this, & that very sincerely . . . that if England is sav'd, it is entirely owing to your good intentions, zeal, & Pains you have taken for it'.[18]

Such well timed flattery and encouragement might help to offset Tory criticism, but the experience of 1705 demonstrated to Sarah for the first of many times the limitations of her interest at St Albans, and made her diffident about taking a personal part in elections there for the immediate future. By the time of the next general election in 1708 she was in any case very reluctant to bestir herself in favour of George Churchill. His open opposition to the ministry in this year was a major source of embarrassment and concern. Marlborough, who regarded his brother's candidacy as a useful means of identifying his own supporters and opponents in the borough, instructed his wife to give Churchill their support as usual, though to spend no money in his favour. It was Churchill who took the matter out of their hands by deciding not to stand.[19] Their efforts could not prevent Gape from regaining his seat, but the more congenial Whig, Joshua Lomax, was elected with their interest. For the rest, Sarah was chiefly concerned during this most promising of Whig elections, with the journalistic projects of her new-found political confidant, the Whig M.P. Arthur Maynwaring, for 'raising a Cry upon the Jacobites'.[20]

But the alliance between the Whigs and the Marlborough-Godolphin ministry with which the duchess and Maynwaring had been so preoccupied in their correspondence of 1708 and 1709[21] proved short-lived. The downfall of the Whig ministry in 1710 led to a premature dissolution of the Parliament in September of that year. Initially the Whigs had hoped to save the majority which they had secured in 1708. When Sarah was approached by the young William Grimston, who had inherited a considerable estate near St Albans, with a request for her interest, she was chiefly concerned to scotch rumours of the dissolution of a Parliament 'which has assisted the Queen so well to get the better of France'. In any case he was not sufficiently a Whig for her taste. She put him off with the excuse that she could do nothing 'in a business of that kind without first acquainting the Duke of Marlborough',[22] and when the dissolution was announced, suggested to Marlborough that they assist Lomax again. But the duke, foreseeing the Tory victory, warned his wife to stay away from St Albans altogether at election time, in case she should 'meet with some insult'. With unaccustomed meekness she took his advice, decamping for the few days of the election to stay with her daughter Lady Bridgwater at Ashridge.[23]

Her intervention at the New Woodstock election showed somewhat less discretion. Since the building of Blenheim Palace was begun in Woodstock Park in 1705, Marlborough's interest had been stronger there than in St Albans. The right of election was in the freemen of the town, and the Duke had taken the immediate precaution of having several of his dependants made free in an honorary capacity. These included William Cadogan and Michael Richards, two of his most trusted army subordinates, his secretary Adam Cardonnel, and John Vanbrugh and Samuel Travers, respectively architect and surveyor-general of the building.[24] The result was that he succeeded with some difficulty in securing first Cadogan's election as one Member in 1705, and in 1708 the election of both Cadogan and a local man, Sir Thomas Wheate, thus entirely defeating the main opposing interest of the Tory Earl of Abingdon. On Sarah's orders, venison from the park was distributed afterwards 'to such Persons of Condition as were serviceable in the late Election, without taking any notice of those Gentlemen who so violently espoused the Lord Abington's Cause'.[25] But perhaps it is significant that Marlborough did not encourage his wife to meddle in the elections themselves, leaving the matter in the capable hands of his agents, Samuel Travers and (in 1705) his Secretary at War Henry St John, the future Viscount Bolingbroke.[26] The duke's interest was so well managed that even at the height of Tory confidence in 1710, Travers was expecting Cadogan and Wheate to be returned unopposed, when a few days before the election Sarah ordered an immediate cessation of the works at Blenheim, pending a decision by the new ministry about payments.

This ill-timed action caused distress both to the workmen who were discharged without pay, and to the townspeople who had given them credit. There were threats of rioting, and Marlborough's agents feared that the discontent would give the Tories an opportunity of setting up a candidate in opposition.[27] The position of Wheate, whose interest was not strong with the corporation, was particularly precarious. Nor was Sarah's attitude notably sympathetic. Dismissing the alarm simply as a ploy to get money, she gave a general assurance that the workmen would eventually be paid what was due to them, and added the sharp reminder that it was not in the interest of the town 'to disoblige the Duke of Marlborough' at the election.[28] But she did write a brief note to bolster Wheate's position:[29]

> I am sory that any concernd in the Building are unruly or like to give any trouble in the Ellection. I will give any derections that are necessary to prevent disorder, so that you may please to shew this leter to any body that you think will bee influenced by it.

On the strength of this Wheate sent urgent messages to his supporters among the out-of-town freemen, and Travers hastily raised £300 on his own credit to distribute among the workmen.[30] But the situation was chiefly saved by the fact that there was not time enough before the election for the unprepared local Tories to take advantage of the crisis. 'We lost the opportunity of throwing out Sir Thomas Wheate at Woodstock', an Oxford Tory complained,[31]

> because we were not provided with one to set up there. The town sent round the neighbourhood and could not prevail with any one to appear, nor could our gentlemen in three days' time find any among themselves that would accept it.

During the general election of 1713 the Marlboroughs were abroad in self-imposed exile, and the duke was under threat of prosecution from a hostile House of Commons. For this reason they were the more anxious to secure the return of their own supporters where they had any interest. In their absence the Tories took the opportunity to make a more systematic challenge at Woodstock. But the creation of a further batch of honorary freemen, a considerable financial outlay, including a judiciously timed programme for paving the town, and above all the continuing dependence of the town on the building works, secured the return of Cadogan and Wheate once again. 'I have ask't not one person for his Vote', an agent of Marlborough reported after paying off some of the Blenheim creditors, 'but I find paying them has the same Effect.'[32] Sarah, no doubt recalling the elections committee of 1705, cynically predicted that Cadogan would be 'voted out of the hous by a petetion, & I think they will doe same by Mr Stanhope, Mr Walpole & every body that will be troublesome in exposing their designs'.[33] But although a re-election was ordered by the Tory Parliament on the grounds of the new honorary freemen, Cadogan and Wheate were again returned. For some time before this, Sarah had had a critical eye on the town clerk, George Ryves, whom she suspected of cheating in his capacity as head keeper and bailiff in Woodstock Park. But the events of the 1710 election had evidently taught her a lesson, for she was careful not to visit her wrath on him until the re-election was well over; 'as long as Mr C[adogan]'s Cause depends on the P[arliament]', she warned her agent on the spot, ''tis not good to disoblige Mr R[yves] or anybody in those Parts'.[34]

It was at St Albans that the duchess's prediction was verified. The Marlboroughs' interest was given by letter and by their agents in person to Grimston and to a young Whig, William Hale of King's Walden. Sarah had been on good terms with the latter's family for some years, having recommended his sister Mary ('a very agreeable young woman of a very good family') as maid of honour to Queen Anne.[35] Grimston and Hale were returned, but Hale was unseated on a petition of John Gape, one of the allegations being that the Marlboroughs' steward had given bribes in favour of both their candidates.[36] Hale had to wait for the first election of George I's reign, when the Whigs were returned to power, in order to unseat Gape in his turn.

By the time of Hale's premature death in 1717, Marlborough had suffered the stroke which left Sarah with a large measure of control over his affairs, and their electioneering was one of the many things to suffer from her remarkable capacity for tactlessness and indiscriminate quarrelling. In Hale's place at the ensuing by-election she decided to put up Robert Jennens of Acton, Suffolk, who had looked after her Hertfordshire properties while she was abroad. Despite the similarity of their names, he was apparently not a relation of hers, but he was connected by marriage with Anthony and William Guidott, who had acted as her family's solicitors for many years.[37]

Sarah made it clear that she expected Grimston's support for her candidate. In a tactless message delivered in Marlborough's name she claimed, as Grimston indignantly reported, that the duke had taken 'a great deale of paines to chuse me when my interest was very little'. When he requested a promise of financial help at the next general election in return for helping Jennens, Sarah chose to regard his attitude as 'insolent' and 'saucy'. Grimston retorted by demanding an apology before he could proceed further. He evidently did not get it, for Jennens, in spite of having spent £800 on the contest,[38] was defeated by Joshua Lomax. Although the duchess had readily given Lomax her interest in the past, she had by this time contrived to quarrel with him also, over a 'false and foolish' letter which he had written concerning Charles Middleton, her gardener and local man of business at St Albans.[39]

Apart from her personal quarrels with Grimston and Lomax, both were government Whigs, with whose politics she had by this time little sympathy. A series of disputes with the Court had left her as hostile to the leading Whigs, Sunderland, Stanhope and Cadogan, as she had once been favourable to them. Discussing her electoral interest with her son-in-law Godolphin in 1719, she wrote:[40]

If I knew any thing in the world that I could do more to procure a good member of Parliament I would not spair my pains, because I must allways desire to preserve so good a fortune as the Duke of Marlborough has in England, but as to party business I have non of that warmth that you have seen in me, for I have been long convinced that there is very few men on either side that really is concerned for any thing but their own present interest . . .

By the 1720s she was firmly entrenched in opposition, and determined to use her electoral interest to 'distress the Court'. This change of attitude meant that for the future she was often to find allies among men whom in the past she had bitterly opposed. 'A Tory & a Whigg', she decided, 'if they have Sense & Honesty, mean the same thing.'[41]

Her candidates for St Albans in 1722 were William Clayton, who had looked after Marlborough's affairs while he was abroad, and a Tory, William Gore, who had agreed to divide the expenses with her. After being defeated, Grimston and Lomax put in a petition alleging a number of irregular practices on the part of their opponents. According to this, Sarah had secured the support of the town clerk, Edmund Aylward, and the mayor, William Carr, and the latter had realized that he could not hope to return two strangers in competition with local Members, 'that deal much in the town and pay well', without a substantial number of honorary freemen created for the purpose. In his office of postmaster, therefore, he sent post horses into 'the adjacent countries and towns' to have supporters of Clayton and Gore 'made free gratis'. When taxed with this, he was said to have repeated Sarah's assurance that 'it would be a Tory Parliament, which with her interest would bring him off'. A further accusation was that Clayton and Gore, realizing that Parliament might set aside the votes of the new freemen, had also attempted to bribe 'every inhabitant and legal freeman that would receive the same'. The duchess, Charles Middleton and Thomas Gape, son of her old enemy, were all accused in this connexion, and 'a public office of bribery' was alleged to have been fixed at the town clerk's house.[42]

There would appear to have been considerable truth in this account. In September 1722 official complaints were laid against Carr for abuse of his office as postmaster during the election. Although she was in deep mourning for her husband who had died three months before, the duchess at once applied to Godolphin to use his influence with Walpole to have the mayor protected. Rather naïvely, she was indignant at receiving only a non-committal response.[43] Aylward's involvement is clear from the details he afterwards supplied of her election expenses. These included over a thousand pounds paid directly to Clayton, 'a great many guineas out of the Duchess of Marlborough's own pocket for votes', and more paid on her behalf by her steward, Charles Hodges, and by Middleton.[44]

When Grimston and Lomax withdrew their petition in November 1722, Clayton wrote to the duchess to thank her for her 'pains, expense and trouble' on his behalf, and added, 'I shall want your Commands about the Woodstock election'.[45] For, as Clayton's opponents did not fail to point out, at the same time as he was petitioned against at St Albans concerning the illegal admission of freemen, he was himself a petitioner on the same grounds at Woodstock.[46]

Clayton had been a Member for Woodstock on the Marlborough interest since Cadogan was raised to the peerage in 1716. When the other Member, Sir Thomas Wheate, had died in 1721, Sarah set up her own candidate, Charles Crisp, against Wheate's son, only to have a new mayor and returning officer appointed in opposition to her interest before the by-election could take place. The rector, Dr Robert Cocks, did his best for her by preaching a sermon on the day of the mayor's swearing-in, in which he reminded the townspeople that Marlborough 'had raised their Streets from the mire, & their fortunes out of the Dust', and 'exhorted them to the Best Returnes of Gratitude very pertinently & seasonably'. Although Sarah predicted bitterly that this would 'do no more good upon such wretches then the reflections of past obligations have had upon the present ministry',[47] she did succeed in securing Crisp's return. But in this victory the building works must have been more instrumental than Cocks's eloquence. To her masons, William Townesend and Bartholomew Peisley, she had written immediately before the election:[48]

> I believe you dont forget what I desir'd of you before I left Blenheim, That you would use all your interest to promote Mr. Crispe's being Chose at the Town of Woodstock. I am told that the Masons That are at Woodstock & in our interest are as good workmen as those that are inclin'd to vote with our enemies, but You are the best judge of that; What I desire of you and of Mr Peisley is that You would encourage those that are inclin'd to be friends as far as You can do it without any prejudice to the work which you have undertaken . . .

But in the six months' interval between the by-election and the general election of 1722, the mayor had been able to create a new batch of hostile freemen, and what made it particularly irksome, to cite similar creations in the Marlborough interest in previous years to prove that it was 'the immemorial Custom & Priviledge of the Councell' to do so.[49] Clayton and Crisp were duly thrown out, and all that Sarah could do to revenge herself was to reject a petition of the townspeople against some aspect of the building work, on the grounds that 'no Body of that Town has Merrit enough to put me to any inconvenience upon Their account'.[50]

For her defeat she chiefly blamed William Diston, George Ryves's successor as head keeper in the park and bailiff of the nearby estates. A member of the Woodstock corporation and the proprietor of a cockpit in the town, Diston revelled in local politics. The original grant in 1715 of the lease for his cockpit had been conditional on the common councilmen having the right to attend any cock-match there free of charge,[51] and his position as head keeper gave him the additional asset of control over the distribution of venison, always a valuable currency for electioneering purposes, as he explained to Sarah:[52]

> When any Freeman came to the Lodge to ask for Venison, I gave it him, and gave him such a diner as I had and a belly full of strong beer into the

bargain . . . By this acquaintance with the Freemen, all Cabals for rebellion soon came to my knowledge, and were allmost as soon defeated.

But Sarah's relations with him followed the same depressing pattern as with George Ryves. By 1719 she was accusing him of profiteering out of the perquisites of his posts and of using his electioneering to maintain his own interest rather than hers. 'If he were in the interest against us by any principle,' she told Godolphin,[53]

> I should have nothing to say against that, but I am thoroughly convinced . . . the mischief which hee has been doing so long to the Duke of Marlborough's friends has proceeded purely from a simple thought that hee would make himself so usefull to the Duke of Marlborough by people's depending upon him, I mean Mr Diston, that the Duke of Marlborough could not part with him whatever hee did in other concerns.

Finally, convinced that he had 'ruined her interest in the corporation', she had persuaded her invalid husband to dismiss him; even though Diston 'was so madd as to come a horseback into Woodstock town with a running footman by his side, making the bells ring for him, & a great mobb hee had got together that cryed a Diston for ever'.[54] Diston was unrepentant, maintaining to the last that it was the interest of Clayton and Crisp that was lost, 'and not your Grace's'.[55] He was far too useful to part with altogether and survived to fight another day.

Marlborough's death in June 1722 without surviving sons left his eldest daughter, Henrietta, Duchess of Marlborough in her own right, and his widow and eldest son-in-law, Godolphin, principal trustees of his great wealth, with instructions to invest it in the purchase of estates. Sarah, exceptionally well provided for under the terms of his will, intended to use part of her own money for the same purpose, to endow her own favourites within the family. As Sir Robert Walpole's power grew in the 1720s, her determination to oppose him with all the interest she possessed increased; and this, coupled with her wealth and the growing extent of her landownership and electoral interest, meant that she was liable to be courted by Walpole's opponents as assiduously as she had once been cultivated by the Whigs when she was a royal favourite. 'You have Friends, you have Credit, you have Talents, you have Power, & you have Spirits stil to do an infinite deal of service', William Pulteney wrote flatteringly, when involving her in one of his electoral projects;[56] and if he and his friends needed her wealth and influence, she needed their advice, based on first-hand experience of parliamentary politics, to exploit these assets to best effect.

It did not take her long to become as disillusioned with Clayton as the Woodstock electorate had been. She suspected that she had been cheated in the matter of election expenses, and accused him of 'under-valuing' her efforts on his behalf at Woodstock and St Albans.[57] Soon she was complaining of Members 'selling their votes' to Walpole's administration, 'after you have been at great expence & trouble to chuse them for very different purposes'.[58] By the general election of 1727 she was well provided with grandsons at or approaching the age when they would be eligible for election. Both on account of their youth and their financial expectations from her, she could expect them to be more amenable to her directions than her previous candidates.

William Godolphin, styled Marquess of Blandford, and his cousins Charles and John Spencer were all travelling on the Continent when she began to lay her plans for them. Blandford, whom she expected to be called to the House of Lords soon after his return, was intended for St Albans, but only to keep 'a place for Johnny to be chose where I have a natural right to recommend when he is of age'. Charles Spencer was to be her candidate for Woodstock.[59] But these plans soon went awry. After her experiences of 1722, she was not anxious for another major contest at St Albans, and when Grimston approached her with the usual project for shared expenses at this notoriously expensive borough she had already learnt that the Nonconformist Caleb Lomax, son of the old Member, had built up a strong interest. Deciding that it was not worth her while to do battle with him, she not only left the field to Grimston, but in spite of their past differences actually gave him her recommendation. Presumably she was intending to claim his support for John Spencer at a later date. She warned him, however, that 'the town may encourage somebody else to oppose you, to get money'.[60] Grimston wrote effusively[61]

> to express my thankfullness and gratitude for your Grace's friendship and recommendation of me to the Corporation of St Albans. Whatever success I meet with will be entirely owing to your Grace's generous interposition . . . The Mayor and Aldermen at present do not shew any inclination to recommend another and I cannot think it will be for Mr Lomax's advantage to promote an opposition which must unavoidably be attended with very great expense and consequently weaken his interest, for very few of the inferiour sort where his strength chiefly lys will resist a temptation.

Although Thomas Gape was set up at the last moment he had no success.

Meanwhile Blandford's services as a stop-gap for his Spencer cousins were required at Woodstock. By joining with another old enemy Lord Abingdon (whom she had dismissed in 1705 as good for nothing but to make 'Jacobit Elections')[62] and his candidate Samuel Trotman, Sarah was easily able to defeat Sir Thomas Wheate and his patron Lord Lichfield. But at the last moment Wheate discovered that Charles Spencer was a few months short of his twenty-first birthday. She was obliged to nominate Blandford, who knew nothing of the matter, in his place.[63] Afterwards she was shocked to reckon up the cost of this relatively trouble-free election: almost £500 laid out in the town itself (including £50 to Diston), besides 'the charge & hire of the freemen from London, all the wine, mead, and strong beer at my own hous & at least 120 bucks'.[64]

By the beginning of 1728 Spencer was of age and returned from his travels, and Sarah immediately proposed that Blandford should stand down in his favour. At this point Blandford's father, the long-suffering Godolphin, showed signs of losing patience with her manipulations:[65]

Really madam tho Lord Blandford was chosen into the house of Commons without his own knowledge or desire, yet I hope you will forgive me if I say that, in my poor opinion, it would give him a most contemptible air, if, now he is in,. He should turn himself out, for any other consideration (at least) than that of being call'd into the House of Lords.

Blandford remained M.P. for Woodstock. It was Charles Spencer who shortly afterwards went up to the House of Lords, succeeding his elder brother as fifth Earl of Sunderland in 1729.

Sarah's alliance with Abingdon and Trotman, a makeshift affair, survived the election of 1727 by only a few months.[66] By this time elections for vacancies to the common council had become necessary, and with the general election safely over, Sarah was determined to build up such an interest for herself there that neither contested elections nor uncongenial alliances would be necessary for the future. For this purpose Diston was an invaluable ally. 'That person that does not think of methods to prevent Electors forming before the vacancies of Parliament happen', he had warned her, 'will never bring his purposes about at the time.' In return for his reinstatement in Woodstock Park, he offered to put it into her power in future to return both Members for the town unopposed and without expense, apart from that of treating on election day. This undertaking immediately plunged him into the round of small negotiations, chiefly involving money and employments, which were his particular talent. One of the councillors whom Diston was trying to detach from his allegiance to Wheate pointed out that if he supported the duchess he would lose Wheate's custom, and required an assurance that he would be given work in Woodstock Park by way of compensation. Once the main building works were over, the townspeople did not benefit as much from the proximity of Blenheim Palace as they might have expected, for Sarah did not like the place and seldom stayed there for long. The town remained predominantly poor (Sarah described one of the aldermen as 'a beggar'), and as Diston candidly explained to her, 'those people that have any mony due to them from any of the necessitous Common-Council men, Take this advantage of pressing 'em for their Debts, in order to get the mony out of your Grace's pocket'.[67]

Godolphin was delighted that she had again secured Diston's services in the cultivation of the electorate, 'a talent he owns himself to be fond of, and thinks himself (as I confess I likewise think him) very able in'.[68] But Sarah was still suspicious of him, and had her own ideas about how matters should be managed. Diston was obliged to go along with these to some extent, using his influence to have her steward Hodges, her grandsons' governor Humphrey Fish and Charles Spencer himself elected to the council: 'the best days work I ever did for your Grace', as he announced triumphantly. For there had been great opposition from the local members of the corporation, who claimed that 'giving such a number of votes to the out-town would render the in-town insignificant, and that the town would be absolutely inslaved and never more regarded'. Diston had been able to succeed only by promising that Sarah would bring no more strangers on to the council for the future. When she again attempted to do so in 1729,

Diston first remonstrated with her, and then abandoned her.[69]

Once John Spencer, her favourite grandson, had come of age in 1729, Sarah did not rest until she had secured his election also. She failed at the St Albans by-election which followed Lomax's death in 1730, when Gape was able to take advantage of the breakdown of her understanding with Grimston to secure his own election.[70] Within a matter of weeks after this she had persuaded Godolphin to approach Walpole with the request that Spencer be allowed to stand unopposed at Lostwithiel, but she cannot have been greatly surprised when Walpole declined to co-operate.[71] It was not until January 1732, following Blandford's early death, that she was finally able to secure Spencer's election for Woodstock, at the cost of setting up a charity for clothing 80 poor men and women of the town.[72]

Later in this year came the violent family quarrel, sparked off when Charles Spencer married without his grandmother's consent, and John Spencer was temporarily cast out of her favour for taking his brother's part. In December 1732 Sunderland took advantage of the breach to make an interest for him, with a view to his being elected for Hampshire, the existing Members, Lord Harry Powlett and Sir John Cope, being both Court supporters. But Sarah suspected that the Court was using the quarrel to try to divide the family and so lessen the collective weight of their opposition.[73] In any case, although she had by no means forgiven Spencer, she was not prepared to relinquish control of the one grandson she had left who was still a commoner. This was made quite clear in the strong letters she wrote to Spencer himself and to his sister Diana, whose husband, the fourth Duke of Bedford, was also involved in the project. In their energy, authority and grasp of detail, these are remarkable documents to come from a woman who was now well into her seventies and immobilized for long periods with 'the gout':

Happening to know a great deal of the Affair relating to the choosing the Knight of the Shire for Hampshire I can easily give my Opinion upon it. I knew long since that Mr Lisle [the Tory candidate, Edward Lisle], had so strong an Interest that about Two Years ago he carry'd the Election for a Verdurer in the Forrest in spite of all the Forces of the Court. The Person who stands with him is Sir Simeon Steward who was never thought to have an Interest equal to the other: But I don't find any impartial Person thinks there is any doubt of Mr Lisle's carrying it. So that 'tis easy to guess whether the Duke of Bolton would not, when he comes to be press'd make single Votes against John Spencer rather than drop my Lord Pawlet, his brother. I am very well Acquainted with Sir John Cope and I will be Answerable from what I know of him that he will not decline standing, unless he finds that he is unlikely to Carry it. Johnny may be Popular (for ought I know) at Stockbridge, but the Chief Weight in the Burroughs is Mony and I believe the first Intention of his making Use of his Interest there was to turn out those the Court set up. If he stands for Knight of the Shire, it is not possible for him to be chose but by joining with the Duke of Bolton, who has no Interest any where but by the Power of the Court . . . On the other Side, if he stands at Woodstock, He is sure to succeed. And in a handsome way, as my Son and Heir, Where he has a natural Call or Right (I think I may say) to be Chose. And he can have no Disappointment or Expence there that will trouble Him or dis-reputation; for if the Court shou'd ever be in the Right (which I very much wish they may, tho' I believe they never will) he may then Vote according to his Honour and Conscience without Suspicion or Reproach.

Spencer, who had evidently thought better of cutting loose from the grandmother from whom he had such expectations, assured her that he would never side with the Court:[74]

I immagined that it was intirely on the Duke of Bedford's interest, & nothing of the Duke of Bolton's (who to be sure is as vile a man as any in the World) but you may be sure, Madam, that I shall never think of standing any where else whilst you are so good as to let me be chose at Woodstock.

But Spencer, young and easy-going, continued to be manipulated by his relations for their electoral ends.

It was at about this time that Sarah formed her close alliance with Walter Plumer, a relation of the Hale family and M.P. for Appleby. By 1733, having been at considerable pains to cultivate her friendship,[75] he was installed as her chief electoral adviser; and in November of that year he and Pulteney tempted her with a proposal for challenging the Court in general and William Clayton in particular at the Westminster election, with himself and Spencer standing jointly. 'I am very sorry your Grace did not let me know your intentions sooner . . .', the Duke of Bedford wrote to her, 'for at present I am engaged to Sir Charles Wager, tho' not to Mr Clayton. If you should think proper to set up either Mr Spencer or Mr Plummer singly against Mr Clayton, your Grace shall entirely command my interest.'[76] On this news Plumer gave up the plan, and Charles Spencer warned the duchess that 'if my Brother should stand alone & not carry it, which may be the case, it would be great cause of Triumph to the court, to say they kept him out by the Duke of Bedford's interest'.[77]

Bedford, in fact, had more ambitious plans for his brother-in-law. In December 1733 he proposed to Sarah that Spencer stand with Charles Leigh for Bedfordshire at the next general election. Somewhat reluctantly she agreed.[78] But she did not let this affect her own plans for him. She owned estates at Wimbledon and Crowhurst in Surrey, and in August 1733 she had been applied to by an impressive group of Surrey freeholders and City merchants, opponents of the Excise Bill, with the proposal that Spencer be put up for the county against Speaker Onslow. Although the Onslow interest had hitherto seemed unassailable, 'the Cry of no Excise on Epsom Green' when the Surrey freeholders had met there to decide on the candidates, had convinced the Court opponents that Spencer could make a successful challenge. He was also, Sarah was told, 'the most probable Person' that Onslow's fellow candidate, the opposition Whig Thomas Scawen, would agree to join with, 'his Lady being a near relation of his Grace the Duke of Bedford'.[79] Although, after some consideration, the duchess did not consent, she did intend that Spencer should stand for both Woodstock and St Albans; 'and when I see I can [nominate?] him in both places, I can just before the election at St Albans recommend a proper man to that town instead of him'.[80]

But complications arose in the execution of these manoeuvres. In the first place, Bedford quarrelled with Charles Leigh, of whom Sarah approved, and proposed to join Spencer instead with Sir Rowland Alston, a Court supporter. This, to her mind, obviated the whole purpose of Spencer's standing, for their votes would cancel each other out, 'which is doing no good as to the public'. It was with difficulty that she was dissuaded from withdrawing Spencer from the contest altogether. But when the time came, she contented herself with insisting that he put in his first appearance at Woodstock, to make sure of his election there.[81] In spite of Diston's efforts and her own, this borough was still not entirely at her command. 'The town is certainly poor', Diston had warned her during a former dispute over the mayoralty, 'and I am afraid they buck 'em on to keep up two parties.' As the election of 1734 approached the mayor did attempt to organize a contest which would have been more lucrative to the town. But when it came to the point Spencer and his fellow candidate, James Dawkins, were elected, 'and not so much as a Pole demanded'. 'The Person spirited up to stand by the Roguery of the Mayor has left a Debt upon the Town', Sarah added vindictively, 'which they deserve to loose who could be base enough to encourage such an Opposition.'[82] Since the St Albans and Bedfordshire elections were appointed for the same day, she had the former put off for a day or two, so that Spencer 'may come to St Albans to give countenance to my recommendation to that town'.[83]

The St Albans election was initially managed for her by Spencer's fellow candidate, Thomas Ashby, who encouraged her to believe that she would have little trouble; when the London freemen were reported 'Inclinable to Rebel' in the months preceding the election, he proposed that he and Spencer attend a meeting with them, and 'I make no Doubt, but One Huzza to your Grace's Health will settle 'Em to a Man'.[84] And it was certainly true that her candidate John Merrill, a client of William Pulteney's and her own relation by marriage, had been successful at the by-election which followed Gape's death early in 1733.[85] The disadvantage that she now seldom visited the town would, she hoped, be counteracted by her recent endowment of almshouses there. 'The only thing they want is to have money spent at the Ale houses', she told her granddaughter as the election approached.[86] But the St Albans electorate was larger and less manageable than that of Woodstock, and subject to a number of opposing interests which were at least as powerful as her own. At the last minute she had to contend with unforeseen local opposition from Grimston, and this was a particular disadvantage since Spencer's substitute, adopted on Plumer's recommendation, was the stranger Sir Thomas Aston. Plumer, however, managed to capture the Nonconformist interest which had formerly been the preserve of the Lomaxes. 'I had a vast deal of trouble', the duchess recalled,[87]

> and I verily believe I should not have carried the Election, tho it cost me a great deal of Mony, if it had not been for the Pains Mr Plummer took in it . . . I

believe the greatest Interest about St Albans are the Dissenters, which Mr Plummer found ways for me to compass a great many of them, But I know none of them my self.

The real difficulty came at the first session of the new Parliament, when John Spencer, returned for both Woodstock and Bedfordshire, had to choose which seat to retain. Normally the county seat would have been considered the more desirable, but Sarah snappishly rejected any suggestion that it would be a 'Diminution' in this case for her grandson to opt for Woodstock; she had always thought it best for him 'to stick to his own Burough'. What particularly annoyed her was Alston's election in place of Charles Leigh:[88]

> I think 'tis very plain from Mr Leigh's having 1020 votes against the Duke of Bedford's Interest join'd with Sir Rowland's that the Duke of Bedford would have carry'd it with Leigh or any other good Man against Sir Rowland, since Sir Rowland's own Interest joined with the Duke of Bedford's made only 1287, And Leigh's came so near him tho' the Strength of the Country united against him.

After the election she made it clear that she expected Bedford to patch matters up with Leigh and let Spencer stand down. The duke resisted.[89]

Sarah then discovered that if she allowed Spencer to resign Woodstock, Sir Robert Walpole had systematic plans to challenge her interest there at the ensuing by-election. At first she had thought this just another 'alarm to get money', until she discovered that Walpole had captured her 'chief Manager', Edward Ryves, who had succeeded his father as town clerk and had 'two or three hundred Pounds a Year in Employments' under the recorder of London. He had also tried unsuccessfully to remove the elderly Henry Beeston, recorder of Woodstock, who had been a loyal supporter of the Marlborough interest since his first appointment under Queen Anne; and his agents at London, Oxford and Woodstock were holding frequent convivial meetings with the freemen, in order to win them over. Two possible candidates were put forward: Thomas ('Butcher') Hope, a former Member for Maidstone, and an East India Merchant, Captain Stockwell.[90] Having conducted what she called a muster of her forces in December 1734, Sarah finally announced:

> I find it impossible to get the better of Sir Robert's Corruption at Woodstock. The Country Gentlemen hate him; And . . . they would certainly oppose whoever Sir Robert recommends. But there is not a great Number of Voters that are Gentlemen: And they live at such a Distance that they cannot at this time of year be depended upon to come to the Election. The Voters that depend any way upon the Crown, who are in Town (except a very few Gentlemen, who would be ashamed to go down to Woodstock to vote for such a low man as Sir Robert would have chose) will certainly go to Woodstock, & vote as they are directed; I mean, the little People. And the best I can expect from a few Gentlemen in the Army is, that to be easy with Sir Robert, they will not vote at all.

In spite of the almost irresistible consideration that 'if I don't fight, it looks as if I was afraid of Sir Robert',[91] she decided that she could not risk parting with Spencer at Woodstock. In fact it is probable that she had never seriously intended to do so. Bedford gave way with a very bad grace,[92] and recommended not Leigh, but Sir Roger Burgoyne in his brother-in-law's place.

In spite of this competition for Spencer's candidacy, it cannot be said that he had a great deal to recommend him as a Member, apart from his impressive family connexions, the fact that he was 'a fine young man' to present to the electors on polling day, and the certainty that he must always vote against the Court if he wished to remain his grandmother's heir. That his use was chiefly as a make-weight for the opposition is clear from Sarah's account of his part in a debate some years later. 'Of those days that he could not attend', she reported, 'he took a very rank Pensioner away with him, which, as he never speaks in the House, is just the same thing as if he had been there.'[93]

Although the duchess's principal electoral efforts were reserved for St Albans and Woodstock, where she had power to nominate candidates, she had some influence as well in less expected areas, and this too was carefully managed for her by her advisers. In November 1734 the Provost of King's College, Cambridge, Dr Andrew Snape, was believed (mistakenly as it turned out) to be 'on the point of death', and the political forces on both sides were mustered with indecent haste for the selection of a successor. 'Sir Robert flatters himself that if he carrys this Point, he shall intirely get Possession of the University of Cambridge & secure the Members of Parliament there for the time to come', William Pulteney explained to her, in terms most calculated to arouse her alarm and combativeness. Pulteney's clerk, Merrill, was organizing the campaign of the opposition candidate, 'an Honest Whig & no Courtier', and wanted Sarah to use her influence over one of the Councillors who had a vote. Sarah hastened to do her part, though the effort proved premature.[94]

Also, of course, she had interest in the counties where she owned or administered estates. Her electoral control over the properties which she had bought in her capacity as trustee of Marlborough's will was limited before the death of her eldest daughter in 1733; for Henrietta's husband was a member of Walpole's administration, and it was to him that the stewards and bailiffs of the trust estates chiefly looked for their instructions at election time. Thomas Norgate, chief steward of the estates until Sarah broke with him in the early 1730s, also had some influence, and he too was 'a courtier'; not, according to Sarah, 'from principle, for I believe he has none', but because he had a place in the customs office.[95] After Henrietta's death, however, Sarah hastened to point out to Godolphin that he must no longer expect to give instructions in electoral matters.[96] Charles Spencer, as the eldest surviving grandson, inherited the Marlborough title, and during the five-year interval before he went over to the Court in 1738, Sarah was delighted to discover that politically he was 'made in some parts like his old Grand-mother'.[97] But since the trust estates had been bought simply as a form of investment for capital, and were seldom if ever visited by the duchess personally, the electoral interest which they provided did not extend much beyond the tenants. 'I have bought a great many Estates in that Country', she wrote when asked to intervene in a Wiltshire by-election in 1736, 'but I doubt my Interest can't go far in a Place where I know no body.'[98] The same applied to the extensive property which she had purchased in her own right, chiefly in Buckinghamshire, Oxfordshire, Bedfordshire, Northamptonshire and Huntingdonshire.[99] But as far as her interest did extend she was strenuous in exercising it against Walpole. She assisted the Tory Sir Justinian Isham in his Northamptonshire by-election in 1730,[100] and in 1734 threw all her weight into the Buckinghamshire contest on the side of Sir William Stanhope, younger brother of her great favourite Lord Chesterfield. 'I have writ four Letters just now, very Strong ones, to assist Sir William Stanhope . . .', she noted in April 1734, 'the Trust and I together have £8000 a Year in that Country: And if he should loose his Election I think it must be from his Neglecting it himself.'[101]

Her position as Ranger of Windsor Park also carried some weight, at least when exercised in conjunction with that of her grandson Marlborough, on whom she had bestowed the lodge in the Home Park. Having received the grant of the Rangership for life from Queen Anne at the height of her favour,.she had clung to it jealously in defiance of the Court during the two succeeding reigns, even when her allowance for salary and expenses was withdrawn in 1737. It was in alliance with Marlborough that she conducted what was, even for her, an outstandingly vituperative campaign against the Court interest of the detested Duke of St Albans and his brothers ('a Family of Idiots . . . who value themselves on being Bastards of a Player'), at the New Windsor by-election in 1738. The attempt was thwarted when the House of Commons determined against her candidate,[102] and since Marlborough himself went over to the Court shortly afterwards, it was never repeated. But her attitude to an earlier Windsor election provides what is perhaps the most striking illustration of the power of her opposition to the Court at this period to override even the bitterest of her former antagonisms. For at one point before the election of 1734, she had believed that a son of Abigail Masham, her cousin and one-time rival for Queen Anne's favour would be set up as a candidate; 'And if he had,' she told the Duchess of Bedford,[103]

> I do really believe my Interest, with the assistance of your two Brothers would have carried it. And to shew what a publick Spirit I have, the unparalleled Ingratitude of the Father & Mother would not have hinder'd me from exerting myself to get one Vote for the Publick.

Well before each election, and before she knew what candidates would be set up, she was at pains to write to 'all my tenants and people that I have influence over, to desire that they would not engage to promise anybody their votes till 'tis seen what members will offer'. When the candidates were named, the voters were instructed 'never to be for any man that has an employment, since experience shows us how few there are that have virtue enough to vote on the side of reason and justice when they must lose by it a profitable place or the hopes of a title'. If no suitable candidates offered, 'I will do all I can to perswade those I can influence not to vote at all. And if there be any one set up that is tolerable, I will endeavour to make them give single Votes for them'. She adopted a similar policy herself, when neighbouring landowners requested her interest.[104]

By 1741 she was over 80 and largely bedridden, but her interest in the forthcoming election was as passionate as ever. Months beforehand she began writing to those who managed her estates 'to engage as many as they can, besides tenants, to vote against pensioners and placemen, in order to save, if possible, the last stake'.[105] Woodstock by this time gave her no trouble; Dawkins and John Spencer were elected unanimously.[106] But the St Albans electorate was a perpetual thorn in her side: 'the most ungrateful Creatures upon Earth', even though 'for many years the Duke of Marlborough did great Kindnesses to the whole Town; & since I have done a great deal for them.' But with the encouragement and assistance of a new ally, the Jacobite leader Sir John Hynde Cotton, whose directions together with Walter Plumer's she promised to take 'in everything concerning it', she prepared to face another contest there. Ashby, 'certainly a very honest man', was to have her interest once more, but Sir Thomas Aston, having 'proved at last a sad choice', had to be replaced.[107] As in 1734, she was advised to put Spencer up initially for both St Albans and Woodstock, but Ashby, able to stand on his own foundation as a local man, did not trouble to manage matters for Spencer. Sarah's reaction when she learnt that the corporation was to oppose her interest, showed that her pugnacity remained unaffected by her great age; she 'thumped her cane to the ground in a rage', and swore 'to be even with them'. She did not live to see another general election, but when Ashby died in 1743 she kept her word to the extent of securing the return of her candidate as his successor, though she had to resort to bribery to do it.[108]

The spectacle of the duchess, who had been so vehemently anti-Jacobite in Queen Anne's reign, joining cordially with an acknowledged Jacobite in her last years, is a strange one. But she considered that Cotton, 'though they call him a Jacobite . . . has too great an estate and too much sense really to be for a Popish government'.[109] Even in extreme old age, it was the contest of the moment that mattered to her, and when her granddaughter broached the subject with her, she made a reply which shows how thoroughly, in spite of her age, she had adapted to the different world of Hanoverian politics and the characteristically heterogeneous oppositions which it produced:[110]

> Considering the vast power that ministers have by disposing of places, honours and money I can't see how it is possible to keep them within just bounds, but by the help of some that have not thoroughly the principles that one wishes, and some of them may assist those that wish what is for the true interest of England, without being able to effect their own designs.

Notes

1   *Letters of Sarah, Duchess of Marlborough . . . at Madresfield Court* (1875), p.37.
2   Devon R.O., 1392 M/L 18 (Seymour of Berry Pomeroy MSS.), to the Duke of Somerset, 30 Aug. 1723.
3   Mary Frear Keeler, *The Long Parliament 1640–1641* (Philadelphia, 1954), pp.233–4.
4   Note by W.D. Pink, *Notes and Queries*, 7th ser., XII (1891), 244–5; P.R.O., S.P. 77/52, f.151; R.H. George, 'Parliamentary Elections and Electioneering in 1685', *Transactions of the Royal Historical Society*, 4th ser., XIX (1936), 176–8.
5   *Private Correspondence of Sarah, Duchess of Marlborough* (2 vols., 1838), II, 27.
6   *Letters of Two Queens*, ed. B. Bathurst (1924), pp.251–2; E.G. Forrester, *Northamptonshire County Elections and Electioneering 1695–1832* (Oxford, 1941), p.27.
7   Dormer was married to her only sister, Mary; for their close relations, see Mrs Burnet's *Method of Devotion* (2nd edn., 1709), p.xii.
8   [B.L.,] Add. [MS.] 61458, ff.31–42.
9   *The Marlborough-Godolphin Correspondence*, ed. H.L. Snyder (3 vols., Oxford, 1975), I, 405.
10 Victoria County History, Hertfordshire, II, 428.
11 Add. 61474, ff. 131–2.
12 *C.J.*, XV, 37–8.
13 Add. 61458, ff.158–9.
14 *Ibid.*, f.50.
15 Add. 61455, f.103; H.M.C., *Buccleuch MSS. (Montagu House)*, I, 354; *Marlborough-Godolphin Corresp.*, I, 468; H.M.C., *Portland MSS.*, IV, 273.
16 *C.J.*, XV, 38. *Cf.* Add. 61453, ff.27–9.
17 G. Burnet, *History of His Own Time*, ed. M.J. R[outh] (2nd edn., 6 vols., Oxford, 1823), V, 230; Add. 61474, f.132.
18 Add. 61443, ff.5–6; 61474, f.144.
19 *Marlborough-Godolphin Corresp.*, II, 966, 976.
20 H.L. Snyder, 'Daniel Defoe, the Duchess of Marlborough, and the Advice to the Electors of Great Britain,' *Huntington Library Quarterly*, XXIX (1965–6), 58–62.
21 Add. 61459–60, *passim*.
22 H.M.C., *Verulam MSS.*, p.177.
23 *Marlborough-Godolphin Corresp.*, III, 1605, 1646.
24 Woodstock Town Hall, Borough Records, box 86, acts of the common council, 19 Mar., 23 Oct. 1705.
25 Add. 61353, f.5.
26 *Marlborough-Godolphin Corresp.*, I, 417; Add. 61353, f.36; 61131, ff.124–8.
27 Add. 19606, ff.33–4; 19609, f.56.
28 Add. 19606, ff.31, 35–6; 61356, ff.127–8.
29 Add. 61468, f.162.
30 Sir Winston Churchill, *Marlborough: His Life and Times* (2 vols., 1947), II, 763.
31 H.M.C., *Portland MSS.*, VII, 21.
32 Woodstock Town Hall, Bor. Recs., box 86, acts of the common council, 28 May, 25 Aug. 1712, 23 Feb. 1713; Add. 28057, f.287; 19606, f.54; 19609, f.136.
33 Add. 61463, f.107.
34 *Letters . . . at Madresfield Court*, pp.44, 59.
35 H.M.C., *Verulam MSS.*, p.114; *Cowper MSS.*, III, 83. *Cf.* R. Clutterbuck, *The History and Antiquities of the County of Hertford* (3 vols., 1815), III, 133.
36 *C.J.*, XVII, 597.
37 For their correspondence, see Add. 61466, ff.1–51, and 62569–70, partly printed in *Letters . . . at Madresfield Court*. See also W.A. Copinger, *The Manors of Suffolk* (7 vols., 1905–11), I, 11–12. The name of the duchess's candidate is given as '—— Jennings' in *The History of Parliament: The House of Commons 1715–1754*, ed. R. Sedgwick (2 vols., 1970) [hereafter cited as *HP 1715–54*], I, 262; but he is referred to as Mr Jennens by Grimston (H.M.C., *Verulam MSS.*, p.115), and identified as Robert Jennens in Add. 62570, f. 114v.

[38] H.M.C., *Verulam MSS.*, p.115; Add. 62570, f. 114v.

[39] *Ibid.*, p.176.

[40] *Catalogue of the Collection of Autograph Letters and Historical Documents Formed . . . by Alfred Morrison*, ed. A.W. Thibaudeau (6 vols., 1883–93), IV, 155.

[41] H.M.C., *Verulam MSS.*, p.117; Add. 61468, f.177.

[42] H.M.C., *Verulam MSS.*, pp.117–9.

[43] Add. 61436, ff.20–1.

[44] Add. 61476, ff.96–8.

[45] Add. 61463, f.190.

[46] *The Case of the Right Hon. William Lord Viscount Grimston and Joshua Lomax; against William Clayton and William Gore, Esquires* [1722], note to the docket title.

[47] Add. 61468, ff.168–74.

[48] 'Some Unpublished Letters of Sarah, Duchess of Marlborough, Relating to the Building of Blenheim Palace', ed. W.J. Churchill, *Transactions of the Birmingham and Midland Institute: Archaeological Section*, XII (1884–5), 6.

[49] Woodstock Town Hall, Bor. Recs., box 87, acts of the common council, 1 Jan. 1722.

[50] 'Some Unpublished Letters', p.9. A poll for the election is at Add. 61468, ff.200–1.

[51] Woodstock Town Hall, Bor. Recs., box 86, acts of the common council, 20 June, 17 Aug. 1715.

[52] Add. 61468, f.96.

[53] *Letters . . . at Madresfield Court*, p.132; Add. 61468, f.61; *Catalogue of the Collection of . . . Alfred Morrison*, IV, 155.

[54] *Sotheby's Sale Catalogue*, 26–27 Oct. 1959, lot 434, the duchess to [Godolphin], 11 Jan. 1720.

[55] Add. 61468, f.96.

[56] Add. 61477, f.89.

[57] H.M.C., *Verulam MSS.*, p.121; Add. 61476, f.98.

[58] Devon R.O., 1392 M/L 18, to the Duke of Somerset, 19 Mar. 1726.

[59] A.L. Rowse, *The Later Churchills* (Penguin edn., Harmondsworth, 1970), pp. 14–15.

[60] *HP 1715–54*, I, 262.

[61] Add. 61476, f.200.

[62] H.M.C., *Buccleuch MSS. (Montagu House)*, I, 354.

[63] Add. 61468, f.149; 61436, f.56; *HP 1715–54*, I, 304.

[64] Add. 61468, f.183.

[65] Add. 61437, f.78.

[66] Add. 61468, f.184.

[67] *Ibid.*, ff. 66, 72, 78, 82, 90, 149.

[68] Add. 61437, f.65.

[69] Add. 61468, ff.96–7, 143; Woodstock Town Hall, Bor. Recs., box 87, acts of the common council, 18 Jan. 1728.

[70] H.M.C., *Verulam MSS.*, pp.121–2.

[71] Add. 61438, f.5.

[72] Woodstock Town Hall, Bor. Recs., box 87, acts of the common council, 29 Sept. 1731; Add. 61468, f.185.

[73] *Letters of a Grandmother*, ed. Gladys Scott Thomson (1943), p.86.

[74] Add. 61448, f.77; 61447, ff.35–9.

[75] Add. 61477, f.61; 61451, ff. 133v–134.

[76] Add. 61448, f.121.

[77] Add. 61446, f.62.

[78] Add. 61448, ff.144–6.

[79] Add. 61477, ff.52–5.

[80] *Letters of a Grandmother*, p.95.

[81] *Ibid.*, pp.113–14; Add. 61668, f.197.

[82] Add. 61468, f.142; Bedford MSS. (Bedford Estate Office, London), Duchess of Marlborough letters, No.80, to the Duchess of Bedford, 25 Apr. 1734.

[83] *Letters of a Grandmother*, p.113; Add. 61477, f.65.

[84] Add. 61477, f.59.

[85]   P. Langford, *The Excise Crisis* (Oxford, 1975), pp.53–4. Merrill's wife was a daughter of Hugh Chudleigh and Marlborough's cousin, Susanna Strode; Sarah had remained friendly with the family for many years: see Add. 61422, f.194; *Marlborough-Godolphin Corresp.*, I, 57; II, 939; Add. 61448, f.42.
[86]   Add. 61448, f.104.
[87]   Pierpont Morgan Library, New York, Rulers of England, XI, Duchess of Marlborough letters, No.15, to Sir John Hynde Cotton, 13 Sept. 1740.
[88]   Bedford MSS., Duchess of Marlborough letters, Nos.122, 80, to the Duchess of Bedford, 12 Nov., 25 Apr. 1734.
[89]   Add. 61448, f.156.
[90]   Bedford MSS., Duchess of Marlborough letters, No.121, to the Duchess of Bedford, 9 Nov. 1734; Add. 61448, f.156; 61468, ff.193–5; 61477, f.89. For Beeston, see his letters to the duchess (Add. 61468, ff.145–61), and her letter to Lady Hardwicke, 27 Sept. 1741 (Add. 35853, f.19). This episode is misinterpreted in *HP 1715–54*, I, 304–5, owing to a misdating of the letters of Major and Pulteney, Add. 61468, ff.193–4 and 61477, f.89 (1733 instead of 1734).
[91]   Add. 61468, f.198; 61448, f.156.
[92]   *Letters of a Grandmother*, pp.176–7.
[93]   Pierpont Morgan Library, Rulers of England, XI, Duchess of Marlborough letters, No.13, to [Sir John Hynde Cotton?], 31 Jan. 1741.
[94]   Add. 61477, ff.87–9. These letters (rightly from 1734) are misdated 1732 in *HP 1715–54*, II, 253, and taken to refer to Merrill's candidacy for St Albans.
[95]   *Letters of a Grandmother*, pp.114–15. *Cf.* J. Chamberlayne, *Magnae Britanniae Notitia* (1735), pt. 2, p.76.
[96]   Add. 61438, f.121.
[97]   Bedford MSS., Duchess of Marlborough letters, No.81, to the Duchess of Bedford, 27 Apr. 1734.
[98]   Add. 47012B, f.10.
[99]   For her estates, see *A True Copy of the Last Will and Testament of her Grace Sarah, late Duchess Dowager of Marlborough* (1744).
[100] Forrester, *Northamptonshire Elections*, pp. 50, 52.
[101] Bedford MSS., Duchess of Marlborough letters, No.82, to the Duchess of Bedford, 30 Apr. 1734.
[102] Add. 61451, ff.148v–149, 152; *Christie's Sale Catalogue*, 1 July 1970, lot 11, the Duchess to 'Mr Davis, Smith at Windsor', 6 Mar. 1738; Rowse, *Later Churchills*, p.63; *HP 1715–54*, I, 193.
[103] Bedford MSS., Duchess of Marlborough letters, No.81.
[104] Maud M. Wyndham, Baroness Leconfield, *Chronicles of the Eighteenth Century, Founded on the Correspondence of Sir Thomas Lyttelton and his Family* (2 vols., 1924), I, 33–5; Add. 61478, f.28; H.M.C., *Manchester MSS.*, p.110; Add. 61477, f.56.
[105] *A Selection from the Papers of the Earls of Marchmont*, ed. G.H. Rose (3 vols., 1831), II, 233–4; for an example of her distribution of election propaganda, see Add. 61478, f.30.
[106] Woodstock Town Hall, Bor. Recs., box 87, acts of the common council, 4 May 1741.
[107] Pierpont Morgan Library, Rulers of England, XI, Duchess of Marlborough letters, Nos.15, 16, to Sir John Hynde Cotton, 13, 20 Sept. 1740.
[108] Add. 34734, f.3; *HP 1715–54*, I, 262–3.
[109] *Memoirs of Sarah, Duchess of Marlborough*, ed. W. King (1930), p.306.
[110] *Letters of a Grandmother*, p.95.

Parliamentary History, Volume 2 (1983)

CHARLES LUCAS AND THE DUBLIN ELECTION OF
1748–1749

SEAN MURPHY

Alongside such episodes as the struggle between Whigs and Tories during the last four years of Queen Anne's reign, the Wood's Halfpence controversy in the 1720s and the Money Bill dispute of 1753–6, the Dublin election of 1748–9 ranks as one of the occasions when the (perhaps overstated) calm of Irish politics in the first 60 years of the eighteenth century gave way to turbulence. Mainly as a result of the efforts of one of the candidates, Charles Lucas, his natural talent for raising controversy, his campaign for reform of Dublin corporation, his vigorous attacks on the Irish administration and his revival of the earlier arguments of William Molyneux and Swift concerning Irish legislative independence, the 1748–9 election campaign generated great political heat. It was probably the most fiercely contested since the general election of 1713, which in Dublin had taken place against the background of the bitter mayoralty dispute then in progress; and, as well as being one of the most important of eighteenth-century elections, it is also, because of the enormous pamphlet literature to which it gave rise, one of the best documented.

Of Cromwellian stock, Charles Lucas was born in County Clare in 1713. Having served his apprenticeship as an apothecary he opened a shop in Dublin in the mid-1730s and in 1741 was elected as a representative of the barber surgeons' guild on the common council of Dublin corporation.[1] In alliance with James Digges Latouche, a member of a wealthy Huguenot banking family, Lucas soon commenced a campaign to reform the corporation. Lucas's and Latouche's main objection was to the fact that the upper house of the corporation, the lord mayor and aldermen, formed a self-perpetuating clique which dominated municipal affairs and excluded the lower house, the sheriffs and commons, from any real share of power. The lord mayor and aldermen justified their oligarchy by referring back to the

'New Rules' of 1672, a series of restrictions imposed on Irish corporations by the government of Charles II. These rules granted the lord mayor and aldermen a virtual monopoly of power in the election of principal officers of the corporation, as well as enabling them to vet carefully the appointment of guild representatives on the common council.[2] Lucas and Latouche claimed that the New Rules were 'unconstitutional' and agitated for the limiting of the aldermen's privileges and a re-enactment of the provisions of the corporation's ancient charters and by-laws.[3]

The campaign for municipal reform attracted the support of a majority of the corporation's lower house and the issue remained constantly to the fore during the years 1742 and 1743, leading to frequent disputes and disruption of corporation business.[4] All other methods of seeking redress having failed, an application in the names of Lucas and Latouche was made to the court of King's Bench in June 1744 for a writ of *quo warranto* against a named alderman, on the grounds that his election was invalid. After a hearing of two days in November 1744, the courts found in favour of the alderman and against the plaintiffs.[5] Both Lucas and Latouche lost their places on the city council in December of the same year, and this, together with the failure of their lawsuit and the crisis caused by the Jacobite rising of 1745, resulted in an effective lull in the municipal dispute until the by-election of 1748–9 provided an opportunity for reactivating the campaign of reform.

Lucas's attention was also temporarily diverted by an occurrence of rioting in the Smock Alley Theatre in early 1747. Adopting the pseudonym 'A. Freeman, Barber and Citizen', Lucas issued a series of pamphlets in which he endeavoured to prove that the disturbances were the work of a group of 'professed papists' and 'mercenary converts' attempting to foment an insurrection.[6] This absurd charge was accompanied by crude invective against 'papists' in general and the Barber's letters became the main basis for Lucas's reputation hitherto as an ultra-Protestant bigot (a reputation which, it will be shown, requires some revision).

2

Though the control of 'patrons' over parliamentary representation was not as tight in Irish cities as it was in the counties and smaller boroughs, the nominees of the corporations tended to prevail in elections. Hence most of Dublin's M.P.s since the beginning of the eighteenth century had also been aldermen, and the sitting Members in 1748 were Alderman Sir James Somerville (first elected 1729) and Alderman Nathaniel Pearson (first elected 1737). On 16 August 1748 Somerville died,[7] and as the writ for a by-election would not be issued until the next biennial session of Parliament in October 1749, prospective candidates for the vacancy faced a long campaign of over 14 months.

The first candidate to come forward was Latouche, and in a newspaper advertisement he entreated the favour of the 'votes and interests' of the gentlemen, clergy, freeholders and freemen of the city.[8] Just over a week after Somerville's death, the aldermanic candidate, Alderman Sir Samuel

Cooke, declared himself. Cooke was a former lord mayor of the city whose father had incurred the wrath of the then predominantly Whig aldermen by refusing to step down as lord mayor during the mayoralty dispute of 1711–14. Latouche could consider himself in a strong position if he faced Cooke alone, as he aimed to win the support of the moderate Tories, old Whigs and traders of the city. However, the possibility that the vote of the anti-aldermanic party would be split arose with the announcement by Lucas on the same day as Cooke that he also was in the running for the seat. Lucas's advertisement declared that he would endeavour in Parliament to vindicate 'those rights and liberties' of which the electors had been stripped, and that their 'instructions' would be the invariable guide of his actions.[9] Unlike the other candidates, Lucas did not request the favour of 'votes and interests', a practice which he abhorred on the grounds that each voter should be left free until polling day to weigh up the relative merits and demerits of each candidate.

A total of six candidates declared their intentions of running for the vacant seat, but of these only Latouche, Sir Samuel Cooke and Lucas really counted, as the others would drop out before the election. The electorate to which the candidates directed their appeals was small by modern, but not by contemporary, standards, and was probably in the region of 4,000 voters,[10] composed of about 3,000 freemen and the rest freeholders, clergy and holders of certain offices, as compared to a total city population of about 130,000.[11] As Catholics were excluded from the franchise by law, the voters were entirely Protestant, with members of the established Church of Ireland predominating.

In view of the lengthy period before the actual casting of votes, it is not surprising that the election campaign got off to a comparatively quiet start. Since April 1748 the most recurrent item of Dublin news had been faction-fights between the Ormond and Liberty Boys. A truce was agreed in June but soon collapsed, and by September engagements between the two sides were taking place every Sunday. Order was restored in October following stern action by the newly appointed lord mayor, Robert Ross, who issued a proclamation and went with the sheriffs, constables and watchmen to Bridewell Bridge, the usual rendezvous of the rioters, and had several of the ringleaders imprisoned. Troops had also been drawn up in readiness to give assistance, and the Catholic clergy threatened to excommunicate those of their communion who continued to participate in the encounters. Faulkner's *Dublin Journal* calculated that over 300 had lost their lives or limbs in engagements between the Ormond and Liberty Boys in the previous two years.[12] A year later in October 1749 mobs would be active in Dublin again, though this time their activities would be in support of Lucas and Latouche and of an avowedly political nature, and thus even more worrying to the authorities.

Lucas was the busiest of the election candidates at this early stage, and on 18 August 1748 commenced the publication of a massive series of addresses to the free citizens and freeholders of Dublin.[13] These lengthy and wordy pamphlets were designed as much to educate the electors in correct constitutional and political principles as to support their author's candidature. Inevitably, Lucas also devoted some space in his addresses to the less lofty task of besmirching the rival candidates, especially his former ally Latouche.[14]

Lucas's first nine addresses were devoted to an exhaustive analysis of the British constitution which laid great stress on the importance of maintaining a correct balance between the three estates of King, lords and commons.[15] In his tenth address of 13 January 1749 he endeavoured to show that the British constitution was also the birthright of the Irish. He rejected the claim that Ireland was a conquered kingdom subject to the government of Great Britain and paraphrased Molyneux's arguments concerning the antiquity and long-standing independence of the Irish Parliament. Having stated that all past general rebellions in Ireland had been fomented by 'the oppression, instigation, evil influence or connivance of the English', Lucas devoted his eleventh address of 31 January to an exposure of English misgovernment in Ireland. Basing himself on the authority of Sir John Davies, he claimed that despite their submission to English law, the native Irish in medieval times had been treated as badly 'as the Spaniards used the Mexicans, or as inhumanly as the English now treat their slaves in America'.[16] Lucas's revival of the question of Ireland's constitutional status provoked strong criticism from his opponents, and the extreme utterances in his tenth and eleventh addresses in particular were eventually to land him in serious trouble with the authorities.

In his fifteenth address of 16 March Lucas progressed from description to prescription and set out to provide remedies for the political 'distempers' caused by arbitrary lords lieutenant and corrupt officials. In the last analysis the remedy for such ills lay with the people, for the health of every state depended on their being free and virtuous. Hence the voters should freely and fairly elect the best and most thoroughly qualified persons to represent them in Parliament if they wished to heal the wounds in the constitution and restore the political system to a healthy condition.[17]

3

The election campaign entered a more intense phase with the death on 12 May 1749 of Dublin's second M.P., Alderman Pearson. Alderman Charles Burton immediately declared himself a candidate for the second vacant seat, and as he came from a family noted for its opposition to 'High Church' and Toryism, he presented a more serious threat to Lucas and Latouche than the other aldermanic candidate, Sir Samuel Cooke.[18] Because they both now stood a chance of being elected and their rivalry was deflecting attention from the task of keeping the aldermen out, Lucas and Latouche found it expedient temporarily to forget their differences, and a somewhat strained reconciliation took place.[19]

The campaign styles of the candidates of the pro- and anti-aldermanic parties differed markedly. Lucas and Latouche made frequent speeches in the guild halls and the former also deluged the voters with pamphlets.

Before the second vacancy, Alderman Cooke had toured the guild halls and in a short, set speech had based his appeal for votes on his many relations and acquaintances in the Irish House of Commons. Alderman Burton took the lead after the second vacancy, and in his guild speeches he apologised for his lack of skill in oratory, similarly stressed his connexions in Parliament and defended the integrity of the aldermen. Burton also committed the *faux pas* of anticipating the death of the King by pointing out to the voters that if he proved an unsatisfactory M.P. they would soon have an opportunity of electing another, as the then Parliament could not last more than a session or two longer (at this time, before the passage of the Octennial Act, the Irish Parliament was only dissolved at the sovereign's will, or at his decease). Henceforth Cooke and Burton were content to leave the guild halls to Lucas and Latouche and concentrated instead on canvassing citizens in their homes and places of business.[20]

On 3 June Lucas supplemented his already copious election propaganda by commencing the publication of a weekly newspaper, *The Censor, or the Citizen's Journal*, the forerunner of the better known *Freeman's Journal*. Lucas did not publicly acknowledge that he was editor of the *Censor*, but it was an open secret in the city that he was, and later in exile he reprinted leading articles from the paper along with his election addresses and letters. In the first issue he stated that the purpose of the new paper was to monitor abuses and corruption and observed that arbitrary government could exist only where there was no freedom of the press.[21] Coverage of the election campaign in the *Censor* was much fuller and less restrained than in other Dublin newspapers such as Faulkner's *Dublin Journal*, though it was of course biassed in favour of Lucas's party.

Temporarily suspending his plan to move on in his election addresses to an analysis of Dublin's municipal constitution, Lucas directed a series of letters to the commons and citizens in May in which he claimed that the aldermen had concocted a scheme to lease the city tolls and customs to one of their own number. He also alleged that some councillors had not been summoned to an assembly on 9 May in order that the measure might more easily be rushed through.[22]

These accusations were to provoke a strong backlash from both houses of the corporation, but in the meantime Lucas had decided that the cause of corporation reform now required a bold approach to the Crown itself. The Lord Lieutenant, Harrington, not being due from England until September, Lucas waited on the Lords Justices at Dublin Castle on 12 June and presented them with copies of the Latin text and his own translation of one of Dublin's charters (issued by Edward IV in 1462 and styled by Lucas the 'great charter').[23] Lucas requested the Lords Justices to transmit a copy of this presentation to the King, and for this purpose prefaced the work with a dedication to His Majesty. Lucas commenced the dedication with the complaint that the Parliaments of England had for some time treated Ireland as 'a conquered province or a dependent colony'. He went on to describe the decline of Dublin's municipal constitution and recounted the attempts to secure its restoration made by his supporters and himself. He recalled how the failure of the 1744 lawsuit in the King's Bench had moved him to appeal to the Lord Lieutenant, but to no effect. Lucas then commenced a tirade against 'evil ministers' and pointed to the wisdom of the maxim, 'remove the evil counsellor from before the king; so shall his throne be established in righteousness'.[24]

The last was an obvious demand to have Harrington removed, and coupled with the strength of expression elsewhere, it ensured that Lucas's presentation never reached the eyes of the King. The authorities immediately showed their disapproval by arresting Lucas's printer, James Esdall, and binding him by recognizance to appear in court on the first day of the next term.[25] On 4 August the Lords Justices returned to Lucas the 'great charter' and dedication to the King, informing him that they did not think them fit for transmission to His Majesty.[26]

At the midsummer assembly of Dublin corporation on 21 July the sheriffs and commons decided to investigate Lucas's charge that some of their members had not been properly summoned to the assembly held on 9 May. Samuel Morgan, the officer responsible for summoning councillors to meetings, denied that he had ever neglected his duties and none of the councillors present could charge him with any neglect. The sheriffs and commons then passed a motion declaring that Lucas's allegation was 'false, malicious and scandalous' and ordered that the proceedings of the day should be published in the city's newspapers.[27] Lucas published further letters to the commons and citizens in late July and early August, in which he attacked Morgan's veracity and claimed that the proceedings against him had in fact been 'hatched' by the aldermen and carried out by their 'creatures'.[28] The lord mayor and aldermen responded to this attack without delay and on 4 August issued a public notice denying any prior knowledge of the proceedings of the sheriffs and commons on 21 July, accusing Lucas of spreading malicious falsehood and challenging him to name the source of his allegations.[29]

The combined censures of both houses of the corporation constituted a severe blow to Lucas's reputation and popularity, and whether or not they had been engineered by the aldermen and their supporters for the purpose, they also adversely affected his hitherto favourable prospects of winning a seat in Parliament. Undaunted, Lucas turned to the guilds, and from early August a stream of supportive notices from these bodies appeared in the newspapers. Fifteen of the city's 25 guilds expressed their disapprobation of the proceedings of the sheriffs and commons against Lucas, and where appropriate, censured their representatives for not standing by him.[30]

As well as addressing the guilds, it was customary for election candidates to be presented with their freedom, and Lucas was voted free of a total of 21 guilds in the course of the election campaign.[31] It was later to be alleged during the parliamentary inquiry into the Dublin election in November and December 1749 that Lucas's activities in the guild halls had been accompanied by riots and intimidation. Witnesses claimed that Lucas and Latouche had attended the shoemakers', tailors', cutlers' and weavers' halls in August and October accompanied by mobs composed of persons not free of these guilds, had forced through motions of support drawn up by themselves and had been admitted to membership against a background of shouts of 'Free! Free!'[32] On the other hand, it was claimed elsewhere that the masters of several guilds had obstructed the granting of freedom to Lucas and Latouche by quitting their chairs and thus bringing the meetings to a close prematurely.[33]

Lucas resumed his series of addresses to the electors on 9 August and in the seventeenth gave a brief history of Dublin corporation from the time of its institution, listing its constituent parts and principal officers.[34] This account was mostly a reworking of the contents of his earlier tracts on municipal affairs, the *Remonstrance* (1743) and *Divelina Libera* (1744). In his eighteenth address of 15 September Lucas described the 'breaches' made in the constitution of the corporation, such as the New Rules and the encroachments of the aldermen, again basing himself on the work of his earlier pamphlets.[35] Lucas's nineteenth address of 25 September was devoted to a summary of his first 15 addresses on the political constitutions of Britain and Ireland, in which he reiterated his controversial claims concerning Ireland's status as an independent kingdom bound only by laws passed by its own Parliament, and the ill effects of English oppression and misgovernment in Ireland.[36]

In his twentieth and final address of 29 September Lucas outlined a programme for the reform of Dublin corporation. He pointed out that even allowing for the restrictions imposed by the New Rules, it was possible to secure municipal representatives of the right calibre who would limit the powers of the aldermen. This goal could be achieved if the members of the guilds took care to nominate 'men of good sense and strict probity' as their representatives on the common council. However, such measures were at best palliatives, as only Parliament would be able to provide 'a radical cure' for the city's ills. It was therefore the duty of the citizens, Lucas concluded, to elect only virtuous and qualified men as their M.P.s.[37] Lucas thus brought to a close his monumental series of election addresses and letters on the British constitution, the state of Ireland and the municipal government of its metropolis. Exclusive of other pamphlets such as the 'great charter', his addresses and letters of 1748–9 total over 200,000 words, and few election candidates can have expended such energy in striving to achieve their goal.

4

Irish newspapers during the first half of the eighteenth century were extremely wary of dealing with controversial domestic political issues, and the kind of detailed information we now expect to find in newspaper articles must generally be sought in the tracts and pamphlets of the period, the average length of which was eight to 16 pages. The large volume of surviving publications relating to the Dublin election of 1748–9 indicates that it was an affair which aroused considerable public interest. The Haliday collection in the Royal Irish Academy alone contains over 150 election pamphlets, and additions are to be found in the National Library of Ireland, the Bradshaw collection in Cambridge University Library, and in some other repositories.

None of the other election candidates matched Lucas's prolific output, and Aldermen Cooke and Burton do not appear to have engaged at all in pamphleteering, being no doubt content to let their mostly anonymous defenders tackle Lucas in this arena. On 2 October 1749 Latouche issued a second and in his case final address to the citizens, in which he concentrated on the issue of corporation reform. Perhaps conscious of the fact that despite their truce he had continued to be overshadowed by Lucas's more daring propaganda, Latouche went on to praise the spirit which had 'defeated Wood's vile scheme to ruin us'.[38] An unexpected addition to the list of election candidates was Richard Poekrich, the eccentric inventor of a musical instrument constructed of drinking glasses, but a reading of his three election addresses suggests that his candidature was not really serious.[39] The great majority of election pamphlets were in fact written either to attack or defend Lucas, a reflection of the fact that his personality dominated the entire campaign.

Among Lucas's supporters during the early phase of the election campaign was a certain 'Helvidius Priscus' or 'Free Briton' who wrote four pamphlets late in 1748.[40] These papers were lofty in style and written by one with a marked interest in the histories of ancient Greece and Rome. Referring only obliquely to Lucas and the controversies surrounding the election, the author used examples from ancient history to demonstrate how 'the virtues of a single person have rous'd a sinking nation from despondency, to assert her former freedom, or prop'd her fame, when even the spirit of liberty was decay'd'.[41]

Justice Arthur Warren Samuels, completing a work commenced by his deceased son, Arthur P.I. Samuels, claimed in 1923 that the 'Free Briton' pamphlets were in fact written by the young Edmund Burke, while he was a student at Trinity College. In support of this claim, Samuels declared that the pamphlets were 'redolent of Burke' in their 'style and substance and lofty political wisdom'.[42] Samuels also listed certain other pamphlets from the 1748–9 paper war as Burke's,[43] as well as five articles in Lucas's *Censor*, some of which were signed with the letter 'B', like Burke's articles in his own journal, the *Reformer*.[44]

Samuels's claims ran counter to those of the majority of Burke's earlier biographers, who repeated a Trinity College tradition that Burke had in fact written pamphlets satirizing Lucas during the Dublin election. In 1953 G.L. Vincitorio pointed out that Samuels had not produced any hard evidence to show that Burke was the 'Free Briton', or that the various writings he had listed were even the work of the same author. Vincitorio stated that it was inconceivable that Burke could have supported Lucas, who was 'a virulent bigot' and a demagogue who 'pandered to the mob'.[45]

While Vincitorio was undoubtedly too preoccupied with vindicating Burke's conservative credentials, it is equally true that Samuels sacrificed objectivity in endeavouring to remove what he considered to be a blot on Burke's reputation. With one exception, Samuels produced no plausible evidence that Burke was the author of the election publications he listed. The exception is the series of five articles in the *Censor*, and it would appear highly probable that if Burke was the author of the *Reformer* articles signed 'B', then he was also the author of the *Censor* articles so signed. Quantitative stylistic analysis, such as the 'stylo-statistics' of Alvar Ellegard,[46] might provide a conclusive solution to this problem of literary detection.

Given Lucas's reputation as an anti-Catholic bigot, it is surprising to find that his leading opponents in 1749 were Protestant zealots who attempted to link him with 'popery' and Jacobitism. William Henry declared that the 'violence and plunders of the Pretender and his Highland rebels' were not half so dangerous as Lucas's attempts to create disunity between Great Britain and Ireland, and he stigmatized Lucas's doctrines as those of the 'popish' rebels of 1641.[47] By far the most virulent and dangerous of Lucas's opponents was Sir Richard Cox, M.P. for Clonakilty, County Cork, a grandson and namesake of the former Tory lord chancellor and lord chief justice of Queen Anne's day whom Lucas had attacked in an edition of the *Censor* in June 1749.[48] Using the pseudonym 'Anthony Litten' or the 'Cork Surgeon', Cox issued a series of pamphlets in which he lashed at Lucas for 'meddling with the dependency of Ireland upon Britain' and for justifying 1641 and other Irish rebellions. In a paroxysm of fury, Cox described Lucas as an 'incendiary' and 'the offspring of an Irish popish priest', as well as an agent of the Pretender.[49]

Charles O'Conor of Belanagare, the Catholic historian and leading publicist for the claims of the oppressed Irish Catholics in the later eighteenth century, was sufficiently interested in the controversy surrounding the Dublin election to pen a response to Henry and Cox. O'Conor's anonymous pamphlet commenced with some complimentary remarks concerning Lucas and ended with an exhortation to the freemen of Dublin to elect the 'champions of liberty' to 'the grand council of the nation'. The greater part of the pamphlet was devoted to a defence of ancient Ireland from charges of barbarism levelled by Henry.[50]

As none of O'Conor's correspondence for this period has survived, we cannot tell whether his support for Lucas was as wholehearted as this anonymous pamphlet suggests. However, it is likely that O'Conor's attitude was not far removed from that of his relative Michael Reilly, who wrote to him from Dublin on 12 October 1749:[51]

> Indeed the greatest aversion I have to him [Lucas] proceeds from his Barber's letters, for a true patriot would not betray such malice as he has shown in those papers. His behaviour at that time makes a blot in his character that we can never overlook, otherwise I could wish him success.

It would not be unreasonable to conclude that O'Conor and other Irish Catholics, while repelled by Lucas's Protestant prejudices, were attracted by the comments on Irish rebellions and English misgovernment contained in his tenth and eleventh addresses and were moved to support him by an emergent sense of national solidarity. In this connexion, it may not have been entirely coincidental that the few passages in Lucas's writings in 1749 which touched on the subject of Catholics and Catholicism[52] tended to be much mellower in tone than the Barber's letters of 1747.

5

As the storm raged about Lucas's head, the Lord Lieutenant arrived in Dublin on 20 September 1749 in preparation for the biennial session of Parliament commencing in October.[53] On Tuesday, 3 October, Lucas waited on Harrington at the Castle and presented him with copies of the 'great charter' and the prefixed dedication to the King, together with a new address to the Lord Lieutenant and copies of his election publications. In his address Lucas endeavoured to acquit himself of the charge of being 'a riotous, tumultuous incendiary' and recapitulated his attempts to achieve a reform of Dublin corporation. He then explained that the refusal of the Lords Justices to transmit the charter and dedication to the King made it necessary for him to appeal personally to Harrington to forward them. Lucas's impressions of this audience were that he had been favourably received and that he was free to attend again, but he was rudely disabused of these notions when he arrived at a levee at the Castle on Friday, 6 October, and was almost immediately ordered to leave.[54]

Harrington opened the session of Parliament on Tuesday, 10 October, and in the course of his speech to the Lords and Commons observed that the encouragement lately given to the Irish linen manufacture by the British legislature must incline them to cultivate 'that reciprocal confidence and harmony which will at all times be found essentially necessary to the interest of Ireland'. He continued:[55]

> Every audacious attempt to create a jealousy between the two kingdoms and to disunite the affections of his majesty's common subjects, so closely connected by the same civil and religious interests, must excite the highest indignation in all true lovers of their country.

This was a clear reference to Lucas, and on the day following, Wednesday the eleventh, a complaint was made in the House of Commons by Sir Richard Cox concerning Lucas's dedication to the King, several of his addresses and letters to the citizens of Dublin, and several editions of the *Censor*, on the grounds that they highly and unjustly reflected on the King, Lord Lieutenant and Parliament, justified the 'bloody and barbarous rebellions' in the kingdom, and tended to create jealousy between Great Britain and Ireland and disunite the affections of His Majesty's common subjects. It was accordingly decided that a committee of the whole House should meet the following morning to consider this complaint, and Lucas was ordered to attend, together with his printers James Kelburn and James Esdall.[56]

On Thursday the twelfth Lucas appeared before the committee, and, having been presented with a book composed of his writings, was asked to state whether he was the author. Rather than answer directly and thus incriminate himself, Lucas asked to what end he was being examined and stated that he hoped to have an opportunity of vindicating himself. Here he was interrupted by the chairman of the committee, Marcus Anthony Morgan, Member for the borough of Athy, County Kildare, who informed him that he must confine himself to the established order of Parliament and that he would not be indulged. Lucas thereupon flung the book in his hand on to the table and declared with some passion that if he was not to have indulgence, he knew not what business he had before the committee. Outraged by this behaviour, which contrasted strongly with the usually contrite demeanour of those who had incurred the displeasure of the House, Morgan angrily ordered Lucas to withdraw. Esdall did not appear when called to give evidence, as he had absconded, but Kelburn appeared when called, and admitted that he had arranged the printing of eleven addresses for Lucas. Lucas was called in again and asked if he was the author of the dedication and addresses. Once more he declined to answer, this time on the grounds that several incorrect and spurious copies of his works had been published. The committee then agreed to allow him several days in which to examine the writings of which complaint had been made, and adjourned until the following Monday (16 October).[57]

Harrington had not named Lucas in his speech to Parliament, but in his correspondence with the English ministry he was more specific. He explained to the Duke of Bedford (Secretary for the southern department and his official correspondent) that 'the seditious and dangerous behaviour' of Lucas had caused 'his majesty's principal servants' in Ireland to desire him to touch on the subject in his speech from the throne. Harrington then gave a summary of Lucas's activities, commencing with his campaign for the reform of Dublin corporation and culminating in his unwelcome appearance at the Castle levee, when, as Harrington had been informed, Lucas had intended to demand publicly of him whether or not he had transmitted his dedication to the King. Regretting that he had been obliged to enter into such long and tiresome detail upon an affair which considering the 'meanness and insignificancy of the principal actor in it', was not of so great importance, Harrington added:[58]

> But the truth is that the turbulent and factious spirit of this incendiary, and in particular his bold opposition to the government in the city, has gained him so many converts that it is become absolutely necessary to put an immediate stop to his proceedings, and that in a parliamentary way, by declaring the sense of the nation thereupon, and their abhorrence of his rebellious doctrines.

On Monday 16 October Lucas was accompanied to the Parliament house by a large group of supporters and sympathizers, and the size of the procession may be gauged by the fact that there were an estimated 40 coaches in attendance. In front of the committee, Lucas thanked the House for the indulgence of the extra time granted him, but still declined to say whether or not he was the author of the writings of which complaint had been made. The flight of Esdall and Lucas's refusal to answer incriminating questions had placed the committee in some difficulty in obtaining positive proof of the authorship of Lucas's publications (this despite the fact that with the exception of the *Censor*, they were all signed with his name).

Accordingly, the Commons asked the Lord Lieutenant to lay before them the dedication to the King and several addresses to the citizens of Dublin presented to him by Lucas, a request he complied with. These were then produced to Lucas, who confessed that he had given books of like titles and bindings to the Lord Lieutenant, adding that he did not imagine the Lord Lieutenant would give evidence against him. Lucas was again turned out, and as it was obvious that he would continue to refuse to answer the questions put to him concerning his authorship of the offending works, he was discharged from further attendance.[59]

After some further deliberations the committee drew up several resolutions and these were reported to the House of Commons on its reassembly. It was the opinion of the committee that Lucas was the author of the dedication to the King and a second, fourth, eighth, tenth, eleventh and fifteenth address to the free citizens and freeholders of Dublin; that these papers contained several paragraphs falsely and scandalously reflecting on the Lord Lieutenant; that they tended to promote sedition and insurrection, openly justify past rebellions in the kingdom and create jealousies between His Majesty's subjects; that Lucas had in some of the papers scandalously and maliciously misrepresented the proceedings of the House of Commons and highly reflected on the honour and dignity thereof. The House agreed to these resolutions *nem. con.* and went on to resolve, again without opposition, that Lucas was an enemy to his country, that an address should be presented to the Lord Lieutenant requesting him to direct the Attorney-General to prosecute him for publishing scandalous and seditious papers, and that he should be committed to Newgate for this infringement and violation of the privileges of the House.[60]

After being dismissed by the Commons committee, Lucas, still accompanied by a large crowd, went to a meeting of the merchants' guild then in progress at the Tholsel. When news of the resolutions of the Commons was received the crowd at the Tholsel became angry and clamorous, whereupon Lucas addressed them, asking them to disperse and declaring that he was determined to adhere to legal methods to secure redress.[61] Lucas (or an anonymous supporter) later recalled that he was resigned to imprisonment at this stage and sent some of his friends to Newgate to arrange decent accommodation. However, he was allegedly informed on the following day that he was to be refused a separate apartment in the gaol and would be confined among common criminals. Fearing that his health would not stand up to these conditions and that his enraged supporters would attempt an insurrection which would be suppressed with bloodshed (death threats were in fact made against Sir Richard Cox and others), Lucas yielded to the pleas of his friends and fled by boat to the Isle of Man, leaving his family behind.[62]

Harrington's letter to Bedford of 12 October makes it clear that the parliamentary managers in Ireland, 'undertakers' ('his majesty's principal servants'), had been the chief instigators of the parliamentary proceedings against Lucas. Furthermore, the general similarity of the language of the resolutions of the House of Commons concerning Lucas to that of the 'Cork Surgeon's' pamphlets shows that the influence of Sir Richard Cox was predominant. The political turbulence of 1749 therefore took the form primarily of a dispute between the 'undertakers' and an extra-parliamentary opposition led by Lucas. Lucas's attacks on the Dublin aldermen and his campaign for reform of the corporation, his unrestrained comments on the sensitive subject of the relationship between Ireland and Great Britain, his reflections on the judiciary and Parliament, his unwise aspersions on Cox's forbear and demands on the Lords Justices and Lord Lieutenant, all combined to raise him many enemies of power and influence. The support of the middle- and lower middle-class merchants and tradesmen of the guilds was not sufficient to counteract these in an undemocratic age, and the only wonder is that Lucas survived relatively unscathed for as long as he did.

6

On the evening of 17 October about 150 supporters of Lucas and Latouche met at the Rose Tavern in Dame Street to select a new anti-aldermanic parliamentary candidate to replace Lucas. The latter had by this time withdrawn his candidature and was preparing to flee the country, but he was consulted about the meeting and asked to nominate a suitable replacement. The meeting, chaired by George Thwaites, Latouche's brother-in-law, considered several names before finally deciding on Thomas Read, who had been recommended by Lucas. Read was master of the merchants' guild and one of the leaders of a group which had temporarily wrested control of that guild from the aldermen. Latouche, hitherto overshadowed by Lucas, now assumed the leadership of the anti-aldermanic party.[63]

A week before polling, and following the withdrawal of all other candidates, the election had become a straight contest between 'the aldermen', Cooke and Burton, and 'the merchants', Latouche and Read. The parliamentary proceedings against Lucas and his flight abroad had dampened the spirits of his supporters and effectively excluded anything as radical as national grievances from the list of election issues. In a final notice to the voters on the eve of the poll, Cooke and Burton asked for the 'votes and interest' of the gentlemen, clergy, freemen and freeholders, proclaimed themselves 'enemies to faction' and 'zealous supporters of our present happy establishment under the illustrious house of Hanover', and requested the attendance at the place of polling of 'all real friends to the liberty and welfare' of the corporation. Latouche and Read also based their final appeal for 'votes and interest' on their support for the constitution and the house of Hanover, mentioned their promotion of trade and manufacture and zeal in the defence of the rights and privileges of the freemen of the corporation, and requested the attendance at the poll of 'all true friends to this corporation and their country'.[64]

The Catholic clergy continued their policy of supporting law and order by issuing directions from the pulpits on Sunday, 22 October, which strictly forbade persons of their communion 'to join in any mob, tumult or meeting . . . or even to appear about the place of election, as they have no manner of concern whatsoever therein'.[65] This injunction would appear to indicate that though they were deprived by law of the franchise, Dublin Catholics were taking as keen an interest in the election as was Charles O'Conor of Belanagare. As already noted, the Catholic clergy had threatened a year earlier to excommunicate those Catholics who participated in the Ormond and Liberty Boys' feuds, and it is likely that Dublin election gatherings also contained a fair sprinkling of Catholic tradesmen, journeymen and apprentices.

Polling to fill the two vacant parliamentary seats commenced on Tuesday, 24 October, under the supervision of the sheriffs and lasted for 19 days. The court in the Tholsel was used for the taking of votes, and according to custom the freeholders and merchant freemen voted separately while the other freemen voted in order of precedence of their guilds. The powerful and influential cast their votes for the aldermanic candidates with a suitable flourish of publicity. The Speaker of the House of Commons, Henry Boyle, Lord Chief Baron Bowes and Lord Chief Justices Marlay and Singleton all declared for the aldermen. Other pillars of the establishment who voted for the aldermen included Nathaniel Clements, Warden Flood and Luke Gardiner. Following the lead of the chapter of Christ Church, a majority of Church of Ireland clergymen also voted for the aldermen. Yet at least two aldermen, both Protestant Dissenters, broke ranks to vote for the merchants: James Dunn gave one vote to Cooke and the other to Latouche, while Nathaniel Kane voted for both Latouche and Read.[66]

The recording of votes was a slow process, as there was no secret ballot and each side challenged the validity of votes cast for their opponents on the slightest excuse. Among the objections made were that some voters had 'popish wives', which disqualified them by law from voting. As the number of freeholders was seen to be greater than in previous elections and as they were voting mainly for the aldermen, the merchants began to insist that they should take an oath as to the location of their freeholds. As soon as the guild of freemen began to vote, agents of the aldermen objected to several on the grounds that their votes had been procured by 'undue influence'. Ominously, those who asked for this objection to be explained were told that it would be considered in another place. Despite these differences, the casting of votes proceeded without any disorder or disturbance.

Though the aldermen were in the lead during the early stages of the poll, the merchants slowly began to gain ground, a reflection of their support in the 'inferior' guilds. When the poll closed on Saturday, 11 November, the results were as follows:

Sir Samuel Cooke	1,543
James Digges Latouche	1,499
Charles Burton	1,411
Thomas Read	1,283

Scrutinies being demanded, the election court adjourned until 16 November, when the sheriffs dismissed the aldermen's objections of undue influence and Latouche's counter-objections, declaring Cooke and Latouche to be duly elected.[67]

A total of 2,906 freemen and freeholders polled at the election, and as Latouche defeated Burton by only 88 votes and Cooke was a mere 44 votes ahead of Latouche, the voting was extremely close. Though the aldermen won only one of the two seats, they received an overall majority of all votes cast, their strongest support coming from the merchants' guild and the freeholders. The merchants' party won a majority of the votes of the guild freemen only, and the weavers were their strongest supporters. The polarization of voters is shown by the fact that the great majority supported candidates of one side only, a mere 14.8% splitting their votes. Finally, a large majority of Dissenter and Quaker guild freemen voters supported the merchants, indicating the existence of a further religious dimension to the political divisions in Dublin.[68]

Though the sheriffs had declared Latouche duly elected, the aldermen were by no means content to let the matter rest there. On 21 November Burton submitted a petition to the House of Commons alleging that Latouche, in conjunction with Lucas, had prevented him from being fairly elected by using 'undue and corrupt means' and publishing seditious writings. This petition was referred to the committee of privileges and elections which commenced its deliberations on 28 November and did not conclude until 7 December. Counsel for Burton produced witnesses whose evidence portrayed Lucas and Latouche as joined in the same interest, disrupting the proceedings of guilds with the assistance of mobs of non-freemen and generally using discreditable means to dissuade voters from supporting the aldermanic candidates. Counsel for Latouche endeavoured to show that far from being in conjunction with Lucas, Latouche had publicly opposed his principles, and witnesses were called who supported this claim and denied that disorder had been fomented in the guild halls.

A long debate then followed, with Latouche's few friends and sympathizers in the committee arguing against Burton's petition, and Sir Richard Cox and others arguing that Latouche should be excluded from the House. The committee finally resolved that Latouche was not duly elected and that his seat should go to Burton, a decision ratified by the House on 18 December by 112 votes to 60.[69]

Contested or controverted elections were as common in the eighteenth-century Irish Parliament as they were at Westminster, and there too the outcome usually depended less on the relative merits of each side's case than on the strength of the influence they could command in the House of Commons. The earlier proceedings against Lucas and the manifestly unjust ejection of Latouche from his hard-won place show the lengths to which the Dublin aldermen and the 'undertakers' were prepared to go to exclude from Parliament anyone whose principles savoured in the least of radicalism.

7

While his flight abroad had placed him safely beyond the reach of his opponents, what can only be described as the persecution of Lucas continued unabated. On 6 November Lord Chief Justice Marlay delivered a charge to the grand juries of the city and county of Dublin in which he accused Lucas of 'preaching up anarchy' and exhorted the jurors to 'free us from these insolent libellers, these abandoned printers and publishers, these Jack Straws, Wat Tylers and Jack Cades of the age'.[70] Accordingly, in late November/early December the grand juries presented Lucas for being the author of the papers censured by the House of Commons, as well as 'a common libeller' and 'an enemy to his country'.[71]

In compliance with the request of the House of Commons, the Lord Lieutenant issued a proclamation on 11 December for the apprehension of Lucas so that he could be proceeded against according to law,[72] while on 15 December the Attorney-General, St George Caulfield, filed an information against Lucas in the King's Bench,[73] and at its Christmas assembly on 19 January 1750 Dublin corporation ordered that Lucas be deprived of his freedom of the city.[74] What seem to be the last recorded legal proceedings against Lucas took place the following May, when yet another grand jury of the city of Dublin presented as seditious libels publications by Lucas and some of his supporters and prayed that they might be 'burned by the hands of the common hangman'.[75]

On 18 April Harrington embarked for England from the North Wall, and the *Censor* sarcastically remarked that the crowd in attendance had 'expressed their just sense of his excellency's wise administration and their own loss, by repeated groans'.[76] Shortly before his departure, Harrington had rewarded Sir Richard Cox for his distinguished support of the government in Parliament by having him appointed collector of Cork, this despite opposition from some of the revenue commissioners, which Harrington dismissed as politically motivated.[77]

The affair thus ended in complete victory for the political establishment and defeat for Lucas, Latouche and their supporters. Yet the issue of the reform of Dublin corporation was now raised to the level of a standing grievance, and from his beginnings as a municipal politician, Lucas had entered the field of national politics and revived the debate concerning Irish national rights. His emphasis in 1748–9 on an Ireland oppressed by a foreign power was so marked, especially in his tenth and eleventh addresses, that the term 'nationalism' is a perfectly valid description of his ideology. This ideology was also, of course, distinguished by an oft-repeated respect for the authority of the British Crown, which made it a forerunner of the constitutional nationalism of Grattan and O'Connell rather than the republican separatism of the United Irishmen. And for all Lucas's reputation as a bigot, there is evidence that his agitation in 1749 gained the sympathy and support of at least some Irish Catholics. Finally, the most immediate significance of the events of 1748–9 was that they proved in many ways to be a rehearsal for the 'Money Bill' dispute of 1753–6, and the subsequent growth of a coherent patriot party which could successfully challenge both the administration and the 'undertakers'.[78]

Notes

1   *A Handbook to Lisdoonvarna and Its Vicinity* (Dublin, 1876), p. 66; *D.N.B.*; *Calendar of Ancient Records of Dublin* . . ., eds. Sir John and Lady Gilbert (19 vols., Dublin, 1889–1944) [hereafter cited as *Anc. Recs. Dublin*], IX, App. 2, pp. 449–50.
2   *Anc. Recs. Dublin*, I, 56–67; *The Statutes at Large, Passed in the Parliaments Held in Ireland* . . . (20 vols., Dublin, 1786–1801), III, 205–12.
3   Lucas, *A Remonstrance against Certain Infringements on the Rights and Liberties of the Commons and Citizens of Dublin* (Dublin, 1743); *idem, Divelina Libera: An Apology for the Civil Rights and Liberties of the Commons and Citizens of Dublin* (Dublin, 1744); Latouche, *Papers Concerning the Late Disputes between the Commons and Aldermen of Dublin* (Dublin, 1746).
4   P.R.O. of Ireland, Dublin corporation records, journal of the sheriffs and commons, 1; *Anc. Recs. Dublin*, IX, App. 13, pp. 498–625.
5   *Anc. Recs. Dublin*, IX, 200; A. Briton [?Latouche], *The History of the Dublin Election in the Year 1749* (1753) [hereafter cited as *Dublin Election 1749*], p. 16; *Faulkner's Dublin Journal* [hereafter cited as *F.D.J.*], 10 Nov. 1744; Lucas, *The Complaints of Dublin* (Dublin, 1747), pp. 12–16; Appendices 1–5, pp. 29–48.
6   A. F[reeman], Barber and Citizen [Lucas]. *A [First] - Third letter to the Free-Citizens of Dublin* (Dublin, 1747).
7   *F.D.J.*, 20 Aug. 1748.
8   *Ibid.*
9   *Ibid.*, 27 Aug. 1748; *Dublin Election 1749*, pp. 18–21.
10 Calculated on the basis that the 2,906 voters who polled in 1749 represented about three quarters of the electorate.
11 M. Craig, *Dublin 1660–1860* (Dublin, 1969), pp. 178, 341.
12 *F.D.J.*, 14 Apr., 6 Sept. 1748 *et seq.*, 4 Oct. 1748.
13 Lucas, *A [First]-Twentieth Address to the Free Citizens and Freeholders of the City of Dublin* (Dublin, 1748–9). Lucas republished these addresses from exile in *The Political Constitutions of Great Britain and Ireland Asserted and Vindicated* (1751), and it is to this edition that reference is hereafter made [cited as *Constitutions G.B. and Ire.*].
14 *Constitutions G.B. and Ire.*, pp. 14–16, 192–216.
15 *Ibid.*, pp. 1–109.
16 *Ibid.*, pp. 109–53.
17 *Ibid.*, pp. 216–41.
18 *F.D.J.*, 13, 16 May 1749; *Dublin Election 1749*, pp. 26–8.
19 *Dublin Election 1749*, p. 29; *Constitutions G.B. and Ire.*, p. 192.
20 *Dublin Election 1749*, pp. 30–4, 120–1; *Constitutions G.B. and Ire.*, pp. 438–9; *Censor*, 10 June 1749.
21 *Constitutions G.B. and Ire.*, pp. 451–6.
22 *Ibid.*, pp. 383–93.
23 *The Great Charter of the Liberties of the City of Dublin*, ed. Lucas (Dublin, 1749); *F.D.J.*, 13 June 1749.
24 *Great Charter*, ed. Lucas, Dedication, pp. i–xliv.
25 *Censor*, 17 June 1749; [? Sir Richard Cox], *An Examination of the Facts* . . . *Contained in a Pamphlet Intitled A Critical Review of the Liberties of British Subjects* (1750), p. 44.
26 *Constitutions G.B. and Ire.*, p. 445.
27 P.R.O. Ire., Dublin corp. recs., jnl. of sheriffs and commons, 1, pp. 236–7; *F.D.J.*, 22 July 1749.
28 *Constitutions G.B. and Ire.*, pp. 402–23.
29 *Anc. Recs. Dublin*, IX, App. 5, pp. 463–4; *F.D.J.*, 5 Aug. 1749.

30 *F.D.J.*, 8 Aug.–2 Sept., 12 Sept., 7–19 Oct. 1749; *Constitutions G.B. and Ire.*, pp. 579–96; *Dublin Election 1749*, pp. 34–7.

31 A Gentleman of the Middle Temple [?Lucas], *A Critical Review of the Liberties of British Subjects* (2nd edn., 1750) [hereafter cited as *Critical Rev.*], p. 34.

32 *Journals of the House of Commons of the Kingdom of Ireland* (3rd edn., 19 vols., Dublin, 1796–1800), V, 33–7, 46.

33 *Censor*, 7 Oct. 1749.

34 *Constitutions G.B. and Ire.*, pp. 265–87.

35 *Ibid.*, pp. 292–331.

36 *Ibid.*, pp. 331–54.

37 *Ibid.*, pp. 355–79.

38 Latouche, *A Second Address to the Citizens of Dublin* (Dublin, 1749).

39 Poekrich, *A [First] - Third Address to the Gentlemen, Clergy, Freeholders and Freemen of the City of Dublin* (Dublin, 1749); *D.N.B.*

40 Helvidius Priscus, *A Free Briton's Advice to the Free Citizens of Dublin*, Nos. [1]–4 (Dublin, 1748).

41 *Ibid.*, [No. 1], p. 4.

42 A.P.I. and A.W. Samuels, *The Early Life, Correspondence and Writings of the Right Honourable Edmund Burke* (Cambridge, 1923), pp. 190–1; App. 3, pp. 331–55.

43 *Ibid.*, pp. 191–202; App. 3, pp. 356–89.

44 *Ibid.*, App. 3, pp. 389–95. See *Constitutions G.B. and Ire.*, pp. 487–91, 501–5, 517–21, 563–7, 568–72.

45 'Edmund Burke and Charles Lucas', *Publications of the Modern Language Association of America*, LXVIII (1953), 1047–55.

46 *Who Was Junius?* (Stockholm, Gothenburg and Uppsala, 1962), pp. 97–119.

47 W. Britanno-Hibernus [Henry], *An Appeal to the People of Ireland, Occasioned by the Insinuations and Misrepresentations of the Author of . . . the Censor* (2nd edn., Dublin, 1749), pp. 6–8.

48 *Constitutions G.B. and Ire.*, p. 466.

49 Anthony Litten [Cox], *The Cork Surgeon's Antidote against the Dublin Apothecary's Poison* (Dublin, 1749), No. 2, p. 5; No. 6, pp. 4, 5, 8–11, 18.

50 [O'Conor], *A Counter-Appeal to the People of Ireland* (Dublin, 1749).

51 Royal Irish Academy, MS. B.I.1, 'Civicus' [Michael Reilly] to O'Conor, 12 Oct. 1749. It should be noted that the Rev. Charles O'Conor, D.D., embellished this passage and falsely attributed it to Charles O'Conor of Belanagare in order to minimize his grandfather's support for Lucas: *Memoirs of the Life and Writings of the Late Charles O'Conor of Belanagare* (Dublin, 1796), p. 212. This deception has been at least partly responsible for the tendency of later historians to portray Lucas's attitude to his Catholic fellow countrymen as one of unrelieved contempt and hostility: see, for example, W.E.H. Lecky, *A History of Ireland in the Eighteenth Century* (2nd edn., 5 vols., repr. 1913), II, 205–6.

52 See *Constitutions G.B. and Ire.*, pp. 442–4, 497, 551–7.

53 *F.D.J.*, 23 Sept. 1749.

54 Lucas, *An Address to His Excellency William Earl of Harrington . . . As It Was Presented to Him on Tuesday the Third Instant* (Dublin, 1749), Preface, pp. 12–13; Address, pp. iii–vi; *Censor*, 7 Oct. 1749.

55 *C.J. Ire.*, V, 9. The House of Commons also ordered on 10 Oct. that writs be issued for elections to fill the vacancies in Dublin and 14 other constituencies (*ibid.*, 10–11).

56 *Ibid.*, 12; *Critical Rev.*, p. 50.

57 *C.J. Ire.*, V, 12–13; *Critical Rev.*, pp. 52–6; [? Sir Richard Cox], *An Examination of the Facts . . . Contained in a Pamphlet Intitled A Critical Review . . .* (1750), pp. 24–5.

58 P.R.O. of Northern Ireland, typescript calendar of State Papers (Ireland) 1745–55, Harrington to Bedford, 12 Oct. 1749.

59 *C.J. Ire.*, V, 14, 44; *Critical Rev.*, pp. 59–66; [?Cox], *An Examination of the Facts*, pp. 30–1; *Dublin Election 1749*, pp. 45–6.

60 *C.J. Ire.*, V, 14.

61 *Dublin Election 1749*, p. 49; *Critical Rev.*, pp. 71–3.

62 *Critical Rev.*, pp. 75–8; *Anc. Recs. Dublin*, IX, 316–17.

63 *C.J. Ire.*, V, 37, 45; *Dublin Election 1749*, pp. 49–50; *Critical Rev.*, pp. 76–7.
64 *F.D.J.*, 21 Oct. 1749.
65 *Ibid.*, 24 Oct. 1749.
66 *Dublin Election 1749*, pp. 53–8; *An Alphabetical List of the Freemen and Freeholders of the City of Dublin who Polled at the Election for Members of Parliament . . . 1749* (Dublin, 1750), pp. 7, 10, 18, 74, 76, 78, 79.
67 *F.D.J.*, 28 Oct.–18 Nov. 1749; *Dublin Election 1749*, pp. 58–63; *An Alphabetical List*, p. 89.
68 Details of voting patterns abstracted from *Dublin Election 1749*, p. 63; *An Alphabetical List*, pp. 3–89 and MS. annotations on a copy of the same, showing the religious denomination of voters, in Royal Irish Academy, Haliday Pamphlets, CCXIV, 1749.
69 *C.J. Ire.*, V, 31–56; *Dublin Election 1749*, pp. 80–150.
70 *The Charge of the Right Honourable Thomas Marlay Esq., Lord Chief Justice of His Majesty's Court of King's Bench . . . to the Grand Juries of the County of the City of Dublin, and County of Dublin* (Dublin, 1749), pp. 9, 14.
71 *F.D.J.*, 2, 12 Dec. 1749; *Constitutions G.B. and Ire.*, pp. 158–9.
72 *F.D.J.*, 16 Dec. 1749.
73 Pearse St. Library, Dublin, Gilbert Collection, MS. 32, ff. 219–33; [?Lucas], *Remarks on the Examiner and Examination of the Critical Review . . .* (1750), pp. 73–8.
74 *Anc. Recs. Dublin*, IX, 323–5.
75 Pearse St. Lib., Gilbert Coll., MS. 31, ff. 85–7; *F.D.J.*, 15 May 1750; *Constitutions G.B. and Ire.*, pp. 159–60.
76 *Censor*, 21 Apr. 1750.
77 P.R.O.N.I., *Eighteenth Century Irish Official Papers in Great Britain. Private Collections: Volume I* (Belfast, 1973), pp. 72–3; *F.D.J.*, 24 Mar. 1750.
78 Lucas's stand on municipal reform was vindicated to a great extent by the passing in 1760 of the act 33 Geo. II, cap. 16, which broke the aldermen's monopoly of power over Dublin corporation. As a result of the more relaxed political circumstances following the accession of George III, Lucas was able to return unmolested to Ireland in 1761, and was elected M.P. for Dublin. Thenceforth until his death in November 1771 he remained a thorn in the side of government, being dubbed 'the Wilkes of Ireland' by Lord Lieutenant Townshend in 1768.

Parliamentary History, Volume 2 (1983)

THE PARLIAMENTARY REFORM MOVEMENT IN CORNWALL, 1805–1826

EDWIN JAGGARD

Western Australian College of Advanced Education

While much is known about several strands of the early nineteenth-century parliamentary reform movement in England, there continues to be a comparatively narrow concentration of historical effort. For example, the dynamics of politics in 'Radical Westminster' are still being unravelled, as are the activities of such figures as Sir Francis Burdett and Major John Cartwright.[1] The fluctuating attitudes of the parliamentary Whigs towards reform have also been analysed and of course there has long been a focus upon the importance of the radical movement which swept through London, the provincial cities and manufacturing districts after 1815.[2] Although relatively little is yet understood about provincial ultra-Tory disenchantment with Wellington's government at least it has been delineated as another thread in the reform tapestry.[3] The same cannot be said for the long-term role of those rural gentry who, meeting in London as the Friends of Reform in 1811, later became the nucleus of Cartwright's short-lived Hampden Club. Their impact in their various counties is unknown, yet judging by the political activities of the 14 Cornishmen who attended the Freemasons' Tavern meeting, and developments in their native county after 1805, it should not be neglected.

For almost a century Cornwall has served as the exemplar of all that was wrong with the unreformed system. Forty-two M.P.s were returned by mostly tiny boroughs with restrictive franchises. Grampound, Tregony, Mitchell and Penryn were among the most infamous, while local patrons such as the Boscawens, Eliots, Edgcumbes, Bullers and Sir Christopher Hawkins controlled a majority of seats. Election petitions were frequent, and flagrant law-breaking notorious. Historians have told us that electoral politics in Cornwall in the reign of George III were a bad joke, a parody of the representational system. However, with the notable exception of W.B.

Elvins's comprehensive study of the county reform movement, their generalizations have ignored important political undercurrents.[4] There has been a tendency to overlook the variety of motivational forces operating during changes in borough patronage and, more importantly, in a gentry-led reform movement, as well as to tar county politics with the same brush as the 21 boroughs. True, between 1790 and 1831 all county elections were uncontested; and, with the exception of an 18-month period from January 1825 to July 1826 the seats were shared between Whigs and Tories. Outwardly county politics was a succession of aristocratic and gentry manipulations, of compromises and representation by imposition. The reality was very different. These political methods became increasingly unpopular with many Cornishmen, because of the remarkable activism of a gentry group who stimulated a greatly heightened level of political aware-ness and participation among the rural middle classes. The eventual product was the total frustration of the county's political wirepullers — most of whom were Tories.

Who were the Cornish reformers? From where did they gain their inspiration, and in an era when parliamentary reform was bandied about by groups often sharply divergent in political outlook, with whom did they align themselves? What tactics did they employ? These are some of the questions which can lead to an assessment of the reformers' efforts, and shed fresh light on the reform movement outside the large provincial cities before 1832.

2

By the close of the eighteenth century, when Britain was totally involved in the Napoleonic Wars and simultaneously undergoing an epochal econo-mic transformation, Cornwall's economy was already highly diversified, its society unusually mobile.[5] Besides the profitable agricultural mix of wheat, oats and barley, particularly east of Truro where the peninsula thickens, there were the internationally renowned copper and tin mines, pilchard fisheries, shipbuilding and shipping, general merchandising, textile and quarrying industries. There were myriad opportunities for large and small investments, especially in mining which like all gambling could produce enormous profits — and losses. Landowners, miners, merchants and lawyers, the latter often amassing great wealth because of a notably litigious society, placed some of their fortune in status-giving landed estates. But few wealthy families relied solely upon rents for income. The result was a volatile society with continual jostling for pre-eminence among families of old and new wealth.[6] These struggles repeatedly overflowed into county and borough politics.

In such circumstances, with constant changes among the ranks of the political *élite* as families vied for status and power, county politics were rarely free from conflict. In fact there was a tradition of political dissidence, of challenge and response after 1770. Evidence of this is not hard to find. Before 1770 Cornwall's two county seats were monpolized by four families

— the Molesworths, St Aubyns, Bullers and Carews. They overcame a well planned challenge from the Boscawens in the 1750s and '60s, but were far less successful thereafter when Sir William Lemon (whose family had risen from blacksmithing to a baronetcy in two generations), Edward Eliot and Francis Gregor sought the prestigious positions.

Lemon, a county M.P. from 1774 until his death in 1824, repeatedly voted for and supported parliamentary reform. Gregor and many of his influential supporters in 1789–90 had been openly sympathetic to Wyvill's Association movement, calling a county meeting on reform in 1782. But after his victory in 1790 Gregor was absorbed into that coterie of families which still attempted to dominate county politics, and there was a temporary hiatus in the phases of political challenge and response.[7] The lull ended in 1805 with the first public appearance of two men who were to lead the Cornish reformers until 1832.

Neither John Colman Rashleigh (1772–1845) nor the Reverend Robert Walker (1754–1834), vicar of St Winnow, had played a conspicuous role in county political life before 1805, the year in which a scandal over peculation in the Admiralty sparked a public outcry. In Cornwall as elsewhere, parliamentary discussion of the degree to which Lord Melville, Treasurer of the Navy, was aware of the fraud prompted a group of magistrates — all lesser gentry — to demand that the sheriff summon a county meeting. Most of the requisitioners merely wished to express indignation at the recent exposures, thereby making it a typically 'Country' versus 'Court' assembly, but among the magistrates were two who had been directly involved in the short-lived Cornish reform movement of the 1780s, Robert Gwatkin and the Reverend Jeremiah Trist. The latter was now a good Tory; but Gwatkin (1757–1843) was a lifelong reformer, and it may have been he who drew in Rashleigh and Walker, encouraging their help in the drafting of the petition as well as a motion demanding Melville's impeachment.[8]

Rashleigh was related to one of Cornwall's best known landed families, being a cousin of William Rashleigh of Menabilly, the highly independent M.P. for Fowey from 1812–18. Much of his early life was spent outside Cornwall. After attending Trinity College, Cambridge, Rashleigh led a rather feckless life until he was stirred by the political questions being raised by the French Revolution. He wrote:[9]

> I, though never at any time a Republican enlisted myself into the ranks of the popular party which though never, that I know, meditating the abolition of monarchical government or establishing an actual equality — certainly were more democratic in their leanings than even the most liberal of Whigs could be said to be.

Soon political questions dominated his life; he joined a debating society and the Society of the Friends of the People, a Whig group favouring temperate rather than radical reform, though it had many radical members. Later he drifted into the often conflicting political orbits of Major Cartwright (whom he considered 'a perfect fanatick in politics') and Sir Francis Burdett, apparently remaining in touch with both until their deaths. Cartwright was for many years a neighbour of Rashleigh's brother-in-law, Thomas Holt White of Enfield, Middlesex, and it was through White's involvement that Rashleigh was drawn into assisting Burdett in his campaign for a Middlesex seat in 1802.[10] It should be added that Holt White was a foundation member of the Friends of the People and remained a dedicated reformer thereafter. Of Walker we know little except that he was an innovative farmer and like his contemporary Gwatkin, a lifelong reformer.

This then was the background to Colman Rashleigh's political début in April 1805. He and Walker strongly argued that Lord Melville should be impeached — that he should be answerable to the Commons, the people's representatives. Many Tories present were aghast at this, one unwittingly aiding the case by angrily exclaiming:[11]

> The people of this County should be the last to complain of violation of the Acts of Parliament. There is little else to be heard of in Cornwall but the breaking of acts, defrauding the revenue, and people cheating their next door neighbours. Surely the House of Commons knew what they were about better than half-a-dozen gentlemen assembled at the Fag-end of the Kingdom?

This was hardly calculated to bring a chorus of approval from the listening freeholders and Rashleigh's impeachment motion, supported by Walker, was passed with near unanimity. Both men showed that they were willing to give the lead on contentious public issues. Their outspoken criticisms heralded the birth in Cornwall of an opposition party whose existence was confirmed four years later.

Once again it was a national scandal, this time over the sale of commissions by the Duke of York's mistress, which aroused the country.[12] Many believed that the King's ministers were, through the powerful borough patrons, controlling debate in the House of Commons. Therefore the crucial question of the representational system moved to the forefront of public discussion. Such was the case in Cornwall where, to the consternation of the Tories, for the first time since 1782 a group of reformers requested a county meeting. Heading them were Rashleigh, Walker and Gwatkin, all men of relatively small property, but nevertheless gentry and magistrates.[13]

Also among the signatories were John Trevanion, Edward Stackhouse, Henry Peter, Nicholas Kendall, William Hocker and several other reformers. Most of the group were under 40 in 1809, lived within a radius of 15 miles of each other in central southern Cornwall, were of similar economic and social status to Rashleigh and had been university-educated. The same could be said of Peter's sons William and Robert, and the Reverend Darrell Stephens, who also took a prominent part in the reform movement during the next 20 years.

From one point of view the 1809 meeting was similar to that of four years earlier; there was open, public conflict between Tories and Whigs over the petition to be sent from Cornwall. Nevertheless there were also important differences. This time the Tories were prepared for opposition. In fact one aristocrat boasted that it was, 'intended to put down for ever the factious spirit which had begun to show itself in Cornwall'.[14] Another difference was in the wording of the petition, which naturally enough reflected the concerns of the originators. According to them corruption within departments of state could be attributed to 'the defective state of the representation'. Reform, therefore, was the only solution to such abuses. Furthermore the state of the public mind demanded constitutional reform, they claimed.[15] Led brilliantly by Rashleigh, who used the Duke of York scandal as an opening to present his arguments for moderate reform and to highlight the evils of the corrupt borough system, with suitable Cornish examples, the reformers had the best of a debate lasting almost five hours. Unfortunately for the Tories Lord De Dunstanville, one of their leaders, made a poor and rambling speech during the course of which he disparaged many of his audience. Speaking of the people's rights at the time of Magna Carta he asserted that, 'the ancestors of the greater part of those who hear me, were probably at that time, slaves attached to the soil and possessed of no rights or privileges'.[16] The reformers and many freeholders present did not forget this, and it widened the growing political rift in the county.

Writing much later Colman Rashleigh looked back to the occasion at Bodmin in May 1809 as a political landmark:[17]

> The meeting laid the foundations of those unremitting and systematic exertions of the popular party in Cornwall through good and evil report and in the teeth of nearly the whole aristocratic interest and the most unscrupulous use of a prostitute press which after twenty one years struggle were crowned by complete success.

He was right, for this new political party remained a cohesive force until the first Reform Act. What Rashleigh failed to mention was that from 1809 onwards he became the acknowledged leader and foremost spokesman of the reformers. What then were the grounds upon which he and his supporters based their arguments?

Between 1809 and 1832 Rashleigh, Walker and later William Peter were the principal speakers at a succession of county meetings. In addition Rashleigh rehearsed his major arguments in letters to Holt White, so there is no shortage of evidence about their ideas. Among the clearest of them was one, first elaborated in the 1790s by the Society for Constitutional Information and the Friends of the People (F.O.P.), that the existing borough system was grossly defective. The latter organization went to great lengths to show that through the power of nomination and influence 154 individuals returned 307 Members of the House of Commons. Because of the control of the borough patrons, Rashleigh, among others, claimed that political power was in the hands of an oligarchy. It was a theme he developed in 1809, at another county meeting in 1811 and frequently in the years that followed. He argued[18]

> that by the limitations and distribution of the elective franchise the people are neither fully nor fairly represented: that from the description of those communities which possess the power of returning a majority of the House of Commons; from the nature of the Influence exercised over them in elections

and nominations: from the *degree of weight* which they possess, and *from the lands* in which that weight in truth rests 1st the people are not only not adequately represented, but not represented at all: their share in the public voice being entirely countervailed and stifled . . . . .by an oligarchy; by a corrupt oligar-chy: the number of patrons etc being so few as to make it an oligarchy.

Like the F.O.P., Rashleigh, Walker and other reformers frequently disting-uished between legitimate and illegitimate aristocratic influence, the latter arising from fear and misuse of the power of wealth which ultimately contributed to the unrepresentative nature of the Commons. Conversely, legitimate influence should be preserved and vindicated.[19] An anonymous contributor to the *Gazette* in 1809 (probably Rashleigh) wrote:[20]

I will allow . . . that besides the representation, the influence of large properties *will have* — in the nature of things *must have* great weight. The possessor of large property whether Peer or Commoner [who uses his influence wisely] . . . deserves to have great weight. . . But if he makes use of the powers of large property, to purchase the elective franchise of others, for the purposes of personal ambition or family aggrandisement, he must not be allowed to plead this as a natural or constitutional influence of property.

Elimination of rule by oligarchy, and illegitimate aristocratic influence, shorter Parliaments (without commitment to a specific length) and electoral redistribution to eradicate some of the more gross anomalies, were the reformers' chief concerns. Economical reform was far too mild, while Cartwright's radicalism, resting on the triad of annual Parliaments, secret ballot and universal suffrage was, Rashleigh believed, highly dangerous.[21]

In terms of ideology it was parliamentary Whigs like Burdett and Thomas Brand with whom the Cornish reformers were most compatible. They applauded Brand's motions for reform in May 1810 and 1812. Similarly, in June 1811 when the Friends of Reform met at the Freemasons' Tavern London, 14 Cornishmen attended, Rashleigh, Walker, Gwatkin, Trevanion and Stackhouse prominent among them. Major Cartwright was present too, not because he hoped such a gathering would agree to his radical programme first published in 1776, but because he was currently absorbed in promoting a reform party in Parliament. With Burdett and Brand also in attendance the meeting argued that the House of Commons did not speak the sense of the nation and that reform of the House was as essential to the independence of the Crown as it was to the liberties of the people.[22] Later Rashleigh, Glynn and Stackhouse joined Cartwright's Hampden Club, eager to support him, Burdett and others in their en-deavours to promote reform.[23]

However this did not mean that the Cornish tail was being wagged by the Westminster dog. Between 1812 and 1815, while Cartwright and Burdett compromised on a petitioning campaign embracing equal electoral districts, annual Parliaments and the vote for all those subject to direct taxation, Rashleigh and his friends continued to attack 'oligarchy', corruption and electoral abuses, as well as unreservedly supporting Catholic emancipation and repeal of the Test and Corporation Acts. By contrast with the insipid

Whiggery of many in Parliament Rashleigh promoted a far more vigorous ideology, yet he never flirted with radicalism. So in 1815 when Burdett identified himself with the advocates of universal suffrage, he wrote, 'and as to his [Burdett's] opinions on reform . . . they are wild, crude and untenable; nor will it do for us to have anything to do with him. We must look elsewhere for a leader'.[24] Three years later, following the general election of 1818, Rashleigh reiterated these comments, pinning his hopes on George Tierney (a former member of the F.O.P.) leading the struggle in the House of Commons.[25] By this time too he was thoroughly disenchanted by the 'radicalism' of the Hampden Club.[26] Yet, though occasionally Rashleigh and his friends were heartened by events at Westminster, more often the parliamentary Whigs' indecisiveness forced them along their own path. They never wavered in their determination to encourage popular support for their principles. At the same time, the extremism of Henry Hunt and William Cobbett held no attraction for a gentry group who hoped above all else that the Westminster Whigs would stop vacillating and put themselves at the head of a campaign for reform.

In spite of their fixity of principles Cornwall's reformers were willing to adapt to changing circumstances. Thus in 1813, as will be seen presently, they took advantage of an acrimonious debate within the county on religious questions, attending and speaking at a county meeting called by the Tories. One year earlier when Sir William Lemon and his colleague John Tremayne (who represented the county's leading Tories) were re-elected unopposed, they used the proceedings on election day to embarrass Tremayne and forcefully present their arguments for reform.[27] Then, from 1815 to 1822 they initiated a series of meetings on the property tax, government economy and retrenchment, economic distress, the assassination attempt on the Prince Regent, Peterloo, the Queen Caroline affair and reductions in tithes and rents. At these meetings the reformers generally addressed themselves to the topic of the day before offering reform as the ultimate solution to most grievances, particularly those which weighed so heavily upon agriculturalists. During the comparative economic prosperity of the mid-'20s the only public forums at which reformers appeared and spoke were the county by-election of 1825, the general election one year later and various town anti-slavery meetings. Then the crisis over Catholic emancipation in December–January 1828–9 revitalized them; until the end of 1831 they called a succession of county meetings, whipping up popular feelings and excitement as their long awaited goal drew closer.

Unwavering adherence to the moderate reform espoused by the F.O.P. in 1793, skilful utilization of the corruption and anomalies in Cornish borough politics, unity and powerful leadership, were the hallmarks of the Cornish reformers. Colman Rashleigh led by example, usually making the most telling speech at any meeting he attended, and tirelessly demonstrating how unrepresentative was the existing constitutional system. He often employed historical precedents to bolster his arguments, especially an elaborate version of the American catchcry 'No Taxation Without Representation', but always he, Walker, William Peter and others fell back on the

Whig ideals of the early 1790s. These became their creed, and in a county so rife with electoral corruption it was understandable that many clear-thinking men among the small town and rural middle ranks found it attractive. How did the gentry reformers build up a widely supported movement?

3

From December 1812 until late in January 1813 the Cornish press was preoccupied with an often emotional debate over Catholic emancipation. So determined were the principal Tories to resist a relief act that they called a county meeting, one of the very few times there were to do so between 1805 and 1832. Colman Rashleigh and the reformers attended in force. More importantly, they urged many non-freeholders to journey to Bodmin to judge the issue for themselves. During the meeting the prominent Tory solicitor Charles Rashleigh (Colman's cousin) explained that while riding into Bodmin he had met one of his tenants, the captain of a tin mine. Rashleigh questioned him about why he was attending when not a freeholder. The man replied that Colman Rashleigh had ordered him to be present. Charles Rashleigh triumphantly crowed amid the mounting up-roar, 'how was it to be supposed that such persons could be masters of the subject; the idea of a captain of a tin mine, followed by his labourers, coming forward to vote for Catholic emancipation, was absurd in the extreme'.[28] In reply his cousin contended that any person who paid the county rate should be eligible to attend, and that, 'the unsophisticated understanding of the tinners would lead them to as safe political conclusion as the understanding of any person present'.[29] The meeting quickly bogged down on this point, but like the landmark of 1809 this was a turning-point for the reformers. Thereafter they began a protracted and finally successful campaign to open county meetings to freeholders *and* inhabitants.

The elimination of attendance restrictions at the largest public forums was one of several tactics used by the reformers in order to broaden their support. They realized that step was essential if they were to maintain credibility and continue to attract large audiences to their meetings. Consequently they shrewdly developed two other lines of attack which complemented the first. In 1810, frustrated by the evident and unabashed Toryism of Cornwall's single newspaper, the *Royal Cornwall Gazette*, they established the rival *West Briton*, Edward Budd a reformer and Wesleyan lay preacher becoming the editor.[30] The other tactic was to enlarge their support by establishing strong ties with an influential but hitherto mute segment of the population — the yeomen and tenant farmers. By publicly sympathiz-ing with their post-war grievances and proposing remedies they forged an alliance which was instrumental in electing Edward Pendarves as a county Member in 1826.

Within a year of the first public arguments about attendance restrictions at county meetings, the issue, like reform, clearly divided Cornish Tories and Whigs. In June 1814 the lord lieutenant, the Earl of Mount Edgcumbe, the other Cornish peers, De Dunstanville, Falmouth and Eliot, as well as Reginald Pole Carew, William Rashleigh, Francis Gregor, Francis Glanville, F.H. Rodd and several more well known Tories headed a requisition for a county meeting to address the Prince Regent on the restoration of peace with France. Only 'Noblemen, Gentlemen, Clergy and other Freeholders' were invited to attend, a provocative step as far as the reformers were concerned.[31] They immediately applied to the sheriff, Rose Price, a one-time reformer, for a counter-meeting including *inhabitants* of Cornwall. He refused. So Rashleigh and his allies, after first seeking legal opinion, decided to summon the meeting on the basis of their authority as magistrates. Thus two meetings took place, on 11 and 16 July, each group re-emphasizing its previous stand. The Tories quoted precedent in their defence; for at least two centuries they said, meetings had been restricted to freeholders. To that Trevanion, Rashleigh and Walker replied that no legal usage or statute could be quoted to defend the status quo, therefore custom should be ignored.[32] They did that with a vengeance in the years that followed, and judging by press reports their action was highly popular with non-freeholders.

Having established the precedent in 1814 of calling meetings on their authority as magistrates if the sheriff refused a request, and of inviting freeholders and inhabitants, the reformers used this to their benefit. In February 1817, following the Spa field riots and opposition to a meeting from the Tory sheriff W.A. Harris, they nevertheless proceeded, Colman Rashleigh outlining the direct connexion as he saw it between recurring economic distress, the suspension of Habeas Corpus and the evils of the 'rotten borough' system.[33] The same procedure was followed for a county meeting in 1819 to recommend an inquiry into Peterloo, and again in February 1821 when, under the pretext of demanding the restoration of Queen Caroline's name to the liturgy, the reformers petitioned for 'a rigid system of economy and retrenchment in every branch of the public expenditure, a full enquiry into the present distress especially of the agricultural interest, and an immediate consideration of the state of the representation'.[34] Parliamentary reform preoccupied most speakers, and thereafter it was always raised before freeholders and inhabitants at county meetings, regardless of the ostensible purpose.

By the early 1820s the Cornish reformers had made their point. Through legally sidestepping the sheriff's authority if he rejected a requisition, they could assemble whenever the need arose. More importantly, by insisting upon the admission of freeholders and inhabitants they not only enlarged the audience to whom they could explain their principles, but also earned the gratitude and support of those formerly excluded. In turn many of the tenant farmers who were now drawn into political debates played an active rather than a merely passive role. This is illustrated by the county meeting of April 1822, for the requisition was signed, not by the principal Tories or Whig magistrates, but by nearly 500 freeholders and leaseholders who wished to consider ways of relieving distress among farmers and, 'to take into consideration the defective and unequal state of the Representation of the people to which the burthens and privations under which they suffer are principally to be attributed'.[35] In fact the farmers, having been encouraged to become political activists, were now prepared to proceed with or without the reformers.

The same meeting underlined another now obvious feature of county politics — the reluctance of the Tory magnates to offer political leadership other than at elections. Colman Rashleigh pointedly drew attention to this when, during the course of his speech he observed that[36]

> it will be deeply felt and long remembered. The landed Aristocracy were the natural leaders of the People. When the Yeomanry and the country were breaking down under the burthens, how were the people to act when those who from their stations should lead them, deserted them in their dilemma?

It was a rhetorical question, for the answer was obvious to everyone listening. Only the reformers appeared genuinely interested in the plight of the farmers — and only they were prepared to initiate county meetings. Why did the Tories, the traditional leaders of a community in which the farmers were an important element, allow their position to be undermined?

The answer lies in the fact that until 1809 despite periodic but short-lived challenges, the aristocracy and wealthy gentry directed county politics and opinion. They also dictated the frequency and topics of public debate. Petitions despatched from Cornwall to the monarch or Parliament were usually reflections of their viewpoints. However after 1809 they began to lose the initiative to the reformers, opponents whom they labelled 'factious', 'Jacobinical', and 'obscure persons'. The Tories were willing to contest any issue so long as it was primarily a struggle within the ranks of the aristocracy and gentry. But once the reformers made attendance restrictions at county meetings a central issue, and once meetings convened by reformer-magistrates were opened to the 'lower orders', they refused to attend. Their stand was one of principle; the Tories contended that the meetings were illegal. Charles Rashleigh's contempt for the lower orders (so publicly expressed in 1813) was shared by all of the principal members of the party — and this was another reason for non-attendance. They had no wish to be associated with those whose opinions they regarded with disdain. Thus in 1825 Lord De Dunstanville wrote, 'it will be a disgrace to have a member forced upon the County by a party chiefly composed of the lower orders'.[37] Finally, the leadership of the Tories was undermined because they feared the numerical strength of those supporting the gentry reformers. There was the real possibility that they could be publicly humiliated at county meetings, particularly those on reform. Reflecting on the past in 1832 Pole Carew admitted that 'I have never been a friend of the measure of attending the county meetings when we have always been beaten and shall infallibly be beaten as long as this popular delusion and phrenzy lasts'.[38] It was these attitudes which led the Tories (probably unwittingly) to neglect the farmers' interests, so making the farmer-reformer alliance a certainty.

While the series of county meetings had an undeniable impact upon emergent public opinion, the *West Briton* constantly reinforced the reformers' position. It was, from its foundation, a mouthpiece for them. Colman Rashleigh and the Reverend Walker were certainly among the original proprietors, and within months the paper was on a sound financial footing.[39] No records survive of the comparative circulations of the two papers before 1831 when the *Gazette*'s yearly total was 27,000, the *West Briton*'s 50,900.[40] Under Budd, the first editor, the paper remained in that position until his death in 1835. Throughout he never wavered in his support of parliamentary reform, nor did he shrink from attacking the *Gazette* with skill and gusto. Furthermore the *West Briton* brought many examples of Cornish borough corruption to the public's attention, while the weekly editorials were invaluable for propagating reform principles. Universal suffrage and annual parliaments were sternly disapproved of and generally Budd was content to agree with the Whig ideals espoused by the principal reformers. During general elections the manipulations and shenanigans of various borough-mongers, particularly Lord Falmouth and Sir Christopher Hawkins, were mercilessly exposed, and there was always a detailed coverage of the progress of radicalism and the reform movement elsewhere in England. Unquestionably some of what the *West Briton* printed was blatant propaganda and exaggeration: nevertheless by 1825 its political reporting was far more accurate and detailed than that of the *Gazette*. In short the *West Briton* kept the question of parliamentary reform continually before the Cornish reading public in a way that public meetings, however numerous, could never do; and it probably won over many waverers on what might otherwise have remained a relatively abstract issue.

Yet it would be wrong to regard the *West Briton* as a single issue paper. Evidence suggests that, important as were the public roles of Rashleigh, Walker, Trevanion, Pendarves (who usually chaired the reformers' county meetings), Glynn, and William Peter, it was the editor Edward Budd's obvious concern about the causes and effects of the post-war economic distress which did much to forge the farmer-reformer alliance. Through the columns of the *West Briton* he attacked the levels of government expenditure, taxation and the undue burdens which tithes and local rates placed upon Cornish farmers. Equally sigificant was the paper's encouragement of farmer activism. The outcome was that the agriculturalists concluded that their complaints and the reformers' objectives were complementary.

Whether or not Cornwall's reformers consciously wooed the farmers into an alliance is debatable. Obviously the campaign over county meetings opened an avenue of complaint to them, drawing the farmers into political discussions. Of course after 1815 the reformers helped that process by taking up their various concerns (often economic) as a prelude to their principal objective — parliamentary reform. Yet, these developments notwithstanding, there were two other circumstances which aided the union. One was the economic hardships endured by the agriculturalists between 1815 and 1822, the other the energetic proselytizing of John Penhallow Peters, a notable yeoman farmer and political activist.

The course of the national post-war depression is so well known that except for several Cornish peculiarities it needs little discussion. Unlike their contemporaries elsewhere Cornwall's farmers did not become agitated about the malt tax. Certainly barley was widely grown in the eastern hundreds, but perhaps because only moderate amounts were destined for the maltsters, opposition to the tax was sporadic and geographically isolated. The same may be said of the currency issue. Peel's act of 1819 produced no more than occasional comment. With agricultural protection a very different situation developed. Under the leadership of Penhallow Peters the Cornwall Agricultural Association adopted a solidly protectionist attitude. Through Peters and the Association's secretary John Bligh, Cornwall became affiliated with George Webb Hall's Central Agricultural Association, a short-lived national protectionist pressure group. Although it enjoyed support in many agricultural counties the Association achieved little, Hall's arguments about the benefits of protection finally being discredited before a parliamentary select committee in 1821. Despite this Peters and the Cornish farmers rallied to Hall's support by expressing their appreciation of his efforts at a Truro meeting in December 1821.[41] The farmers decried the judgments of the select committee and dispatched another petition, before turning away from protection to complain about more immediate problems — the levels of tithes and rents. Once again it was Penhallow Peters who led them, just as it was he who played a pivotal role in the farmer–reformer alliance.

Peters, a farmer on the Veryan peninsula east of Falmouth was a mountainous figure who regularly held court at the Red Lion Inn, Truro, during farmers' ordinaries. Once described as 'a sane madman' he was no one's fool, either as a farmer or as a politician; he pioneered the crossing of Leicester and Cotswold sheep, and was instrumental in drastically increasing Cornish wool yields through regular sales of his long-wool Leicester rams. Politically his position was defined by his fervent Whiggery and by the realization that parliamentary reform could lead to a government more responsive to agriculturalists' complaints. Therefore it was natural that he should join the gentry reformers in their protests after the meeting of 1813, when they not only supported the Catholic claims, but also began their campaign for the rights of inhabitants to attend.[42] Henceforth Peters's name was usually among the reformers requesting meetings and he became the unofficial leader of the farmers.

His pivotal role between reformers and farmers began to emerge in 1816. Two county meetings were held to approve petitions to the government demanding economy, retrenchment and relief for the alarming rural distress. Peters was prominent at the second meeting in October and it was reported that the farmers were there in force too. Colman Rashleigh told them that only through an independent Parliament could financial changes be secured, and no doubt the message was heeded.[43] In the same year Peters, obviously a natural leader, used both Cornish newspapers to address himself to the gentry, clergy and farmers of Cornwall on the annual burden imposed by tithe payments. He initiated a petition and undertook a well supported campaign against the tithes, arguing that they were unfair and promoted divisiveness within the community.[44] One of the most interesting aspects of this episode was the decision by Peters and his principal allies to channel surplus funds into the Cornwall Agricultural Association. Peters, George Simmons and John Bligh, all farmers, were leading members of that organization and Simmons, like Peters, was on the list of requisitioners for both county meetings in 1816. Here were the seeds of a future alliance.

From then until 1822 it seems that the embryonic union was carefully nurtured by Peters, Bligh and Simmons on the one hand, and the gentry reformers on the other. Time and time again it was Peters who organized the rural middle classes, the climax coming in 1822 when many freeholders and leaseholders requested the sheriff, David Howell (a reformer) to call a county meeting. No reformers signed yet the connexion was unmistakable; the farmers stated that, 'labouring under unexampled distress from the unprecedented low prices of all Agricultural produce, and oppressed by an excessive weight of Taxation, which added to the payment of Rent, Rates, Tithes, and an enormously increased Poor Rate, has become intolerable'. Pleading for urgent relief they then added that the House of Commons should seriously consider parliamentary reform.[45] It was an open invitation for the reformers to join the farmers at the meeting — which they did. And although Peters proposed the list of resolutions, as we have already seen it was Colman Rashleigh who dominated the meeting, supported by Walker, Trevanion and William Peter. The farmers enthusiastically endorsed their reformist ideals and from then until 1832 their support for parliamentary reform never wavered. Politically, the consequences were far-reaching.

When Sir William Lemon died in December 1824, having been a county M.P. for 50 years, the ensuing by-election in January 1825 and the general election of 1826 gave both farmers and reformers the opportunity to demonstrate their political strength. Throughout his long life Lemon had favoured parliamentary reform. One Tory critic wrote of him: 'I have long ceased to be surprised at any opposition vote for Sir William — he is just as systematic an opposer of the measures of the Government whether right or wrong as the most devoted tool of administration is a favourer of them.'[46] Shortly after Lemon's death the sharing of county seats was shattered when the Tories brought forward Sir Richard Vyvyan to join John Tremayne. In doing so they made it obvious that they intended to re-create the old monopoly of seats which had aroused great bitterness in the past. The same feelings of opposition recurred in 1824–6, with Edward Pendarves, one of the best known reformers, challenging the proposed supremacy before it was established.

Pendarves had initially decided to contest the by-election against Vyvyan, but the realization of a possibly expensive general election in 1826 made him reconsider and withdraw. Then at the nomination meeting on 26 January 1825 Penhallow Peters and Abraham Hambly unexpectedly proposed Pendarves on behalf of the yeoman and tenant farmers. They pointedly remarked that 'the yeomanry know their rights and strength and will never allow two members to be thrust on them by the aristocracy in this way'.[47] In spite of Pendarves's protestations the farmers insisted that he go to the poll, but after an evening of much arguing Pendarves finally persuaded them to bide their time. One notable feature of this episode was Pendarves's lack of support from the great landed interests in Cornwall. However, it was compensated for by the remarkable show of strength from the farmers throughout the prolonged canvass of 1825–6. Independence from aristocratic influence and parliamentary reform were their catch-cries and Pendarves eagerly identified himself with both while Vyvyan, perceived by everyone as the representative of the 'aristocratical interest', laboured under what had now become an electoral handicap. The outcome was that in mid-1826, shortly before the election, it was acknowledged on all sides that should there be a poll Pendarves would head it, the contest being between the ultra-Tory Vyvyan and the moderate Tremayne. As the latter was reluctant to empty his pockets for what undoubtedly would have been an expensive contest he withdrew at the very last moment, leaving Pendarves and Vyvyan to represent the county.[48]

This reversion to shared county representation in 1826 was for several reasons a milestone in Cornish politics. Firstly, Pendarves made sure that questions of principle came to the fore, something hitherto unknown in county politics. Parliamentary reform, Catholic emancipation, the abolition of colonial slavery, and to a lesser degree the corn laws were the paramount issues during the unprecedented 18-month period of canvassing and electioneering before the election. None of the candidates could avoid them, especially the ultra-Tory Vyvyan. In January 1825, when he was unopposed, his speeches and published addresses were consistent with those of his Tory predecessors who did no more than suggest their independence from parties, generally approve of the government's attitudes and claim support as protectors of Cornwall's extensive mining interest.[49] By nomination day Vyvyan was clearly identifiable as a staunch 'Protestant' Tory who vehemently opposed Catholic emancipation and parliamentary reform, and seemed uncertain about the rising tide of anti-slavery sentiments throughout the country. Much of this was a reaction to positions openly taken by Pendarves and his supporters.[50] Secondly, the political potency of the farmer-reformer alliance could no longer be doubted. Thoroughly disenchanted by the aristocracy's lack of interest in their problems and viewpoints the farmers were prepared to favour a Whig candidate who could be identified with parliamentary reform. Pendarves was supported because of what he stood for rather than who he was. As for the gentry reformers, after some early misgivings and jealousies they supported him solidly. It was also very evident that several among his principal backers — the Williams and Davey families — were representative of powerful western mining interests and comparative newcomers among the reformers.[51] Thus parliamentary reform was now drawing adherents from families of 'new' wealth, as well as the rural middle classes. The long standing political wirepullers among Cornwall's Tories, men such as Lords De Dunstanville, Mount Edgcumbe, Eliot and Falmouth and Reginald Pole Carew failed to realize that by abandoning the agriculturalists after 1816, by failing to sympathize with their plight or even appear at county meetings, their own political leadership was being badly eroded. So they inadvertently encouraged Cornwall's farmers to enter and remain consistently involved in county politics.

It might well be argued that between 1805 and 1826 Cornwall's gentry reformers achieved comparatively little, At the national level this is certainly true. They had no spokesman in Parliament, for Sir William Lemon was a passive though consistent reformer, and they apparently exerted no influence over the vacillations of the parliamentary Whigs. However in Cornwall their impact was enormous and far-reaching. Divorcing themselves from the twin radical demands for annual Parliaments and universal suffrage, they presented the county with what Christopher Wyvill, Major Cartwright and Sir Francis Burdett at various times advocated — a gentry led reform movement. It was a movement which derived much of its impetus from irregularities in the existing constitutional system and from the beginning it was firmly organized and led. In fact the *Gazette* grudgingly admitted this as early as October 1812 after Colman Rashleigh, John Trevanion and the Reverend Walker had severely embarrassed Cornwall's Tory county Member John Tremayne on the hustings. Financially very few of the reformers could afford to stand for the county, but light purses were no hindrance to continuous political activism which annoyed and frustrated the leading Tories.[52] By utilizing county meetings, the *West Briton* and post-war distress of the agriculturalists, they took the cause of parliamentary reform to the people of Cornwall. Many among the rural middle classes needed little persuasion to take a far more active, and as 1825–6 revealed, even decisive political role.

Naturally enough in the aftermath of the 1826 general election reformers and farmers were jubilant. While the latter group busied themselves on the land, the gentry reformers, recognizing that rural prosperity would provide them with few opportunities for public meetings, now took a new direction. They became enmeshed in small town anti-slavery societies — Rashleigh, Pendarves, Walker, William Peter and the others using these groups to engender political activism in several of Cornwall's largest boroughs. At a series of borough public meetings in January 1829 they also spoke out strongly for Catholic emancipation, and their eventual reward was the blooming of a dynamic small town reform movement. In fact well before the general election of December 1832 it was obvious that the spirit of Whig liberalism had gripped corrupt Cornwall. The farmer-reformer alliance stood firm, the farmers demonstrating again in March 1830 that they believed parliamentary reform would be their economic salvation.[53] These triumphs gave the reformers immense satisfaction; and they had laid the foundations of Liberalism's nineteenth-century dominance in part of England's 'Celtic-fringe'.

Notes

1   W. Thomas, *The Philosophic Radicals: Nine Studies in Theory and Practice 1817–1841* (Oxford, 1979), esp. Chapter 2; J.M. Main, 'Radical Westminster 1807–1820', *Historical Studies, Australia and New Zealand*, XII (1966), 186–204; J.R. Dinwiddy, 'Sir Francis Burdett and Burdettite Radicalism', *History*, LXV (1980), 17–31; N.C. Miller, 'John Cartwright and Radical Parliamentary Reform, 1808–1819', *E.H.R.*, LXXXIII (1968), 705–28.

2   For example see J. Cannon, *Parliamentary Reform 1640–1832* (Cambridge, 1972); A. Mitchell, *The Whigs in Opposition 1815–1830* (Oxford, 1967); E.P. Thompson, *The Making of the English Working Class* (1972).

3   D.C. Moore, 'The Other Face of Reform', *Victorian Studies*, V (1961), 7–34, and *The Politics of Deference* (Hassocks, 1976).

4   Sir Lewis Namier, *The Structure of Politics at the Accession of George III* (2nd edn., 1961); E. and Annie G. Porritt, *The Unreformed House of Commons* (2 vols., Cambridge, 1903); W.B. Elvins, 'The Reform Movement and County Politics in Cornwall 1809–1852' (Birmingham M.A. thesis, 1959).

5   According to Dr John Rowe in his excellent *Cornwall in the Age of Industrial Revolution* (Liverpool, 1953), the revolution came earlier to Cornwall than elsewhere in England, beginning in the 1740s.

6   A penetrating study of this development is Mrs V.M. Chesher's 'Some Cornish Landowners 1690–1760, a Social and Economic Study' (Oxford B. Litt thesis, 1957).

7   Gregor was a follower of William Pitt and reacted strongly against the French Revolution, as did his contemporary Davies Giddy (later Gilbert) who was a self-confessed radical until he realized his property would be threatened by English Jacobins.

8   Cornwall R.O., Sir John Colman Rashleigh, *Memoirs of Sir Colman Rashleigh Bt. : In Four Parts (1772–1847)*, Part II, p.14.

9   *Ibid.*, Part I, p.39.

10   Rashleigh's correspondence with Thomas Holt White may be found in the Gilbert White Museum, Selborne, Hampshire, Holt White MSS., nos. 302–319.

11   *Royal Cornwall Gazette*, 1 June 1805, p.3.

12   An excellent account of the Cornish reaction to this scandal, and the emergence of the reformers in county politics may be found in Elvins, 'Reform Movement', Chapter 2.

13   Gwatkin's appearances among the reformers were spasmodic in later years. However he also openly supported the anti-Boscawen reform party in Truro in the 1830s.

14   Cornw. R.O., *Rashleigh Mems.*, Part II, pp. 31–2.

15   *Ryl. Cornw. Gaz.*, 20 May 1809, p.1.

16   *Ibid.*, p.2.

17   Cornw. R.O., *Rashleigh Mems.*, Part II, pp. 37–8.

18   Gilbert White Mus., Holt White MSS., no. 316, J.C. Rashleigh to T. Holt White, [1819?].

19   Christopher Wyvill, *Political Papers . . .* (5 vols., York, n.d.). III, App., pp.231–2.

20   *Ryl. Cornw. Gaz.*, 3 June 1809, p.3.

21   Miller, 'Cartwright and Reform', p.707.

22   *West Briton*, 21 June 1811, pp.1 and 4.

23   Gilbert White Mus., Holt White MSS., no. 455, 'List of Members of the Hampden Club 1812'.

24   *Ibid.*, no. 310, J.C. Rashleigh to T. Holt White, 2 Apr. 1815.

25   *Ibid.*, no. 314, 15 Aug. 1818.

26   *Ibid.*, no. 312, 25 Jan. 1817.

27   *W. Briton*, 23 Oct. 1812, p.4. Colman Rashleigh challenged Tremayne to explain why he had voted against Thomas Brand's motion in 1810 and 1812, for committees to consider various aspects of parliamentary reform. Walker and Trevanion joined Rashleigh in his attack on Tremayne.

28   *Ibid.*, 29 Jan. 1813, p.2.

29   *Ibid.*

30   Elvins, 'Reform Movement', Chapter 2, pp.1–7.

[31]   *W. Briton*, 15 July 1814, p.1.
[32]   *Ibid.*, 12 Aug. 1814.
[33]   *Ibid.*, 7 Mar. 1817, p.1, and 14 Mar., 1817, pp.1 and 4.
[34]   *Ibid.*, 23 Mar. 1821.
[35]   *Ibid.*, 29 Mar. 1822, p.1.
[36]   *Ibid.*, 5 Apr. 1822, p.3.
[37]   Elvins, 'Reform Movement', Chapter 4, n. 70.
[38]   Carew MSS. (Sir John Carew Pole, Antony House, Cornwall), CC/N/65, Reginald Pole Carew to Lord Falmouth, 18 May 1832.
[39]   Elvins, 'Reform Movement', Chapter 2.
[40]   *Ibid.*, App. 4.
[41]   *W. Briton*, 14 Dec. 1821, p.1.
[42]   *Ibid.*, 29 Jan. 1813, p.1.
[43]   *Ibid.*, 18 Oct. 1816, p.3.
[44]   *Ryl. Cornw. Gaz.*, 8 June 1816, p.1.
[45]   *W. Briton*, 29 Mar. 1822, p.1.
[46]   Cornw. R.O., DD(R) 5313 (Rashleigh MSS.), Canon Rogers to William Rashleigh, 24 Jan. 1820.
[47]   *W. Briton*, 28 Jan. 1825, p.2.
[48]   Tremayne believed that he should be guaranteed a seat, without incurring any expense, in return for his 20 years of service as a county M.P. He quoted the election of Sir William Lemon in 1790 as a precedent, but this was false.
[49]   For elaboration see E.K.G. Jaggard, 'Patrons, Principles and Parties; Cornwall Politics 1760–1910' (Washington University, St Louis, Ph.D. thesis, 1980), Chapter 4.
[50]   *Ibid.*
[51]   Members of both families later entered Parliament: Richard Davey, Liberal M.P. W. Cornwall 1851–68; Michael Williams, Liberal M.P. W. Cornwall 1853–8. In mid-century the families also intermarried, forming a powerful alliance.
[52]   Edward Pendarves could afford to contest a county seat in 1826 only because of a fortuitous inheritance.
[53]   *W. Briton*, 26 Mar. 1830, p.2. The farmers prompted a meeting to discuss the existing agricultural distress. They agreed with the leading speakers, William Peter and Walker, that the pernicious effects of a contracted currency would eventually be overcome by a more representative House of Commons.

Parliamentary History, Volume 2 (1983)

THE ORGANIZATION OF THE CONSERVATIVE PARTY 1832–1846
PART II: THE ELECTORAL ORGANIZATION

NORMAN GASH

[*Continued from ante*, I, 159]

Between the machinery of the parliamentary management and what might be called for the sake of clarity the central electoral organization, no clear-cut division existed. The distinction in these terms is not a contemporary one and the participation of the same group of men in both aspects of party work further obscures the difference between them. Yet it was a difference which after the Reform Act became increasingly important and self-evident. The task of the parliamentary organization was the efficient conduct of the parliamentary party in being; the task of the electoral organization was to give the parliamentary party a majority in the House of Commons. The hardening of party divisions in the post-Reform years made it practically impossible to secure a majority by means of manoeuvres within Parliament. Peel's failure in 1834–5 either to win over Stanley's 'Third Party' or to attract the support of moderate Whigs, demonstrated the growing reluctance — or the increasing inability — of ordinary M.P.s to change sides. The decisive shifts of power had to come as a result of elections. It was to the electoral contests therefore that an increasing amount of party attention was devoted. Moreover, the altered condition of those contests demanded a more continuous and detailed activity than could be provided by the whips alone, or even the whips in conjunction with the constituency organizations. The emergence of Bonham as the specialist electoral expert of the party was a mark of this growing complexity.

Even before the Reform Act, however, the advent of a general election was normally marked by the formation of a small committee prepared to devote itself entirely for two or three weeks to the supervision of the party's electoral activities. Some such committee was clearly necessary; all the more because of the general exodus of Members to their constituencies at election time. The besetting defect of election committees was that they were apt to include men who were attracted by the self-importance and access to party intelligence offered but were little disposed to take their share of the hard work. The party election committee of 1832 may have suffered in this way from a superfluity of ornamental members, to judge from a hint from Bonham to Arbuthnot about the need for 'having some *working* friends in London'. Nevertheless he cautiously shared the general optimism of the party over the prospects of the first election under the reformed system. The Duke of Wellington, who still ranked as the party leader, was even more sanguine. According to Arbuthnot, 'the D. of Wn. who has no exaggeration in his mind thinks that with so many in the field we shall do still better than you expect'.[1] Not surprisingly therefore, when telling Sir George Clerk after the election that the returns in England were not at all satisfactory, Peel added 'far less so than our too sanguine friends in Carlton Terrace anticipated'.[2] The principal members of the 1832 election committee were probably the Earl of Rosslyn, Bonham, and Holmes, though there was certainly a much longer list of well-meaning if amateur helpers and hangers-on. The next election committee was formed two years later in readiness for the dissolution of Parliament consequent on the formation of the first Peel ministry. 'Already a dissolution is expected', wrote Dawson, Peel's brother-in-law, on 22 November 1834, 'and a Committee is active at the Carlton. The reports are very favourable.' But this committee too was a large and inefficient body in which the chief 'working members' were Lord Granville Somerset, Rosslyn and Bonham. Writing to Rosslyn on election prospects at Leith, Lord Melville begged him not to disclose the information to 'the electioneering committee in London where I suspect that secrecy is not the order of the day'.[3] The elections represented a distinct success for the party but Bonham writing a few months later was inclined to assign most of the credit to Granville Somerset. 'I know', he told Peel, 'what G–S did at the last election, by his almost single exertions, for some of our friends did us more harm than good.'

It was probably the experience of the 1835 election that prompted Bonham to propose to Peel in the following May the creation of a small standing election committee. The idea was something of a novelty and drew its immediate justification from the fear of an unexpected Whig dissolution. But the advantages of such a permanent piece of machinery were obvious. What Bonham advised was[4]

> a very small and *quiet* but active committee to obtain information and prepare for such an event. For myself I am ready *to devote my whole time* out of the H of C to this work and with a very small committee, hardly more than 7, composed of G. Somerset (above all others), Lord Lincoln, Clerk, Fremantle and any others whom you might wish to recommend, I feel confident that we might so work the Constituency as would perhaps even deter them from the attempt.

Bonham's suggestion was probably taken up, for an election committee was certainly in existence the following year (1836) although there was no general election. Thereafter the party organization grew visibly more effective and self-confident. The general election of 1837 was in many ways the decisive battle of the campaign between Whigs and Conservatives after 1832 even though the fruits of victory were not plucked until 1841. In that encounter the party reduced its opponents to virtual impotence and from that point onward it was only a matter of time before Peel returned to office.

The effective members of the central committee during Peel's period of leadership were substantially the same from one election to another. From 1835 at least Granville Somerset was head of the organization. Rosslyn up to his death in 1837 and Sir James Graham after that date were powerful coadjutors, though as the latter was not a member of the Carlton until 1841 it is doubtful whether he was formally on the committee. Bonham, who after 1837 had no parliamentary or electoral cares of his own, was the permanent and indispensable official round whom the organization was built; and the whips were co-opted to give as much of their time as they could afford. Other men such as Hardinge, Herries, and Goulburn, seem to have taken a prominent part at different times. No doubt when the elections were actually in progress a number of hands were required to deal with the physical work of correspondence and members of the committee who were themselves candidates would necessarily be absent at crucial moments. The activities of the committee were numerous and valuable. They corresponded with local Conservative Associations and gave warning of imminent elections. They collected reports from all over the country and produced a unified view of election prospects which was of political use for their leaders. They supplied candidates to constituencies and constituencies to candidates; they dealt with the mass of letters which any general election evoked — queries, difficulties, protests and requests; they kept an almost daily account of the progress of elections; and by the time the last contests were being decided, they could report in detail on the result of the general election and the composition of the new House of Commons. Afterwards they could examine the number of lost contests where an appeal might be successful and arrange for petitions to be presented. Primarily perhaps the function of the committee was to collect exact information upon which the internal management of the party and its external tactics could be based. They ensured as far as possible that no important constituency lacked contact with the party and that no important information was lacking to the leaders. The attention paid to the constituencies was an obvious and important part of their work; but the importance of the constant flow of information to the leaders on the state of the party in the country should not be underestimated. The central committee was of course very far from being universally influential. Moreover its power did not extend much beyond England and Wales. Scotland, that distant and clannish kingdom, was prudently left to men with local connexions such as Lord Melville, Aberdeen, Graham, and Lamond of Glasgow; while responsibility for Ireland was placed almost entirely in the hands of Shaw who corresponded directly with Peel on election matters. 'With Ireland', wrote Bonham to Peel in a survey of the 1837 election, 'I can give no opinion or attempt to reason on anything that may happen in that most eccentric land.' But though the Irish Conservatives had unpromising material to work on, the reports that came in from Dublin suggested that Shaw was an energetic and strong leader. 'We have 69 Candidates now in the field in Ireland', he wrote to Peel in January 1835, 'having had but 28 members in the last parliament & tomorrow morning I expect to have an excellent second candidate for this city which will make 70.' Hardinge writing a week later added that they expected to gain about ten or 12 seats. At the next general election the going was harder and though Shaw wrote in good spirit about the prospects and did not reckon more than five lost seats, Hardinge would have been glad to compromise at seven or eight.[5]

But even excluding Scotland and Ireland there was a substantial area under the immediate influence of the central organization and from their headquarters in London they were enabled to exercise a light but important and continuous supervision of much of the party's activities in the country. In the matter of election petitions they could even initiate policy. After the general election of 1837 Granville Somerset was urging election petitions in every case where there were the slightest grounds for them. Not only was there the opportunity thereby of securing more seats but a strong Conservative attack, he thought, would counteract the efforts of the Whigs if they tried to employ similar tactics. 'I am convinced', he told Peel, 'that the only chance we have of tolerably Fair play on the score of Bribery and of treating will be to attack the Ministerialists strenuously on these grounds, more especially as I believe them to have been guilty of both those Practices to an *infinitely more extensive* Degree than our Friends have.'[6] The same methods were used after the election of 1841. The central managers could thus institute an offensive to cover the delinquency of their friends in the country. At the same time election petitions offered a chance of further increases in the party strength. In August 1837 Hardinge was hoping for eight or ten additional seats as a result of Conservative petitions. At the next election Parkes, who knew as much as anyone of the management of the Liberal Party, complained bitterly of Tory activity in getting up election petitions. He estimated that about 54 petitions in all were presented, about one tenth of the whole representation. 'Old Bonham, Sir G. Clerk, and Fremantle', he wrote, 'have been regular procurers of petitions, daily and hourly in the recognizance room to watch and see'; whereas on the other side there was scarcely any effort, 'not a soul on our side on the move'.[7] Even when allowance is made for the exaggeration of domestic criticism, there is good evidence that by 1841 if not earlier the sense of superiority and initiative was with the Conservative Party organization.

One other weapon remained to the central election committee — money.[8] The financial burden of the general election fell mainly of course on the candidates themselves. Radical Members and radical constituencies might sometimes successfully limit electoral expenditure and transfer what financial obligations remained from the candidate to his supporters. But local Conservatives, possessing wealthier candidates, and more deeply imbued with aristocratic notions of society, tended to look upon their men as sources of wealth rather than as political protégés. Not only was the candidate expected in general to meet the costs of election but even in ordinary years calls would be made upon him for subscriptions to local charitable, social, party, and association funds. If a Conservative politician lacked what was called in the apt jargon of the day 'the necessary', he lacked the essential basis of a political career. This was true even of those better-known party members whose past services or future prospects might seem to qualify them for outside assistance. Sometimes the friends and supporters of a candidate would come to his rescue by raising a fund by subscriptions drawn not only from the constituency but also from the principal members of the party at large. At the 1837 general election for instance the committee of A.G. Stapleton, the Conservative candidate for Birmingham, applied to Peel for a subscription to his electioneering fund.[9] In the by-election at Taunton in April 1835, when Disraeli unsuccessfully opposed Labouchere, he was supported by the financial as well as the political strength of the party headquarters. Granville Somerset gave him an interview and told him that he would be started by the party at the first opportunity. Bonham introduced him by letter to the local Conservatives in the constituency and was active in raising the sum of £300 which Disraeli requested to support his contest. 'It is astonishing how well they are informed in London of all that passed here', wrote Disraeli to his sister on the eve of nomination day, 'and how greatly they appreciate my exertions. They have opened a subscription for me at the Carlton, headed by Chandos, who has written twice to me in the warmest manner.'[10]

The most striking example of an individual subscription fund was that offered to Lord Ashley in 1846. In spite of his differences with Peel and Graham over the Factory Bill, Ashley had supported the policy of repealing the Corn Laws. Nevertheless, sitting for an agricultural constituency, and after convincing himself of the strong feelings of his electors, he deemed it his duty to retire from the seat. He applied for the Chiltern Hundreds at the end of January 1846. Less than a week later Bonham came to him privately to say that a few members of the party, including Peel and Graham, had subscribed £2,000 towards the cost of his re-election, and that he was instructed to inform Ashley that acceptance would impose no obligation on his political conduct. 'If I were returned', wrote Ashley, recording the conversation, 'and the next night moved the Ten Hours Bill and by success drove them from office, they should consider that it was simply within the compass of my inevitable duty.' But as Ashley clearly perceived, though the donors might expect nothing, the receiver would feel fettered. The next day he wrote to refuse. 'It would have been very inconsiderate and ungracious on my part', he told Bonham, 'had I, at once, declined to accept the kind and liberal offer you made to me in the name of certain Gentlemen who were desirous of contributing largely towards the expenses I should be subjected to in standing a contested election for the County of Dorset. I fully appreciate the generosity as well as the *delicacy* of the proposition, but I cannot conceal from you that I should feel myself embarrassed were I to accept it.'[11]

Occasionally, important opponents and prestigious constituencies were singled out for particular efforts by the party organization. 'We have raised here', wrote Hardinge from London on the eve of the 1837 election, '£2,400 for Dublin City and £3,300 for Westminster — the Candidates and their committees must do the rest.'[12] The two capitals, London and Dublin, were among the greatest prizes of the election campaigns; and Ireland in general, since it represented the antithesis to Conservative thought and interests, tended to receive special attention. A fund was raised after the 1837 election, for instance, to fight Irish election petitions. Early in 1842 Lord Eliot, the Chief Secretary, made an appeal for a party subscription of £2,000 or £3,000 to assist in a Dublin by-election. Similarly when a by-election was anticipated in Middlesex the following year a party subscription was opened for the Conservative candidate, though Fremantle told Peel that 'it is doubtful in the present state of the party whether the Conservatives will come forward as readily as they have done on former occasions'.[13] There is some indication that O'Connell was made the object of a formidable attack by the central Conservative organization which took the form both of contesting elections and petitioning against returns. The most notable of these personal onslaughts came in 1835 when a petition was brought against O'Connell's return for Dublin and enormous sums expended in the effort to unseat him. O'Connell himself estimated that he spent between £1,000 and £1,500 in defending the petition; and he reckoned that this was only a fifth of the expenses of the prosecution. This would make the Conservative expenses something between £5,000 and £8,000 which though a high, and probably exaggerated, was not an impossible figure. Whatever the amount, the costs of the petition were alleged to have been borne by Carlton Club subscriptions and certainly few private individuals could or would have undertaken such an expenditure. But it is clear that the Conservatives made a special and expensive attempt to unseat the great Catholic agitator who at the same time was the firm prop of the Whigs.[14]

Petitions were perhaps more favoured as occasions for party subscriptions than elections. The reasons for this are comprehensible. The number of such petitions was considerably fewer than the number of contested elections. Coming after the immediate election results the issue of a controverted return possessed a marginal and in aggregate possibly decisive importance. There was the human desire to reverse in the committee room the verdict of the hustings and the tactical consideration that this was the last opportunity of challenging seats otherwise lost for the duration of a septennial Parliament. But candidates who had just borne unaided the expense of an election contest could scarcely be expected to meet a second expense which might be as great or greater than the first. Consequently general subscriptions for fighting specific election petitions were a common feature of party warfare as waged by the Conservatives. In April 1840 Lord George Bentinck was at Newmarket where among more characteristic activities he canvassed for subscriptions to the Cambridge election petition. He confessed to Graham, however, that it was a bad place at which to try to raise money. He obtained £20 from the Duke of Beaufort, £20 from Lord

Chesterfield, and added a similar stake from himself. But that, he added, would hardly suffice for one day's work on the election petition.[15] When Dick Dyott, after his narrow defeat at Lichfield in 1841, was contemplating a petition against one of his opponents, he received cordial advice and support from Bonham whom he met at Peel's house shortly afterwards. A conference between Dyott, Bonham and Fremantle was held at Drayton in which Peel showed a neighbourly interest and Bonham promised on his return to town to discuss the matter with the two barristers whom Dyott had already consulted 'as he said he knew how to judge of Parliamentary petitions as well as they did'. After the decision had been taken to proceed with the petition Bonham seems to have obtained £250 from central sources to add to the local subscriptions raised on Dyott's behalf in Staffordshire. Fremantle, too, whom Dyott visited in London, showed every desire to assist and placed at his disposal a situation in the customs 'for a good Lichfield Conservative'.[16]

The financing of election petitions was for the most part beyond the resources of the two or three high-minded electors who were usually put up to assume nominal responsibility for initiating proceedings. The costs would normally fall on the unsuccessful candidate and he in turn would try to get financial help from his supporters and from his party. Without such backing the private elector was helpless. Election petitions were not intended to check bribery and corruption within the constituencies, though they sometimes had that effect. They were merely extensions of the party conflict. The proceedings were therefore very much under the control of parties and candidates and very far removed from the wishes and initiative of the constituency. Some light is thrown on this by an incident at Evesham after the election of 1837. Lord Marcus Hill, the Liberal candidate, promised to pay a certain sum to his local party organization if he were returned. He was defeated at the polls but one of his opponents was unseated on petition and the seat awarded to Hill. When asked for the promised subscription he refused on the grounds that he had been returned not by the Evesham Liberals but by a committee of the House of Commons. Such an attitude was perhaps rare and, as Ellenborough joyfully pointed out, if Lord Marcus Hill persisted in his refusal, it was all over with him at Evesham.[17] But the incident clearly brought out the distinction between the contested election and the controverted return.

Money from the central organization even if merely for prosecuting or defending specific election petitions was certainly forthcoming in this period. The more obscure question was whether there was a central fund for general electioneering uses. Little was known to the general public of such resources; even the critical account of Conservative organization and tactics that appeared in the *Edinburgh Review* in 1835 did no more than allude in vague language to the probability of finance being one of the responsibilities which the Carlton had taken over. Even inside the party there was no question of there being a party chest in which all could dip. 'I hear', said one of Herries's correspondents in 1832, 'that there is no idea of assisting any candidate with money, so Holmes tells us, and Bonham, and all who can be supposed to have means of knowledge.'[18] The same story was heard two years later. On the eve of the 1835 election, Rosslyn told Lord Melville that there would be no fund for electioneering expenses. 'I am sorry to hear it', wrote Melville in reply, 'not with reference to Leith or even to Scotland generally — but to England, where I am quite sure it will be wanted. I am not aware that such a fund will be of any avail or will be required in Scotland; I think we get on very well without it, or at any rate, with local subscriptions where necessary.'[19] In 1837 Lyndhurst wrote tentatively to Bonham to say that Smythe had informed him that he had been put to such continual expense in politics that he would be unable to stand without some pecuniary assistance. 'Can it', asked Lyndhurst, 'be obtained?'[20] Or again, in connexion with a by-election in January 1840, the Newark Conservative Association sent in an application for financial assistance to the Carlton Club which was refused in such uncompromising terms that it evoked the suggestion from the disappointed constituency that such a central fund for assisting Conservative candidates should be started.[21]

Yet for all the lack of public comment, and despite the private complaints, a central electioneering fund did exist. It may not have been present in 1832 but there was certainly one in the general elections of 1835, 1837 and 1847; and there can be little doubt that one existed for the 1841 election. Rosslyn's statement to Lord Melville seems, to say the least, to have been misleading or else misunderstood. There may not have been a central fund to which all members could indiscriminately apply for help, but there was a sum of money administered by the party managers for election purposes and in 1835 Rosslyn himself was one of the principal executors of the fund. A good deal of secrecy surrounded this aspect of the party organization and probably only a small number of men knew of its existence. The actual amount moreover was probably not very great in relation to the purposes for which it was to be applied. No party could undertake to assist, still less maintain, candidates in every contested constituency and secrecy was the necessary safeguard of small resources. To advertise the existence of such a fund without the means to satisfy the demands which would inevitably follow would merely provoke disappointments, jealousies, and suspicions that would injure the party more than the money would assist. The fund was raised by subscriptions from the wealthier members of the party, though sometimes there might be a surplus left over from previous occasions. A note of the 1837 election fund is preserved among the Hardinge papers which is no doubt characteristic of the general procedure. Almost all the subscribers noted were peers and their contributions totalled nearly £7,000. The Duke of Newcastle headed the list with £2,000; the Duke of Wellington and Lord Lonsdale each gave £1,000; and among the other donors were the Earl of Ripon (£100), Lord Brownlow (£300), Earl Howe (£300) and Lord Ashley (£10). The list is not necessarily comprehensive nor are the details all clear.[22] In particular it cannot be assumed that this was the total amount raised for the election. Peel's name, for instance, does not appear, although Peel was an extremely rich man. On the other hand a general subscription list opened for the party at large would be impossible to keep secret and it may well have been customary for the bulk of the election fund subscriptions to be raised by the peers who, unlike their colleagues in the lower House, had no election contests to face.

But even if the sum of £7,000 is doubled or trebled, it is obvious that it could not meet more than an insignificant fraction of the total outlay by one side in a general election. This in itself was reason enough to keep the existence of such a fund as little known as possible. The election fund was therefore used to assist a limited number of candidates who from their personal circumstances or official position, seemed to deserve exceptional support. Some evidence is available for the distribution of subsidies from the central fund in the 1835 election. In that year the Conservatives put up Sir John Chetwode as candidate for Buckingham. After a preliminary canvass, however, Chetwode resigned, or in the language of party managers 'bolted'. Sir George Rose and another Conservative supporter then wished to bring forward another candidate, Watts, and assured their leaders that they were confident of success if they could obtain £500. They applied to Rosslyn, who seems to have been the party treasurer for this election; but he told them he could neither give nor promise them anything. Nevertheless he wrote to Peel, describing the situation and asked whether he wished to give any instructions on that matter. The question was complicated by intervention from another quarter. Simultaneously Rosslyn was approached by Lyndhurst, probably following an earlier and unsuccessful application, who informed him that nothing less than the £500 demanded would enable another Buckinghamshire candidate, Disraeli, to start for Wycombe and that if it was not forthcoming he would resign the next day. This second request on behalf of another Conservative candidate in the same county evidently embarrassed Rosslyn. Disraeli was not a candidate who possessed the confidence of the leaders but on the other hand it would be a delicate task to assist Watts and at the same time refuse to help Lyndhurst's protégé. 'There is rather more difficulty in giving money here', wrote Rosslyn in a second letter to Peel, 'than in any other place from D'Israeli's connection with this county.' There is mention too of other candidates backed by the central fund in this connexion. The following day Rosslyn reported that he had started Farrand for Peterborough upon letters from Lord Westmorland and the Duke of Wellington. But fortunately 'Mr. Farrand pays for himself and saves £500 which the Duke would have given'. As for the earlier problem, 'the Duke has authorised me to give £500 to D'Israeli besides Sir Harry Smith.[23] I have seen the Chancellor[24] and told him — I know not if it be in time'.[25]

In this election the repetition of £500 in the three instances reads like a routine subsidy and it seems clear that Peel and the Duke were trustees for the sums which Rosslyn administered. Given this kind of discreet and parsimonious handling, it is probable that a certain amount of money remained in the party chest even between elections. Some of this would go towards election petitions but it is possible that at most times between 1835 and 1847 there existed at the disposal of the leaders a small fund for extra-ordinary expenses or special grants. An example of the latter was provided by Lord Lincoln's case in 1847. The previous year his loyalty to Peel had involved him in two contested elections in rapid succession; the first in Nottinghamshire he lost, the second at Falkirk burghs he only narrowly won. At the general election of 1847 he was obliged to defend the seat at Falkirk so recently secured. This, his third contest in 18 months, cost him some £2,000. It was an expense he could ill afford in view of his early marriage and the absence of much financial support from his father; and was all the more painful to incur since it had not been anticipated that his return for Falkirk would be challenged a second time. Indeed Young the party whip had advised him to remain at Falkirk rather than accept any of the offers made to him by other constituencies. Feeling some degree of personal responsibility, therefore, the latter put the case before Peel as one justifying special financial assistance. 'The subscribed fund', he added, 'has been very little trenched upon, and you will perhaps think L's case one which deserves aid.'[26]

But not all grants from party funds concerned elections. After the party took office in 1841 there were negotiations between Fremantle and Painter, the editor of the *Church of England Review*, over the issue of a new weekly paper, to be called the *Journal of the Working Classes*, designed to appeal to the popular taste and counteract radical influence. Fremantle suggested to Peel that if he thought the paper likely to do good, they could give Painter £1,000 or £2,000 to meet its initial expenses.[27] In 1843 the chief whip passed on to Peel a proposal to lend financial assistance to a Dr Hugh who was running an anti-'Anti-Corn Law League' campaign in the industrial areas of Lancashire and Yorkshire. Peel was sceptical of Dr Hugh and his claims, and wanted no personal connexion; but he told Fremantle that if he thought some use might be made of the man, 'I make no objection to the employment of a specific sum entailing no further liaison with the Doctor'.[28] And in November 1844 Bonham was promising a sum of £30 for purposes connected with electoral registration though it is not clear in what constituency.[29]

However much the central organization endeavoured to draw together the scattered elements of the party, the main conduct of affairs in the provinces was in the hands of local men. It was inevitable that this should be so. Local knowledge, local influence, and local subscriptions, were indispensable for the work of electioneering in the distant counties and boroughs. Any attempts at central domination would have been both unpopular and unsuccessful. There was of course often direct communication between local Conservatives and the central managers. Graham, for instance, wrote in detail on the situation and prospects in the Border districts and the Lowlands of Scotland. Ellenborough kept Bonham constantly and minutely informed of Conservative activities in Gloucestershire and Worcestershire. These reports in themselves contain wide proof of the extraordinary amount of hard and thorough work done by local agents and committees. Ellenborough's letters are a case in point. The area with which they dealt was Gloucester, Evesham, Cheltenham, Stroud and Tewkesbury. For all these constituencies reports were periodically sent in containing statistics of electoral divisions, results of registration revisions, and local news bearing on the issue of elections. A Mr Lawrence was Ellenborough's agent in collecting this information and he in turn acquired his knowledge from local Conservative agents.[30] Besides sending to Bonham this mass of detail, Ellenborough also advised him on the impression made by Conservative candidates in these constituencies, any source of friction which might be removed by timely intervention from the centre, and the chances of attacking seats held by the enemy. Similarly Lord Mahon, at Bonham's request, was in the years 1838–9 sending him regular and copious reports on certain Kentish boroughs — Canterbury, Deal, Dover, Hythe and Sandwich — which included information on municipal politics and the state of the registration. These letters, like those from Graham and Ellenborough, were preserved by accident. They were set aside by Mahon himself when, as one of Peel's literary executors, he came into possession of Bonham's papers in 1855. When it is recollected that 'the greater portion' of Bonham's 'very voluminous correspondence' was burnt by Mahon 'as no longer of interest'[31] one can only speculate on the total amount of electoral information that was flowing in to Bonham in these years from the minor M.P.s, candidates, constituency agents, and local Conservative politicians who probably constituted the mass of his correspondents.

Often, however, the local politicians pursued their party warfare without reference to headquarters and with little expectation of recognition. Joseph Neeld of Chippenham was an example of the active, independent, provincial politician. After the general election of 1837 Granville Somerset took the unusual step of drawing Peel's attention to Neeld's services, both by way of personal effort and financial contribution, in the recently concluded Wiltshire elections. As on the previous occasion he had returned himself and Boldero as Members for Chippenham and put his brother at the top of the poll for Cricklade. Not content with this he had by his own exertions 'lugged in Goddard' as the second Member for Cricklade, thus keeping out Lord Suffolk's son; and had been instrumental in bringing in Burdett and Long for the northern division of the county. His activities at previous elections and registrations had been the main reason for the overwhelming success of the Conservatives in north Wiltshire; and Granville Somerset suggested that a letter of appreciation from Peel would give him considerable pleasure.[32] The work of such men as these, mainly unrecorded and forgotten, was at the root of the party's strength in the provinces.

Even before 1834 a variety of local organizations existed to supplement the work of individual politicians. The Reform Bill excitement stimulated the formation of innumerable clubs and associations; and if the reformers took the lead in organizing the mass of the people, the opposition did not disdain to copy their methods. Such Tory associations as the *Conservative Operative Society* at Bristol or the *Union* at Hertford, both founded in 1832, or the *Constitutional Pruning Society* at Lewes, and the *Orange and Purple Club* at Norwich, all dated from the period of the Reform Bill. Often these clubs were set up by individual efforts; by the borough magnate, the sitting Member, or the opposition agent. Few of them perhaps represented much more than the intensely local fight of colours and factions within each constituency. Of rather more elevated description were the various local registration societies to which the Reform Act gave birth. These, as their title indicates, were simply designed to support party interests at the annual revision courts. Their work in consequence was largely confined to raising money for that purpose from local subscribers and feeing local solicitors and agents. Often the main burden of expense fell upon the candidate or chief electoral magnates and for the most part their membership was not very large. At one remove further may be counted the Orange Lodges which under the energetic leadership of Colonel William Fairman took on some electoral importance between 1832 and 1835. There were nearly 300 lodges in England and Scotland and the whole tone of the Society was violently political and partisan. The movement was the more significant since the centres of Orange activity in Great Britain were Lancashire, Yorkshire, the Midlands, and the west of Scotland — districts not otherwise favourable ground for Conservative opinions. It was perhaps not entirely coincidental that the spread of Conservative operative societies a few years later was most clearly marked in the industrial areas where the Orange lodges had flourished.

For a while at any rate the Orange Society acted as some kind of link between political Toryism and the lower classes in the industrial North; and might have been developed as a useful electoral adjunct had not the movement been cut short by the parliamentary inquiry of 1835.[33]

The development which finally organized and consolidated Conservative feeling in the country in direct support of the party's electoral efforts was of course the formation of Conservative Associations in the constituencies. Here, as in other aspects of the party reconstruction, the starting point is not so much 1831–2 as 1834–5. It was the unexpected stimulus provided by the emergence of a Conservative ministry in 1834, after only two years of the reformed system, that really started the work of reorganization within the party. The central managers, in office and fighting for a majority; the local Conservatives, snatching at the royal-sent opportunity of recovering their ascendancy, all laboured with a common zeal. Though they did not succeed in winning the election, because so much had previously been left undone, yet what they achieved gave a certain promise of success in the future. 'Then', wrote Bonham a few months after the 1835 general election, 'we had to find candidates, organisers and friends in almost every place. *Now that work is done*, and a tenth part of the exertions then applied would at least preserve if not increase our present strength.'[34] The influence of the new and invigorated party machinery was clearly visible in the election campaigns of 1837 and 1841. In the general election of 1837 Granville Somerset reported to Peel that the party had candidates for every important constituency in England except Stroud and that in the whole of the United Kingdom they had put forward 445 candidates with the probability of more to come. In 1835 the number of candidates had probably been less than 390. As the number of sitting Members in 1834 had been less than 180, and in 1837 about 310, there was every reason to hope that this great army of candidates would secure a proportionate number of victories.[35] In the general election of 1841 the party's effort reached its peak with almost 500 candidates put into the field.

The factor which more perhaps than any other made possible this deployment of party strength was the organization of local Conservative Associations throughout the constituencies of the kingdom. In many of them Tory clubs under various names had existed earlier. In a few, actual Conservative Associations had come into existence even before Peel's Hundred Days. At Newark one had been established as early as 1831 to preserve the long-standing electoral influence of the Duke of Newcastle. Some such support certainly seemed advisable. At the general election of that year, in the political excitement that followed Grey's dissolution of Parliament, all eight seats in Nottinghamshire had been captured by the reformers, the duke's own particular borough of Newark, to his great aggravation, for the second time. The new Newark Association, however, was not a very active body and was apparently content to leave the electoral initiative in the hands of its ducal patron. Its role was ancillary rather than that of a principal.[36] In Canning's old constituency of Liverpool, where the electors had heard so often his Tory views on reform and the constitution, a Conservative Association had been founded in August 1832. This, by a rare inversion of events, preceded by three years the formation of a Conservative Registration Association. It owed its precocious appearance to the need felt in Tory circles for some counterpoise to the two existing Liberal reform organizations in the borough.[37] Lord Londonderry's Durham Conservative Association of 1833, of which he was vastly proud, was claimed by him as the first county association of its kind. Its activities, especially through its registration committee, certainly had a heartening effect on the party's fortunes in County Durham. Like the Duke of Newcastle, however, Lord Londonderry was something of a political liability. Unlike its counterpart in Newark, the Durham Association owed its continuing existence partly at least to the desire of the county aristocracy to have some check on his autocratic influence.[38] The evidence suggests that these early examples of Conservative Associations were isolated phenomena born of unusual local circumstances.

It was the period from November 1834 to April 1835, that is to say, the period of Peel's first ministry, which witnessed the first national mobilization of Conservative feeling in the provinces. The South Lancashire Conservative Association dated from November 1834. In December was founded the Birmingham Conservative Union under the presidency of the Earl of Dartmouth when a Conservative candidate was put up to oppose the radicals. In March 1835 the Westminster Association was started, with a subscription of one guinea *p.a.* and a substructure of committees, to promote the election of a Conservative Member. April 1835, which saw among others, the formation of associations in Staffordshire, Denbighshire and Hampshire, was perhaps the most fruitful month of all. On 23 April *The Times* printed on its leader page an extract from the *Liverpool Standard* exhorting its readers to 'become a member of the Conservative Association formed in his own immediate vicinity'.

It is with no small degree of pleasure [continued the *Standard*] we perceive that these valuable and important institutions are spreading far and wide, taking for their model the principle on which the South Lancashire Conservative Association has been established.

During the next few years the number of associations continued to grow. The first (South) Buckinghamshire Association, for example, in a county which by 1837 could boast no less than three, was founded in June 1835. The South Lincolnshire Association, and the Glamorganshire Constitutional and Conservative Society, in 1836; the borough associations in Banbury, Buckingham and Reading, and the Berkshire county association, in 1837. By that date the movement had already assumed national proportions.

A pamphlet published that year, entitled 'Thoughts on the State and Prospects of Conservatism', by an author who concealed his identity under the initials R.S.S., declared that 'at this moment there is scarcely a county in England which cannot boast of its Conservative association of gentry'.[39] The new organizations, however, were not confined to the aristocracy. They were to be found in industrial towns such as Coventry, Halifax, Preston and Warrington, as well as in more old-fashioned boroughs like Thirsk, Lewes, Ripon, Winchester, Cambridge and Canterbury. In the sprawling metropolitan area associations were founded in the separate constituencies, as for example, Lambeth and Tower Hamlets; and even such small, outlying suburbs as Hackney and Croydon started their own associations. It is difficult even to guess at the total number of Conservative Associations founded in this decade. In all probability many of the smaller societies have left little trace of their existence other than stray references in local newspapers. The Conservative disruption of 1846, the competition of Protectionist societies, and the somnolence that overcame British party politics between 1856 and 1865 were all powerful dissolvents of conventional local party organizations. Both small and large associations proved vulnerable in the changed circumstances of the middle of the century. The South Lincolnshire Association, for instance, completely disappeared and its role was taken over by a system of private subscriptions; not until 1880 was it revived.[40] The county of Buckinghamshire, which yielded to none in the militancy of its Conservative politics in the 1830s, saw a total collapse of constituency party effort in the following decade. The Bucks. Conservative Club, founded in the autumn of 1841, was in the nature of a despairing effort. It is doubtful whether it ever attracted much support or collected many subscriptions; and it seems not to have lasted even to the following general election. 'The 1840s', writes Professor Davis, the historian of Buckinghamshire politics, 'saw the end of any enduring political organizations in either the boroughs or the county for at least twenty years.'[41] It is true that the Buckinghamshire collapse was intimately connected with the financial disasters which overtook the second Duke of Buckingham, the Lord Chandos of Reform Act fame. But finance was a perennial problem for all associations and the Buckinghamshire society was not the only one to depend heavily on one or two wealthy magnates. The known disappearance of some, and the presumed disappearance of many others of these early associations, make any inferences drawn from statistics of Conservative Associations a generation later of little value.[42]

What is clear is that well before the general election of 1841 the party possessed a widespread if loose connexion of local organizations throughout England. Less headway seems to have been made in Wales and Scotland, though even in those more distant parts of the kingdom there were imitations of the English models. Moreover, the new associations were not confined to the areas of traditional Tory influence. Indeed, some of their strongholds did without these newfangled devices. In North Lincolnshire, where the two parties divided the seats from 1832 to 1846, there was no Conservative Association until after the second Reform Act; but this did not prevent the Protectionists from capturing both seats in 1847 and 1852. In Dorset the Conservatives held two of the three seats from 1832 to 1841 and all three from 1841 to 1857. Yet Dorset had no Conservative Association until the 1880s, nor, from 1832 to 1857, did it witness a contested election. It was in more demanding situations that the value of a constituency association was most keenly appreciated. After 1835 there must have been many Darlfords that 'had now a Conservative Association, with a banker for its chairman, and a brewer for its vice-president, and four sharp lawyers nibbing their pens, noting their memorandum-books, and assuring their neighbours, with a consoling and complacent air, that "Property must tell in the long run"'.[43]

A parallel, if more localized development, was the growth of Conservative Operative and Tradesmen's Societies, to which *The Times* was giving publicity and support in the autumn of 1836. These organizations, designed as lower-grade auxiliaries to the main Conservative Associations, were particularly prominent in Lancashire, the West Riding, and the Midlands. The Leeds Operative Society, claimed as the first of its kind, was started in March 1835 in support of Conservatism, the Peel ministry, and the local Conservative M.P., Sir John Beckett. Another was formed in Liverpool and furnished the occasion for *The Times*'s encouraging notice in October 1836. But more was happening in the industrial areas of the North than was known to the metropolitan journalists. An indignant Conservative wrote up a few days later to point out that so far from setting an example, Liverpool was merely following in the wake of Bolton, where three months previously a Conservative Operative dinner had been given to 600 operatives and gentlemen.[44] Operative Societies, however, were not confined to the Midlands and the north-western industrial districts; nor did they only emerge after 1835. At Bristol there was a Conservative Operatives Association as early as 1832. It was started by a group of wealthy citizens, including some half-dozen members of the predominantly Tory corporation, and its ostensibly charitable expenditure seems to have been no more than a cloak for a system of electoral rewards.[45] In many towns the new Operative Societies were clearly continuations of older political clubs and even in their new form must often have retained something of their pre-Reform characteristics of benevolent and entertainment clubs for the lower classes of the electorate. Yet it would be a mistake either to dismiss all these societies as no more than vehicles for electoral bribery or to draw no distinction between operatives' and tradesmen's organizations. At Liverpool, where the Tories appear to have been better than their Liberal opponents at mobilizing middle-class support and more generous in admitting tradesmen to seats on the council, the Tradesmen's Conservative Association (founded in 1836) had as its first chairman Samuel Holmes, a master-builder and railway contractor who became an important figure on the town council. The impetus here was provided not so much by the Reform Act of 1832 as by the Municipal Corporations Act of 1835. With a middle-class electorate in a position of dominance in local politics, it made good political sense to bring this new and influential class of voter into the old alliance of wealthy merchants and poorer, venal voters that had characterized Liverpool politics in the past.[46] Together, Operative Societies and Tradesmen's Associations represented a significant widening of the party's social base and had a direct electoral value in both local and national politics. The author of the 1837 pamphlet was sufficiently persuaded of their numbers and usefulness to suggest that while county registration could be supervised by the local Conservative Associations, the work of registering supporters and eliminating opponents in the boroughs could be undertaken by the Tradesmen's and Operative Societies.

In this remarkable growth of the Conservative provincial organization, often in politically unpromising circumstances, immediate electoral success was not always to be achieved. Yet even where a Conservative Association saw its newly fledged candidate at the foot of the polls, it had the satisfaction of knowing that a nucleus of strength had been created from which sooner or later important results might emerge. Their opponents at least were impressed by these Conservative activities and paid them the sincerest of all tributes by imitating them. It was a mark of the resilience and vigour of Conservative feeling in the country that these associations spread so rapidly. For there is no evidence that the leaders of the party took any initiative in proposing or encouraging them. Once started, they spread by a process of spontaneous emulation. Indeed, writing only six years later, R.C. Scarlett, the son of Wellington's Attorney-General, attributed the real authorship of the Conservative Associations to the comparatively unknown figure of Beckwith, the town clerk of Norwich, who was an active party organizer in Norfolk and Suffolk during the '30s.[47]

> His popularity at Norwich . . . enabled him to found a conservative club at Norwich under the name of the Orange and Purple Club at the time of the Reform Bill and this club may fairly be said to have been the origin of all the rest, since it was at the suggestion of Mr. Beckwith that in 1835 I had the honour of proposing at a dinner given after the elections to Sir Thos. Cochrane at Westminster the general adoption of those societies, a proposition which was followed by the immediate adoption of one in Westminster and afterwards throughout the country.

This credit is doubtful since some Conservative Associations had certainly been formed before the dinner at which Scarlett made his suggestion. Nevertheless, the fact that in writing to the chief whip of the party Scarlett could put forward such a claim argues at least that the establishment of the associations was not due to any deliberate policy on the part of the leaders.

Apart from the general stimulus to Conservative party spirit in the provinces, the main function of these associations was to attend to that novelty which the Reform Act had presented to the nation, the list of registered voters and its annual revision in the barristers' courts. It was their task to organize Conservatively-minded electors, to defend their franchise against attack, place new adherents on the rolls, and disqualify as many of their opponents as the revising barrister would allow. In this never-ending work even the smallest contribution was of value. Thus the Croydon Conservative Association in the autumn of 1836 could proudly publish its balance-sheet for the year.[48]

Conservative claims sent in by the Association	46	
Conservative names struck off	20	
Increase of Conservatives		26
Radical claims sent in by the Reform Club	23	
Radical names struck off the list	27	
		− 4
Total increase of Conservatives on the list for Croydon parish only		30

This primary electoral activity led on the one side to various devices for assembling supporters and raising subscriptions and on the other to frequent contact with the central organization of the party for advice, information and candidates. But the fundamental feature was registration. In any constituency where the parties were at all evenly matched, management of the register was imperative. In itself it might not bring victory; but without it a candidate might have lost the seat before canvassing was begun or the writ issued. And since no one could be sure, least of all in the '30s, when the next general election would come, unremitting attention was required.

Moreover registration was a matter of local tactics that could only be effectively conducted by local men. The annual battle in the courts demanded knowledge of local conditions, much preparation, and the ability to meet a recurrent and sometimes heavy expense. The central organization could be of little assistance here. There was, at one point, in the general enthusiasm for organization which seemed to possess the Conservatives at this period, a vague and completely unofficial attempt to control or at least finance registration through a committee of the Carlton. Those with experience of such work would have nothing to do with it but one of the promoters was, characteristically, Disraeli. It was perhaps another small item in the general score of distrust which he seems to have run up with the party authorities at this time.

Perhaps you may have heard [wrote Bonham to Peel in 1838] that some more zealous than wise friends of ours, Lords Strangford, Exmouth, de Lisle, Bob Scarlett, D'Israeli, *cum multis aliis*, and two or three attornies formed themselves into what they called a 'Registration Committee' to *manage* the Registration of the Empire ! ! ! and they collected a certain number of five pound subscriptions. On writing to me at Brighton to join and aid them personally, I pointed out the inefficiency and utter absurdity of such a plan, and unless they collected a sum that would enable them to fee all the hungry registration Tories and retainers, who most certainly claim their assistance, the mischief that might result from the attempt. However, they persisted, and as I hear that the Committee is dissolved, they probably have satisfied themselves that my advice was good.

The triple exclamation mark alone was enough to indicate Bonham's opinion of this plan.[49]

Certainly £5 subscriptions would need to come in remarkable numbers for any central assistance in the work of registration to be effective. As it was, local associations felt the expense keenly enough and were often obliged to fall back on the long purse of a local magnate or wealthy candidate. At Cheltenham, for example, the Conservative club, which had been extraordinarily active at the registrations (in 1838 they expunged 170 Liberal and added 101 Conservative voters), was by 1840 between £200 and £300 in debt. In such circumstances they could justifiably look forward to assistance from the Conservative candidate who was to benefit from their labour and expense.[50] In East Cumberland the Conservative Association decided at the end of 1839 to prepare for a contest in the hope of getting at least a compromise that would give them one seat. But the burden of expense here seems to have fallen mainly on Sir Charles Musgrave, the high sheriff, who was ready with money to start some local county gentleman as candidate, and on Sir James Graham, the president of the Association, who undertook to bear the cost of the canvass and poll in his district.[51] Where so much was done through local relationships and local efforts, it was clearly impossible to set up any form of extensive control.

A good case-study is provided by the Staffordshire Association on which an unusual amount of information is available, partly from Mr Kent's researches, partly from the printed diary of General Dyott, Peel's friend and neighbour.[52] It was founded after the general election of 1835 at a time when all four county seats were held by the Liberals. The first general meeting took place on 9 April, the day after Peel's resignation. Political inducements for action were therefore not lacking. It being quarter sessions day a good number of gentry and aristocracy were present, headed by Lords Talbot and Dartmouth. At the meeting a president and two vice-presidents were chosen, together with a committee of 24; the annual subscription was fixed at not less than 5s. or more than £2. Electoral registration was recognized as the most urgent task but at the general meeting the following January it was clear that much remained to be done. From the start the southern division showed greater activity and initiative, winning a by-election in 1835 and perfecting its organization over the whole area. But though the southern

Conservatives retained their seat at the general election of 1837, it was at the expense of a hard-fought contest which ran them deeply into debt. At the election of 1841 there was a peaceful division of the two seats between the parties, an economical practice which persisted for several more elections. The northern division was slower to get under way. For some time it lacked both a secretary and a candidate and it was not until the autumn of 1836 that a start was made in supplying the first of these deficiencies. Old General Dyott remarked, in words where sense triumphed over syntax, that 'it is grievous to observe the want of energy that ought to prevail, unless the Radicals are to ride triumphant'. The early enthusiasm certainly seemed to have waned. In April 1837 Dyott attended an Association meeting where there were present only himself, two other members, the secretary and the treasurer. His disappointment was not sweetened by the secretary's list of complaints and his emphasis on the need to pay agents for their services. The summer meeting that year was better attended though it had to spend most of its time on straightening out the society's tangled finances rather than on preparations for the dissolution of Parliament which the King's death a few days earlier had made inevitable.

The lack of long-term planning was doubly irksome to General Dyott since it was probably a partial cause of his son's narrow defeat in the southern division in the following August. In the northern division Baring's return at the top of the poll, more than 1,000 votes ahead of his nearest Liberal opponent, showed the potential strength of the Conservative vote, even though his nomination was a last-minute decision following his defeat at Stafford borough. After this slow start, the situation in the northern division steadily improved. A great Conservative Association dinner was held in November 1838 at which it was announced that there was a Conservative majority of over 1,000 votes on the new register for the division. The dinner itself became an annual event; the district committees seemed to be meeting regularly from 1839 on; and in 1840 the general committee of the northern division recommended the adoption of Charles Adderley as prospective candidate in place of Baring who had announced his wish to retire. In the end the efforts of the previous six years had their reward in the return of two Conservatives for the northern division at the general election of 1841. Perhaps most associations suffered from the inefficiencies and inexperience which vexed the soldierly mind of General Dyott. But shortcomings of this nature were not the monopoly of one side; and any organization is apt to look less impressive from within than from without. However wasteful and amateurish these early associations may have been, the cumulative effect over the country as a whole must have been considerable.[53]

The real significance of the growth of the local associations was that they tended to transfer the parliamentary party rivalry into the ordinary framework of social and political relationships in the provinces. Local feeling was not subordinated at one stroke to central control; such a revolution was out of the question. But a measure of local organization had been introduced which would have the effect of approximating the constituencies more and more to the outlook of the central parties at Westminster. No doubt divisions on the old party lines of Whig and Tory already existed in some counties to a marked degree. But the emergence of local party associations necessarily had the effect of hardening these divisions and making them more embracing. Charles Wynn distrusted the new Conservative Associations precisely on that account.[54]

> I much dislike all Political Associations, [he wrote in perplexity to Peel in April 1835] as I consider them always liable to be perverted from their original object and tending to produce irritation and reaction, and usually to check the exercise of individual judgement and opinion. At the same time I see our friends promoting them all over the country and there is frequently utility in acquiescing in what one cannot prevent. The circumstances of the present time also in some degree justify it.

But Wynn came of an old-fashioned family in a county, Denbighshire, where local feeling had more than once overridden party connexion. His attitude may not have been unique but it was certainly rare. The Denbighshires and the Cornwalls were counties on the fringe of England and hardly representative of the mass of the country. And even they were not unaffected by the general movement of consolidation. It had been the formation of a Conservative Association in Denbighshire that had been the occasion of Wynn's letter in the first instance. The old county feeling that sent a man up to Westminster to represent his neighbours and his neighbourhood rather than any party or programme had not yet disappeared; but it was at least weakening. The rapid growth of Conservative Associations in the constituencies was at once a proof of the decline of that feeling and an important strengthening of the parliamentary party. Certainly Peel was right at his election victory dinner at Tamworth in July 1841 to pay tribute to the work of the thousands of 'unobtrusive individuals' up and down the country who (he added) had exerted themselves in the cause of the party more energetically than candidates themselves had been accustomed to in an earlier era.

Notes

1. [B.L.,] Add. MS. 40617, f. 4.
2. Scottish R.O., Clerk Papers, Peel to Clerk, 27 Dec. 1832.
3. Add. MS. 40405, f. 28.
4. Add. MS. 40420, f. 126.
5. Add. MS. 40409, ff. 168–9; 40314, ff. 9, 177. In the 1837 election Shaw told the party headquarters that he could guarantee 36 Irish Members, a figure of which Bonham was inclined to be sceptical (Add. MS. 40424, f. 42). But in the event Shaw was only two out in his calculations, 34 Conservative M.P.s being returned.
6. Add. MS. 40424, f. 82.
7. Add. MS. 40314, f. 182; J.K. Buckley, *Joseph Parkes of Birmingham* (1926), p. 175.
8. The section which follows is an expansion of the short note on party funds which forms Appendix C of my *Politics in the Age of Peel* (1953, 2nd edn., 1977).

[9]   Add. MS. 40423, f. 351.
[10] W.F. Monypenny and G.E. Buckle, *Life of Disraeli* (6 vols., 1910–20), I, 281.
[11] Add. MS. 40617, f. 218; E. Hodder, *Life of the Seventh Earl of Shaftesbury* (1890), p. 341.
[12] Add. MS. 40314, f. 177.
[13] Add. MS. 40476, ff. 298–301.
[14] W.J. Fitzpatrick, *Correspondence of D. O'Connell* (2 vols., 1888), I, 525; II, 6, 13, 29–35.
[15] Add. MS. 40616, f. 168.
[16] *Dyott's Diary 1781–1845*, ed. R.W. Jeffery (2 vols., 1907), II, 347–9, 354–6.
[17] Add. MS. 40617, ff. 50–2.
[18] E. Herries, *Memoir of J.C. Herries* (2 vols., 1880), II, 162.
[19] Add. MS. 40405, ff. 30–2.
[20] Add. MS. 40617, f. 45.
[21] Add. MS. 40427, f. 259.
[22] I owe this reference to the kindness of Mr Michael Brock.
[23] Presumably Sir George Henry Smyth, Bt, of Beerchurch Hall, Essex, who was returned as Conservative M.P. for Colchester in this general election.
[24] Lord Lyndhurst.
[25] Add. MS. 40409, ff. 114–15, 146–7.
[26] Add. MS. 40599, f. 217.
[27] Add. MS. 40476, ff. 70–3. Extracts from this correspondence are printed in A. Aspinall, *Politics and the Press c.1780–1850* (1949), App., p.409. The *Journal of the Working Classes* duly appeared in 1842 but failed to outlive the year of its birth. After 15 numbers it ceased publication.
[28] Add. MS. 40476, ff. 290–5.
[29] Add. MS. 40617, f. 188.
[30] E.g. Add. MS. 40617, f. 50.
[31] Stanhope MSS. (Chevening, now deposited in the Kent Archives Office), note by Earl Stanhope, July 1863. I am indebted to Dr Aubrey Newman for bringing this correspondence to my notice.
[32] Add. MS. 40424, f. 82.
[33] For the history of the Fairman movement see H.C.605 (1835). XVII (Orange Institutions in Great Britain and the Colonies); and R.B. O'Brien, *Life of Thomas Drummond* (1889), pp. 133–95. Fairman at any rate was keenly aware of the electoral value of the Orange organization and endeavoured to establish a close connexion between it and the official Conservative Party. His *Appeal to the Conservatives of England* urged them to join a society which could 'enable men possessing wealth and patronage in their command to distinguish the true supporters of constitutional principles and to reward merit and honesty'. Another manifesto, the *Address to Members of the Carlton Club and the Conservatives of England*, composed in the summer of 1834, argued that 'a large portion of the community must be bound in union for the support of the institutions of the country' and pointed out that there could be found no 'better means for securing so desirable a result at any election . . . than the co-operation of Orangemen': H.C.605, pp. 93–100, 117 (1835). XVII, 289–96, 313.
[34] Add. MS. 40420, f. 126.
[35] Add. MS. 40423, f. 346.
[36] R. Stewart, *The Foundation of the Conservative Party 1830–1867* (1978), pp. 130–1. Mr Stewart's book, which appeared after this article was originally written, contains the fullest account of the early Conservative Associations. I have revised this part of my article to take into account his work and that of a number of other recent historians bearing on the subject. For the extra-parliamentary organization of the Conservative Party in this period see generally Mr Stewart's valuable Chapter 7.
[37] D. Fraser, *Urban Politics in Victorian England* (Leicester, 1976), p. 190.
[38] T.J. Nossiter, *Influence, Opinion and Political Idioms in Reformed England: Case Studies from the North East 1832–74* (Hassocks, 1975), pp. 29–31, 64.
[39] *The Times*, 11 Aug. 1837.
[40] R.J. Olney, *Lincolnshire Politics 1832–1885* (Oxford, 1973), pp. 102, 160, 201.
[41] R.W. Davis, *Political Change and Continuity 1760–1885: A Buckinghamshire Study* (Newton Abbot, 1976), p. 142.

[42]   In 1874 only 44 of the 82 English county constituencies had Conservative Associations (Stewart, *Foundation of Conservative Party*, p. 131).

[43]   B. Disraeli, *Coningsby*, Bk. IV, Chapter V. See also R.L. Hill, *Toryism and the People 1832–1846* (1929), pp. 43 *et seq.*

[44]   *The Times*, 1 Nov. 1836.

[45]   G. Bush, *Bristol and its Municipal Government 1820–51* (Bristol Rec. Soc. XXIX, 1976), p. 39.

[46]   B.D. White, *History of the Corporation of Liverpool 1835–1914* (Liverpool, 1951), pp. 28, 86–9; Fraser, *Urban Politics*, pp. 161, 190.

[47]   Scottish R.O., Clerk Papers, Scarlett to Fremantle, 6 Oct. 1841.

[48]   *The Times*, 29 Oct. 1836.

[49]   Add. MS. 40424, f. 277.

[50]   Add. MS. 40617, ff. 50–2, 94.

[51]   Add. MS. 40616, f. 133.

[52]   G.B. Kent, 'The Beginnings of Party Political Organization in Staffordshire 1832–41', *North Staffordshire Journal of Field Studies*, I (1961), 86–100, and his unpublished M.A. thesis 'Party Politics in Staffordshire 1830–1841' (Birmingham, 1968); *Dyott's Diary*, II, 196–349.

[53]   See *Edinburgh Review*, LXII, 167, 'Tory and Reform Associations'.

[54]   Add. MS. 40420, f. 74.

Parliamentary History, Volume 2 (1983)

GLADSTONE, LAND AND SOCIAL RECONSTRUCTION IN IRELAND 1881–1887[*]

ALLEN WARREN

University of York

In April 1881, as the protracted Cabinet discussion on Irish land came to an end and as the Liberal government prepared to introduce its legislation, Gladstone, around whom the mass of Cabinet papers had circulated, made two complementary, if perplexing, remarks. In the first he claimed the honour of being the second most conservative land reformer in the Cabinet after the Duke of Argyll, and in the second that he remained as opposed to the principles of the 'Three Fs' as he had been in 1870.[1] Yet, paradoxically, the second Irish Land Act has been regarded as one of Gladstone's greatest personal achievements, outraging the ideas of his age, and as providing a link between the reforms of land tenure and the later creation of a peasant proprietorship.[2] Indeed, Gladstone also came to regard his second Land Act as a central element in his attempts to grapple with the distinctiveness of Ireland. Five years after its passing in the autumn of 1886 and following the failure of the first Home Rule Bill, Gladstone could still write to Harcourt in the following terms: 'I am of course in a special position with regard to the Land Act of 1881 and I have never committed myself to reopening any of its provisions . . . No one is as bound as I am.'[3] At first sight such a remark might seem disingenuous to say the least. Gladstone had, after all, explored many other avenues of reconciliation since 1881, and the largest and latest of these, Home Rule, had been combined with a land measure which would

---

[*] The author would like to thank the Warden and Fellows of New College, Oxford, for enabling him to conduct the original research upon which this article is based and also Dr Boyd Hilton and Professor John Vincent for their comments upon it. The Librarians of the British Library and the University of Birmingham kindly allowed him to consult the Gladstone and Chamberlain collections in their keeping. The late Viscount Harcourt, the late Earl Spencer and the late Marquess of Aberdeen and Temair, Sir William Gladstone, Bt, and Mrs V. Rowe also gave permission to consult manuscripts in their keeping and to quote from them.

have totally altered the pattern of social and economic relationships in the Irish countryside.

Such obvious ambiguities in Gladstone's attitude and behaviour may legitimately lead the historian to claim that little sense can be made of such remarks outside their immediate political context. As a result he is inexorably drawn into the hot-house world of high politics and the 'governing passion'. Such an approach has created in this period an historiographical rain forest through which the Gladstone scholar travels at his peril. The work of Andrew Jones, A.B. Cooke, John Vincent and others, so thorough as to source material, so discriminating as to the nuances of political action and motivation, warns off those who still think that some connexion might be established between Gladstone's political and moral worlds.[4] Even so, the attempt should be made because, like Andrew Jones, I think that governing is about the use of words (in part at least) and that it is possible for the language of political behaviour to be the way to an understanding of intention, perspective and explanation in the political world.[5] This article is therefore an attempt to see whether any coherent pattern of attitudes can be discerned in Gladstone's approach to the Irish land question in the 1880s, something which may also cast some light on the wider ambiguities and tensions inherent in the Anglo-Irish relationship.

Traditionally 1868 and 1885–6 have been seen as the great flash-points in that combustible material which constituted Gladstone's Irish involvements and, in a very different sense, recent scholarship had tended to confirm this view. While it is obviously true that the political class looked forward to an uncertain future in 1884, the world of Westminster and Downing Street was not quite as unstable as an exclusive concentration on the years 1885–6 might suggest. In fact, it was not a mere accident of the struggle for power that focused political attention upon the issue of Ireland and its government during those years. Rather, in Gladstone's case at least, policy, politics and more deeply reflected preoccupations were coming together to give the Irish issue that multi-dimensional significance which was to dominate both his thinking and that of the political class for a generation. To make any real sense of this development and of Gladstone's particular contribution to it the historian needs to be aware of that complex of attitudes, opinions and actions which had constituted the Liberal government's Irish experience since 1880. This is particularly important in the case of Gladstone, whose mind moved slowly in any great matter. Once this is done, the years between 1880 and 1882 become critical, marking, through the debates over the second Irish Land Act, the reintegration of Gladstonian and Irish concerns, a dialogue which had lain dormant since the early 1870s. While the Irish question could and did acquire new dimensions throughout the 1880s — some related to immediate circumstance, others reflecting more fundamental shifts in the culture and language of politics, for Gladstone certain socio-political preoccupations, highlighted by the pressure of events between 1880 and 1882, were to re-emerge as dominant elements within his political personality.

2

What therefore was Gladstone attempting to achieve by the introduction of the 1881 Land Bill and what did he mean by remarks about his own conservatism in landed matters and his hostility to the 'Three Fs'? Before answering this question it is worth being reminded that on coming into office in 1880 Gladstone had no clearly formulated view about the agrarian situation in Ireland. While it may be true, as Dr Steele has argued, that Gladstone was both enthusiastic and advanced on land questions in 1869, this was certainly not the case in 1880.[6] He had not given any thought to Irish questions for some years, and, in so far as he had any opinion, it was that the 1870 act had provided an adequate recognition of the peculiarities of Irish land law and custom. As a consequence, when Forster, the Chief Secretary, in the summer of 1880 urged the introduction of a temporary relief measure in the form of compensation for disturbance, Gladstone was genuinely able to reassure the Duke of Argyll that he had not deviated from his firm adherence to the principles of 1870. Gladstone gave Forster his full support over the ill-fated Compensation Bill but it is clear that his mind was principally engaged in the reacquired delights of Treasury finance and the prospective repeal of the malt tax.[7]

It was, in fact, only in the late autumn of 1880 and in response to powerful letters from Forster outlining the need for substantial reform that Gladstone was to give his attention to the complexities of the crisis affecting the Irish countryside. His response was cautious and conservative. To Forster's already clearly formulated view that nothing less than the 'Three Fs' would be sufficient, Gladstone at first proposed the adoption of a scheme along the lines proposed by Mr Justice Longfield. This involved establishing a flexible procedure of compensation for eviction, through which a stability would be built into landlord–tenant relations by making it *financially* disadvantageous for either landlord or tenant to make fair rent claims which were substantially different from what the market would determine. As the evidence already being collected by the Bessborough Commission indicated, such a sophisticated mechanism would hardly meet the crude realities of the crisis. Even so, Gladstone remained sceptical about the need for land reform and was still toying with improved compensation mechanisms long after such ideas had become redundant.[8]

The winter of 1880–1, therefore, reintroduced Gladstone to the complexities of the Irish land system and, by the following spring, he recognized that the weight of the evidence and argument had moved him substantially towards the 'Three Fs', a policy which had been continuously urged by his Chief Secretary. In making these admissions Gladstone had not simply accepted a more radical scheme of reform. Throughout the discussions his own preoccupations appeared again and again, and, in a situation in which the precise nature of the Irish crisis was itself unclear, Gladstone was able to mould and shape the final legislation, so that his own basic principles should not be obviously compromised.

Above all, Gladstone was concerned to maintain what he regarded as the basis of rural society — the interdependence of landlord and tenant. The core of this relationship as Gladstone saw it lay in the right of the landlord in the last analysis to dispose of *his* property as he willed. While Gladstone recognized that circumstance had moved him closer to the ideas of Forster in the early part of 1881, he could still report his views in the following terms at the beginning of March:[9]

> I stated to the Cabinet some of what I may call 'limiting conditions' which affect my own actions; not to transfer the kernel of the property to the tenant from the landlord, to leave open the way for an eventual return to free contract as far as possible, and to reduce to a minimum the disturbance of existing relations, not compelling people to do things on the passing of the Act, but only empowering them.

As a result it was the principle of fixity of tenure that Gladstone found most difficult to swallow and, in fact, he was never to admit that the 1881 act had granted anything more than greater security of tenure.[10] This view was in striking contrast to that of the Duke of Argyll, who saw free sale as the most noxious feature of the bill, involving the compulsory and confiscatory transfer of property from landlord to tenant.[11] For Gladstone this ultimate right of disposal remained the kernel of the landed relationship, constituting the privilege of the landed proprietor from which derived the whole complex of consequent duties and obligations which combined to make an harmonious society.

It is perhaps not surprising, given Gladstone's reluctant approach to land reform, that we get only occasional glimpses of what he saw the bill as attempting to achieve. While Forster regarded it as a necessary complement to the coercive legislation as the means whereby the Land League could be destroyed through a necessary adjustment to changed agricultural conditions, Gladstone's aspirations were less explicit. Having vigorously opposed coercive legislation, he never laid down a grand strategy for the restoration of social peace and harmony in Ireland. What Gladstone did return to again and again was the need to preserve and revive this central core of the landed relationship. It was this concern that led him more easily to accept fair rents and free sale than fixity of tenure. What he was not prepared to tolerate was any flirtation with schemes of land purchase, which would have the effect of replacing both landlord and tenant by peasant proprietors, thereby abolishing that interdependent relationship. So vehemently hostile was Gladstone to extensive land purchase that he became more flexible over reforms in Irish land tenure, in part at least, to deflect the rising enthusiasm for purchase among some members of the Richmond and Bessborough Commissions.[12]

Of course Gladstone rarely expressed any opinion unambiguously, especially if questions of political management were involved — as they clearly were over the land purchase question in 1880. With Bright, Shaw Lefevre and other radicals interested in ideas of proprietorship Gladstone was only able to accept tenant purchasers if they could demonstrate qualities of independence, industry and thrift through an ability to put down a portion of the purchase price as well as pay an annuity higher than a judicially adjudicated rent. Such a class, hardly a large one in 1881, would be a valuable and responsible support for the social system. But to any purchase scheme on a substantial scale and centrally funded Gladstone remained unalterably opposed. Even here however he was able to gloss his fundamental opinion with qualifying conditions. Publicly, his opposition to purchase schemes was explained by Gladstone's view that such plans involved a totally illegitimate use of central public funds for essentially local purposes. As a result Gladstone was frequently able to declare that once local government institutions were established in Ireland his opposition to purchase schemes — administered and financed by such responsible local bodies — would be diminished. Once given local responsibility, however, Gladstone was privately confident that local communities would be equally cautious about any schemes to abolish landlordism at public expense. From the beginning of the second ministry therefore a connexion was established between the policies of land reform and the introduction of local government, as basic prerequisites in the process of stabilizing Irish society. In the context of 1881, however, when few saw local government as the immediate Irish priority, what emerged in the debates over land reform was Gladstone's determination to resist, if possible, all schemes of peasant proprietorship.[13]

If Gladstone was opposed to anything which sapped traditional landed relationships in any fundamental way, he was similarly hostile to actions which might more subversively undermine that system or prevent the restoration in the future of what he regarded as the ideal of the English pattern. Such an attitude makes one sceptical about Gladstone's grasp of the reality behind Irish conditions and it led him to some perplexing conclusions. While Gladstone could readily accept free sale, he remained implacably opposed both to the admission of leaseholders to the benefits of the bill and to the defraying of tenants' arrears. In both cases contractual considerations seem to have been crucial. The leaseholder was seen as having bound himself to the landlord in an explicit manner, different from that of the tenant at will, although often experiencing similar economic difficulties. By admitting leaseholders, Gladstone commented, 'it would be impossible to strike more directly at the very root of contract itself, as it is understood in Ireland, than to give relief in that form'.[14] Similarly arrears were contracted debts, which it was the duty of the tenant to pay off, *before* he could be admitted to the benefits of the act.[15] But perhaps most revealing of all was Gladstone's insistence on preserving the often academic distinction between present and future tenancies, thereby leaving open the possibility of a return in the future to landlord-tenant relations upon the English model. These largely scholastic distinctions perhaps make the point that in 1881 Gladstone had not accepted that Ireland in its rural relationships was other than a local and temporary variant of an English ideal.[16]

It is also clear that initially Gladstone saw the work of the Land Commission as a short-term and small-scale operation whereby social harmony might be restored and a basis for local government established. He saw the act as the means whereby an ascendancy class might be enabled and encouraged to reassert their natural social authority. Vexed and perplexed in the winter of 1880 that the landlord class seemed so feeble in controlling its own country Gladstone saw the Land Act as forcing the landlords to be free. Here Gladstone's concerns over land complemented his attitude to the restoration of law and order. Gladstone saw social and political harmony as being created in the locality through the active participation of the landlord class and he could not understand why that class was so inert in the face of the Land League agitation:[17]

> Is it really quite hopeless to expect that the community itself may do something against the Land League? Can there be no *strong* counter-association to condemn and discountenance a combination aimed at the repudiation of contracts? It is difficult to feel much admiration for those landlords whose Resolution you sent me; it would not be fair, in the circumstances, to say they only howl and whine; but surely they ought to have gone beyond the scope of mere complaint.
>
> Not all the Governments upon earth can do for a community certain things it ought to do for itself.

What Gladstone certainly did not understand in 1881 and possibly never did was that the upper class were no longer in a position to exercise that kind of authority — even assuming they had ever been so placed. While historians may now take a more tolerant view of the ascendancy after the Famine than they did formerly, it is nevertheless clear that by the 1880s their authority was being undermined by an increasingly articulate, assertive and Catholic subculture, of which Parnell was to be the first beneficiary. Gladstone's petulance about the ascendancy is perhaps some indication of the gap that was opening up across the Irish Sea in the early 1880s.

3

As the Land Bill made its slow progress through the House of Commons during the early summer of 1881 it was Gladstone, ironically enough, who gradually became its most loyal and enthusiastic supporter. Perhaps aware of how close had been the threat of a major restructuring of Irish society, Gladstone more than most began to see the bill as the basis for re-establishing social harmony. Spencer was quick to pick up this change of mood:[18]

> As to the Land Bill you will be glad to know that amidst all his worries . . . the Prime Minister turns for comfort to the Land Bill which the more it is discussed the more its perfection is proved to his mind. I do not say this sardonically, I tell you as a matter of fact.

While it is unwise to see fundamental breaks in the pattern of Gladstonian thinking about Ireland, it is nevertheless true that 1881 does mark his critical re-involvement in Irish affairs. Even though the years 1885–6 mark a more dramatic reassertion of Gladstonian authority in a political sense, the discussion over the Land Bill created a frame of reference within which most of Gladstone's later Irish attitudes developed. Similarly the years 1881–5 created that climate of administrative and governing experience within which many of the later political battles were to be fought out. Much of that experience was itself to derive from a continuing determination to make the settlement of 1881 effective. In particular it is clear that both the Kilmainham imprisonments and later negotiations in the spring of 1882 were closely linked to the establishing of an administrative and political framework within which the Land Act could operate more easily. It is some indication of the prominence which the land legislation had by then acquired in Gladstone's mind that in the autumn of 1881 he was prepared apparently to reverse totally his position on coercion, from being the Cabinet member most opposed to extraordinary legislation to that of being in total accord with his Chief Secretary. Unappreciative of the difficulties of Parnell's own position Gladstone increasingly saw the Irish leader's attitude to the land settlement as malevolent and by late September 1881 Edward Hamilton is describing his temper as having reached 'boiling point'.[19] Through the crisis over the arrest of the Irish leaders and the proclamation of the Land League Gladstone fully supported Forster within the Cabinet and reinforced that position through his speeches at Leeds and Knowsley.[20] Nor was this just the temper of the moment, as Gladstone's report to Ripon in India at the end of November makes clear:[21]

> As to Ireland we are still in conflict with the last and basest result of the *delicta majorum*: in the shape of the most immoral, most wicked assault not only on law and order but on private rights, and not only on private property, but yet more upon personal liberty, the direct offspring of the abominable teaching of Parnell and his friends. Much has been done by putting down the external and visible action of the Land League; but much more remains to be done . . . Our great object I hope has been effectually, and all but universally, secured: that is the free access of the Irish people to the Land Court, which six weeks ago appeared to be placed in the greatest jeopardy.

Despite such firm action against the Land League the land settlement was in fact already running into difficulties by the first few months of 1882. Internally it was not operating smoothly as it became clear that the arrears question could not be simply ignored and as the integrity of Healy's clause protecting the value of the tenant's improvements was undermined in the courts through judicial decisions like that in Adams *v.* Dunseath.[22] Externally the early decisions of the Land Commissioners had provoked a full-scale Tory attack upon the credibility of the act through the establishing of Lord Donoughmore's select committee.[23] More ominous still were the hints that the Tory party was putting together an alternative Irish strategy, which anticipated the *rapprochement* of 1885, and which could have very real attractions to the Parnellites themselves. By early April 1882 this Tory new departure was sufficiently far advanced as to allow both Salisbury and Stafford Northcote to make major speeches in favour of land purchase and Tory Members to put down motions in the House urging both extended purchase provision and the release of the Kilmainham prisoners. All of these developments were taking place in a parliamentary context, in which Tories and some Irish Members were already working together to resist the government's closure proposals.[24]

In such an uncertain political and administrative climate the announcement by the Irish Members of a Land Act Amendment Bill and the hints that Parnell was prepared to negotiate with the government were an enormous relief to a hard pressed Cabinet. Gladstone recognized immediately the importance of these initiatives on the part of the Parnellite Members as implying both a repudiation of the 'no rent' manifesto and outright hostility towards the Land Act and also of any idea, in the short term at least, of Irish/Tory collusion. It is true, of course, that the Irish amendments to the Land Act contained all kinds of provisions totally unacceptable to Gladstone, like the admission of the leaseholders and an extended land purchase provision. But what was important was that through introducing amendments to the act the Irish were implicitly accepting the principle of the 1881 settlement. Furthermore, the negotations through O'Shea and others quickly centred on the arrears question, a subject upon which the government in its private discussions had already decided to legislate, in order to preserve the integrity of that land settlement. Over this question the government were prepared both to bargain and concede by agreeing to finance any arrears legislation on the basis of a government gift rather than through a Treasury loan as they had originally intended. This bargain was in fact the *substance* of the Kilmainham negotiations. Everything else was left in the air and to the hoped-for improvement in the social and political climate. Questions of further land reform, the details of further coercion and of co-operation with the Parnellites themselves were all left as matters of future discussion rather than present agreement. Much was made of the so-called Kilmainham agreement both at the time and subsequently but it is clear that if anything more substantial in the way of direct concession had been explicitly involved Lord Spencer would not have been offered and certainly would not have accepted another Irish term. What Gladstone had wanted from the Kilmainham negotiations he had secured — the free working of the 1881 Land Act satisfactorily amended as to the arrears and within a parliamentary and Irish context where the decisions of the Land Commissioners were not going to be constantly harassed by obstruction in the countryside or party collusion in the Commons. Seen in this light the Phoenix Park murders tragically aided Gladstone's purposes since the Kilmainham negotiations had necessarily left much that was ambiguous. The events of 6 May on the other hand gave a brutal clarity to the situation. Coercion was now a public and political necessity as all recognized including Parnell. Arrears legislation could also now go forward freely, unencumbered by Tory remedial or diversionary tactics, since for the moment at least there could be no question of Tory/Parnellite collaboration around the issue of land purchase. Paradoxically, therefore, the Phoenix Park murders probably made it easier for the Kilmainham understanding to hold, than if it had been put immediately to the test by the government's clear intention, despite the agreement, to introduce new crimes legislation on the expiry of the Protection of Person and Property Act later in the summer.[25]

The events of April and May 1882 were, therefore, directly related to the workings of the 1881 Land Act, which remained the centrepiece of Gladstone's policy towards Ireland. Lord Spencer was now sent to Dublin, not only to break up the murder gangs, but also to provide the Irish countryside with a period of calm, during which the Land Act could have its harmonizing and stabilizing effect. His appointment, agreed before the negotiations started, indicated that, as far as Gladstone and his colleagues were concerned, the field for action had now shifted from London and Westminster to Dublin and the Irish countryside. Even so, the historian should be careful not to see the Kilmainham episode exclusively within an administrative framework. Although the negotiations did not create the kind of concordat that Chamberlain was looking for, they nevertheless brought a political dimension openly into the Parnellite/Liberal relationship for the first time. As we have already seen, Gladstone had not formulated a comprehensive strategy towards Ireland in 1881 beyond a desire to restore the integrity of the landlord-tenant relationship and had only dimly discerned the implications for the Anglo-Irish relationship of the rise of Parnell. Initially therefore Gladstone had in 1881 been prepared to go along with Forster's overriding desire to destroy the Land League. The Kilmainham negotiations had shown, however, that there could be a political dimension to the government's strategy, something which Forster was unable to accept. Although tinged with bitterness Forster's own commentary on those negotiations indicates a political sophistication no less acute than Gladstone's, even if it had led him in the direction of an aggrieved resignation:[26]

> Then came the question which is the gist of the whole matter, how far is it politic to purchase an immediate cessation of outrage and apparent pacification of Ireland by the unconditional release of suspects — the virtual revocation of Government policy. One thing to be considered, says Father, is that such a course would be a tremendous step towards Home Rule. It would be equivalent to admitting that these men are what they claim to be — but are not — the leaders and representatives of the Irish people, and that the Government releases them in order to effect maintenance of law and order. It will be open to Mr Parnell to represent the transaction in this light before the Irish people. 'I got you the Land Act — the Government shut me up for what I had done — but now finding they cannot quieten Ireland without my influence they have let me out to help amend the Land Act and pacify the country . . .'
>
> It would seem with Mr Gladstone, all his ideas concerning agitation and lawlessness in Ireland are more or less connected with opposition to the Land Act; provided the Parnellites show a disposition to use the Land Act, all danger must needs be over, and the necessity for repressive legislation ceases.
>
> The truth is, says Father, that in a great proportion of cases the crime and defiance of law have nothing to do with opposition to the Land Act as such, and therefore acceptance of the Land Act by the Land League chiefs and the people does not necessarily imply the absence of intimidation and outrage for the furtherance of Land League principles. It is none the less true that for the people

to venture to use the Land Act freely and still more for the Parnellite leaders to come forward and openly accept it (as they do by bringing forward such a Bill as Mr Healy's) shows plainly to what extent the Government has triumphed in establishing the law of the land as opposed to the law of the Land League. This has been done under a system and by methods which it is now proposed to repudiate. *Because* the policy carried out by the Chief Secretary has been so far successful that the Land League chiefs instead of breathing out defiance and contempt against the Government, and teaching the Irish people to despise the 'Parchment Law' (as they were adjured in poetry) and to 'avoid the Land Courts' (as they were exhorted in prose) — now come forward in the House to propose reasonable amendments of the Land Act, and to present themselves in the light of misunderstood politicians whose one aim is to assist the Government in making their useful legislation in Ireland still more effective — because this is the result, the logical Radical sequence is to reverse the policy and to turn out the Minister who carried it into effect.

Few of Forster's gloomy predictions were obviously apparent in the months following the Phoenix Park murders as the Government forced through its Prevention of Crimes Act. Nevertheless, the years 1882–5 are marked by a shaping of this socio-political dimension modestly introduced in 1882. In particular the experience of the Spencer administration in Ireland, coinciding as it did with the rise of the National League, highlighted for both Gladstone and his colleagues the urgent need for local government institutions in Ireland. This was, of course, no new Gladstonian concern. Principles of self-government and responsible self-dependence were central to his view of the political world and he had constantly emphasized that local institutions were the means whereby an organic and fully integrated United Kingdom could be created. He had, in fact, chosen this particular theme when speaking in Dublin in 1877 and there is no evidence of a change in principle in the years that followed. In his 1877 address, after commenting on how little had been achieved in the direction of greater local responsibility in England, Gladstone had continued:[27]

> Not only have we done nothing for the purpose, but by a system of dealing out large doles of public money we have been abridging local institutions and taking powers which were formerly local into the hands of central authorities. My Lord, in my opinion we have been moving in that sense in the wrong direction. Central control undoubtedly must accompany the grant of local money to local institutions, but instead of abridging the power of those local institutions we ought to seek to extend it, and that is the principle which in my opinion lies at the root of all sound agitation. I look, indeed, to fundamental principles which I do not believe that any one will question or deny. I am persuaded that we are at one in holding that these three kingdoms should be one nation in the face of the world — one nation for every purpose of duty and power, and that an Imperial Parliament should give effect to that principle in all things that fall legitimately within its scope, subject to those paramount and admitted principles. I, for my own part, can set no bounds to the desire that I feel to see all through these three kingdoms the people brought politically to learn in narrower spheres the public duties which belong to narrower spheres and strive to fit themselves for those higher duties which are involved in the

material work of the Government. I do not believe that anything has contributed, perhaps nothing so much contributes at this moment, to the solidity of British institutions as the fact that the people are trained politically in the habits of self-government, that they understand political rights and understand political duty, and, understanding the relations which prevail between right on the one side and duty on the other, they carry with them a talisman which is a safeguard in the main and in the long run invaluable against those dangers which have threatened and those mischiefs which have lacerated other great and distinguished nations.

If the political implications of the rise of the National League gave an urgency to the introduction of local government into Ireland so, even more emphatically, did the partial success of the Land Act. The settlement in 1881 had not been a comprehensive one in solving the problems of a diversified, depressed and regionalized economy. In fact the effects of the Land Act had been very much as many of its critics had predicted — a piece of legislation simply to reduce rents and to confirm the tenant in his holding. Non-tenurial problems such as the conditions in the crowded districts, the recurrence of famine and the deteriorating position of the agricultural labourer were largely ignored. Similarly, little thought had been given to the longer-term implications of turning the landlord into little more than a rent charger with its deterrent effect on agricultural improvement and the mobility of the land market. Basically, any problem involving finance had been ignored in 1881 as the original treatment of the arrears question had shown. These limitations did not disappear, indeed they became more prominent as the Land Act had its undoubtedly pacifying effect. In the face of public demand for relief of famine in the bankrupt unions of the far west in the winter of 1882–3 Gladstone had urged the immediate introduction of local government institutions. In that case Spencer was able to agree a more immediate remedy with the Treasury, but increasingly the Liberal administration in Dublin found itself facing a growing number of problems which required constructive solutions involving imperial finance. In areas as diverse as assistance to emigrants and labourers, housing, fishing and agricultural improvement and the development of communications, the Spencer administration was pressed by the various interest groups to take an initiative. The response was cautious but between 1882 and 1884 the modest foundations of what was later to become Balfour's policy were being laid. The lesson that Gladstone drew from such experiments was that the need for local government had become the more pressing.[28]

If the problems ignored in 1881 remained to trouble Dublin Castle so also did the alternative solutions to the land question. Whether as a direct consequence or not, it did appear that the Land Act had had the effect of freezing the land market, creating a dangerous agrarian stasis at a time when economic margins were being squeezed. In addition during 1883 it became clear that the 1881 act had not dissolved the more general desire for easier land purchase facilities. It was, of course, easy to argue, as some radicals were inclined to do, that land purchase was merely a relief policy for landlords. Unfortunately the issue was not quite so simple, given that the abolition of landlordism was an ostensible long-term aim of the National League. In addition it was clear that the purchase issue was not just a landlord fad since other radicals like Bright, Shaw Lefevre and Morley were enthusiasts for peasant purchase as but the the first step in a more general dismantling of landlord privilege throughout the United Kingdom. The purchase issue, therefore, remained both politically and administratively complex, a fact amply confirmed by the public attention given to the question by the Tory party leadership through Lord George Hamilton's parliamentary motion urging extended purchase provision in June 1883. It was becoming clear, therefore, that not only would Liberals have to face the challenge of problems left untreated in 1881, but that the basis of their own settlement, the Land Act itself, might come under threat through the demand for an extended peasant proprietorship.[29]

The response of the Liberal government and of Gladstone in particular was unambiguous. It had not altered its attitude to land purchase and peasant proprietors in any way and Gladstone remained firmly convinced that the landlord-tenant relationship was fundamental to the future well-being of the Irish countryside. It is true that Gladstone was prepared, where large-scale tenants showed evidence of reliability and thrift, to tolerate a modest encouragement of purchase through Treasury loans and thereby supply a ballast to local society. But to any extensive or generous scheme of proprietorship Gladstone was still hostile. Even so, Gladstone had to recognize that a fairly wide discussion of land purchase schemes was taking place and it highlighted the need for local government in Ireland in his mind, as it had done in the spring of 1882.

Any viable scheme of land purchase would almost certainly involve central government funding, and Gladstone was concerned, if purchase or improvement schemes were to become (albeit against his will) instruments of Irish policy, that there should be local bodies which would act as a security for the repayment of such government monies. Possibly more importantly, Gladstone also saw such purchase and improvement schemes as much from a social as from a strictly financial perspective. Land purchase, if based on central government funds, would be a direct encouragement to economic plunder by putting the beneficiary into a dangerously direct relationship to the state. It was Gladstone's view that if local institutions could be introduced then not only would a safety barrier be established between the imperial Treasury and the borrower, but a framework of local responsibility would also be created, through which foolish schemes would be discouraged and landed society preserved, while local society would be revived around traditional rights, duties and mutual responsibilities, just as he had outlined in his speech in 1877. Local government therefore, as well as being the proper way to administer purchase and improvement schemes, was also the best means through which the long-term objectives of 1881 could be best met and defended.[30]

This dialogue between a demand for increased land purchase provision and the government's wish to introduce local institutions continued until the fall of the ministry itself in June 1885, and at the same time as the political world was becoming aware of future Parnellite power. In the past the prominence given to the discussion over Chamberlain's central board scheme has tended to highlight the growth of this latter political dimension. However, well before Chamberlain floated his own devolutionary scheme the evidence suggests that it was the land question that made the introduction of local government a matter of urgency for the Liberal Cabinet. In 1883 the government had been able simply to reject Lord George Hamilton's purchase motion. During the following year the reaction was very different and Lord Spencer and his Dublin Castle colleagues found themselves forced by both Irish and domestic political pressures in London into adopting a purchase bill after months of protracted ministerial correspondence. The measure that was ultimately introduced by Trevelyan in 1884 was both complex and almost certainly unworkable, involving intricate guarantee mechanisms which bore little relation to Irish circumstance. Indeed, there is more than a hint that the government had consciously introduced an inadequate measure, and it was certainly a matter of some relief to the Cabinet when they were later able to drop their proposal in the face of the increasing parliamentary difficulties over the reform of the franchise on 10 July 1884. The purchase issue had consumed a considerable amount of Cabinet and ministerial time during early 1884 and throughout those discussions both Spencer and his principal adviser, Sir Robert Hamilton, had never retreated from the view that all such schemes should be preceded by the introduction of responsible and representative local government, something clearly out of the question until at least the franchise question had been settled.[31]

By late 1884, however, Spencer, who had for the previous two years resisted all but the most modest alterations in the strategy adopted prior to the Kilmainham negotiations, became convinced that a new initiative was necessary in Irish policy, something which the discussions over the central board scheme have tended to obscure. In the first place Spencer now thought the introduction of county government was both practicable and desirable in order to secure the pacification achieved as a result of the Land Act. Secondly such a move was also politically expedient in order to balance the fact that Spencer did not believe that all extraordinary powers could be done away with on the expiry of the Prevention of Crimes Act in mid-1885. Thirdly such local institutions were required because Spencer now understood that a land purchase measure was inevitable. Opinion in Ireland was almost unanimously in favour of such a scheme including the Land Commissioners themselves and all the various pressure groups and interests had also agreed a scheme of purchase which had been widely circulated by Lord Castletown's committee. Such united pressure could neither be argued against nor ignored as it had been in 1883 or earlier in 1884 and thus the need for local government had itself become more pressing, something on which Sir Robert Hamilton was especially insistent.[32]

The coupling therefore of land and local government — the essence of the administrative side of the crisis of 1885–6 — was present well before the 'governing passion' began in earnest and particularly in the minds of the two figures almost least involved in the scramblings for power — Spencer and Hamilton. Early in 1884 Hamilton had vehemently resisted the demand for extended land purchase in Ireland as both unnecessary and undesirable and that in relation to public finance Ireland needed to learn the lessons of self-dependence. Later in the year he made his view even more clear in a letter to Henry Fowler:[33]

> At the bottom of all real reform lies the introduction of a system of local government. This is a matter not alone of Irish but Imperial importance, and concessions made in the direction of spending more public money in Ireland as it is at present governed will only increase the difficulties of arranging matters hereafter. Short of separation, which is out of the question and which at present is only desired by a very small minority in Ireland, the fullest measure of self-government should be granted. If this is not done and done quickly we may have the bigger question of separation to combat. Under such local government mistakes would be made, but the people would be educated in self-dependence, and without this Ireland will be a constant and increasing source of trouble to successive administrations who will be attempting the impossible task of governing an educated people from outside instead of showing them and helping them to govern themselves.

How therefore did Gladstone view this reopened debate on Irish policy placed as it was within the context of the battle for the new democracy? So far this article has been trying to highlight two Gladstonian preoccupations — the centrality of the 1881 act and the importance of the introduction of local government, as the necessary culmination of the pacification effected by the Land Act and as the best defence of its social principles. These two themes remain of continuing importance through all the twists and turns of the years 1885–6, linked as they were to a changing attitude towards Parnell, the first signs of which had been visible in April 1882.

Looking across the battle ground of politics which made up the years 1885–6 Gladstone seems to demonstrate two principal concerns from September 1885 and both involved the issue of Ireland and a resumption of his own political authority. Firstly he desired to restore the 'morality' of British politics, a process involving the idea that national politics was a great moral debate conducted through firmly delineated party politics. This necessarily required both the subjection and perhaps the destruction of Chamberlain and, if possible, a revamping of the Whig household through men like Spencer and Rosebery. There is not the space in an article of this length to discuss all of Gladstone's more gloomy forebodings about the state of the nation in 1885, except to quote Gladstone's own thoughts in a letter to Argyll on 30 September 1885. Having commented on the unfavourable contrast between the Conservative Party of Peel and that of 1885 Gladstone continued:

> Why do I mention all these things? They are very bad, but their badness is not the reason. I mention them
> 1   because out of such a Conservative party you will never get conservative work, and specially
> 2   because they are the men who play directly into the hands of the extreme

wing of Liberalism. To whatever point Churchill and the boasted Tory democracy drag the Conservatives that very point supplies *a new point of departure* for what you would call the Chamberlain section. This is a slight and very imperfect indication of very important and painful topics.

I was not and am not afraid of the natural democracy (an exceedingly mild one) of the rural constituencies. But when they have been well dosed with the factious Tory democracy, and when that has had its natural fruit in a further large addition of alcohol from extreme men on our side, then it is a different affair.

There are other chapters which I have not time to open. I deeply deplore the oblivion into which public economy has fallen: the prevailing disposition to make a luxury of panics, which multitudes seem to enjoy as they would a sensational novel, or a highly seasoned cookery and the leading of both parties to socialism of which I radically disapprove. I must lastly mention among my causes of dissatisfaction the conduct of the timid and reactionary Whigs. They make it day by day more difficult to maintain that most valuable characteristic of our history which has always exhibited a good proportion of our great houses at the head of the Liberal movement.

Home Rule was therefore to become the means whereby Gladstone restored health to British politics.[34]

But Gladstone's second aim in 1885 also involved Home Rule since he saw it as the final solution to the problem, which he had been tackling since 1881 and whose full implications became only slowly clear to him, that of creating a socially integrated Ireland and establishing thereby that true union of the United Kingdom of which he had spoken in 1877. Gladstone had seen in 1882 that the political forces led by Parnell might be the instruments of social stability in Ireland and events since Phoenix Park had not changed his view. Even the Tory/Parnellite association of 1885 demonstrated not so much the opportunism of Parnell as the depraved state of the English political parties. Moreover if the Nationalist Party was going to dominate the Irish political landscape it became all the more important that it should rapidly acquire the shackles and duties of representative responsibility. By 1885 Gladstone had accepted that in political terms the Irish upper class were a spent force, although he still retained the hope that a properly devised scheme of devolution might induce the Irish minority into a proper and local concern for their own interests. But at a more basic level Gladstone was preoccupied with the problem of social relationships, because he now saw the Parnellites as allies in his social conservatism. Gladstone was now convinced that Parnellism did not necessarily imply the abolition of landlordism in Ireland, more particularly if it was the Irish themselves who had to supervise the pattern of landed relationships.

What is one to make, therefore, of the land purchase scheme that was initially associated with the first Home Rule Bill and against which Gladstone subsequently reacted because of its domestic divisiveness and unpopularity. In my view political considerations, as emphasized by Professor Vincent, only partly explain Gladstone's gyrations over the land question in 1885 and 1886.[35] In fact Gladstone remained committed to the land policy he had been pursuing since 1881 and continued to be hostile to any idea of replacing the landlord class by peasant proprietors. It was not possible, however, to be straightforwardly hostile to such ideas, just as it had not been possible in 1884. Experience had shown since 1881 that land and local government issues were inextricably intertwined. Moreover the actions of the Tory government in 1885, through the passing of the Ashbourne Act and the non-renewal of coercion had limited Gladstone's freedom of manoeuvre and confirmed him in his view of the baseness of Tory politics. Although constrained by illness and the understanding with the minority Tory government Gladstone was deeply hostile to the Ashbourne legislation, seeing it as a major breach in the 1881 settlement and as unsettling all that had been achieved since that time. Just as in 1882, when the Tory threat of pressing land purchase had forced Gladstone rapidly to construct a local government structure to contain such a threat, so the passing of the Ashbourne Act increased the need for devolution to be undertaken as a matter of urgency.[36]

Two factors remained critical, however, if Gladstone was even partly to achieve his dual aims in 1885 and 1886 of restoring principle to British politics and stability to Ireland. It was essential, in the first place, that he have the capacity to form a Home Rule ministry and secondly that such a ministry should be so composed as to be the basis for a revived and multi-faceted Liberalism. In adopting Home Rule Gladstone probably recognized that he might, thereby, exclude both Hartington and Chamberlain, and in the context of the 1885 general election such an exclusion might be positively beneficial, especially if Whiggishly inclined figures like Henry James could be retained.[37] If, however, the Liberal Party was to remain a great national party, it was essential that Home Rule should not become just a sectarian fad. As a consequence the support of two figures in particular was crucial for Gladstone if he was to succeed in establishing a credible Home Rule ministry, and these were Spencer and Morley. Spencer was critical because of his Irish experience, his disinterested and administrative approach to politics and because he demonstrated that the great Whig households could still provide authoritative, aristocratic leadership. In a more junior way Rosebery was regarded by Gladstone in the same light. Morley, on the other hand, was a vital figure because of his close connexion and now disagreement with Chamberlain. Through his support for Home Rule, Morley made it clear to the party (if it needed convincing) that it was Chamberlain and not Gladstone who was following the sectarian and divisive course. As for Gladstone himself, Morley increasingly came to demonstrate the true morality of English radicalism in person and in contrast to the factious socialism of Chamberlain. The problem was that for both of these men, Spencer and Morley, a settlement of the land question through a buying out of the landlords was a necessary prerequisite for a successfully introduced Home Rule scheme. He had little choice therefore in early 1886 but to accept that a grand land solution was a necessary concomitant of Home Rule.[38]

But it was clear that Gladstone was no enthusiast for the buying out of the landlords, and after the defeat of Home Rule he persistently maintained that the land scheme had been one of the main causes of that rejection both in the House and in the country. After the 1886 election Gladstone made strenuous efforts to uncouple the land and Home Rule issues. Now although it is true that the Land Bill was an unpopular and divisive element within Liberal policy, no doubt strengthening Gladstone's hostility to it, this political factor was not the basis of Gladstone's own opposition to the scheme. In spite of the Ashbourne Act Gladstone still fundamentally held to the land policy as laid down in 1881 and to the view that Home Rule should precede the land question. Recognizing once again the interdependence of the land and local government questions it was Gladstone's view that a traditional and harmonious society would be best maintained in Ireland not by an Ireland socially transformed and also self-governing, but by a self-governing Ireland which would then understand the logic of preserving traditional social relationships. As Gladstone commented in the middle of his travails, 'I am indeed in very rough waters, but, according to all that my poor vision can discern, it is a conservative work, adapted to restoring the tarnished honour and augmenting the strength of my country'.[39]

Therefore although the Land Bill was introduced it was never seriously proceeded with, and any idea that it was to be a comprehensive solution was abandoned when its financial provisions were halved — much to the irritation of Spencer who took a rather more radical view of Home Rule as a new departure for Irish society.[40] But perhaps most revealing of all are Gladstone's attitudes towards Irish land after 1886, which confirm the statement to Harcourt, with which this article began. In the autumn of 1886, when Parnell introduced his own Land Bill, Gladstone still opposed the admission of leaseholders to the benefits of the 1881 act. During the following year Gladstone was now able to use his commitment to Home Rule as the reason for his opposition to Conservative land proposals. His mode of argument is, *ceteris paribus*, very similar to that pattern of attitudes adopted in 1882. For Gladstone in 1887 it was the problem of arrears of rent consequent upon another fall in agricultural prices and not the need for additional purchase funds, that was critical. Secondly just as in 1882 Gladstone stated that no additional purchase funds should be made available prior to the establishing of responsible local government institutions (now expressed as Home Rule) within Ireland. Taken in isolation these arguments look like mere political posturing but put into the context of the discussions over land and society in Ireland which had taken place since 1880 they represent a consistent and remarkably resilient line in Gladstonian thinking.[41]

It is inevitable in a paper of this length that certain elements in the argument should appear excessively generalized given the extraordinary complex of ideas, politics and policy which constituted the British experience in relation to Ireland in the years following the Land War. This is particularly so in the case of Gladstone as it is not possible to separate his own thinking from wider considerations of government action and the general pattern of politics. Nor is it suggested that this article has provided a comprehensive answer to that range of interpretative problems raised by the politics of the years 1885–6. Indeed, the treatment adopted has involved a deliberate exclusiveness in order to show a continuity in Gladstone's thinking and approach in relation to Ireland, which transcended and partly moulded the politics of the 'governing passion'.

As a conclusion it may be useful to highlight some of these elements which are fundamental in any understanding of Gladstone's involvement with Ireland after 1880. Firstly, it is clear that Gladstone's mind moved slowly in any substantial matter. In relation to Ireland the 1881 Land Act was critical in two respects, in that it marked the reinvolvement of Gladstone in the affairs of Ireland for the first time since the early 1870s, and that the discussions leading up to that legislation reveal and mould a pattern of thought in Gladstone's case from which he was subsequently extremely reluctant to depart. This cluster of attitudes centred on Gladstone's determination to maintain the landlord-tenant relationship in Ireland as the foundation upon which the institutions of society and the functioning of its politics should rest.

Secondly, having been brought to accept the necessity of a 'Three Fs' policy, partly from a fear of more subversive alternatives, Gladstone became passionately attached to that settlement so that many of his later actions, including both Kilmainham and even Home Rule itself, can be related to securing its implementation and long-term objectives.

Thirdly, from 1881 at least the policy issues of land reform and local government for Ireland were closely linked and related to Gladstone's wider views about a restoration of socio-political harmony in Ireland, free from central government money and policing. As a result the introduction of local government became an urgent necessity, not only as the culmination of the government's attempts at Irish pacification, but also as the best defence of that policy. Within this policy area three interdependent processes can be discerned. Firstly, if the Land Act aimed at encouraging social harmony based on a reformed Irish land tenure, then locally devolved government was the political dimension to that social system. Secondly, as the limitations of that 1881 settlement became clear through the continuing economic problems of the west of Ireland, through the arbitrary exclusion of leaseholders, and those in arrears from the act, and particularly through a renewed enthusiasm for a larger peasant proprietorship, local government became the Liberal government's positive answer to both its critics and those articulating alternative remedies. These latter alternatives became increasingly vocal and powerful in the years after 1883 and helped to confirm Gladstone in his gloomy speculations about the state of English party politics, something which eventually required a new initiative on his part. The third process was Gladstone's own increasing understanding that Parnellism almost certainly represented a permanent geological shift in the political landscape. Dimly discerned in 1882, Gladstone had accepted this new pressure by 1885, and, although recognizing its capacity to dislocate imperial politics, also perceived its potential for long-term conservation and consolidation within the United Kingdom as a whole. Provided that Parnell and the forces he led could be kept within a framework of locally devolved institutions Gladstone felt confident both that constitutionalism could be encouraged and extremism contained by the forces of domestic Irish opinion rather than through imperial control.

Finally, while Home Rule and the crisis around devolution can be seen from many angles and clearly had different implications for the parties involved, for Gladstone it can be seen as a necessary, if not inevitable, development of a view of Irish society brought into focus by the debates over the 1881 Land Act and which remained fundamentally the same six years later.

Notes

1 [B.L.,] Add. [MS.] 44105, ff. 66–7, 86.
2 The most eloquent statement of this view is to be found in J.L. Hammond, *Gladstone and the Irish Nation* (1938; new impression 1964, with introduction by M.R.D. Foot).
3 Add. 44200, ff. 160–1.
4 For the work of the 'high politics' school of historians working in this period see particularly A.B. Cooke and J. Vincent, *The Governing Passion: Cabinet Government and Party Politics in Britain 1885–6* (Brighton, 1974); A. Jones, *The Politics of Reform 1884* (Cambridge, 1972); R. Jay, *Joseph Chamberlain: A Political Study* (Oxford, 1981); R.F. Foster, *Lord Randolph Churchill: A Political Life* (Oxford, 1981) and J. Vincent, 'Gladstone and Ireland', *Proceedings of the British Academy*, LXIII (1977).
5 A. Jones, 'Where "Governing Is the Use of Words"', *Historical Journal*, XIX (1976).
6 E.D. Steele, *Irish Land and British Politics: Tenant Right and Nationality 1865–1870* (Cambridge, 1974).
7 George Douglas, *Eighth Duke of Argyll . . . Autobiography and Memoirs*, ed. the Dowager Duchess of Argyll (2 vols., 1906), II, 349–53; Lady Frances Balfour, *Ne Obliviscaris . . .* (2 vols., 1930), I, 285–7; Add. 44544, ff. 17, 19; *The Diary of Sir Edward Walter Hamilton 1880–1885*, ed. D.W.R. Bahlman (2 vols., Oxford, 1972), I, 11–12.
8 Mr Justice Longfield, 'Land Tenure in Ireland', *Fortnightly Review*, Aug. 1880; Add. 44157, ff. 177–85; Bodl., Harcourt MSS., Forster Cabinet memorandum, 27 Dec. 1880; Add. 44126, ff. 13–20.
9 Add. 44544, ff. 141–2.
10 Hansard, [*Parl. Deb.*, 3rd ser.,] CCLXIII, 56–62.
11 Add. 44625, ff. 10–12; 44624, ff. 13–14. Also see Argyll's correspondence with Gladstone in *Argyll . . . Autobiography*, II, 356–62.
12 Add. 44158, f. 34.
13 Add. 44625, ff. 24–5; Aberdeen MSS. (the Marquess of Aberdeen and Temair, Haddo House, Aberdeenshire), Gladstone to G. Shaw Lefevre, 22 Dec. 1880.
14 Hansard, CCLXII, 1673.
15 Add. 44544, f. 187.
16 Hansard, CCLXI, 585–609.
17 Add. 44158, f. 63; Bodl., Harcourt MSS., Gladstone to Harcourt, 12 Dec. 1880.
18 Katherine, Countess Cowper, *Earl Cowper, K.G.: A Memoir* (privately printed, 1913), pp. 502–3.
19 *Hamilton Diary*, ed. Bahlman, I, 170–1.
20 Add. 44159, ff. 22–3, 27–8. For Gladstone's speeches at Leeds and Knowsley, see *The Times*, 8 Oct. 1881, p. 6a–f; 28 Oct. 1881, p. 8a–c.
21 Add. 44545, f. 59.
22 For the Healy clause and the decision in Adams *v.* Dunseath, see *The Times*, 1 Mar. 1882, p. 10a–b; and also Hammond, *Gladstone and the Irish Nation*, p. 229.
23 For the nomination of the Donoughmore select committee on 24 Feb. 1882 see Hansard, CCLXVI, 1501–22.

[24] For Irish-Tory collusion see F.H. O'Donnell's letter to *The Times*, 26 Nov. 1881 (p. 11e–f); Flintshire R.O., Hawarden MSS., Herbert Gladstone diary, 16 Mar. 1882; Add. 44160, ff. 92–6. For the speeches of the Tory leaders in Liverpool see *The Times*, 13 Apr. 1882, p. 6a–d.

[25] There is a great deal of printed primary and secondary material relating to the Kilmainham negotiations. The most useful is to be found in Hammond, *Gladstone and the Irish Nation*, pp. 263–82; Joseph Chamberlain, *A Political Memoir 1880–92*, ed. C.H.D. Howard (1953); J.L. Garvin and J. Amery, *The Life of Joseph Chamberlain* (6 vols., 1932–69), I, 349–58; Jay, *Chamberlain*, pp. 58–64; F.S.L. Lyons, *Charles Stewart Parnell* (1977), pp. 170–207; C.C. O'Brien, *Parnell and His Party 1880–90* (Oxford, 1957), pp. 76–9; A.B. Cooke and J.R. Vincent, 'Herbert Gladstone, Forster and Ireland 1881–2', *Irish Historical Studies*, XVII (1970–1) and XVIII (1972–3); R. Hawkins, 'Gladstone, Forster and the Release of Parnell 1882–8', *ibid.*, XVI (1968–9); and J.E. Powell, 'Kilmainham — the Treaty that Never Was', *Historical Jnl.*, XXI (1979). On the government's intended coercion policy see Add. 44643, ff. 85–6; University of Birmingham Library, Chamberlain MSS., JC 5/7/19, Bright to Chamberlain, 6 May 1882; and Add. 56453 (unfoliated), extract from the journal of Lady Frederick Cavendish, enclosed in Lucy Cavendish to Morley, 31 Jan.–2 Feb. 1902.

[26] Trinity College, Dublin, Rowe MSS., extract from the journal of Florence Arnold-Forster, 30 Apr. 1882.

[27] For Gladstone's speech in Dublin see *The Times*, 8 Nov. 1877, p. 7c–e.

[28] For Gladstone's repeated association of improvement schemes and the need for representative local government see Add. 44546, ff. 43, 62–3, 116; *The Political Correspondence of Mr Gladstone and Lord Granville 1876–1886*, ed. Agatha Ramm (1962), No. 963.

[29] For the Commons debate on Lord George Hamilton's motion, 12 June 1883, see Hansard, CCLXXX, 412–67. Both Trevelyan and Gladstone spoke in the debate, the latter reaffirming that the Land Act had gone to the root of the land question in Ireland and also that Treasury loans for purchase implied a dangerously direct relationship between England and Ireland particularly if they did not include a down payment by the purchasing tenant as evidence of character: *ibid.*, 427–35, 446–54.

[30] From late 1883 the Spencer administration faced a varied range of pressures to introduce easier land purchase facilities, not least from some of its own Irish supporters: see Spencer MSS. (Lord Spencer, Althorp, Northamptonshire), C.S. Roundell to Spencer, 23 Oct. 1883; T.A. Dickson to same, 9 Feb. 1884; Lord Monteagle, 'Address at the Close of the Thirty-Sixth Session of the Statistical and Social Enquiry Society for Ireland', *Journal of the Statistical and Social Enquiry Society for Ireland*, VII, No. 6, Part xvi. The resulting ministerial correspondence was brought together by Spencer in a Cabinet memorandum, 3 Apr. 1884, proof copies of which exist in the Spencer MSS.

[31] For the introduction of the government's legislation see Hansard, CCLXXXVIII, 1510–26; CCXC, 692–6. Lord Carlingford for one had expressed the lively hope that the legislation would come to nothing: see Spencer MSS., Carlingford to Spencer, 30 May 1884.

[32] Campbell-Bannerman, the new Chief Secretary, had made public this desire for a new local government initiative in a speech at Stirling: see *The Times*, 13 Dec. 1884, p. 6d. This is confirmed in Spencer's own correspondence: Spencer MSS., Spencer to Harcourt, 19 Jan. 1885; R.G.C. Hamilton to Spencer, 25 Apr. 1885; Add. 44312, ff. 1–8. For the views of the Land Commission on the purchase question see Spencer MSS., E. Litton to Spencer, 27 Jan. 1885; T.C.D., E.W. O'Brien MSS., J.E. Vernon to E.W. O'Brien, 5 May 1885; J. Vesey-Fitzgerald to same, 8 Feb. 1885. Campbell-Bannerman was also an enthusiast for land purchase: see J.A. Spender, *The Life of the Right Hon. Sir Henry Campbell-Bannerman . . .* (2 vols., 1928), I, 72–3.

[33] Spencer MSS., R.G.C. Hamilton to H. Fowler, 8 Sept. 1884.

[34] Add. 44548, ff. 45–6. For similar gloomy thoughts about the state of politics see *ibid.*, ff. 47–8.

[35] For this view see Vincent, 'Gladstone and Ireland', pp. 226–30.

[36] For Gladstone's reaction to the Ashbourne Bill and the political situation in late July 1885 see Add. 44142, f. 137; 44548, ff. 40, 41.

[37] Cooke and Vincent, *Governing Passion*, pp. 124–5, 340–2, 344–6.

[38] For Spencer's and Morley's views see Spencer MSS., Spencer to Lansdowne, 2 Feb. 1886;

to Sir Rowland Blenerhassett, 7 Feb. 1886; to Gladstone, 24 Mar. 1886; Add. 44255, ff. 54–6, 111–12; Univ. of Birmingham Lib., Chamberlain MSS., JC 5/54/681, Morley to Chamberlain, 3 Feb. 1886.

³⁹   Add. 44548, f. 77.

⁴⁰   For Spencer's irritation with the amended land scheme see Spencer's speech at Newcastle-Upon-Tyne in the company of Morley: *The Times*, 22 Apr. 1886, p.6a–e. Spencer commented to Gladstone that except for electioneering meetings it was the first popular meeting he had attended since 1857: Add. 44313, ff. 68–71.

⁴¹   For those later attitudes see Add. 44200, ff. 160–1; Gladstone to Harcourt, 1 Jan. 1887, quoted in M. Hurst, *Joseph Chamberlain and Liberal Reunion: The Round Table Conference of 1887* (1967), p. 158; Add. 44255, ff. 184–5. See also Gladstone's statements in the Commons attacking proposed amendments to the 1881 legislation, extension of the Ashbourne purchase provisions and the granting of aid to the congested districts: Hansard, CCCIX, 1044–60; CCCXVII, 876–83; CCCXXX, 1531–52; CCCXLIII, 1287–1301; and CCCXLIX, 358–66.

Parliamentary History, Volume 2 (1983)

NOTES AND DOCUMENTS

THE ABJURATION VOTE OF 27 JUNE 1702
IN THE SCOTTISH PARLIAMENT

P.W.J. RILEY

University of Manchester

There seemed, on the face of it, no reason why the Scottish Parliament of 1702 should have split so dramatically over the issue of abjuration. That Parliament, after all, had been composed entirely of Court adherents. The Country party's secession in protest against the alleged illegality of the 1702 session had left a rump of something under 120 Courtiers though, by reason of late arrivals, early departures and one expulsion, the number was subject to fluctuation. This remnant had, with little incident, passed the bulk of the Court's programme. Anne's title to the throne had been ratified, supply voted, the presbyterian establishment confirmed and an act passed allowing negotiations to take place for a union with England. The Duke of Queensberry, as Lord High Commissioner, had a further instruction permitting him to give assent to an Act of Abjuration directed against James Francis Edward Stuart, formerly 'the pretended Prince of Wales' and, in the view of the Jacobites, since his father's death 'James VIII of Scotland and III of England'. This precaution would have been in accord with the example of England where an abjuration oath was being imposed.

Committed adherents to the Protestant Succession — in the jargon of the day 'Revolution men' or, as their opponents tended to call them, the 'presbyterians' — expected such an act to pass as a matter of course. And so did others. The sudden emergence of the abjuration as a divisive issue came as a surprise to many, inside and outside Parliament.[1] Queensberry himself does not seem to have envisaged the possibility of any split. Faced with opposition to the act he wrote to court for guidance and received very little. The Queen, he was told, 'observing the great difference of opinion even amongst those you represent are well affected to her service' would 'give no directions from hence but wishes such measures may be taken as may not tend to make further divisions'.[2]

At this Queensberry tried to produce an abjuration formula acceptable to both sides. The 'Revolution men' would accept no less than the most stringent abjuration. Members of the Scottish Parliament and office-holders were to 'refuse, renounce, disclaim and abjure any allegiance or obedience' to James Francis Edward Stuart 'according to the plain and commonsense meaning of the words, without any equivocation or reservation whatsoever'.[3] It was an oath which, in what Lockhart described as its 'most horrible scurrilous terms',[4] would have permitted little scope for evasion or reservation on the part of any who took oaths seriously. A number of Members refused to entertain such a form of words.

In this *impasse* Queensberry conferred with the leading supporters of abjuration. He pointed out the dangers of making the oath a public issue and asked them to abandon the act for that session. With the single exception of Marchmont, all those present agreed not to introduce an Abjuration Act although indicating that were one to be introduced they would feel obliged to support it. Marchmont declined to give any such assurance unless Queensberry issued a direct order to that effect. The Commissioner accordingly gave him a formal instruction which Marchmont acknowledged and at once left the meeting.[5]

Thus Queensberry assumed that the danger of an open split had been averted although, in view of the 'heats and divisions' which were spoken of and the 'great caballing on both sides', not everyone shared his conviction.[6] The Lord Commissioner went to the sitting of 27 June with the full intention of adjourning Parliament without any fuss. He was, in fact, just after the commencement of the day's proceedings, scribbling a few words for his adjournment speech when Marchmont, as Chancellor and president of the Parliament, introduced an Act of Abjuration and moved a first reading. In an assembly composed entirely of Courtiers 'mark a first reading on the act' was carried by only four votes. Hamilton professed himself amazed by the narrowness of this division.[7]

The split was now not only wide but well-publicized. Both groups prepared for a trial of strength. On 30 June the non-abjurors proposed to clog the act by an addition: 'that, after the death of her majesty, and failing issue of her body, no successor should enter to the legal government, until the parliament first met and declared their right and title.' But by this time Queensberry had decided to cut short public displays of acrimony by adjourning Parliament. The proposed amendment gave him the excuse. On the ground that he had no instructions covering this new development, and protesting 'his constant adherence to the present settlement', he announced an adjournment till 18 August.[8]

The immediate effect was to transfer the dispute to the Privy Council. Sir James Stewart, Lord Advocate and a prominent 'abjuror', proposed in Privy Council that, in view of changed circumstances, a proclamation should be issued tightening up the terms of the assurance. To the designation 'the pretended Prince of Wales' would be added the additional words 'who hath now taken upon him the title of king of this realm'. Opposition came at once from Mar, Tarbat, Murray of Philiphaugh and the President of Session, Sir Hugh Dalrymple — 'all those members of council', as Carstares put it to Harley, 'that were in parliament against the abjuration'.[9] Such an amendment, they claimed, could be authorized only by Parliament, being beyond the Council's competence. Stewart maintained that the additional words were merely explanatory and required parliamentary sanction no more than earlier changes made on the deaths, respectively, of King William and King James.

Very probably because the advocate had given no general notice of his intention, the rival groups in the Council were evenly matched. There was a tied vote decided rather oddly by Marchmont who, having expressed at some length the view that the proposed change was *ultra vires*, concluded by giving his casting vote in favour of it. The opposers safeguarded themselves against misrepresentation by emphasizing their ostensible reason for objecting. They refused to sign the proclamation but nevertheless took the assurance as amended, declaring their willingness to have signed had the revised wording been sanctioned by Parliament.[10] Subsequently the abjuration dispute was absorbed into the general issue of the Scottish Succession which occupied the next Parliament from 1703 to the Union.

The abjuration vote left many in a state of complete mystification. Others, who claimed to know what it signified, professed themselves unable to entrust the information to the public mails.[11] Historians, for the most part, have either ignored the episode completely or accepted the official argument against abjuration in spite of its being inherently dubious. But further evidence is now available through the discovery, in the Blair Atholl muniments, of a Scottish parliamentary list.[12]

The list was written on one sheet on paper and consists of 107 names arranged in two groups headed respectively 'pro' and 'contra'. The former contains 56 and the latter 51 names.[13] All those listed were members of the Convention Parliament. From the total absence of committed Country Members and the inclusion of some who first took their seats in 1702[14] it appears that the list relates to the Convention's final session. Since Archibald Douglas of Cavers is included, who attended in 1702 for the first time on 25 June, it must be assumed that the list arose from a vote on or after that date. There are two possibilities: 'the act concerning the union betwixt the two kingdoms' voted on 25 June[15] and the Act of Abjuration on 27 June.[16] The former involved no such tight division. Furthermore, Stewart of Pardovan and Moncrieff of Reidie, who protested against the Union Act, are both listed as 'pro'. The latter division seems the more promising. Since the first reading of the Abjuration Act was carried by a majority of four, the close correspondence between that vote and the list is quite striking as unofficial parliamentary lists go.[17] Both this and the absence of numerous emendations seem to rule out the possibility of the compilation being a forecast or a working list. A further shred of corroborative evidence lies in the absence from the list of James Brodie, who took his seat for the first time that session on the following day.[18] What we seem to have, in fact, is a marginally inaccurate voting list for the first reading of the Abjuration Act, an episode which needs to be reviewed.

Those opposed to the act were not short of reasons. Philiphaugh told Carstares that that act 'would be no effectual security, and that it was not proper for this limited parliament to put limitations upon members of a subsequent parliament, but chiefly, that such a step would carry us so far into the measures of England about the Succession, that they would become careless and indifferent about the union'.[19]

Of course those opposing an Act of Abjuration needed unexceptionable reasons. The non-abjurors were to be Scottish constitutionalists devoted to the national interest and anxious to hold on to their main, and perhaps their only, bargaining counter in any negotiations with England. By implication their opponents were lacking certainly in vision and very probably in patriotism, blinded to Scotland's long-term interests by their fears for the presbyterian establishment, their devotion to the Hanoverian Succession, or both. These opposition claims proved to be one of the foundations of the myth that the Queensberry Court group consistently refused to compromise on the issue of Scotland's Succession before union negotiations took place. Perhaps no one has endorsed this version more extravagantly than Trevelyan. 'All true Scots', he wrote, on the subject of the abjuration vote, 'Presbyterian no less than Jacobite, knew that the only method by which they could bring pressure on their purse-proud neighbours and extort leave to trade with England, was to keep the succession to the Scottish Crown an open question.'[20]

The voting list on the Act of Abjuration certainly establishes that the division was largely one between the 'Revolution' group supporting abjuration and the Queensberry-Dalrymple interest opposing it. Amongst the 56 in favour of abjuration there were at least 26 who were looked on as 'high presbyterians' of long standing or men who had more recently adopted that stance.[21] No more than two ostentatious 'Revolution' names appear on the other side.[22] On the other hand, at least 20 Members of the Queensberry-Dalrymple interest appear amongst the opposition to the abjuration oath compared with only two who supported it.[23]

But, quite apart from the fact that doubts concerning the powers of a limited Parliament had not inhibited the Court in other respects, there has always been cause for scepticism about the alleged reasons for this split. Of course the Scots had cause for annoyance in that the English Succession had been settled on Hanover without any previous consultation between the kingdoms. They had also the fate of the union overtures of 1689 to reflect upon, with the emergence subsequently of the disagreeable English attitude to Scottish trading ventures. And it is true that Philiphaugh had earlier argued along the same lines, privately, to Queensberry. When the death of the Duke of Gloucester in 1701 had left the Succession open, Queensberry had spoken of a possible settlement on English lines and said that 'this nation should not make one step that way before the case existed, unless the English gave us good conditions as to our liberty of trading'. Philiphaugh had sought to confirm the duke in this resolution.[24] Such views did circulate and were occasionally expressed in speeches and pamphlets.[25] Some might have believed them to form the basis of a carefully considered policy of applying pressure on the English such as the Scottish Parliament was subsequently to blunder into, unwittingly for the most part.[26] If so it was not one that the leaders of opposition to the oath were prepared to act upon. So much was quite apparent even in 1702. During Queensberry's unsuccessful attempt to find a compromise formula, the anti-abjuration group expressed a willingness, whilst not abjuring the Pretender, to 'disclaim' him on oath. Marchmont remarked: 'the promoters of the abjuration . . . could not see how the disclaiming upon oath would be a lesser hindrance of the union than the abjuring.' This seems a fair comment. The difference would have been appreciated only by those intending to make mental reservations. So the core of the opposition's argument seems to have been unsound and the fact occasioned the anti-abjurors some unease. In the course of his lengthy and detailed account to Carstares of proceedings on the act, at no point did Philiphaugh mention that the opposition had been prepared to 'disclaim' James Francis Edward Stuart.[27]

The list seems to confirm the lack of substance in the anti-abjurors' main argument. No Scottish Courtiers were more likely to be predisposed towards patriotic arguments about trade than those who had been sufficiently incensed by the Darien episode to have associated, however briefly, with the Country opposition in 1700 and 1701. No such correlation appears. Very slightly more of these men supported abjuration than opposed it.[28] Even were no other evidence available this would leave a question hanging over both men and motives.

The Revolution men were at least acting consistently. What seems to require explanation is the conduct of the Queensberry-Dalrymple interest. When Lockhart was speculating on what could have led a group of Courtiers to oppose abjuration, the issue of Scotland's bargaining position was not one which occurred to him although he must have been familiar with the argument. Quite conceivably he was unwilling to credit Courtiers with any patriotic intent. More probably he felt his own conjecture to be more soundly based. He referred to 'the uncertainty how affairs would go in England; the queen was but newly come to the crown, and not well fixed in the throne, and they foresaw they might expect little thanks if she afterwards should favour the interest of the distressed royal family'.[29] Nothing was further from Anne's mind than respect for her brother's claim to the throne but Lockhart's suspicion that the key lay in England was well founded.

Throughout much of William's reign the Queensberry-Dalrymple interest and the 'Revolution men' in the Court had been in conflict. Queensberry had enjoyed some success in advancing his personal supporters regardless of their political views, greatly to the anger and alarm of his 'high presbyterian' colleagues. For long enough Queensberry had found the presence of the latter in the ministry uncongenial, not least because he wanted their jobs for his followers. Pressure from the Queensberry interest had intensified to the extent that by 1701 the duke had alienated his erstwhile ally, Archibald, first Duke of Argyll. By the end of William's reign Argyll had been transformed into Queensberry's chief rival. He began to talk and act as the self-styled leader of the 'presbyterian interest' although the men he was claiming to lead were only marginally less suspicious of his motives than they were of Queensberry's and rightly so. But they were thankful for any ally who could help in stopping the impetus of the Queensberry-Dalrymple group. With William on the throne, the Convention Parliament still in existence and a presbyterian establishment the preservation of which seemed to call for ceaseless vigilance, the duke's opponents could, with more or less credibility, insinuate that his following was virtually Jacobite. More practically they could, and did, argue that he was putting at risk the management of the next Parliament, due to be summoned in 1702.[30] But when the 1702 Parliament met, William was dead and affairs in England had a different aspect. With Anne on the throne, professing high Anglicanism and Tory sympathies, the division of Scottish politicians into staunch defenders of the Revolution on the one hand and Jacobites on the other, as hitherto alleged, seemed to carry less conviction. When those to be convinced were English Tory ministers, whose own views would have been branded in Scotland as disaffected, some reappraisal was called for.

High Anglicans of the stamp of Nottingham and Rochester, to whom the establishment of presbyterianism in 1690 had remained a festering grievance, favoured elections in Scotland to break the grip of what they took to be a tyrannical religious minority. They envisaged a Parliament dominated by episcopalians, seen as Scottish 'Tories', good 'Churchmen' and natural allies against Whiggery in both kingdoms. At Anne's accession only the disarray of the Scottish Courtiers and their inability to agree on anything but reconvening the old Parliament led the English ministry to acquiesce in this controversial course of action in 1702 and then only as a means of gaining time.

In fact their enthusiasm for new elections was shared in Scotland only by the opposition, both Country and Jacobite, who scented an opportunity of controlling a new Parliament, making a profit and exacting retribution for past humiliations. Within the Court party only a few visionary spirits entertained fantasies of a ministry freed entirely, by new elections, from the presbyterian taint. Tarbat, naturally, was one of them. He wrote to Queensberry, urging him to a complete break with the 'presbyterians' and a purge of the ministry to avoid alienating the 'many I know would prefer your interest to your competitors". Such changes should, he thought, be made before the elections.

> Those who are vested with the beams of the royal power will strengthen their interest whether it be fit for the queen or for yourself or not. On the other hand many who would be just to you both but have not attachment, or rather have averseness for severals of the present ministry will not only sour but despair and will flee to other shores wherein I conceive nobody will lose so much who might have these as your Grace. . .[31]

Tarbat was borne away by his own optimism to the extent that he very soon set himself up as a rival to Queensberry and attempted to create election conditions favourable to the 'episcopalian' interest.[32]

But there was no need to share Tarbat's wilder imaginings to appreciate a need for some readjustment. Even before William's death members of the Queensberry-Dalrymple group had chafed at the obstruction of their progress by Marchmont, Cockburn and the other 'Revolution men'. Argyll's recent stance seemed to have made the situation even more plain. Queensberry could re-establish co-operation with Argyll and the others only by abandoning his followers' claims to preferment.[33] Such a *rapprochement* would produce dismay amongst his lieutenants and on more general grounds might even be ill-advised. Hard-line Revolution principles and presbyterianism could well be out of fashion in the new reign. Perhaps the time had come for Queensberry to dissociate himself from such connexions. His supporters had no wish to see him sink with the weight of the 1690 settlement and the Hanoverian Succession round his neck. Even less did they relish being pulled down with him.

Within the existing political bonds the alternative was even more bleak. Elements in the Country party were extremely antagonistic to Queensberry, some of them — Tweeddale, Tullibardine and Hamilton for example — implacably so and greatly inclined to make his departure from influence a prerequisite of any bargain with the Court.

Since the Queensberry interest unaided was not strong enough to manage Parliament and so monopolize patronage, the possibilities of opening up political activity to people hitherto excluded and reaching some modest accommodation with them must have seemed worth exploring and even attractive. Queensberry's erstwhile episcopalian *persona* could be refurbished for their benefit and that of the new English ministry. He could be represented as one through no fault of his own too long shackled to uncongenial allies. Despite his Williamite past and his fraternization with presbyterians, he was now to be represented as far from zealous for the Hanoverian Succession and not averse from entertaining other possibilities. This was the germ of the policy which, somewhat modified, was to emerge as the 'Cavalier alliance' of 1703. But the *sine qua non* of any such realignment was the avoidance of an oath of abjuration. In fact the composition of the 1703 Parliament, which seemed to make a Cavalier alliance a tactical necessity for the Court, had been deliberately contrived before the elections. The Jacobite presence in that Parliament was not merely the product of an election which had got out of hand but had actually been envisaged as an objective.[34]

The abjuration episode of 1702 was a first step in an intended realignment in Scottish politics. To some extent this was foreshadowed by those Members of Parliament of episcopalian inclination voting with Queensberry's followers and the Dalrymples against abjuration, however the argument had been presented to them.[35] What was at stake was not the principle of abjuration so much as the composition of the next Parliament, whether the 'presbyterian old guard' was to be dismissed and whether the Queensberry interest would be sufficiently reinforced to have a monopoly of power. The issue gave a pretext for approaching younger peers considered to be as yet unsettled in their views. It was calculated, for example, that the young Marquess of Montrose might well be influenced by his family's loyalist tradition and long standing enmity to the Argyll Campbells. The task of recruiting him seems to have been delegated to Boyle, only recently Queensberry's candidate to replace Marchmont as Lord Chancellor. Just after the introduction of the Abjuration Act Boyle, who could usually be relied upon to overdo things, wrote to Montrose in preposterous terms. He represented Queensberry as having been determined not to allow an Abjuration Act to pass, a decision he had taken, Boyle claimed, largely in deference to Montrose's own views. Now that the act had been introduced, Boyle made a show of begging Montrose to intercede with Queensberry for an adjournment to put a stop to abjuration, 'this stroke which will certainly tend to the ruin of the nation'.[36] Boyle's letter is not to be taken as a serious statement of anybody's views, least of all his own. It was, however, a blatant attempt to recruit Montrose into an interest claiming to be rather less than lukewarm towards the Hanoverian Succession.

The professed aims of this projected grouping could not risk being unduly precise. A stance which could be represented as Jacobite but not necessarily so, as one of special allegiance to a Stuart Queen, or as merely a patriotic defiance of English pressures was not without short-term advantages. Little else could have offered a means of unifying a group with virtually nothing in common but dislike of the presbyterian establishment and a wish to dispossess its staunch adherents in the ministry. That apart, such a position was neither safe nor sensible. The Cavalier alliance can be defended as the last resort of a Court party which had suffered an electoral disaster. As a strategy deliberately contrived it was a gross miscalculation.

Marchmont and his associates were quite aware of the dangers threatening them and therefore, as they saw it, the kingdom. In their view, security for Scotland lay in the maintenance of the presbyterian establishment, the settling of the Hanoverian Succession and their own continuance in office. Rather in the fashion of the English Whigs, though with even less justification, they tended to speak and act as if the Hanoverian Succession was already embodied in an entrenched constitutional clause. 'The nature of the monarchy', Marchmont asserted, was 'hereditary in the protestant line' and it seemed to be his conviction that this led inescapably to the Hanoverian Succession. In this belief he denounced the opposition's proposed amendment to his Abjuration Act as one which 'would change the nature of the monarchy from hereditary in the protestant line to elective' in breach of the claim of right.[37] It is doubtful whether Marchmont recognized that some of his opponents were not so much Jacobites as men who had accepted rather than embraced the Revolution and now saw themselves as keeping their options open even though they were not quite sure what the options were. But even had he done so it was not a distinction he could tactically afford to make. The Tory ministers in England had to be convinced that any dithering over the abjuration in Scotland was due to Jacobitism and to nothing else. Their flesh had to be made to creep with thoughts of disaffection rampant. England's having settled the Succession and accepted an Act of Abjuration seemed to him his most effective weapon. Even Tory ministers could hardly watch with equanimity the Scots' refusal to do either. So the issue had to be portrayed in black and white terms. Marchmont wrote to court:[38]

> Why those, who are in their hearts satisfied of her majesty's title to the government and have taken the allegiance and the assurance should now oppose the abjuration is hard to understand, seeing one of contradictory propositions must be true: if the queen have a good title the pretended prince has none, and if the pretended prince have a good title, the queen and her progeny have none. There is no medium. . .

This was clearly an oversimplification since what was at issue for some Scots, as for some Englishmen, was neither the Queen, who was accepted, nor her progeny — all dead and unlikely to be replaced — but the Hanoverian Succession. Perhaps the distinction was over-subtle in speculation and meaningless in practice, but it did exist. Marchmont, however, was not prepared to admit the difference. Shilly-shallying over the Succession was dangerous and the English had to be made to believe it. The 'Revolution men' fully realized that the struggle concerned the composition of the next Parliament and the next ministry. An Abjuration Act would, Marchmont wrote, 'secure the next parliament as well from jacobites as from papists . . . for few, if any, of them, will swallow the word *abjure*'. Failing that, 'it may reasonably be doubted if the next parliament can be got of such a set of men as will be so hearty to. . . [the abjuration] as this', and if the Jacobites were to take advantage of the mental reservation that there was no longer a 'pretended prince of Wales' then 'the next parliament may be a very odd one, and very unsafe for the queen and kingdom'.[39] On the other hand, with an abjuration oath, the next Parliament might be no more than a diluted version of the Convention in which Marchmont and his colleagues might well hold their own better than most. For that reason they were against new elections until an Abjuration Act had been passed and they wanted a further sitting of the Convention in August 1702 for the express purpose of voting it.[40] But a majority of four on the first reading and the threat that, if necessary, enough seceders would return to throw out the act did not augur well for an August session. Under the circumstances the advice to recall the Convention Parliament was disregarded.

Marchmont must have been well aware that the introduction of the Abjuration Act placed Queensberry in a dilemma: either to support abjuration and alienate some of his following or appear, if only tacitly, against it and risk being represented, not as a Jacobite, which was scarcely credible, but certainly as one contaminated by unwholesome company. Since a major aim of Jacobite policy was to avoid any measure, including abjuration, which closed the door on the main Stuart line,[41] the idea of widespread Jacobite conspiracy surfacing over abjuration would have seemed to some anything but far-fetched. Insinuations of this kind concerning Queensberry were made in England[42] and after the adjournment Marchmont exerted himself to place the blame for the failure of abjuration convincingly on the Lord Commissioner without too much concern for the truth. It appeared, according to this version, that the act had been quite properly introduced after consultation and was on the way to being passed handsomely when Queensberry, inexplicably it seemed and greatly to Marchmont's surprise, had adjourned. It 'occasions', Marchmont wrote, 'great speculation, guessing and muttering, that the proceeding upon an act so evidently advantageous to your majesty and your government, did meet with a stop from the throne'.[43] He revealed further how 'it strangely happened that most of the members of parliament upon whom the commissioner and the earl of Seafield are known to have powerful influence, failed them and did not vote for a first reading'.[44] So the responsibility was placed squarely on Queensberry although Seafield, who was always fair game for either side, was not to be allowed to escape.

However, in view of the part undoubtedly played by the Queensberry-Dalrymple interest in defeating the abjuration, it is curious that in many respects Queensberry himself was more in sympathy with the 'Revolution men' than with his own followers. Whatever he might have hinted on occasion, and privately, about the Succession to friends such as Philiphaugh there is little doubt that in 1702 Queensberry had been prepared to carry out his instructions and pass an Act of Abjuration. He did, in fact, according to Marchmont, produce a form of words based on the English abjuration oath which, initially, he seemed confident of persuading his followers to accept.[45] When the Convention Parliament was finally dissolved he shared Marchmont's view that immediate elections were undesirable and that a 'cooling off' period was needed until opinion seemed conducive to the election of a stable Parliament. But under pressure from the Scottish Country opposition and their sympathizers the English ministers decided to hold elections at once. When the news reached Queensberry he was more than a little put out.[46] During the period of preparation for the 1703 Parliament he, like Godolphin, was in favour of the Pretender's being 'disavowed'.[47] Subsequently the ostentatious behaviour of some episcopalians irritated him, as did any proposals for tolerating them. His feeling was that a toleration scheme would cause more trouble than it was worth. When, as Lord High Commissioner in 1703, he was faced with a clear choice between placating the Mitchell's Club Jacobites and a wholesale reassertion of the Revolution settlement including the presbyterian establishment, he chose the latter without discernible hesitation. Seafield and others were left to limp along with what remained of the Court policy of alliance with the Cavaliers whilst Queensberry dissociated himself from it.[48] In the following year he was prepared to undertake to settle the Hanoverian Succession in Scotland[49] and his subsequent instigation of opposition to it was in the main a show of resentment at his dismissal. Altogether, Queensberry's actions from 1702 to the Union were not those of a man who consistently favoured an open Succession for patriotic reasons or, indeed, any other reason of principle. It is difficult to escape the conclusion that his predicament in 1702 was engineered by his followers and allies, very probably in spite of him. In fact, from the time of Queensberry's succeeding to the title in 1695 there is detectable in the conduct of his interest more than a suspicion of the tail wagging the dog. Queensberry was easier in mind when attempting what the Court required of him. His political stance consisted of little more than the doctrine of survival, holding on to what he had and adding to it as circumstances permitted. Such an outlook was not conducive to bold initiatives. Occasionally he found himself caught up in a risky venture emanating from someone else and then his usual reaction was to edge his way cautiously back to a position where he felt more secure. Not a few of the ambiguities in his career can be interpreted in these terms.

So the question arises of who manoeuvred Queensberry into partial acceptance of such schemes that proved to be too clever by half. It could hardly have been Seafield, the voice of the English Court, treated with reserve by most Scots until they had need of him. Tarbat gave advice in plenty but Queensberry took so little notice of it that Tarbat set up a rival interest. But there is evidence of strong Dalrymple influence in Queensberry's counsels. Sir Hugh Dalrymple, the President of Session, and Murray of Philiphaugh, who worked hand in glove with the family, were very close advisers to the duke.[50] Even when taking different sides the Dalrymples worked as a family unit. In 1704, in some exasperation at what he regarded as a typical and fairly blatant piece of Dalrymple equivocation over settling the Succession, Seafield wrote, 'And thus in Queensberry's first session [of 1702] that family acted in the matter of the abjuration, for it is known that. . . [Stair] keep'd Queensberry from passing it'.[51]

Now Seafield was certainly in a position to know what lay behind the episode of 1702. He was, moreover, writing for the benefit of Godolphin and Harley who, by that time, must have been aware of the circumstances concerning the abjuration. And it seems an unlikely story to have invented in 1704 for the purpose of bringing Stair into disrepute. There was no need to resort to fiction to discredit Stair. The truth is that the scheme of 1702 has Stair's imprint all over it. Both before and after the Revolution, in or out of office, his career had been marked by some very sharp practice. He was by no means alone in this, but his schemes tended to be more ingenious, more sweeping and less successful than most. From his conduct as an emissary to William and Mary in 1689 to the affair of Glencoe he exhibited a marked taste for bright ideas aimed at short-term advantage. As a lawyer and administrator he was undoubtedly able but his arrogance and the limits it placed on his imagination made him dangerously inept as a politician. Only someone grotesquely out of touch with his fellow men could have dismissed with contempt an Act of Parliament as 'a decreet of the baron court' only to be forced to a shuffling retraction in face of the consequent uproar.[52] In fact his disregard of the nature and extent of the opposition his schemes might provoke was almost complete and consequently they tended to create far more complication than they were worth. As Queensberry's *eminence grise* from 1696 he showed a certain fecundity in projects which were ingenious but deficient in common sense. It is highly probable that the 'Scotch Plot' of 1703–4, in Scotland the 'Queensberry Plot', ought more properly to have taken its name from Stair.[53] As it developed, the plot became a device to excuse Queensberry's failure in the 1703 Parliament and to purge the Court of such as were not his personal followers. This exploitation of the plot was conducted by Stair, with Queensberry, on occasion, little more than a spectator.[54] Shortly afterwards Stair seems to have been advocating in Council that for the rest of the Queen's reign Scotland should be ruled without Parliament, the Scottish forces being maintained by English money.[55] Both episodes contributed to the disfavour with which Queensberry came to be regarded by many in Scotland, by the Queen and by the English Court. A direct consequence of the 'plot' was his dismissal in 1704.

The abjuration episode, as distinct from the merits or otherwise of the abjuration itself, bore all the characteristics of Stair's political style. The parliamentary structure was treated as a mechanical system, controllable by precise adjustments to achieve some desired effect. Any possibility of hostile reaction was either grossly underestimated or not even allowed for. In many ways, too, the sequel fell into the usual pattern. Immediate aims were achieved. Presbyterian officers of state were purged from the ministry for the benefit of Queensberry's followers. The pro-abjuration group was heavily pruned in the elections of 1702. But the failure of abjuration led directly to the Jacobite entry into open politics in the 1703 Parliament, the 'Cavalier alliance' and the Revolution men's reaction which precipitated the court *débâcle* in that session. When one reflects that Stair seems to have sought a solution to the Court's predicament of 1703 in the 'plot' and a period of non-parliamentary rule it becomes clear that although, as adviser to Queensberry, as earlier to King James and King William, he considerably advanced his family's fortunes, it is very doubtful whether those who listened to him made quite such a good bargain.

APPENDIX: *Blair Atholl MSS., 43/vi/32: A Division over the Proposed Act of Abjuration, 27 June 1702*

Pro:

E of Melvill
Marq Annandaill
Duke of Argyle
E Seafeild
E Crawfurd
E Buchan
E Lauderdaill
E Levine
Lo Forbes
Lo Elphingstoun
Lo Jedburgh
Lo Advocat [Sir James Steward]
Lo Theassr dept [Glasgow]

Contra

The Lo Montgomry
Marq of Loathean
E of Mar
E of Mortoun
E Eglingtoun
   Galloway
   Loudoun
   Dalhoussie
   Finlator
   Kintoir
Vis.: Tarbat
   Stair
   Roseberry
Lord Reay
   Frazier

Barrons

[William Morison of] Prestaingrange
Sr John Swintoun [of that ilk]
John Scot of Well
[William] Denholme of Westshiells
Mr Francis Montgomry [of Griffen]
Sr Coline Campbell of Abrushall
Adam Drummond of Megins
Sr James Elphingstoun of Logie
[Duncan Forbes of] Colloadine
[Sir Colin Campbell of] Ardkinglass
Sr John Campbell of Carrick
Mr John Campbell of Mamore
Mr James Melvill [of Halhill]
George Moncreiff of Reidie
[Patrick] Dunbar of Machriemore
Sr John Johnstoun [of Westerhall]
Sr John Dempster [of Pitliver]

Burrows

Alexr Thomsone
Robert Cruikshanks
Mr Francis Naipier
Walter Stewart
John Anderson of Glasgow
John Muir for Air
Alexr Swintoun
James Mudie
Sr Archbald Muire
John Scrymzeour [deleted]
James Smith
John Bosewell
Mr Alexr Cuningham
Walter Scot
Sr Andrew Home
Mr James Campbell
Thomas Hamilton
John Muire
Patrick Murdoch
Mr Wm Broadie
Sr Robert Stewart
Mr Wm Johnstoun
William Menzies
Wm Alvas
Heugh Brown
Sr Alexr Home
Mr Charles Campbell

56:

Bellendin
Boyle
Lo Justice Clerk [Roderick Mackenzie]

Burrows [*recte* Barons]

Ard Douglass of Cavers
Alex Horseburgh of that ilk
[Sir William] Stewart of Castlemilk
John Sharp of Hodam
Wm Stewart of Castlestewart
Mr John Stewart of Sorbie
John Crawfurd of Kilbirnie
Claud Hamelton of Barns
Mr Wm Stewart of Ambrismore
Robert Pollock of that ilk
Alexr Porterfeild of that ilk
Alexr Arbuthnot of Knox
Mr Keneth McKenzie of Cromarty
James Scot of Logie
Robert Reid of Baldovie
James Scot younger of Logie
Sr James Abercrombie of Birkinbog

Burrows

John Scrymzeour
Robert Johnstoun
William Cultrain
Mr John Murray
Patrick Wallace
James Smollet
Wallaem Ross
Sr David Dalrymple
Sr Alexr Ogilvie
John Ross
David Maitland
Sr James Scougall
Sr Hugh Dalrymple
Mr Robt Stewart
Jo: Anderson Dornoch
Mr Robt Forbes

51:

¹   E.g. National Library of Scotland, MS. 7104, f. 27, Hamilton to [Tweeddale, 28 June 1702].

²   Buccleuch (Drumlanrig) MSS. (the Duke of Buccleuch, Drumlanrig Castle, Dumfries-shire), Letters from Officers of State, Rochester to [Queensberry], 18 June 1702. The Duke of Buccleuch and Queensberry has kindly given permission for reference to be made to the muniments at Drumlanrig Castle.

³   *A Selection from the Papers of the Earls of Marchmont in the Possession of the Right Honourable Sir George Henry Rose* (3 vols., 1831) [hereafter cited as *Marchmont Pprs.*], III, 242.

⁴   George Lockhart, *The Lockhart Papers, Containing Memoirs and Commentaries upon the Affairs of Scotland*, ed. A. Aufrere (2 vols., 1817), I, 48.

⁵   *State Papers and Letters Addressed to William Carstares*, ed. J. McCormick (Edinburgh, 1774) [hereafter cited as *Carstares State Pprs.*], p. 714.

⁶   *Letters Relating to Scotland in the Reign of Queen Anne*, ed. P. Hume Brown (Scottish History Soc. 2nd ser., XI, 1915), p. 113.

⁷   *Marchmont Pprs.*, III, 242; *Carstares State Pprs.*, p. 714; Nat. Lib. Scotland, MS. 7104, f. 27.

⁸   *Carstares State Pprs.*, p. 714.

⁹   H.M.C., *Portland MSS.*, VIII, 105.

¹⁰   Buccleuch (Drumlanrig) MSS., Letters from Officers of State, Sir George Eliot to [Queensberry], 21 July 1702; Queensberry Letters, xvi, Mar to [same], 21 July 1702.

¹¹   Nat. Lib. Scotland, MS. 7104, f.27.

¹²   Blair Atholl MSS. (the Duke of Atholl, Blair Castle, Blair Atholl, Perthshire), 41/vi/32. I am glad to take this opportunity of thanking Mr Clyve Jones of the Institute of Historical Research, University of London, who found the list and most generously made it available to me. The Duke of Atholl has kindly given permission for the list to be printed in full here. It appears as an appendix.

¹³   One name, that of John Scrymgeour, appeared initially in the 'pro' list but was subsequently deleted and transferred to the 'contra' list.

¹⁴   Viz. John Stewart of Sorbie, William Alves (Sanquhar. Admitted 23 June: Sir David Hume of Crossrig, *A Diary of the Proceedings in the Parliament and Privy Council of Scotland. May 21, 1700–March 7 1707* [Bannatyne Club, XXVII, Edinburgh, 1828], p. 92), Sir Alexander Ogilvy of Forglen (Banff) and John Scrymgeour (Dundee).

¹⁵   *Acts of the Parliament of Scotland*, XI, 25.

¹⁶   *Ibid.*, 28.

¹⁷   There is general agreement on the majority, but Murray of Philiphaugh reported the vote as 57–54: *Carstares State Pprs.*, p. 714.

¹⁸   He could of course have been an abstainer: *Acts of the Parliament of Scotland*, XI, 28. Ten others were either absent or abstainers in addition to Sir Alexander Bruce, expelled on 12 June: Hume, *Diary*, pp. 88–9. They were Burleigh, Hyndford, Glencairn, Kellie, March, Northesk, John Campbell of Schankistone, Sir John Clerk of Penicuik, Sir Robert Sinclair of Stevenson and Sir John Hamilton (Cullen).

¹⁹   *Carstares State Pprs.*, p. 714.

²⁰   G.M. Trevelyan, *England under Queen Anne* (3 vols., 1930–4), II, 229.

²¹   Viz. Annandale, Argyll, Buchan, Crawford, Leven, Melville, Campbell of Abrucehill, Campbell of Ardkinglass, Campbell of Carrick, Campbell of Mamore, Cockburn of Ormiston, Dempster of Pitliver, Denholm of Westshiells, Drummond of Meginch, Elphinstone of Logie, Forbes of Culloden, Melville of Halhill, Moncrieff of Reidie, Stewart of Goodtrees (Lord Advocate), Hugh Brown (Inverary), Charles Campbell (Campbel-town), James Campbell (Renfew), Sir Alexander Hume (Kirkwall), Sir Andrew Hume (Kirkcudbright), John Muir (Ayr), Walter Stewart of Pardovan (Linlithgow). Marchmont, as Lord Chancellor, did not vote.

²²   Viz. Sir John Maxwell of Pollock and Robert Pollock of that ilk.

²³   Boyle, Galloway, Loudoun, Mar, Montgomery (sitting for the session as Lord Treasurer), Morton, Rosebery, Stair, Crawford of Kilbirnie, Douglas of Cavers, Horsburgh of that ilk, Sharp of Hoddam, Stewart of Sorbie, Stewart of Castlestewart, William Cultrane

(Wigtown), Sir David Dalrymple (Culross), Sir Hugh Dalrymple (New Galloway), John Murray (Selkirk), James Smollett (Dumbarton), Robert Stewart (Dingwall). Queensberry, as Lord High Commissioner, did not vote. The two voting for abjuration were two whose personal dependence on Queensberry was very close: Morison of Prestongrange and William Alves (Sanquhar).

24 Buccleuch (Drumlanrig) MSS., 'Bundle of Seven Unsigned Letters [from Murray of Philiphaugh], 1707 [*recte* 1701]', 5 Aug. 1701.

25 E.g. *A Letter to a Member of Parliament Concerning the True Interest of Scotland, with Respect to the Succession* [1704]; *Several Reasons Why the Succession Ought Not be Be Declar'd by This Parliament . . .* (1704).

26 *Marchmont Pprs.*, III, 242.

27 *Carstares State Pprs.*, p. 714.

28 Of the 18 Members in this category, 10 appeared in the 'pro' list (55·6%) and eight in the 'contra' list (44·4%) The former were Forbes of Culloden, Morison of Prestongrange, Scott of Wooll, Swinton of that ilk, John Boswall (Kirkcaldy), William Brodie (Forres), Robert Cruikshank (Aberdeen), John Muir (Peebles), James Smith (St Andrews), Walter Stewart of Pardovan (Linlithgow). The latter were Abercrombie of Birkenbog, Arbuthnot of Knocks, Crawford of Kilbirnie, Pollock of that ilk, Scott of Logie, Scott, jr., of Logie, Robert Stewart (Dingwall), Patrick Wallace (Kinghorn). Information concerning attitudes to Darien is tabulated in P.W.J. Riley, *King William and the Scottish Politicians* (Edinburgh, 1979), App. A, pp. 165–78.

29 *Lockhart Pprs*, I, 48.

30 See Riley, *King William*, Chapter 8 for a documented account of this schism in the Scottish Court.

31 Buccleuch (Drumlanrig) MSS., Queensberry Letters, xvi, 1 Aug. 1702. Presumably he had in mind those he was later to describe as 'tory' — 'firm to the monarchy and to the true line in the Protestant religion. The greatest part of these are indifferent as to Church government, providing they encroach not on the monarchy, and be not of a persecuting principle against any of the reformed religion': *Letters Relating to Scotland . . .*, p. 124.

32 This episode is examined in P.W.J. Riley, 'The Formation of the Scottish Ministry of 1703', *Scottish Historical Review*, XLIV (1965), 112–34.

33 Buccleuch (Drumlanrig) MSS., 'Seven Letters . . .', [Philiphaugh] to [Queensberry], 22 July 1701.

34 Those who voted for abjuration sustained a significantly higher proportion of election casualties. If non-elected Members of Parliament, i.e. peers and officers of state, are excluded, 37·2% (¹⁶/₄₃) of the abjurors were returned compared with 60·6% (²⁰/₃₃) of the anti-abjurors. The proportions were made up as follows:

	'pro'	'contra'
Barons	⁸/₁₇ (47·05%)	⁹/₁₇ (52·9%)
Burgesses	⁸/₂₆ (30·76%)	¹¹/₁₆ (68·75%)

35 Apart from the Queensberry-Dalrymple group, the following, for example, are to be found voting against abjuration: Bellenden, Eglinton, Findlater, Fraser, Kintore, Tarbat, Abercrombie of Birkenbog, Mackenzie of Cromarty, Stewart of Ambrismore, Ogilvy of Forglen (Banff).

36 Scottish R.O., GD 220/5/30/1 (Montrose MSS.), Boyle to Montrose, 28 June 1702.

37 *Marchmont Pprs.*, III, 242.

38 *Ibid.*, 250.

39 *Ibid.* Evidence of anti-Hanoverian, though by no means unqualified Jacobite, views appears, e.g. in *A Speech of One of the Barons of the Shire of B[erwick] . . .* (1702) and *Some Reasons Humbly Offered, Why the English Oath of Abjuration Should Not Be Imposed upon the Subjects of North-Britain . . .* [1708].

40 *Marchmont Pprs.*, III, 241.

41 James Macpherson, *Original Papers: Containing the Secret History of Great Britain, from the Restoration to the Accession of the House of Hanover* (2 vols., 1775), I, 626–7.

42 B.L., Add. MS. 6420, f. 7.

43 *Marchmont Pprs.*, III, 242.

44 *Ibid.*, 248. Seafield's father, the Earl of Findlater, and cousin, Ogilvy of Forglen, opposed

the abjuration, as did Abercrombie of Birkenbog who usually associated with them. Seafield voted in favour of the act.

45   *Ibid.*, 242. *Carstares State Pprs.*, p. 714 seems to indicate that Queensberry avoided abjuration to prevent a public brawl within the Court party.

46   *Marchmont Pprs.*, III, 242, 248; H.M.C., *Portland MSS.*, VIII, 106–7; B.L., Add. MS. 28055, f. 3; Buccleuch (Drumlanrig) MSS., Queensberry Letters, xvi, Seafield to [Queensberry], 9 Aug. 1702.

47   Scottish R.O., GD 248/571/2/5 (Seafield MSS.), [Queensberry] to [Seafield], 17 Mar. [1703], printed in H.M.C., *14th Rept.*, Appendix III, pp. 216–18.

48   These episodes are documented in Riley, 'Formation of the Scottish Ministry of 1703' and *idem*, 'The Scottish Parliament of 1703', *Scottish Historical Review*, XLVII (1968).

49   *Marchmont Pprs.*, III, 262.

50   E.g. Buccleuch (Drumlanrig) MSS., 'Letters on the Treaty of Union', i, [President Dalrymple] to [Queensberry], 11 May [1699]; Queensberry Letters, xiv, [same] to [Philiphaugh], 13 May 1699; 'Colnaghi MSS.', bundle 1, 'Memorial' [1700]; 'Seven Letters . . .', [Philiphaugh] to [Queensberry], 22 July, 7 Aug. 1701.

51   H.M.C., *Laing MSS.*, II, 63–7.

52   Hume, *Diary*, pp. 51–2.

53   Nat. Lib. Scotland, MS. 7021, f. 81, Sir A. Bruce to Tweeddale, 7 Dec. 1703; *ibid.*, f. 83, same to same, 11 Dec. 1703.

54   *Chronicles of the Atholl and Tullibardine Families*, ed. John, seventh Duke of Atholl (5 vols., Edinburgh, 1908), II, 20, 21.

55   *Marchmont Pprs.*, III, 263.

Parliamentary History, Volume 2 (1983)

THE DIVISION THAT NEVER WAS: NEW EVIDENCE ON THE ABORTED VOTE IN THE LORDS ON 8 DECEMBER 1711 ON 'NO PEACE WITHOUT SPAIN'

CLYVE JONES

Institute of Historical Research,
University of London

On Friday 7 December 1711 the government of Robert Harley, Earl of Oxford, suffered a humiliating defeat over its peace policy in the House of Lords.[1] In the debate on the reply to the Queen's speech opening Parliament, the Earl of Nottingham had moved to add a clause requesting the Queen not to make peace if Spain and the West Indies were left in the hands of the house of Bourbon. On the previous question the ministry lost by one vote a division in which 17 proxy votes were cast;[2] on the main question the Whig opposition majority rose to eight.[3] This failure in management by Oxford[4] was the following day to be compounded by an apparent ignorance of procedure, and what on the 7th had been a humiliation for the ministry was turned into a complete fiasco. Many Tories who had refused to follow Nottingham over to the Whigs on the 7th (including his brother Guernsey), voted with the Whigs on the 8th so that the opposition majority swelled to between 11 and 22.[5] Disagreement amongst contemporary unofficial sources over the figures in a Lords' vote is quite common,[6] but historians always have the official figures, recorded by the Clerk Assistant of the House in the manuscript minutes, to fall back on.[7] These official figures were, of course, subject to human error, but in the absence of clear evidence to the contrary they should be preferred to any unofficial figures. The curious story of the vote on 8 December 1711 begins with the fact that no figures are recorded in the manuscript minutes for that day, though they and the printed *Lords' Journals* clearly show that the ministry was defeated over the question of whether or not to include in the address of thanks to the Queen the 'No Peace without Spain' clause agreed the previous day.[8] Why is there no record of the voting figures, when unofficial sources are clear that the ministry suffered a defeat by a substantial majority? The simple answer, supplied by the minutes themselves and fully corroborated by a witness of the day's proceedings, is that a division in the accepted sense — as defined by the standing orders and custom of the House — never took place.

It is necessary at this point briefly to outline the procedure concerning the deciding of questions.[9] By the early eighteenth century the most common method employed was the simple 'collective voice', where after the question was put the side which produced the loudest cry of yea or nay carried it. If this proved unsatisfactory then any one peer (provided he was seconded) could call for a division. After 1675 the contents withdrew below the bar of the House and were counted by a teller as they filed back in, while the not contents remained seated in the chamber where they were counted by the other teller. The figures were reported to the Clerk Assistant to be recorded and the Speaker of the House (the Lord Chancellor or Lord Keeper) announced the result.

The attempt by the ministry on 8 December to reverse the vote narrowly lost the previous day produced an undignified spectacle in the House when it came to the question. What happened on that day may well prove to be unprecedented, and it almost certainly was responsible for producing what may well turn out to be a unique document — an attempt to record the voting in a division which was aborted after the telling had begun. This list, probably compiled by the Earl of Loudoun, is to be found in the Loudoun section of the Bute papers.[10]

The whole episode must have come as a shock to Oxford, especially after his unexpected defeat the previous day. The prospect of reversing the votes of the 7th had sustained the Tory ministry overnight.[11] Secretary of State Henry St John 'hoped, that when it [the address] was reported this day in the house of lords, they would disagree with their committee, and so the matter would go off, only with a little loss of reputation to [the] lord treasurer [Oxford]'.[12] Obsessed by the one-vote margin of defeat on the 7th, the ministry embarked on tactics which were to bring down on their heads the wrath of many of their supporters. Oxford's ignorance of Lords procedure had been revealed the previous day when he had attempted to prevent the vote on Nottingham's motion by claiming it was foreign to an address of thanks and should be debated on a later day. 'Hereupon the Earl of Wharton appeal'd to that Illustrious Assembly, whether there were any such Orders; and the Duke of B[uckingha]m, the most vers'd in the Knowledge of Parliamentary Proceedings . . . overrul'd the T[reasure]r's Objection.'[13] Oxford who, it must be remembered, had only been raised to the upper House at the fag-end of the previous session and was demonstrably ill-versed in the finer points of Lords procedure, may well have consulted his Lord President, Buckingham, who had scuttled his attempt on the 7th, on the advisability of his intended action on the 8th. Buckingham, whom one report indicates voted against the ministry on the 8th,[14] would undoubtedly have informed him that by custom of the House no matter that had once been decided could be considered again in the same session. A letter by Peter Wentworth, quoted below, clearly shows that there was uncertainty amongst Court supporters about the propriety of such a move.

None the less the ministry, according to Lord Cowper, 'fix'd their thoughts on making up that one, sought Lord Carmarthen[15] and thought to have got Lord Hunsdon, who wou'd not Unless they doubled his Pension,[16] so he came now. They did not consider the whole to Secure them again'.[17] The crude attempt of the ministry to circumvent the rules of the House backfired. 'This rule was so sacred', said Bishop Burnet, 'that many of those who voted with the court the day before, expressed their indignation against it, as subverting the very constitution of parliaments, if things might be thus voted and unvoted again from day to day.'[18]

We are fortunate, however, that Peter Wentworth, brother of the Earl of Strafford, was in the House that day, and as was usual with him, recorded proceedings with an eye for detail which makes his letters one of the two best unofficial sources for proceedings in the Lords in this period.[19] On 11 December he wrote to his brother who, as one of the plenipotentiaries at Utrecht, had an obvious interest in parliamentary debates on the peace proposals, that Lord Guernsey, who on the 7th had voted that the 'No Peace without Spain' clause should not be part of the address, had said on the 8th that

> 'twas carried by a majority [and] 'twas not Parliamentary, when they thought they had muster'd up more of their opinion, to endeavour to alter it. Then some lords desired if it was to stand part of the address, that they might have the liberty to protest, and 'twas answered readly, yea, yea; when the Speaker [Lord Keeper Harcourt] said "is it your pleasures that this advise stands part of your address", and the noise for the affirmative was greatest, then the Keeper said "the yeas have it, let it be order'd". My Lord Anglesea rise up and desired the question might be put, whether that shou'd stand part of the address. The Lords of the other side said no such question cou'd be put after once the Keeper had said let it be order'd.[20] My Lord Anglesea insist'd that till the Keeper had said "as many as are content, say content, and as many as are not say not content", and this saying "yeas have it", without divideing the house wou'd not do, whilst there was any Lord who'd say he had said no. My Lord Rivers, Lord Carmarvene, said they had said no, upon wch the house divided. They that were for having the advise part of the address was order'd without the bar, and they that staid in the house saw they wou'd loose several they had the day before, cry'd yeild, th' other cry'd tell, tell, so that for some time there was a great noise in the house. The Keeper appointed two tellers, Lord Abington and Lord Sunderland; Lord A[bingdon] wou'd not tell because those of his part said yeild, Lord Sunderland said if he did not do his duty he wou'd his, and tell without him, and so begun. But they that wou'd not be told hop'd and skipt about, wch was sport for us that were spectators.[21]

Clear and useful as this description is, it still leaves unanswered the question of what finally happened in the division. Fortunately the occasion was so unusual, if not unique, that the Clerk Assistant, John Walker (who had been a clerk in the House since 1660 and Clerk Assistant probably since 1682)[22] recorded it. Having entered the names of the two tellers and the words 'Cont' and 'Not', next to which he would normally have entered the voting figures, he continued:[23]

E[arl of] Sunderland told the other [Abingdon] did not. The lords divided and it was yeilded. The contents had it yet those below the Bar [the Contents] refused to accept their own opinions without telling — [a]gred after debate to declare it myself. Ordered that the Adress be presented to her Majesty by the whole house.

Thus it is clear that the division was finally abandoned, leaving the Clerk Assistant to declare that the question was carried by the contents. The telling of the contents may have been completed, but as the not contents never told no figures could be entered. At the most, only half a division took place.

If there was no division on 8 December, in the strict procedural sense, where did the unofficial figures for the size of the majority come from? Some of the reporters of these figures may themselves have witnessed the proceedings (as did Wentworth, who records no figures) and thus have been able to assess the respective numbers of those within and without the bar of the House, though an accurate counting of the former would have been made difficult by their cavorting. The chaos in the House would account for the varying figures. Many so-called division lists in the Lords are in fact a recording of one side only in a division, usually on a list of the peers and bishops present in the House that day, drawn up early in the day's proceedings by the Clerk Assistant.[24] The use of such a presence list enabled the recorder of the vote quickly to mark off one side of the division (usually the contents who had to leave the chamber and go below the bar), while the unmarked lords (usually the not contents) could be considered as the other side of the division.[25]

The use of a presence list would thus make it possible in the chaotic conditions of the attempted vote on 8 December 1711 to arrive at an estimate of the numbers on both sides. The recently discovered list in the Bute (Loudoun) papers is, it will be argued here, despite some deficiencies and demonstrable inaccuracies, an assessment of the contents in the aborted division on that day.

This list, reproduced below, is based on the presence list of 7 December 1711, being laid out in order of precedence and corresponding exactly to the list as printed in the *Journals*, with the exception that the Lord Steward is placed with the other officers of state at the head of the list instead of coming first in the rank of earls. Also Lords Lexington, Westmorland, Hunsdon, Carmarthen and the Lord Great Chamberlain are tagged on at the end out of precedence, and these do not appear on the printed list for 7 December.[26] The list is marked in various ways, the most frequent being 'x' and 'I' by the names of some lords. At first sight it might seem reasonable to think that this was a list showing the voting pattern of one of the divisions of 7 December on Nottingham's motion. It is true that the bulk of those marked with a 'x' were Whigs or Court Whigs who are known to have voted against the peace, as are some of those marked with a 'I'. There are, however, a substantial number of Tories so marked, and we know that no Tory followed Nottingham on the 7th, whereas we do have some evidence to show that some Tories (most notably Guernsey and Weymouth) did vote against the ministry on the 8th.[27] Both these are marked with a 'x' in this list. An analysis of the markings shows that of the 69 marked with 'x' or 'I', 12 are Tories of various hues (5 marked 'x'[28] and 7 marked 'I'[29]). The rest are Whigs or Court Whigs. The number of lords unmarked is 53: thus the majority of marked over unmarked is 16. When adjustments are made for those who are definitely known to have been absent (Paget and Bishop Fowler from the opposition side)[30] and those who are not officially recorded as present (Howard of Effingham, who was anti-ministry, and Lindsey, who is unmarked and therefore taken as pro-ministry) the majority is 14. Both figures accord closely to the most often quoted unofficial majority figure of 17.

Why was the list of voters on 8 December not marked on a presence list of that day? The presence list in the form that it appears in the printed *Journals*, or as it appears in Loudoun's list dated 7 December (i.e. in order of precedence) was not the form in which the list was originally recorded by the Clerk Assistant, who arranged it according to the actual seating positions of the lords in the House.[31] Rearranging the list in order of precedence for entering in the manuscript journal, the official record of the House, was done at a later stage. Thus the list readily available on the 8th for use as a master list to record the division would have been the presence list of the previous day, not the rough list of seated lords for the 8th.[32] If this is correct, it argues that the recording of the vote on the 8th must have been done on that day rather than reconstructed subsequently, or surely the presence list for the 8th would have been used.

The use of the presence list of 7 December could also suggest that the list we have is not an attempt to record the chaotic vote of the 8th, but an attempt at forecasting the possible division on the 8th. Evidence has been quoted to show that the ministry was confident, if not of the propriety of trying to reverse the previous day's vote, at least of carrying such a vote.[33] As things turned out Oxford was proved wrong, as he had been on the 7th, but this time by a very wide margin. Oxford's previous parliamentary career had shown, as his future one in the Lords was largely to confirm, that he was an expert at parliamentary forecasting, and this occasion (by its very nature unprecedented) was his only serious lapse.[34] If even he was wrong, therefore, could someone else do so much better as to be within two or three votes of the figures which were widely circulated after the abortive division? Certainly not Lord Loudoun, the probable author of the list.[35] The evidence points to this list as an attempt to record the voting on 8 December, the demonstrable errors being easily accounted for by the chaotic circumstances while the telling was in progress. The two types of marks used, 'x' and 'I', can also be interpreted as evidence of the list being a record of a vote. Those marked 'x', overwhelmingly Whigs, may be taken to be those who were (or were thought by the compiler to have been) definitely told before the vote was abandoned, while those marked 'I' were the lords who would have voted against the ministry had the vote continued (i.e. they were already below the bar but had not yet been told).[36] On the other hand if the list is a forecast the two-tier marking system would fit equally well, 'x' indicating those who would certainly oppose the ministry, while those marked 'I' might do so. But who, in the aftermath of Oxford's defeat, when only Nottingham from the Tory ranks had supported the Whigs, could have forecasted that Guernsey, Weymouth and Thanet, and possibly Anglesey and Dartmouth, the Secretary of State,[37] would abandon the ministry the following day?

The importance of the list lies not only in that it gives us some idea of who voted (or would have voted) against Oxford on 8 December, but also confirms that such a vote did take place. The list illustrates with startling clarity the dilemma facing Oxford in the aftermath of the defeats of 7 and 8 December 1711. If he had been inclined to shake off the defeats of the 7th as bad luck, or at worse bad management which could easily be rectified (especially if he could regain the confidence of the Court Whigs[38] and the Scots[39]), the defeat of the 8th showed that he could not tamper lightly with the sensibilities of the House. He must tread carefully if he was not to lose permanently some of his natural supporters.

Lord Wharton of the Whig Junto was not far wide of the mark when on 'coming out of the House after the vote on the address [on the 8th], [he] clapped his hand upon the Lord Treasurer's shoulder, and said, by God, my lord, if you can bear this you are the strongest man in England'.[40] The further catastrophe of Oxford's defeat on 20 December over the Duke of Hamilton's right to sit in the House as a British peer by his title of Duke of Brandon, and the resulting desertion from his fold of the Scottish peers, led him to the desperate, but immediately successful, tactic of persuading the Queen to create 12 new peers during the last days of the year. These were introduced on 2 January 1712 and by the clever use of an uncontroversial procedural vote, Oxford, learning fast the management techniques the House required, was able to demonstrate effectively his new strength.[41] The peace proposals, for the time being at least, were safe. Oxford had turned the tide in the House of Lords.[42]

APPENDIX: *Bute (Loudoun) MSS., bundle A249, 'Lords Present the 7th December 1711'*

The list printed below reproduces the precedence order of the manuscript list, though the spelling of titles has been modernized. The marks as given on the list are reproduced in column 2. Column 3 indicates those peers and bishops whom Oxford recorded as voting against him ('con') on 7 December. There are 20 office-holders and pensioners, and two bishops with financial obligations to the Queen, in column 3. In addition Oxford separately listed 19 loyal peers to be gratified ('pro').[43] Column 4 gives party affiliations based on voting records as printed in G. Holmes, *British Politics in the Age of Anne* (1967), pp. 425–35: T = Tory, CT = Court Tory, HT = Hanoverian Tory, C = Court, CW = Court Whig, W = Whig.

Name	Marked	Vote on 7 Dec.	Party
Ld Keeper [Harcourt]			T
Ld Treasurer [Oxford][44]			CT

Name	Marked	Vote on 7 Dec.	Party
Ld President [Buckingham][45]			T
Ld Privy Seal [Bp Robinson of Bristol]			T
Ld Steward [Poulett]			T
Ld Chamberlain [Shrewsbury]			C
D Somerset	x	con (office)	CW
D Cleveland	I		CW
D Grafton	I		CW
D Ormond			T
D Beaufort		pro[46]	T
D Northumberland			T
D St Albans	x	con (office)	CW
D Bolton	x		W
D Schomberg	I	con (pension)	CW
D Devonshire	x		W
D Marlborough	x	con (office)	W/CT
D Rutland	x		W
D Montagu	x	con (office)	W
D Kent	I	con[47] (office)	CW
M Dorchester	x		W
E Derby	x		W
E Pembroke	I	con[48] (pension)	CT
E Lincoln	x	con[49] (pension)	CW
E Dorset	x	con	CW
E Bridgwater	x	con (pension)	CW
E Leicester	x	?con[50] (pension)	W
E Northampton	I	pro	T
E Denbigh		pro	T
E Manchester	x	con[51]	CW
E Berkshire		pro	T
E Rivers		pro	C
E Winchilsea		pro	T
E Thanet	xI	pro	T
E Sunderland	x		W
E Scarsdale			T
E Clarendon			T
E Cardigan			T
E Anglesey	I		T
E Sussex	I		T
E Carlisle	I	con (office)	W
E Radnor		con	CW
E Yarmouth		pro	T
E Berkeley	x	con (office)	W
E Nottingham	x		T
E Rochester			T
E Abingdon		pro	T
E Plymouth		pro	T
E Portland	x		W
E Torrington	x	pro	CW
E Scarbrough	x		W
E Orford	x		W
E Jersey			T

Name	Marked	Vote on 7 Dec.	Party
E Grantham			CW
E Wharton	x	con (office)	W
E Godolphin	x		W/CT
E Cholmondeley	x	con (office)	CW
E Mar			T
E Loudoun			HT
E Orkney			T
E Ilay			C
E Ferrers			T
E Dartmouth	I		T
V Saye and Sele			T
V Townshend	x	con (office)	W
V Weymouth	x	pro	T
V Hatton			HT
V Kilsyth			T
Bp London [Compton]			T
Bp Winchester [Trelawney]		con	T
Bp Rochester [Sprat]			T
Bp Salisbury [Burnet]	I		W
Bp Lichfield and Coventry [Hough]	x		W
Bp Ely [Moore]	x		W
Bp Peterborough [Cumberland]	x		W
Bp Gloucester [Fowler]	x[52]		W
Bp Oxford [Talbot]	x	con	W
Bp Bangor [Evans]	x		W
Bp Carlisle [Nicolson]	x		W
Bp Lincoln [Wake]	x		W
Bp Chester [Dawes]			HT
Bp Norwich [Trimnell]	x		W
Bp St Asaph [Fleetwood]	x		W
Bp Chichester [Manningham]			T
Bp St David's [Bisse]			T
L Delawarr			CT
L Fitzwalter	x	con (pension)	W
L Willoughby de Broke			T
L Paget	x[53]		W
L Howard of Effingham	x[54]	con (pension)	CW
L North and Grey		pro	T
L Chandos			T
L Howard of Escrick	x	pro	T
L Mohun	x		W
L Byron			CT
L Vaughan	x		W
L Colepeper	x		W
L Rockingham	x		W
L Berkeley of Stratton		pro	CT
L Cornwallis	x		W
L Carteret	I		HT
L Ossulston	I		W
L Stawell		pro[55]	T

Name	Marked	Vote on 7 Dec.	Party
L Guilford		pro	T
L Ashburnham	I		W
L Weston			T
L Herbert	I		W
L Haversham	x		W
L Somers	x		W
L Bernard			T
L Halifax	x		W
L Guernsey	x	pro	T
L Conway			HT
L Hervey	x		W
L Cowper	I		W
L Pelham	x		W
L Boyle			CW
L Lexington	I	q pro[56]	T
E Westmorland		con (pension)[57]	CW
L Hunsdon[58]			C
M Carmarthen [L Osborne][59]			T
L Great Chamberlain [Lindsey][60]			W

Notes

[1] For the debate and vote in the Commons which the ministry won, see G.S. Holmes, 'The Commons' Division on "No Peace without Spain", 7 December 1711', *B.I.H.R.*, XXXIII (1960), 223–34.

[2] The figures were *contents* (i.e. against the ministry) 61 + 6 proxies = 67, *not contents* 55 + 11 = 66.

[3] *Contents 62, not contents 54.*

[4] A detailed analysis of Harley's management of the Lords can be found in C. Jones, '"The Scheme Lords, the Neccessitous Lords, and the Scots Lords": The Earl of Oxford's Management and "the Party of the Crown" in the House of Lords, 1711 to 1714', in *Party and Management in Parliament 1660–1784*, ed. C. Jones (Leicester, 1984).

[5] Seven contemporary sources give a figure for the majority on the vote of 8 Dec. 1711: Niedersächsisches Staatsarchiv, Hannover, Cal. Br. 24 Eng. 107, f.47, Kreienberg's despatch, 11/22 Dec. 1711 [hereafter cited as Kreienberg] (17); B.L., Add. MS. 22908, f. 88, — ? to Colebatch, 11 Dec. 1711 (17); B.L., Add. MS. 17677 EEE, f. 390, L'Hermitage's despatch, 11/22 Dec. 1711 [hereafter cited as L'Hermitage] (18); [W. Pittis], *The History of the Proceedings of the Second Session of this Present Parliament. . .* [1712], p. 7 (20); [A.] Baldwin, *The History and Defence of the Last Parliament* (1713), p. 123 (22); A. Boyer, *History of the Reign of Queen Anne Digested into Annals* (11 vols., 1702–13), X, 288 (22); H.M.C., *7th Rept.*, App., p. 507 (11 or 17).

[6] For another example of where unofficial sources disagree over the figures see Eveline Cruickshanks, D. Hayton and C. Jones, 'Divisions in the House of Lords on the Transfer of the Crown and Other Issues, 1689–94: Ten New Lists', *B.I.H.R.*, LIII (1980), 80.

7   These are published in *Divisions in the House of Lords: An Analytical List 1685–1857*, comp. J.C. Sainty and D. Dewar (House of Lords R.O. Occasional Publication No. 2, 1976).

8   *L.J.*, XIX, 339.

9   For a fuller description of voting procedure see *Divisions in the House of Lords*, pp. 7–14; *A Register of Parliamentary Lists 1660–1761*, eds. D. Hayton and C. Jones (University of Leicester History Department Occasional Publication No. 1, 1979), pp. 7–10.

10   Bute (Loudoun) MSS. (the Marquess of Bute, Mount Stuart House, Bute), bundle A 249. I am grateful to the Marquess of Bute for allowing access to his papers and for granting permission to publish this list.

11   Baldwin, *Last Parliament*, p. 123.

12   Jonathan Swift, *Journal to Stella*, ed. H. Williams (2 vols., Oxford, 1974), II, 432–3 (8 Dec. 1711).

13   Boyer, *Annals*, X, 285; Kreienberg, 11/22 Dec. 1711.

14   B.L. Add. MS. 22908, f. 88, — ? to Colebatch, 11 Dec. 1711. This anonymous writer confesses that he was not present at the debate.

15   He had been absent the previous day, preferring a City tavern to the House and had arrived to give his vote only to find the House risen (Berkshire R.O., Trumbull Add. MS. 136/1, Ralph Bridges to Sir William Trumbull, 14 Dec. 1711). According to one observer he was to play his usual role of buffoon on the 8th, giving 'occasion for more confusion and disorder than has been usual in that Honble House': Bodl. MS. Ballard 21, f. 176, [W. Delaune] to Dr Charlett, [8 Dec. 1711]. For other occasions when Carmarthen jumped in feet first see C. Jones, 'Debates in the House of Lords on "The Church in Danger", 1705, and on Dr Sacheverell's Impeachment, 1710', *Historical Journal*, XIX (1976), 768, 771.

16   He actually acquired a bounty of £1,000: B.L., Loan 29/45A/10. According to Kreienberg (11/22 Dec.) Hunsdon had risked his pension on 7 Dec. by not following the ministry.

17   *The Diary of Sir David Hamilton 1709–14*, ed. P. Roberts (Oxford, 1975), pp. 32–3 (10 Dec.).

18   G. Burnet, *History of His Own Time*, ed. M.J.R[outh] (3rd edn., 6 vols., Oxford, 1833), VI, 83.

19   The other was Bishop Nicolson of Carlisle. Unfortunately, though he attended on 7 and 8 Dec., his diary for that period is lost and does not resume until 1 Jan. 1712. See *The London Diaries of Bishop Nicolson of Carlisle 1702–18*, eds. C. Jones and G. Holmes (Oxford, 1984).

20   According to Kreienberg (11/22 Dec.), Lord Somers, a former Lord Chancellor, insisted strongly on a counting of votes.

21   *The Wentworth Papers*, ed. J.J. Cartwright (1883), pp. 222–3.

22   J.C. Sainty, *The Parliament Office in the Seventeenth and Eighteenth Centuries* (House of Lords R.O., 1977), p. 24.

23   H[ouse of] L[ords] R.O., Manuscript Minutes, XLVII (unfol.), 8 Dec. 1711.

24   See *Register of Parliamentary Lists*, pp. 14–15. For the compilation of the presence list, see C. Jones, 'Seating Problems in the House of Lords in the Early Eighteenth Century: The Evidence of the Manuscript Minutes', *B.I.H.R.*, LI (1978), 139–45.

25   For a similar use of a presence list to record a division see C. Jones, 'Godolphin, the Whig Junto and the Scots: A New Lords' Division-List from 1709', *Scottish Historical Review*, LVIII (1979), 158–74.

26   *L.J.*, XIX, 335. The presence list in the Manuscript Minutes differs from the printed version in that it does not include Lords Northampton and Cornwallis, and has the Bishop of Llandaff instead of St Asaph. For general differences between the manuscript and printed presence lists see Jones, 'Seating Problems', pp. 139–45.

27   L'Hermitage, 11/22 Dec. 1711. The Dutch envoy goes on, 'and two other Tories did likewise'.

28   Thanet, Nottingham, Guernsey, Weymouth, Howard of Escrick.

29   Pembroke, Northampton, Anglesey, Sussex, Dartmouth, Carteret, Lexington.

30   Their proxies had been registered on the morning, see below, n. 39.

31   See Jones, 'Seating Problems', pp. 139–45.

32   All known division lists recorded by marking a presence list use revised presence lists in order of precedence. There is no list known which uses the 'seating order list' of the Clerk Assistant. In this case, the composition of the House was so similar (only three lords

recorded as present on the 7th and not on the 8th — Paget, Howard of Effingham and Bishop Fowler of Gloucester) as to make only a marginal difference, and the addition of five extra names at the bottom represents an attempt to revise the list of the 7th to correspond with those present on the 8th.

33 Swift, *Stella*, II, 432–3; *Wentworth Pprs.*, p. 222. For the truth about the ministry's reported confidence being based on an expected influx of Scottish proxies, see below, n. 39.

34 See Jones, 'The Scheme Lords'; C. Jones, 'The Impeachment of the Earl of Oxford and the Whig Schism of 1717: Four New Lists', *B.I.H.R.*, LV (1982).

35 The handwriting of the presence list is not identifiable, but is probably that of a clerk of the House, though not John Walker, the Clerk Assistant. The markings are also not identifiable. The list, if this analysis is correct and it was compiled shortly after the vote, may have been produced by consultations with several lords. This was not an uncommon practice, see *Register of Parliamentary Lists*, pp. 10–16, 17–18, 26–7.

36 Some credence is lent to this hypothesis by L'Hermitage noting that besides Guernsey and Weymouth only two other Tories voted with the Whigs (see n. 27 above). These would have been Thanet and Howard of Escrick (see n. 28 above), Nottingham not being included as having voted against the Court the day before.

37 Dartmouth was to express opposition to the creation of the 12 new peers at the end of December 1711: Burnet, *History*, VI, 94–5, n.

38 Significantly few of the Court Whigs who voted against the ministry on the 7th and 8th were punished by Oxford, despite the clamour of his Tory supporters. He knew their support in the House was valuable and ought to be cultivated. Only Marlborough and Somerset were dismissed in January 1712. See Holmes, 'Commons' Division on "No Peace without Spain", pp. 231–3. Oxford's views were justified in the first vote after the creation of the 12 new peers. On 2 Jan. 1712 it was reported that four Whigs voted for the ministry 'out of meer Respect to the Court', while 'several others of the same party went out of the House upon the same score': Boyer, *Annals*, X, 316.

39 Only five of the 16 representative peers (Mar, Loudoun, Orkney, Ilay and Kilsyth) were present on the 7th and 8th, and Oxford himself blamed his defeat partly on 'the absence of the Scots peers, whom the floods have hindered': *Letters and Correspondence . . . of . . . Lord Bolingbroke*, ed. G. Parke (4 vols., 1798), II, 49, Oxford to Strafford, [7/8 Dec. 1711]. These five peers, however, held six Scottish proxies between them: Kinnoull and Eglintoun (held by Mar), Balmerino (Loudoun), Rosebery and Home (Ilay) and Annandale (Kilsyth), and all must have been cast at the first vote on the 7th: H.L.R.O., Proxy Book, VII (unfol.), 29 Nov.–7 Dec. 1711. It is possible, though unlikely, that the story that Mar had two unopened proxies in his pocket at the vote may be true: B.L., Add. MS. 22908, f. 88. Loudoun did register the proxy of Earl Marischal on the 8th, but this almost certainly arrived after the start of the debate on the 7th. By the rules of the House no proxy registered after prayers, which opened each day's proceedings, could be used on that day. This is the only new Scottish proxy registered until February 1712. Thus the other stories current at the time that 'the Court Party would, the next Day, have the Majority, by means of the Proxies, which Eight Scotch Peers had sent to the Duke of Hamilton and the Earl of Marr' (Boyer, *Annals*, X, 288), and that the 'D[uke] of Hamilton had the M[arquess] of Annandales proxy in his pocket, which he kept by him and did not exhibit' (Berks. R.O., Trumbull Add. MS. 136/1), are without foundation. Hamilton chose to absent himself to show the ministry his displeasure over their action concerning his British peerage, and therefore only three other representative peers were absent on 8 Dec. — not a bad record for the second day of a session.

40 H.M.C., *7th Rept.*, App., p. 507. A substantial group of Whig lords had dined together both on 7 and 8 Dec., probably to celebrate and discuss tactics: P.R.O., C.104/113, pt. 1 [Lord Ossulston's diary, V (unfol.)].

41 Oxford's majority was 13.

42 H.M.C., *Portland MSS.*, VI, 80.

43 B.L., Loan 29/10/16, endorsed 'List — Dece: 10: 1711'. The list also gives some suggested replacements for those erring Court Whigs. Oxford listed 20 peers with obligations to the Queen who voted against the ministry, whereas two days earlier he had put the number at 14 (*Letters and Correspondence of Bolingbroke*, II, 49).

[44] Kreienberg's report (11/22 Dec.), that Oxford stayed away from the Lords having heard that the Court party was in trouble, is contradicted by the other evidence available.

[45] Noted by one source as voting against the ministry on 8 Dec.: B.L., Add. MS. 22908, f. 88.

[46] Reported by Kreienberg on 4 Dec. (f.43), along with the Bishop of Bath and Wells and Lords Stawell and Lexington, as making excuses for remaining in the country, and not coming up to Parliament, in order to take a neutral stand.

[47] Lady Strafford, not an eyewitness, reported to her husband that, 'the Q[ueen] sent privately for the D[uke] of Kent last night [6 Dec.] and som thinks he will comply for A Garter', and later that 'the night before the Parliament meet the Queen sent for the D. of Kent and talked to him a good while, and the next day he voted with the Tories': B.L., Add. MS. 22226, f. 41, 7 Dec. 1711; *Wentworth Pprs.*, p. 222, 11 Dec. 1711. Kreienberg (11/22 Dec.) states that Kent and Manchester lost the offer of the Garter by voting with the Whigs.

[48] Pembroke's opposition to the peace negotiations is confirmed by Kreienberg in his despatch of 4/15 Dec. (f. 42).

[49] Again confirmed by Kreienberg (11/22 Dec.).

[50] His name was erased by Oxford from his list of 10 Dec.: B.L., Loan 29/10/16.

[51] See n. 47 above.

[52] Bishop Fowler attended on 7 Dec. (the first time for many years) because of his fears over the peace proposals (Holmes, *British Politics*, p. 410). He is reported, however, to have collapsed during the vote 'and thereby being forced to go out of the House, was hinder'd from giving his' (Pittis, *Proceedings of the Second Session*, p. 7). Consequently he was not present on the 8th, his proxy being registered that morning by the Bishop of Norwich (H.L.R.O., Proxy Book, VII, unfol.).

[53] Paget was not present on 8 Dec., as his proxy was registered that morning by Lord Halifax (*ibid.*).

[54] Not recorded as present on 8 Dec.: *L.J.*, XIX, 337.

[55] See n. 46 above.

[56] He is not officially recorded as present on either 7 or 8 Dec.: *L.J.*, XIX, 335, 337. See also n. 46 above.

[57] Not recorded as present on both 7 and 8 Dec. (*L.J.*, XIX, 335, 337). His proxy is recorded as being held by Sunderland between 1 and 9 Dec. (H.L.R.O., Proxy Book, VII). The House did not sit on the 9th, being a Sunday, but Westmorland did take his seat for the first time this session on the 10th (*L.J.*, XIX, 340). However, Sunderland would undoubtedly have cast his proxy against the ministry in the first vote on the 7th.

[58] Not present on the 7th, but present on the 8th (*ibid.*, 335, 337).

[59] Not recorded as present either on 7 or 8 Dec. (*ibid.*). Known by his courtesy title of Carmarthen, he sat by right of his barony of Osborne. Kreienberg reported on 4 Dec. (f.42) that Carmarthen's father, the Duke of Leeds, absent due to old age and infirmity (whose proxy was held by Beaufort), had declared himself against the peace negotiations despite being a staunch Tory.

[60] Not officially recorded as present on both 7 and 8 Dec. Swift, however, recorded that 'yesterday when the queen was going from the house, where she sat to hear the debate, the duke of Shrewsbury lord chamberlain asked her, whether he or the great chamberlain Lindsay ought to lead her out; she answered short, Neither of you, and gave her hand to the duke of Somerset, who was louder than any in the house for the clause against Peace': *Stella*, II, 433 (8 Dec. 1711).

REVIEW ARTICLES

THE LAST OF THE LANCASTRIANS

A.J. POLLARD

Teesside Polytechnic

The Reign of King Henry VI: The Exercise of Royal Authority 1422–1461. By Ralph A. Griffiths. London: Ernest Benn. 1981. xxiv, 968 pp. £25.00.

Henry VI. By Bertram Wolffe. London: Eyre Methuen. 1981. xi, 400 pp. £19.95.

Henry VI is unique among English kings: the youngest ever to ascend the throne and the only king who never knew what it was like not to be king; the youngest king to bring his minority to an end; and the only crowned King of England who was also crowned King of France. He was also a particularly disastrous king who inherited two kingdoms and lost both. It is perhaps because he stands in such contrast to his famous father that Henry's life and reign has had to wait until 1981 before receiving the detailed scholarly attention accorded to other medieval monarchs. Now this has been more than compensated for by the appearance within months of two important works; one a complex study of royal politics, the other, as one would expect of the excellent 'English Monarchs' series, a more straightforward biography.

These two works share much in common, reflecting the accumulated research of generations of scholars (Professor Griffiths cites no less than 61 unpublished theses completed since 1926, the vast majority during the last quarter-century; and a shared conviction that an adult, sane, fifteenth-century king ruled as well as reigned. The role played by the King is the central problem facing the historian of Henry VI. Almost since his first biographer, John Blacman, painted his picture of the simple, saintly man uninterested in the affairs of state and kingship, for one reason or another, Henry has been presented as a mere cipher. In the twentieth century saintliness has been superseded by insanity or inanity. As K.B. McFarlane put it, second childhood succeeded the first without the usual interval. That in the last seven years of his reign and after his deposition Henry was frequently described as simple, easily led, puppet-like or half-witted is by Dr Wolffe amply demonstrated. But, as both authors point out, from the formal ending of the minority in November 1437 until the dramatic collapse of his mental health early in August 1453

Henry was a sane and active king. The main burden of contemporary complaints about Henry before 1453 was significantly that he was not the kind of king his father had been. As Dr Wolffe in particular shows, the idea of the royal saint was always a myth; the more modern idea of the royal simpleton is only true of the final years.

The reign thus divides neatly into three sections; minority, active rule, and the period of ill-health and incapacity following 1453. On this the two authors are agreed. When Henry came to the throne in 1422 the political nation acted with commendable responsibility. Those that inherited power from Henry V in the name of his infant son were the Lancastrian nobles and retainers who had served the new King's father and grandfather, many of them from before the usurpation of 1399. One reason why Henry inherited the throne without challenge, as Professor Griffiths's careful analysis of the composition of the Council shows, lay in the continuity provided by the great Lancastrian affinity. These men, Gloucester as much as Beaufort, shared the one objective of preserving the inheritance which they had helped win in England and France for the time their new lord came of age. The remarkable feature of the minority, 'the period of collective rule' in Professor Griffiths's phrase, is neither the conflict between Gloucester and Beaufort for pre-eminence nor the insidious development of private feuding within the Lancastrian establishment itself, but the success the Council enjoyed in organizing its own affairs (minutes of the Council reveal not only internal stress but also, by their very existence, a determination to act in a business-like manner), in tackling the problems of lawlessness and disorder in the early 1430s, in keeping the Crown solvent, and in holding on to a substantial part of Henry V's conquests.

By 1437 the old Lancastrian *élite* had discharged its duty to its lord. The key to the disastrous nature of the next 13 years thus lies in the King himself. And contemporaries understood this. It was a cruel trick of fate to provide the hero Henry V with a son who was his very opposite. Whereas Henry V was financially provident and prudent, his son was profligate and extravagant. Whereas Henry V was authoritative and commanding, his son was easily led and vacillating. Whereas Henry V stood above faction and showed a determination to stamp it out, his son was never anything but partisan, showing himself gullible and malleable in the hands of those who stood near the throne. But above all, whereas Henry V devoted his reign to conquest and glory, his son ostentatiously turned his back on any personal involvement in the war he was expected to fight. Here lay the deepest and most profound disappointment for those who had nurtured and faithfully served him for the time when he could enter his own. Both Professor Griffiths and Dr Wolffe bring out all the evidence to show how Henry VI in the first flush of manhood rejected his father's militarism, but neither appears to have grasped the full implication of what they establish. At the end of 1439 Henry, at 18, was (if he wished) fully in command at home, peace negotiations had just collapsed, and someone was needed to cross to France to take command of the English forces in the field. What did he do? Three acts in 1440 show the path he chose to follow: the appointment of Richard, Duke of York as governor-general of Normandy; the release of Orléans as a further empty gesture towards peace; and the foundation of Eton College. Perhaps had Henry the character and ability of his father he might have proved a triumphant peacemaker. But his handling of diplomacy was as disastrous as everything else he touched. The demoralization in France and at home followed rapidly after 1440. At the end of the decade, following defeat abroad and mismanagement at home, his regime was severely shaken by aristocratic and popular rebellion.

Nevertheless, it speaks much for the residual loyalty to the house of Lancaster that Henry was able to recover from this disastrous decade and by 1453, when he suffered his paralysing and devastating mental collapse, his reign appeared to be set on a new and more steady course. The political consequences of the King's illness, the special character of the Duke of York's first protectorate and the fuller polarization of faction, complicated by the birth of Edward, Prince of Wales, take on added significance. What both studies suggest (Dr Wolffe's despite the author's suggestion to the contrary) is that the explanation of the final collapse of his regime is to be found in the new and unprecedented circumstances of the King's incapacity (and both authors show how Henry, if not certifiably insane, was rarely after his recovery at Christmas 1454 capable of taking any lead in politics). Thus a new interpretative framework for the reign is presented, central to which is the idea that King Henry before the age of 32 was neither saint nor simpleton, but merely incompetent.

Professor Griffiths's work is by far the more substantial of the two. It is the result of immense labour, is deeply researched and is densely populated by facts and figures. His wide knowledge of the political nation is employed throughout to good effect so that we are constantly reminded of the seething competition for favour and influence both at court and in the country. It is a welcome change to see John, Duke of Bedford portrayed as a man as others pursuing his own personal advantage, perhaps all the more effectively for the respect in which he was held by contemporaries. Likewise, Humphrey of Gloucester is rightly treated more sympathetically. It was he who, as Professor Griffiths shows, as heir presumptive from 1435 to 1447, most consistently stuck to his brother's ideals and was the principal victim of the King's *volte-face* and incompetence. And Professor Griffiths also convincingly delineates Richard of York's hesitant and unwilling progress to claiming the throne, although the argument that early in 1460 he and Warwick were already conspiring to depose the King remains controversial.

For once a full account is given of the actual fighting in France as well as of the shifts and turns of diplomacy, although in this respect it must be pointed out that after the coronation of Henry as King of France, Bedford and his successors as rulers in France no longer enjoyed the title of Regent. Nor is the reader allowed to forget the importance of Scotland as well as France for the politics of the kingdom. A full and thorough discussion of the finances of the Crown is given in which Professor Griffiths gives due weight to the ability of the government to raise loans. The chronic and worsening finances of Henry's regime, he demonstrates, were not due entirely to the cost of the war but were exacerbated by the King's own openhandedness and liberality. Tucked away as Chapter 21 we have the best account now available of Cade's Revolt in which the author skilfully places the surviving rebel manifestos in their precise context and convincingly argues that the pardons granted in such large numbers were taken up not only by rebels, but also by members of the discredited regime in the south-east who feared (justifiably as it happened) the consequences of any judicial inquiry after the dust had settled. But perhaps most valuable of all, we now have at last a full and perceptive account of the most difficult years of 1456–60 for which so little narrative evidence survives. Professor Griffiths reveals how Queen Margaret exploited the rights and claims of her son as Prince of Wales to build up the power of her faction. The real 'end of the house of Lancaster' now receives the detailed analysis which historians heretofore have been unable to supply. There are many other aspects of the work to admire — the discussion of the place of aliens in English society and politics, for instance — which attest to the thoroughness and comprehensiveness of Professor Griffiths's work.

There is, however, one major reservation most readers will have. Professor Griffiths has structured the book thematically within three major divisions corresponding to the major periods of the reign. The reason for so doing, the three kinds of rule exercised in Henry's name, is understandable, but the result does not make for easy reading or for convenience in following up aspects for the whole reign. Unnecessary duplication creeps in; for instance the homecoming of Queen Margaret is discussed twice in different contexts. And with a major topic such as the history of Parliament the reader faces an Herculean task in drawing everything together. To construct a coherent and full account of the Parliament of 1449–50, 'arguably the most difficult assembly with which an English king had to deal since 1399', the reader has to turn to at least six different passages, totalling 20 pages, the longest and most important of which is the last. And this, to a similar or lesser extent, is true of the remaining 21 Parliaments called during the reign. But once he or she has done that, the reader is well rewarded. Professor Griffiths's interest is political not constitutional: there is no reference to the franchise statute of 1429 and elections themselves only feature as part of wider discussions in the context of Cade's Revolt or factions in East Anglia. On the other hand, Parliament's important political role is brought out. It was fully involved in the politics of the realm not just because of taxation (between 1422 and 1429 no lay subsidies were called for) but equally because of its positive and constructive involvement in the government of the minority. Indeed we see Council and Parliament working in these years much as the critics of both Richard II and Henry IV had demanded. Here, if anywhere, lies the Lancastrian constitutional experiment. In 1437 however, Council and Parliament willingly stepped out of the limelight; but rapidly, very rapidly, Parliament came to take up the same issues of complaint as had characterized earlier reigns. By 1439, the first Parliament after the end of the minority, voices were already being raised about the extravagance of the King and the cost of his household. These culminated in 1445 with the attempt to limit the size of the household. But little was achieved and in 1449–50 the attack on waste and corruption was renewed with a ferocity and determination reminiscent of the Good Parliament. The resultant Acts of Resumption were only partially successful and by 1453 Parliament, although very generous financially, was beginning to raise the question of nominated Councils again. The issues and causes, as Professor Griffiths implies, were very much the same as bedevilled relationships between both Richard II and Henry IV and their Parliaments. Henry VI's problems were not solely created by the cost of the war. Here Parliament was not over-generous in its voting of supplies. But it is clear that two standards were applied. When the King himself went to France (as he did as a child in 1430–2) Parliament was generous; otherwise only modest taxation was asked for or voted. Had the King himself gone again to France, matters might have been different. As it was, his unwillingness to take the field coupled with his own lavish lifestyle and improvidence quickly created hostility. One is reminded in fact of Henry's grandfather who likewise compounded real financial need by his own liberality. This is not the only aspect of parliamentary history of value. Apart from this political theme, the historian of Parliament will also find documented in this work the issues and preoccupations of those who collectively or singly brought petitions and bills into the Commons, especially the growing chorus of complaints against aliens and the persistent lobbying of the Staplers to protect their interests.

Dr Wolffe's discussion of Parliament is altogether more straightforward and does provide a brief introduction to its constitutional position. The heart of Dr Wolffe's work lies, however, in his focus on the King in person. This he recognizes is a most difficult task. In addition to excellent discussions of the historical tradition concerning the King and his later apotheosis, he also offers a convincing reconstruction of the King's upbringing (in which he brings out the importance of the two coronations on the precocious child), as well as an informed account of the nature of the King's illness. The most informative and enjoyable part of this book is the discussion of the foundations of both Eton and King's Colleges, although his ascribing the King's motives to pride and ambition is perhaps over-harsh. In many matters he is in agreement with Professor Griffiths, particularly over the King's wastefulness and extravagance. But he differs most markedly in his insistence that Henry was not only incompetent but also possessed a wilful and vindictive streak, especially in his treatment of Gloucester. This attempt to discern a positively unpleasant aspect to Henry's character, although not implausible in itself, runs into the problem both historians face of discerning when Henry's personal initiative ends and the influence of others takes over. It is equally plausible that Gloucester was destroyed by Suffolk and his clique who effectively excluded the duke from the King's presence and poisoned his gullible mind against his uncle. Similarly the historian faces the difficulty of deciding who was responsible for launching the Fougères raid which triggered the renewal of war. While the King himself seems clearly to have initiated the surrender of Maine, perhaps even behind Suffolk's back, it seems less plausible to believe, as Dr Wolffe does, that he had any more control over events in Normandy in 1449 than he had in 1446–8. Likewise, although it is plausible to suggest that in 1453 the unprecedented grant of the provision for the raising of a force of 20,000 archers was an alternative to taxation to support an army to invade France, is it really probable that anyone would still have believed that Henry might have led it in person? Dr Wolffe is not very sound on the conduct of the war, which in truth he considers only cursorily. It is hard to see what grounds there are for suggesting that the Anglo-Norman establishment would have settled for a partition of France after 1439. The efforts to save Pontoise in 1441 represent neither (as he asserts) the abandonment of wasteful and profitless siege warfare as condemned by Fastolf nor a brilliant campaign by York. And the expedition undertaken by Somerset in 1443 was intended to be a *chevauchée* not a conquest. Although, as one would expect, Dr Wolffe gives a precise and clear analysis of resumption, in general the royal finances are also cursorily treated. Furthermore Dr Wolffe is somewhat confusing over the causes of the Wars of the Roses. He is anxious to maintain the view that the wars 'originated from the gross misgovernment and mismanagement of the nation's affairs at home and abroad' by Henry VI, rather than from an escalation of private feuds (pp. 133–4, 332). Yet the comment he cites from contemporary and near-contemporary sources, as well as the account he gives of what happened, serve to demonstrate that the undoubted misgovernment and mismanagement led to the crisis of 1450–2 and that by 1453, on the eve of his mental collapse, the King had succeeded in re-establishing confidence in his regime (p. 262) and was stronger and more active than he had ever been before (p. 267). If this is so, it was the collapse of the King's health, not the misgovernment and mismanagement of the 1440s, that set in train the course of events which was to culminate in the King's deposition and dynastic conflict.

Both books have their slips. In a work as long and densely packed as Professor Griffiths's it is hardly surprising that some have escaped his final scrutiny. The Earl of March who died in Ireland in January 1425 was hardly in a position to cock a snook at authority in London in 1425 or 1426 (p. 138). Harfleur did not fall to the French in December 1438 — it had been recovered by them in January 1436 (p. 456). The correct date of John Talbot's creation as Earl of Shrewsbury is 20 May 1442 as given on pp. 356 and 573, and not 21 July 1441 as given on p. 462. Sandal (as is recognized later) was a property of the Duke of York, not of the Earl of Salisbury (p. 741). It is left unexplained why in November 1456 Sir John Barre is pricked as a

Yorkist sheriff of Gloucestershire (p. 785) but in November 1459 is a *Lancastrian* M.P. for Herefordshire (p. 823). There are as well a few proof-reading oversights, the most unfortunate of which is the statement on p. 573 that Margaret *Berkeley*, spurred on by her husband's creation as Earl of Shrewsbury, forcibly seized some of the Berkeley estates: the lady was in fact Margaret *Beauchamp*. Dr Wolffe too comes occasionally adrift. His index entries for the Talbot family are particularly unfortunate and do not inspire confidence. Beatrice was not a wife of John, first Earl of Shrewsbury: she was the widow of his elder brother Gilbert. And John, Viscount Lisle was not later Earl of Shrewsbury. He was the eldest son of Talbot's second wife; the second Earl of Shrewsbury (also John) was the eldest son by his first wife. John Wenlock, as correctly stated on p. 314, was the Speaker in the Commons in 1455–6 and not William Burley, as stated on p. 298. The point is significant since Burley, as a prominent retainer of the Duke of York, was chosen in place of the Speaker to lead the delegation requesting the appointment of York as Protector for a second term.

These two books are essentially complementary. In this age of consumerism, one would have to plump for Griffiths at £25.00 as a better buy than Wolffe at £19.95. Neither work is definitive: indeed one hopes that Professor Griffiths will follow up with the study of the structure of politics he initially set out to write. However, anyone who wishes seriously to study the reign of Henry VI will now need to start from the basis which Professor Griffiths provides. And while one may not agree with all the conclusions Dr Wolffe draws, his attempt to portray the King in person makes his work a welcome companion. The lasting achievement of both historians is to restore Henry VI to the centre of the stage where he belongs. No longer will it be possible to say of the last Lancastrian that second childhood followed the first without the usual interval.

Parliamentary History, Volume 2 (1983)

THE POLITICS OF THE EXCLUDED: TORIES, JACOBITES AND WHIG PATRIOTS 1715–1760

J.C.D. CLARK

Political Untouchables: The Tories and the '45. By Eveline Cruickshanks. London: Duckworth, 1979. x, 166 pp. £9.80.

The Jacobite Risings in Britain 1689–1746. By Bruce Lenman. London: Eyre Methuen. 1980. 320 pp. £12.00.

Pitt and Popularity: The Patriot Minister and London Opinion during the Seven Years' War. By Marie Peters. Oxford: Oxford University Press. 1980. xvi, 309 pp. £17.50.

In Defiance of Oligarchy: The Tory Party 1714–60. By Linda Colley. Cambridge: Cambridge University Press. 1982. viii, 375 pp. £25.00.

British parliamentary politics in the reigns of George I and George II were shaped not least by an ideological polarity: the doctrinal identities of Whig and Tory at all levels rested ultimately on the choice of Hanover or Stuart, a choice now enforced by the recurring and persistent possibility of a foreign invasion to restore the exiled dynasty. That possibility (despite some modern judgments of its unlikelihood) had much to do with the survival and tactical integrity of Whig and Tory parliamentary parties; with the Whigs' use of the electoral machine to hold power despite a probable majority of electors in favour of their opponents; and with the repeated failure of schemes of alliance between Tories and opposition Whigs which might have broken the Whig stranglehold. The parliamentary historian, here above all, must attend to the ideological dimension and the international context. Jacobitism, by contrast, has usually been written about by specialists, even antiquarians. Dr Lenman and Dr Cruickshanks bring to the subject far wider horizons. Between them, they replace the ideological question so firmly on the agenda for parliamentary historians that it is difficult to understand how it was excluded from it.

To some, it has seemed a moving target. Between Killiecrankie in 1689 and Culloden in 1746, 'the content and meaning of the phenomenon we call Jacobitism had shown no . . . constancy. It was the product not only of a relatively static ideology but also of constantly changing social, economic and political circumstances' (Lenman, p. 283). Dr Lenman's initial stance is that of an economic historian, and his enterprise at first seems to be a reconstruction of the social location of a political movement. But his investigation into the economic fortunes of those who took arms in the '15 falls far short of a self-sufficient economic explanation of the rising. Of the three regions identified as its starting points, the first, north-east Scotland, especially the coastal communities north of the Tay, does not emerge as noticeably distressed; and there, 'the rebellion was very much a revolt of the rich and the powerful' (p. 136), not of the financially embarrassed and the declining. If the region 'merely reflected a general malaise amongst the landed classes of much of Lowland Scotland' (p. 137), this is too generalized to account for a specific outbreak. Much more important, on this showing, is that the north-east was a stronghold of disestablished Episcopalianism, with all that that implied for an embittered and defensive political allegiance. The second focus of the '15, in the south-west Borders, is dismissed as a small rising, running contrary to the traditions of the area (p. 152), the principled protest of a few aristocratic families. The third, in north-east England, Dr Lenman attempts to trace to the declining fortunes of the coal trade of Northumberland and Durham, and low coal prices in the autumn of 1714. The argument is not convincing; more telling is the discovery that 'Jacobite views were widespread amongst the gentry and the clergy' in the countryside, and that 'Non-Jurors and Roman Catholics were extremely numerous' (p. 117). The very lack of support for the rising in the rest of England suggests that its motive force was something much less widespread than economic discontent; and by the time we reach the '45, Dr Lenman attempts to bring forward very little in the way of an economic explanation: the stance has changed markedly.

For neither the '15 nor the '45 have economic motives been established as common or dominant ones among those who rebelled. Nor, we might conclude, were they civil wars, mass risings against foreign domination: the majority of Scots backed the government, and men seem to have been equally reluctant actually to fight for either side. What emerges from Dr Lenman's pages as the overriding common factor was religion: Episcopalians and Roman Catholics (with, in England, a few High Churchmen and non-jurors) against presbyterians. And, with religion, its reflection in political thought. Dr Lenman begins with a brisk dismissal of legitimist sentiment and theory (p. 12), but soon (p. 25) he seems to be asserting it roundly, and the book ends as a convincing and able exposition of the importance of dynastic ideology, embedded in real and concrete social and economic situations. But, as such, it stops at the Border. Dr Lenman argues to minimize the extent and vitality of Jacobite sentiment in England in order to establish a contrast with Scotland, as well as to portray the '15 and '45 as something in the nature of proto-nationalist reactions to Hanoverian oppression. What actually emerges from the book is an appreciation of the continuity and importance of Jacobite ideology, despite its shifting economic and political locations and occasions.

Yet it would better be titled *The Jacobite Risings in Scotland*. The author's research is chiefly in Scottish archives, or on material relating to Scotland; his original arguments are all about that country. To highlight his example, he contrasts it with eighteenth-century England — which he then makes far more modern than it was. His brisk, materialist iconoclasm, and his cynical view of politics, are nothing if not bracing. But something is missing when English royalist allegiance is discounted even from the Restoration; when we are told that 'there never was very much independent vitality' in late seventeenth-century absolutist doctrine; that 'outside court circles it tended to be held with some violence *only* by clerics' (pp. 11–13, italics added). Scholars such as J.R. Jones and John Miller have shown the plausibility of James II's plans; many historians have investigated the English counterparts to the doctrines of Richelieu and Bossuet; and the confusion of 'absolute' and 'arbitrary' is one which there is now no excuse in making.[1] Subscription to an ideology was never a substitute for organized military force, whether in 1660, 1688, 1715 or 1745. But force on either side could evoke substantial active sympathy and even more widespread acquiescence in a profoundly divided society.

Dr Lenman is correct at one point (p. 12) to identify two roots of Jacobitism, before 1690, in the doctrine of indefeasible hereditary right, and the 'cult of martyrdom and loyalty in the Stuart cause'. Equally, he bears out the conclusions of Dr Cruickshanks and others in endorsing Swift's denial of the importance of Jacobitism during Anne's reign: 'It does seem to have been the accession of George I and the establishment of a rabidly partisan minority ascendancy in Whig hands which alienated so large a proportion of the English political nation as to render the whole British political fabric susceptible to revolution' (Lenman p. 287). Dr Lenman argues convincingly against G.P. Insh's thesis that Scottish Jacobitism was the lashing-out of a backward Celtic civilisation threatened by 'improving' Lowland and English commerce and its values. He shows the great diversity of support for the '45, mostly from men who do not fit into a 'Celtic' category. But this successful argument actually frees Jacobite allegiance as an ideology from an economically determined regional or class location and points to how widely available it might have been in early eighteenth-century England also. Dr Lenman finds overwhelming support for the '15 in the Lowlands (p. 133), and even in north-east England: it is a pity that this line of inquiry stops there. In *c.* 1725–39, the Old Pretender failed 'to become the focus of any significant volume of discontent or disturbance': Jacobites derived very little advantage from dissatisfaction at Hanoverian rule (pp. 205, 215). The survival of Jacobitism in these years 'was not based on hope of an impending successful rebellion, for hope there was none. Rather it was the product of deep-seated intellectual attitudes and social structures which . . . continued to exist and indeed develop in their own way' (p. 223) — as was true, it might be added, of England.

A particular strength of the book proves to be Dr Lenman's reconstruction of the mental world of his Scots actors. Weighing 'typical' motives, or assessing sincerity, is a chancy business for the historian. Some slip into the 'Whig' error of assuming the absence of motives from the absence of assumed results: no mass rising in England in 1745, therefore no mass Jacobite sentiment. But this is merely playing the victors' game. What we can now do with more certainty (thanks not least to Dr Lenman) is to reconstruct the world of discourse which those men inhabited and which provided them with reasons which they could adduce as motives. And the rationale which the participants in the risings chose, even after capture and on the scaffold itself, was indefeasible hereditary right (p. 25). It could amount to a 'quasi-mystical political religion' in its most zealous adherents, and drew on 'a whole complex of beliefs' which was widely shared even among prudent and practical men for whom a martyr's death was unthinkable. It does not follow that this argument can validly be turned into a quantifiable one: that the widespread incidence of such motives made a Stuart rising *likely* in 1745. But to take circumstantial evidence (which is most of the evidence we have) as far as it will go, one can say that a Stuart restoration would have been widely justified, defended and interpreted in the light of that body of doctrine.

If 'the Highland aristocracy which came out for the Pretender in 1715 was conspicuously anglicized and indeed rather cosmopolitan' (p. 146), they must have been well aware of the form of government and its rationale which was the norm almost everywhere in Europe: divine right absolutism. What made the nexus of doctrines associated with hereditary, indefeasible right outdated in England while they were perfectly viable on the continent was not some English realization of their objective falsity, some praiseworthy and realistic English awareness of their anachronism in a modern age, some English rejection of feudal obstacles to modern representative democracy, but rather the fact that the regime which appealed to those doctrines as an official rationale suffered military defeat in 1688–9, 1715, and 1745, and political and diplomatic frustration at countless points *en route*.

Historians should beware of allowing their arguments about Jacobitism to centre on an attempt, in some sense, to quantify it. And such attempts often lead to fixed commitments to a definition, isolated, perhaps, from political practicability. If Jacobitism is defined (as Dr Lenman is careful not to do) as the fanatical dedication of the martyr, or of conspirators willing to commit themselves on paper, little enough of the thing will be found. But what matters in either case is their pointing to a broad and deep body of sentiment in the nation at large, restrained by ordinary human lethargy as much as by lack of political initiative, by prudence, by fear and by equivocation. As Dr Lenman rightly concedes of England (p. 32), Tory strength in the majority of elections 1689–1713 (and, one should add, until the 1740s in terms of votes cast) reflected a widespread acceptance of 'deference', a rejection of Whig contractarian doctrines, and a transfer of passive obedience from the King to the 'King-in-Parliament': a shift which, by identifying George I and II as locum tenens, actually served as a reminder of the case for revolution.

If England had one set of incentives to disaffection, Scotland shared them, and added others. The Revolution settlement and the radical presbyterianism it embodied produced a conflict at every level with royalist Episcopalianism. Dr Lenman ably explains the problems which the settlement created for itself, and the exacerbations of Williamite misgovernment and the Union. But if the 'social crisis' took a particular form in Scotland, it is difficult to accept that it 'had no parallel in contemporary England' (p. 55). Dr Lenman is right to lay much emphasis on religion, and the role of the dispossessed Episcopalian clergy in fostering a highly principled and articulate disaffection; but his dismissal of a parallel Jacobitism among the English clergy (p. 67) is unsubstantiated. Oxford's infiltration was even more striking than that of St Andrews, of which he aptly reminds us. The contrast with England throughout (cf. p. 110) is supported by reference to J.H. Plumb's model of a rapidly secularizing, sceptically empiricist society in which a Whig-Tory fight had been replaced by an oligarchical one-party regime by the time of Walpole's fall, soporific, corrupt, complacent and ideologically vacuous. That model is, of course, no longer tenable. But since Dr Lenman's book is mostly about Scotland, and since its merits in dealing with that country are so great, the value of the book is little diminished by the revisions which must be made in its bearing on English society. And that dimension is ably covered by Dr Cruickshanks.

Granted that Jacobitism was a receivable doctrine in England, all hinged on a foreign invasion and the activities of English Tories who might arrange and co-ordinate it. It is these aspects which are explored by Dr Cruickshanks: diplomacy, espionage, war strategy and English politics. Her book is especially welcome since Dr Fritz's pioneering study, despite its title,[2] only covered in detail the period to *c*.1725, and did not drive home its case for the importance of the Jacobite threat in later years. It is currently fashionable to criticize historians who give prominence to manoeuvres at Westminster; they should be given credit when, without renouncing this priority, they place their subject in a long chronological perspective, or within the wide context of European diplomacy.

It is clear from Dr Lenman's work that the Jacobite risings were not peasant revolts — blind, desperate convulsions of early modern societies in demographic crisis. They were marked, on the contrary, by restraint, discipline, legalism, a stress on legitimate authority and its ideology. The Jacobite risings were, in other words, definitely political; and it is the English political dimension which Dr Cruickshanks illuminates, with great lucidity and a classical economy of style. Her research has won support for the idea of a 'social revolution' in 1715 which excluded more than half the political nation from government until the 1760s; the idea that the Tories did not want office and its perquisites under the first two Georges is an historiographical hangover from the Court-Country model of Westminster politics, now discredited. 'It was the proscription which turned the Tory party into a Jacobite one' (p. 6). It is not clear that this amounts to an assertion that all the Tories 'were Jacobites', in some simple sense, though at times Dr Cruickshanks's success in establishing the political potential of that allegiance distracts attention from the problem of how that allegiance itself should be characterized. This is an objection, too, to Dr Fritz's approach in baldly listing Jacobite M.P.s. Dr Colley, in asserting[3] that 'the majority of Tory peers, MPs, and their county supporters were innocent of Jacobitism in 1744 and 1745', more clearly commits this error of method on the other side: to suppose that the question can be solved merely by identifying and counting Hanoverians and Jacobite sympathizers among the Tory ranks. A more realistically political interpretation reveals that neither men nor issues have an autonomous coloration, like pieces on a chessboard; their tone is determined not least by the way they are illuminated in the light of politics. It is Dr Cruickshanks's presentation of the shifting and equivocal commitments both of the people at large, and of many of the *élite*, which is the more realistic in this sense. No useful catalogue of Jacobite Tories will ever be arrived at, because, in principle, political loyalties cannot be treated in this way; but that does not mean that the thing itself did not exist, or was not a powerful alternative.

Not the least of the book's strengths is in relating the wider diplomatic theme for the first time to the history of the Tory party since 1715; and here Dr Cruickshanks draws on the massive work of herself and her colleagues at the History of Parliament Trust. The evidence from the 1720s onward does not sustain a picture of Jacobite M.P.s as a small enclave *within* the parliamentary Tory party (p. 11). There were clearly such men as 'Hanoverian Tories' in c. 1713–17 and the 1750s; the evidence so far fails to establish the existence of such a body between those dates.[4] The long story of uneasy co-operation with opposition Whigs reveals rather the tactical availability of the Stuart option in the eyes of Tory M.P.s as a whole. On two crucial occasions, in 1730 and 1742, the effective union of the two elements in the opposition, remarkably coinciding with letters from James III to the Tories ordering it,[5] can only realistically be ascribed to Stuart intervention[6] (Cruickshanks, p. 12). Clearly it suited Walpole's purposes to brand all Tories as Jacobites; but, as Dr Cruickshanks realizes, this is perfectly consistent with such charges also having a large element of truth. That, of course, is what made them so effective for so long.

It is always possible for historians to belittle the accuracy of Jacobite agents' reports, or the realism of the Stuart and French courts' plans on the basis of them. But Dr Cruickshanks does not attempt to minimize the powerful circumstantial evidence of diplomacy and strategy.[7] In 1739 James III, in response to a Scots initiative, insisted that any rising there must be linked to one in England, and to the intervention of French troops. Colonel Arthur Brett was sent to sound the extent of likely English support: his report was less than enthusiastic[8] (p. 21). It was followed up through trips by Lord Barrymore and others, and by Sir William Wyndham, to Fleury in May 1740; they persuaded the cardinal to despatch another agent to England, but the report was cool. Nevertheless, Chesterfield in turn undertook a mission to Bolingbroke and Ormonde in France in August 1741. Far from the Tories being chiefly Hanoverian, Dr Cruickshanks suggests that even a section of the Whig opposition, around Argyll, Chesterfield and Cobham, was willing at this point to countenance a restoration as a move in the power struggle. Chesterfield did in fact procure James III's circular letter of 16/27 September 1741, which allied the two parts of the opposition and brought down Walpole. Subsequently, it was an English initiative in the spring of 1743 which led to James Butler's mission, and a report on the dispositions of the disaffected, county by county.[9] It was not a list of those pledged to rise, but of 'people expected to declare for a restoration provided a successful landing had been effected by French troops with Charles Edward at their head, conditions which were never fulfilled'. Obviously, argues Dr Cruickshanks, 'the amount of support expected was probably much magnified in order to persuade the French' (pp. 44–5). But although this must have been perfectly apparent, Louis XV was at last persuaded, and induced also to stake everything on an English expedition and refuse a separate one for Scotland. The French were persuaded, that is, after contacts over a number of years with leading Tories, repeated reports of their own agents on the situation in England, and against the background of an increasingly grave situation in Europe. The parallel with 1688 is striking. If the '45 was 'not so much . . . a mass rising as . . . an abortive French-sponsored *coup d'état*' (Lenman, p. 259), it was one made possible, as in 1688, by the widespread unwillingness of the population spontaneously to oppose the invader.

   The problem cannot be dismissed with the remark: 'What would have been the response of English Tories to the arrival on English soil of an expeditionary force of 10,000 veterans under the baton of the first soldier of France remains an academic question' (Lenman, p. 238.) It is one which academics must take seriously; and the chances of success of a French invasion, once ashore, must be weighed. Cumberland and Ligonier were England's most able generals. The Comte de Saxe beat Cumberland at Fontenoy, in May 1745; Ligonier at Rocoux, October 1746; Cumberland again at Laffeldt, July 1747: each time against the most professional and best prepared element of the English army.[10] The result of an encounter with the improvised English defences in 1744 or 1745 is scarcely in doubt. The frustration of the '44 by English naval supremacy, guided by the disclosures of the spy '101', has been revealed by Dr Cruickshanks; the narrow margin of that supremacy is emphasised by Dr McLynn. The key problem then becomes, not 'How much Jacobite sentiment was there in England in 1745?', but 'Why did French military help not reach Prince Charles Edward?'

   As Dr McLynn has shown, French scepticism induced by the failure of the English Jacobites to rise was only a small (though undoubtedly a real) factor. For the '45, as he agrees with Dr Cruickshanks, was finally as much a French-backed enterprise as the '44.[11] It almost secured a repeat of the former plan. With Charles Edward pressing south, Cotton and Barrymore got a message through to France appealing for a landing in Essex, as in the '44. The expedition was already prepared; its departure was set for 14/25 December 1745; and judging by the state of the English naval command, suggests Dr Cruickshanks, it had a good chance of getting through. Princes Charles knew of its imminence at Derby. It was his commanders who insisted on a withdrawal.[12] 'The real reason for their decision to retreat . . . was a narrow kind of Scottish nationalism' (p. 100). Dr Lenman corroborates this: 'There is no doubt that one of the emotional supports of the '45 was a streak of unreconstructed Scottish nationalism' (p. 253). Dr Cruickshanks's conclusion is that the '45 'was a gamble from the beginning, but they threw in their hand when they held most of the trump cards' (p. 100). After Dr Lenman's verdict that the '15 almost succeeded, it now seems that the '45 was nearly successful also.

One may therefore question the argument that it was a lack of popular support in England which led to the retreat from Derby. This has been the received interpretation, since the general acceptance of early Hanoverian England as a one-party oligarchy. As Dr Fritz expressed it, by the time the Jacobites received the French support they had always asked for, 'it was too late. In 1745 the English did not rise in great numbers to support the march south to Derby . . . That they did not do so must be attributed to Robert Walpole and his fellow ministers, who had destroyed Jacobitism as an active force in England' (Fritz, pp. 138–9). Dr Colley echoes this: 'No Tory gentleman joined Charles Edward's standard, and by withholding arms, money and encouragement the party shaped his decision to retreat' (p. 42). But the English gentry had no adequate arms, and a lack of equipment hindered recruiting; few of them were in a position to remit money to the rebel army during its stay in England, without joining its ranks themselves; and Charles Edward had little difficulty in collecting the official revenues in the towns he passed through. Nor was the failure of the English to rise so greatly out of line with the general situation in warlike Scotland. The '45 was everywhere a small rising, not a mass phenomenon. No 'really great' Scottish magnate joined it (Lenman, p. 255). 'In the Highlands active Jacobites were a distinct minority.' It got as far as it did because of Lord George Murray's brilliant generalship, and because 'Hanoverian Britain was a law-bound society with an unpopular, divided and irresponsible political class, and in the '45 the result of this state of affairs was near-paralysis' (Lenman, p. 258). In all rebellions, it may be suggested, the majority of the population prudently attempt to be, and succeed in being, non-combatants. The English may not have risen spontaneously at the first news of a landing; but a widespread reluctance to fight for the Hanoverian regime is equally marked. Even had the French landed, Dr Lenman speculates that the English would probably have awaited the outcome of the decisive battle (p. 238). But James III had been explicit that his English supporters, without arms, could not and should not attempt anything in the face of regular troops. 'English Tories were Jacobites in the sense that their leaders, answering for the party, wanted the restoration of the Stuarts in the person of Charles Edward, hoping he would conform to the Established Church, but they had said again and again that only regular troops could bring it about' (Cruickshanks, pp. 70–1, 98). Sedgemoor was a vivid and sufficient lesson of the futility of popular revolts.

Charles Edward's retreat does not, therefore, prove the weakness of English Jacobitism: it removed a test which was about to supply one sort of objective criterion. In the light of his retreat, the full extent of popular support for him, as Dr Cruickshanks rightly sees, becomes impossible to gauge. Though it is not the subject of her book, she points to enough popular manifestations of disaffection (e.g. pp. 88–91) for historians to feel able to say that a Jacobite victory would have been widely acclaimed. The Tories would have stood forward as the party of government; the Whigs would have been proscribed for a generation. The failure of the '45 cemented the Whigs' hold on power and re-emphasized a traditional ideological polarity as the professed justification for the hostility and unity of Whig and Tory parliamentary parties.

How did this world pass away? A major gap in the historiography has been the absence of a full study of the Tory party under the first two Georges, and it is this gap which *In Defiance of Oligarchy* aims to fill. It combines 'a chronological if sometimes impressionistic survey' of the parliamentary fortunes of the party 1714–60 (112 pp.) with six chapters of analysis (171 pp.) placing the argument at some length within its recent historiographical setting; arguing against those historians who deny the survival of the Tory party after 1715 as well as against those who trace any link between it and Jacobitism; outlining the Tories' surviving ideological identity as 'a constitutional opposition party'; and examining their electoral base.

The diversity of its sources, many of them newly tapped, contributes much of the book's interest. Dr Colley has cast her net wide, and her all-embracing approach has produced some unexpected results. No one who has not laboured in the same local archives, sifting the often scanty and disappointing papers of early eighteenth-century Tory M.P.s, will quite appreciate Dr Colley's achievement in making so many bricks with such little straw. And the most persuasive section of the book is the examination of the party in the constituencies, especially the popular ones like Bristol and Westminster: the local mechanisms of its hold on seats which preserved it from extinction in the face of the Whig electoral machine. Tory decline after 1715 is rightly traced to their loss of power at the centre, not unpopularity or incompetence in the localities. Dr Colley is particularly useful, too, on the policy commitments this entailed: the stand against electoral corruption, but at the same time the limited sense in which their own position allowed the Tories to advocate parliamentary reform.

Two central arguments in the book are, however, unlikely to win acceptance. First, the presentation of Westminster politics is intended to support the contention that the Tories thought 'they could salvage their position by legitimate political endeavour' (p. 26), that is, by a parliamentary campaign which would give them power without appeal to a Stuart restoration. The heart of the book is the claim that the Tories operated as a loyal opposition party, and that they did in fact stand a chance of office under the first two Georges for that reason. There is an element of truth in this argument, but not enough to sustain it. It was certainly a Tory dream at many times after 1715 that a mixed administration might be formed which would break the Whig stranglehold (a dream which finally undid them in the crises of the 1750s). They pursued that possibility, in the hope that they might topple Whig ministers or even, perhaps, create a lasting Commons majority. But it was rarely that they expected George I or II to summon Tory ministers.[13] This scepticism was amply justified. That these two sovereigns were at times restive and dissatisfied with their Whig ministers, and that they occasionally (as in 1746 and 1757) struck out at what they rightly saw as a party-based restriction on their free choice of servants has long been established (especially by the work of J.B. Owen). But there is no evidence that either of them seriously contemplated a complete change to a Tory ministry as such,[14] or that they regarded such a possibility as ideologically sound: that the Tories were a *loyal* opposition, however much their behaviour in Parliament might accord with constitutional convention. This is a major gap in the argument, and without such evidence it cannot be accepted.

If many Tories hoped that their proscription was based on George I's personal prejudice alone, they were undeceived in 1727. It was not a completely hopeless case — some Tories always thought it possible — but those who achieved it did so only by changing (or, like William Murray, concealing) their previous ideological identity. Not until the 1750s did collaboration with Whig governments become a real option for the party, and only with a new monarch in 1760 could Tories seriously entertain hopes of major office. Certainly, Tories engaged themselves in the warfare of Westminster, and Dr Colley makes the most of their hopes of profiting from the ever-changing kaleidoscope of Whig manoeuvre. But this is not inconsistent with an alternative loyalty. If the opposition press in the 1730s and '40s 'only rarely engaged in the mildest of Stuart apologetics' (p. 28), this should not surprise us: most of the press campaign was organized by the Tories' opposition Whig allies, and the penalties attached to open declarations of disaffection lost none of their deterrent effect as the decades went by. If Tories protested their loyalty in 1715 and 1745 'for fear of being suspected', as Horatio Walpole claimed, it is reasonable of Dr Colley to ask 'how were pro-Hanoverian Tories to demonstrate their loyalty?' That was indeed their problem: they could not prove it.[15] But it is unreasonable, indeed simplistic, then to take at face value all such professed gestures of loyalty as 'unequivocal . . . manifestations of Tory probity' (p. 38), and to reinterpret Whig charges of disloyalty as mere attempts to smear rivals.

On Dr Colley's showing, 'Tory proscription was anomalous' (p. 291), an unnecessary refusal of the services of a loyal half of the nation, to be explained only by the success of Whig slanders: 'Whig sabotage of Tory rectitude' (p. 39). But contemporaries should not so readily be written off as fools. Proscription could not have been so effective for so long, nor could the Tories have survived as a party until the 1750s, had not the Jacobite option so often been real; had not very many Englishmen entertained an equivocally expressed but profound and tenacious attachment to a monarchical legitimism which only in 1760 was substantially transferred to a Hanoverian monarch. Consequently, it was not expectation of office as a party, or as a section of a supra-party coalition, as Dr Colley suggests, which restrained the Tories from co-operation with opposition Whigs, but natural distaste for men whose doctrines and dispositions were antithetical to theirs.

The second central prop of Dr Colley's case, then, is related to the first: a denial of the importance of a possible alternative allegiance among the Tories. There was some Tory-Jacobitism in 'the first decade of proscription', but it was 'becoming residual in the later 1720s': 'The Atterbury debacle and morality [*sic; sc.* mortality?] irremediably diminished English Jacobitism' (pp. 33–4). But in view of the admittedly 'limited and patchy' nature of the evidence, it is unsafe to infer that the lack of evidence proves the absence of the thing. Evidence which does exist is too often discounted, like James Butler's list of 1743. 'Was it *really* to be expected' that Whig peers would support a coup? 'Carte's report is *surely* suspect': such are Dr Colley's expedients where it cannot be proved (pp. 36–7, italics added). The improbability mounts when Cotton's request for a delay of the French expedition in December 1744 is held to prove that he and his party did not want it (p. 37), an unsupported speculation; and the strange Tory quiescence at Westminster in that month is most implausibly ascribed to 'dazed euphoria' at the inclusion of some of them in office (p. 245). Dr Cruickshanks's account has at last shed a flood of light on this crucial episode, and disproved also the suggestion that 'the Tory-Jacobite liaison acquired prominence only when the Tories were temporarily deprived of Whig allies' (Colley, p. 41); it was, on the contrary, the Tories' revived hopes which led them to distance themselves from opposition Whigs.

It is armed rebellion that strains this insistence on the unimportance of Jacobitism. If the '15 merits only half a paragraph in its place in the narrative (p. 187), the landing of Charles Edward in 1745 is there introduced as an aside (p. 249) and the '44 not mentioned at all. But when Sir Watkin Williams Wynn (who was in it up to his neck) appears as only a '*semi*-Jacobite'; the Oxford riots of 1748 are described as 'some *quasi*-Jacobite demonstrations'; and Dr William King's oration at the opening of the Radcliffe Camera is allowed to have been interpreted as 'pro-Stuart in impetus' by only '*some* of its audience' (pp. 227, 256–7, italics added), it is difficult not to smile: the denial of Jacobite allegiance has become almost a parlour game.[16]

One reason why Dr Colley denies the existence of Jacobitism as a political force is that she denies its existence as a theoretical position, a body of doctrine. Yet if Jacobite commitment in England can often seem to have a 'curiously insubstantial nature' (Lenman, p. 67), that is in large part because it is a subject which has been neglected by historians. We have no work on early eighteenth-century legitimist theory and sentiment to place beside that of Caroline Robbins, J.G.A. Pocock, Isaac Kramnick and others on radical Whig ideologists in the neo-Harringtonian, civic humanist, Country tradition.[17] Yet their theories were those of the study: they wrote primarily for each other. The broad channel, the main stream of opposition to the house of Hanover was still, in church and state, in high theory and in popular sentiment, expressed in a dynastic idiom. Its neglect is curious; and it is strange that many historians of the political left, after objecting so loudly to what they saw as the Namierites' dismissal of the importance of ideology, should now be so unwilling to admit its significance in the form of Jacobitism under the first two Georges.[18]

In Defiance of Oligarchy goes part of the way towards an acceptable account of Tory ideology, but regrettably stops short. The author rightly and importantly maintains, contrary to the general current of modern scholarship, and to J.H. Plumb's commonly acclaimed model, that not only did the Tories consistently act together as a parliamentary party, but 'they also preserved a distinct ideological entity' (p. 24, *sic*; *sc*. identity?). A chapter is devoted to reconstructing it. Dr Colley perceptively and correctly sees that the Tories were capable of employing both legitimist and Lockeian Country doctrines; and that the opposition to Walpole does not embody a single, neo-Harringtonian ideology (pp. 28–9, 90). The Tories pursued many plans for tactical alliance in Parliament with opposition Whigs; but they never sought an ideological *rapprochement* with them (p. 261). If the Tory party was not Jacobite, then, what held it together? Dr Colley concedes that 'organisational expedients were . . . a less material component of the Tory party's durability than the persistence of its traditional and distinctive policy attitudes' (p. 82), which is true. The components of this Tory tradition are presented as the cult of the Stuarts; the antipathy to Dissent, and championing of the Church of England; and the veneration of the Crown, now transferred to the Hanoverians: 'for the majority of Tories concern "for the Prerogative abstractly considered" survived the change of dynasty and checked the temptation to disaffection' (pp. 88, 102). It is this transference which is crucial to Dr Colley's argument, but it is not proved — for the simple reason that it did not generally occur until 1760. Because it is unproven, and because it was not so in fact, Dr Colley fails to establish, further, that it was the Tory policy commitments she enumerates which 'prevented the party's amalgamation with dissident Whiggery' (p. 101): a key component is missing.

The existence of a Tory political option with dynastic overtones was made possible by two mutually reinforcing factors: the diplomatic context, carrying at times the threat of a foreign landing, and the survival in England of a substantial and viable body of legitimist ideology. It is a pity that neither of these things are dealt with in a book which otherwise seeks to portray the Tory party 'in the round'; and it may be thought myopic in some quarters to write so exclusively about England, without that attention to Scotland and France which Dr Lenman's and Dr Cruickshanks's books now demand.[19] For what made Jacobitism plausible over time, as we now see, was not the independent ability of the English gentry to rise and lead their tenants, armed with a body of rigid and fanatical opinion, to effect a restoration, but the possibility of military backing from outside, and a liaison with disaffected politicians at home — as in 1688. To dismiss Jacobitism in early eighteenth-century England because there was no prospect of a spontaneous rising is even more historically perverse than, say, to discount socialism in twentieth-century England on the grounds that there was little prospect of an armed Marxist revolution on the Russian model. A whole ideological dimension is missed.

One cause of these problems is perhaps, the subordination of the narrative.[20] This is unfortunate, since the history of one party can properly be understood only in relation to all other parties, and because, where primary evidence is scanty, the circumstantial evidence of context and strategy assumes a much greater importance. To neglect this allows a dubious thesis to be espoused despite the inconclusive nature of the arguments which can, in the nature of things, be brought to bear in its favour. Much of the book has, unhappily, been moulded, and the argument often disorganized, by being drawn into a debate about Jacobitism, and by Dr Colley's efforts to deny, on point after point, any importance to that political loyalty. It is a pity that the first full-length study of the Tory party should be characterized by this polemical insistence on the unimportance of ideology, for this preoccupation may distract attention from the book's real merits.

The survival of Whig and Tory parliamentary parties into the 1750s was amply demonstrated in 1970 by Romney Sedgwick's volumes of the *History of Parliament*. This was not widely accepted partly because of the contentiousness of the volumes' asserted link between Toryism and Jacobitism, and Dr Colley's endorsement of the thesis of the survival of party is welcome despite her residual problems about reasons. But what happens after the 1750s? Dr Colley still seems to believe that there was a 'Tory bloc' at Westminster into the 1770s (p. 267), which will scarcely do. But the problem is as difficult for any historian willing to accept mid-eighteenth-century political ideologies for what they were. To throw light on the transformation of Toryism is not the least of the achievements of Dr Peters's handsome book.

For in the 1750s first City Toryism, then the parliamentary party, were taken over with remarkable speed by outsiders, William and Richard Beckford, and steered in a new direction: endorsement and support of William Pitt. That they could effect this coup says much for the ineffectual nature of the party's leadership by that date and something for its lack of alternative tactical options after its damaging involvement in Whig manoeuvres during 1754–6. Dr Peters documents the way in which its various strands — 'old high Toryism', the Toryism of the independent gentry, and the Toryism of radical London — were merged into and transmuted by the now-stereotyped Country Whig Patriot tradition (p. 25). This has not been studied before, and Dr Peters ably explores the realm of day-by-day argument in a book which breaks much new ground in its study of the press.

It is a mark of the self-contained nature of this aspect of the work that its success is not invalidated by the political model taken as the point of departure: the existence in Parliament of a large bloc of independents, 'outnumbering both committed politicians and placemen', whose opinion is 'to some extent' a gauge of that in 'the political nation' (p. 3); a Tory party in the Commons which was merely a subdivision of the independents, and which 'seldom acted as a disciplined group' because its members 'lacked political ambition' (p. 11). In the light of recent research, this model is untenable. But it is largely irrelevant to Dr Peters's main purpose, which is to assert the importance of extra-parliamentary opinion — 'What these people thought about politics could powerfully influence events when circumstances were ripe' — by tracing its 'connections' with 'the political fortunes of a leading statesman' (p. vii).

The attempt raises two unresolved problems. First, Dr Peters insists that Pitt 'is unique among politicians of the eighteenth century, not least because a claim to "popularity" was a substantial element of his political strength' (pp. 1, 271). But why, if popularity was such a potentially powerful force, could others not exploit it? Of course they could, and did, but not in the way that legend has pictured Pitt sweeping to power on a wave of popular acclaim. And Pitt's tenure of the highest office was very short: those who lasted there were men like Walpole, Newcastle, North or Liverpool, who scarcely posed as popular idols. The problem is especially pressing for Dr Peters's argument if, indeed, 'the boundaries of the political nation were widening again' from the 1750s and '60s, as she believes they were, citing Dr Brewer (p. 273). It is not enough to dismiss 'Pitt's indifference to popularity in the sixties' as simply a mistake — that, by using it, 'he could have solved his dilemma . . . and created the circumstances in which his undoubtedly creative vision could have continued to find realization' (p. 275). Equally unacceptable is the grand imprecision of chronology and method in the culminating claim that the growing scope for the use of 'popularity' meant that 'realities were beginning to change, even if the change was not to be fully apparent until the next century' (p. 276).

The second unresolved problem is Dr Peters's claim to have shown the *links* between high politics and popular opinion. This she has seldom done. Her book is a detailed and valuable study of the *second* of those two things, as revealed by the press, but it pays too little attention to the complexity and detail of the *first* to establish many links between them. In the political narrative, Chapters 1–3, covering 1754–7, are based largely on familiar printed sources and add nothing to the received understanding of those events. The narrative of 1757–60 could have been much improved in the light of Dr Fraser's important thesis,[21] which, though listed in the bibliography, seems to have contributed little to the text. A more adequate narrative would have guarded against the errors of supposing that public opinion and Pitt's popularity played a large part in his rise to power in 1756 and Newcastle's fall (pp. 2, 28, 62); in ensuring Pitt's place in the coalition of 1757; or his pre-eminence throughout the war. Often, Dr Peters is perfectly aware of the problems of assessing 'popularity' in the eighteenth century — 'Comment was written more for, than by, public opinion. It shows not the spontaneous concerns of the political nation but rather what various interested parties thought they could excite opinion about' (p. 23; cf. pp. 24, 89). But elsewhere she seems carried away by enthusiasm for her theme. It is not at all clear, for example, how to prove assertions like 'the *Monitor*'s reaction directly reflects not its patron's wishes but the strength of feelings among the readership it wanted to keep' (pp. 98–9).

What is needed is an appreciation of the awareness of other eighteenth-century politicians of 'public opinion' in the proper sense (that is, as evoked by the political class); and a better understanding of the cynical and often unsuccessful use Pitt, in common with them, actually made of it. Too often, in modern accounts, he stands out with melodramatic brightness from a background which has been dark only because of our relative ignorance of it. And the background must be lit first by a study of politicians *as politicians*; to dismiss their art as 'subtle politickings' (p. 62) hints at a coy unwillingness, shared, alas, by other recent writers, to get to grips with a complex, tough and ruthless world.

In fact, a close examination shows that Pitt himself was not greatly interested in propaganda. It was arranged for him by his allies. His famous empathy for his public, whether with the Commons or 'the people' at large, is mostly legend. His rise to power in 1754–7 was unexpected, the result of his skills in devious and unscrupulous manoeuvre, given significance not chiefly by the public dimension but by their significance for the evolution of parliamentary parties and for Britain's astonishing military success in the Seven Years' War. It was the course taken by the party political battle, not a reaching-out by Pitt himself to join hands with 'the people', which explains why he came to be hailed as the heir and champion of the Country tradition of 'popularity'.

Pitt and Popularity is a good study of how Pitt's image was projected and managed, what limitations this must have placed on his strategy, and the fluctuations in the opinion of the press concerning him and his government during the war. It is less good on the exact interaction between all this (or between public opinion itself) and political tactics, and the attempt to imply that a valuable but clearly defined study establishes things which it does not extend to, entails unnecessary weaknesses.

Nevertheless, our understanding has been carried a considerable distance by these books. We now know much more about Jacobitism, its social location, and its involvement with the Tory party as late as the 1740s. We know more than we did about the Tory party itself, its organization, local bases and bids for power. We can begin to see its final self-abasement in the service and ideology of a dissident Whig politician, Pitt. There is little room, now, for theories of a single-party 'Whig oligarchy'; for a 'growth of political stability' which discounts the threat of revolution; for a retrojection of 'Court' and 'Country' to the reigns of the first two Georges, or for a dismissal of Jacobite ideology as a quaint and irrelevant survival into the modern age. All this is new, and of major importance.

These books have already given rise to heated and trenchant controversy, and rightly so. The real sense in which Britain under George I and II was an 'oasis of tranquility between two agitated epochs', in Basil Williams's well known phrase, has been in its stifling imprisonment within the 'Whig interpretation' of G.M. Trevelyan and his intellectual and political heirs. Controversy about fundamentals is both inevitable and desirable if this cosy historiographical oligarchy is to be broken. Even more enjoyable than the sight of this process being undertaken is the pleasure of reading such good scholarship; and at the risk of taking the edge off the exchanges, it may not be improper to suggest that more already unites the revisionist historians of eighteenth-century British politics than divides them.

Notes

[1] Cf. J. Daly, 'The Idea of Absolute Monarchy in Seventeenth-Century England', *Historical Journal*, XXI (1978), 227–50.

[2] P.S. Fritz, *The English Ministers and Jacobitism between the Rebellions of 1715 and 1745* (Toronto, 1975).

[3] *Ibid.*, pp. 156–9.

[4] There are only a very few instances of identifiably pro-Hanoverian Tories contesting parliamentary seats against identifiably Jacobite Tories, as Dr Colley briefly concedes (p. 136): a fact of considerable importance.

[5] Dr Colley's denials of the importance of James III's interventions (pp. 209–10, 230) are unconvincing.

[6] Professor Speck has objected to this argument as likening the Tories to 'a Western European communist party in the 1930s under orders from Moscow': *The Whig Ascendancy: Colloquies on Hanoverian England*, ed. J. Cannon (1981), p. 59. This rejected analogy actually seems strikingly apt, though in one way not strong enough: the probability of a Stuart restoration in the England of 1715–45 was far greater than of a Marxist revolution at any time in the twentieth century.

[7]   *Political Untouchables* links the French and English arenas, focusing on the second. F.J. McLynn, *France and the Jacobite Rising of 1745* (Edinburgh, 1981) has since provided a detailed and thoroughly researched account of diplomatic and military policy from the French perspective.

[8]   A previous report by James III's agent William Hay, before the outbreak of war, had been similarly cautious: McLynn, *op. cit.*, p. 12. Dr Colley's reference to 'the unfailing optimism of Stuart agents' (p. 31) is unjustified.

[9]   McLynn dismisses it as a 'farrago of half-truths and nonsense' (*op. cit.*, p. 16) and argues in general against the extent and vitality of English Jacobitism. This is not justified by his research, which draws almost wholly on French sources, and which is not addressed to the question.

[10] Cf. J. Colin, *Les Campagnes du Maréchal de Saxe* (3 vols., Paris, 1901–6); J.E.M. White, *Marshal of France: The Life and Times of Maurice, Comte de Saxe 1696–1750* (1962).

[11] Again, in response to English initiatives, carried to France by Sir Watkin Williams Wynn in October 1744 and Lord Clancarty in August 1745: McLynn, *op. cit.*, p. 29; Cruickshanks, p. 77.

[12] McLynn, *op. cit.*, pp. 143–63 shows how this contributed to the abandonment of the French invasion plans. It was not the sole cause; they might have gone ahead notwithstanding.

[13] Dr Colley's 'definite evidence' that mixed administrations were seriously considered by the sovereign in 1717, 1721, 1725, 1727, 1744 and 1746 (p. 50) proves, on examination, very weak. Sunderland's interest in this option in 1721–2, for example, was rejected by George I as the thin end of a Jacobite wedge (Cruickshanks, p. 9), which it was.

[14] Only a minimum of Tories were given office in the 'Broad Bottom' administration of December 1744, and their inclusions as individuals, leading to the defection of some of them, including their chief, Gower, caused turmoil in the party. The offer of more Tory j.p.s at the same point scarcely marked the end of the party's proscription.

[15] It is less than generous to label the historical reconstruction of this problem 'double-think', or a suggestion of the significance of the sparseness of Tory M.P.s' archives as 'Titus Oates-like': Colley, pp. 31, 311.

[16] Dr Colley's efforts to pin a simple 'Hanoverian' label on Sir John St Aubyn, Lord Barrymore, the first and third Earls of Oxford, Sir William Wyndham and others are similarly dubious: pp. 309, n.23, 317, n.55; Cruickshanks, 'The radicals' predicament', *Times Literary Supplement*, 28 May 1982, p. 581.

[17] It would not be unfair to say that the high calibre of this scholarship, and the deserved acclaim it has won, has led to a considerable over-estimate both of the importance and the typicality of its subject matter.

[18] The present author attempts an historiographical explanation of this reluctance in a forthcoming study.

[19] It is a legitimate complaint against all the books discussed here that they fail to deal with Ireland — the dog that did not bark in the night, as far as English politics is concerned until the 1780s.

[20] The recent tendency of some historical works to abbreviate their narrative chapters and relegate them to the end of the book, as if included at all only as a reluctant concession, is regrettable. It reinforces a familiar willingness to rest content with a certain level of generalization in historical explanation, so that narrative functions rather as a mode of presenting conclusions previously arrived at than as a method of inquiry in its own right.

[21] E.J.S. Fraser, 'The Pitt-Newcastle Coalition and the Conduct of the Seven Years' War 1757–1760' (Oxford D. Phil. thesis, 1976).

REVIEWS OF BOOKS

History and Imagination: Essays in Honour of H.R. Trevor-Roper. Edited by Hugh Lloyd-Jones, Valerie Pearl and Blair Worden. London: Duckworth. 1981. ix, 386 pp. £25.00.

This is a book for those who read history for pleasure: a welcome demonstration that weighty scholarship and light reading can coexist in the same well constructed piece. Like most *festschriften*, it has no common theme, but it enjoys a common style. Enjoys, indeed, is the operative word.

Among the individual pieces, Robert Lopez on Dante is pleasant and thought-provoking. Jeremy Catto produces a valuable discussion of the religion of the English nobility in the later fourteenth century. The main outlines of the piece support the picture painted by K.B. McFarlane, but many of the details of that picture are filled out by evidence shrewdly chosen. This piece ought to be read by anyone tempted to take a teleological approach to the Reformation. David Katz on the language of Adam captures something of the essence of the seventeenth century in an exceptionally amusing piece. T.C. Barnard on Sir William Petty's Irish estates produces a well researched example of the disappointment which has attended to many English hopes of Ireland. Richard Cobb, though he at times seems to be attempting to parody himself, has a solid point to make.

For parliamentary historians, some pieces will inevitably be of more interest than others. William Thomas on Lord Holland suggests a comparison between the first Reform Bill and a pamphlet from Holland's circle called *Suggestions on the Cortes*. John Elliott, on 'The Year of the Three Ambassadors' sheds much light on the might-have-beens of 1640. Might-have-beens, of course, they remained, but the knowledge of Charles I's discussions with Spain undoubtedly hardened the minds of some of his critics. Blair Worden, in a valuable piece, discusses the influence of classical republicanism in the 1640s. Perhaps this influence contributed something to the growth of the notion of an impersonal 'state' or *respublica* as something to which loyalty could be owed, a development without which the political history of 1642 would have been impossible.

The most specifically 'parliamentary' of these essays, it is not surprising to find, is that by Professor Elton. His discussion of 'Arthur Hall, Lord Burghley and the Antiquity of Parliament' offers the expected revision of the work of Sir John Neale. Instead of the collective might of an outraged House of Commons, finding Arthur Hall standing between them and the future, we now find a Council feud, with Burghley on one side and Mildmay on the other. The evidence is powerful, especially Arthur Hall's knowledge of a decision of the House of Commons eight days *before* it was taken. This reconstruction is persuasive, yet it would be nice to know *why* Mildmay and other Councillors selected the case of Arthur Hall for the matter of a feud with Burghley. Having reconstructed other incidents in parliamentary history in a similar manner, I hope I may be allowed to say (without any criticism of Professor Elton) that it would be a pity if a few successful examples led to this pattern of conciliar faction being enshrined as a 'model' for parliamentary research. It explains many incidents, but it should not replace 'government' and 'opposition' as an all-purpose explanatory tool.

Professor Elton amuses us considerably with his reasons for admiring Hall as an historian. It would, incidentally, be nice to know the exact words in which Hall showed that he was 'conscious of a revolutionary movement in the 1530s'. This collection includes more good things than a reviewer can find room to mention. It is a book to be bought and read at leisure.

CONRAD RUSSELL
Yale University

Studies in Irish History Presented to R. Dudley Edwards. Edited by Art Cosgrove and Donal McCartney. Dublin: University College. (Distributed in Great Britain by Colin Smythe Ltd., Gerrards Cross.) 1979. [ix], 253 pp. IR £12.00.

Ireland under the Union: Varieties of Tension. Essays in Honour of T.W. Moody. Edited by F.S.L. Lyons and R.A.J. Hawkins. Oxford: Oxford Univeristy Press. 1980. x, 337 pp. £15.00.

Plantation to Partition: Essays in Ulster History in Honour of J.L. McCracken. Edited by Peter Roebuck. Belfast: Blackstaff Press. 1981. xi, 292 pp. £8.95.

The scope of these tributes is a measure of the contribution of three of the pioneers of modern Irish historical studies, Professors Edwards, McCracken and Moody, in transforming their 'subject and its place in Irish intellectual life'. *Studies in Irish History*, the tribute to Professor Edwards, is a miscellaneous collection of 16 essays by a variety of young and well-established scholars on subjects ranging from the later Middle Ages to the first half of the twentieth century, with notable gaps in the eighteenth century and in the economic history of Ireland. These gaps are, to some extent, filled in *Plantation to Partition*, in honour of Professor McCracken, which confines itself to the province of Ulster and whose 15 articles consist largely of essays on economic questions by younger scholars. The volume dedicated to Professor Moody, *Ireland under the Union*, is even more coherent and apposite. It gains coherence by being confined to a critical period of direct British rule, while eight essays on the consequent varieties of tension, national, sectarian and agrarian, are contributed by young scholars associated with Professor Moody's historical seminar at Trinity College, Dublin.

Aspects of the Roman Catholic church are treated in all three volumes, albeit on largely traditional lines, ignoring the French school with its emphasis on *'mentalités'*. In the Edwards volume, the episcopate is favoured. Professor F.X. Martin uses the career of Bernard O'Higgins, Bishop of Elphin, 1542–61, to illustrate the confusion which beset clerical life in Tudor Ireland after the Reformation. A genuine secular and religious reformer, O'Higgins made little headway in Donegal in face of local opposition, and the Counter-Reformation effort there was not resumed until the following century. The sort of men to carry through this work are discussed by Dr D. Cregan in his prosopographical analysis of the 37 bishops who took up residence in Ireland between 1618 and 1660. Irishmen of elevated social status and continental education, they comprised an episcopate which was 'almost a blue-print for the type of bishop which Rome of the counter-reformation wished to provide for the universal church'. Other essays reach beyond the bishops. S.J. Connolly's study of Catholicism in Ulster, 1800–50, in the McCracken volume, has some interesting things to say about the Catholic church establishment, particularly the restricted nature of Catholic religious practices and the limited provision for a sound Catholic education. Poor though educational provision may have been in pre-Famine Ireland, the pattern of clerical control was firmly established even before the setting up of the national schools, as is made clear by Dr M. Daly in her original contribution to the Edwards volume on the development of the national school system, 1831–40. This theme of clerical influence is also pursued in the Moody volume by C.J. Woods, who argues that in the general election of 1892, the Catholic clergy contributed to the defeat of the Parnellites not by, as is usually said, 'hectic electioneering' but by 'steady influence' in rural areas.

Another theme common to all volumes is a revisionist view of the Anglo-Irish and associated landlordism. Dr A. Cosgrove, one of the editors of *Studies in Irish History*, rightly maintains that, despite the misunderstandings engendered by the phrase 'more Irish than the Irish themselves', the Anglo-Irish 'retained a distinctiveness based on national origin'. A good example of this vanished breed appears in *Plantation to Partition*. Dr A. Malcomson presents 'The Gentle Leviathan . . . . [the] Second Marquis of Downshire, 1753–1801', an opponent of both the Act of Union and Catholic Emancipation, as 'an Irishman rather than an Englishman . . . emphatically not an Ulsterman', attempting a 'balancing act and a mediating role' between Orange and Green. Other contributors also rescue landlords from the traditional charges of excess. Dr M. MacCurtain's review in *Studies in Irish History* of post-Cromwellian rural society concludes that despite their 'dark and penal side', the plantations of Ireland had a beneficial long-term effect on methods of farming and estate management. Dr P. Roebuck, the editor of *Plantation to Partition*, emphasizes both the good intentions of Ulster landlords and the difficulties they, unlike their English counterparts, encountered, particularly peculiar tenurial conditions and the province's hectic economic growth in the later eighteenth century. In the end, however, landlords proved unequal to their task and Dr W. Vaughan delivers a well balanced verdict in *Ireland under the Union*. After the Great Famine, landlords simply failed to take advantage of their powerful position in society either to maximize their own income or to transform the countryside.

A third theme common to all volumes is the attitude of British politicians towards Ireland and Irish questions. Two contributors to *Studies in Irish History*, Dr F. D'Arcy and Dr E. Steele, suggest that Charles Bradlaugh and Gladstone had a more accurate understanding of Irish social and political conditions than previously allowed. It was just that for Gladstone, patriot and imperial stateman, the claims of Irish nationalism had to be subordinated to the interests of Britain and her empire.

Moreover, in *Ireland under the Union*, Mr D. Haire's original study of the military's peace-keeping role in Ireland, 1868–90, shows how even such a conservative machine as the British army could respond to changing conditions in Ireland. On the other hand, Dr R. Foster's essay on Randolph Churchill in *Ireland under the Union* and Dr R. Fanning's discussion in *Studies in Irish History* of the Asquith government's Irish policy both indicate that the British response to Irish affairs was normally characterized by opportunism and incomprehension.

There is relatively little about the nature of Irish politics before the nineteenth century, but the quality of some of the later material more than compensates. Particularly rewarding in *Studies in Irish History* is Dr T. Hoppen's reappraisal, foreshadowed elsewhere, of Irish politics in the mid-nineteenth century. His suggestion that 'fragmented localism' was the usual state of affairs does really make possible a more convincing view of Irish history, particularly in the 1850s and 1860s, where the absence of national issues is usually regarded as an aberration, attributable to inadequate leadership or such unfavourable conditions as government jobbery and clerical opposition. With fascinating detail, Dr Hoppen shows that mid-century elections and politics, often violent and tumultuous, were determined 'by considerations more pragmatic than ideological, more shifting than permanent'. The relationship of 'broker' with 'client' more often than not determined the outcome. As the Bishop of Kilduff lamented in 1865, 'I do not attach so much value to the six votes the Murtaghs have in the boro' as I do the *painful* influence they have over their customers and creditors, the publicans and bankers of Athlone'.

Disappointingly, and a reflection of the drift of historical studies in the south, only the McCracken volume faces up to the Ulster question and the complex intertwining of 'the various pivotal influences on the process of historical change (local and national, internal and external, political and religious, economic and social)'. Mr W. Crawford provides a framework for the study of Ulster towns, 1750–1850, against the evolving economy of the province. Similarly, Mr D. Macneice's study of industrial villages throws light on both their physical evolution and the nature of the paternalism that helped bridge the gap between employers and employed in Ulster. Less easy to absorb, but instructive nonetheless, is the use made by Dr A. Hepburn and Mrs B. Collins of the 1901 census enumerators' schedules to probe the nature and extent of sectarianism and segregation in 'clanging Belfast'. Catholics were disadvantaged in relation to their Protestant neighbours, particularly in the manufacturing sector of the economy and 'the stable population pattern and segregation level of the twentieth century was established by 1901'. Finally, Dr D. Johnson, although too attached to global figures and underestimating the political consequence of the harm done early to individual trades in particular areas, is broadly right in concluding that partition inflicted no serious damage on the Irish economy until 1931, but after that 'the two parts of the island began to move more rapidly apart under the impact of world depression and even more so of the "economic war"'.

In all, students and teachers of Irish history should welcome the publication of these three volumes. There are shortcomings and omissions, particularly of the new Marxist historians. Nevertheless, each volume is worthwhile in its own way and most of the essays are lucid, original, even provocative and certainly useful, such as Professor H. Kearney's stimulating reappraisal of Father Matthew's temperance campaign, which provides a readable and brief corrective of the outmoded views of pre-Famine Irish society still prevalent in Great Britain.

PATRICK BUCKLAND
University of Liverpool

Documents Illustrating the Crisis of 1297–98 in England. Edited by Michael Prestwich. London: Royal Historical Society (Camden Fourth Series, Volume 24). 1980. vii, 216 pp. Available from Boydell and Brewer Ltd., Woodbridge, Suffolk. £10.00 plus postage and packing.

Curiously, in view of the great interest which the crisis of 1297 has aroused in historians of the medieval constitution, a good deal of vital evidence concerning Edward I and his ministers has never been published. Dr Prestwich's purpose in assembling this welcome collection of documents is to make good the omission by printing a wide range of representative examples which illustrate the major problems facing the English government in a particularly troubled period. Almost all of the 208 items selected for this purpose are from the Public Record Office, and of these the majority comprise royal writs issued under privy seal and enrolled on the Memoranda Rolls of the Exchequer. A number of letters and petitions have also been selected to reveal the attitudes of Edward's opponents, although inevitably the choice here is far more limited. Enough material has, however, survived to show, for instance, how strongly and widely felt was the opposition to military service in Gascony voiced by magnates and knights alike in the Salisbury Parliament of 1297. This was no empty rhetoric, as one example after another so clearly proves. Protests too against the constitutional propriety of the tax authorized in July of that year by a 'Parliament' which was demonstrably little more than a collection of placemen were also very real. Although described with a detachment common to bureaucrats of all periods, the account of Bigod and Bohun's confrontation with the barons of the Exchequer in August 1297 reminds us clearly enough that the conflict was a matter of personalities as well as economic and political issues. With the exception of certain crucial texts (such as the *Confirmatio Cartarum*, which could hardly have been excluded from such a volume), very few of these documents have appeared in print before; and some, most notably the list of the household of Roger Bigod, Earl of Norfolk, are of general as well as specific importance.

This apt choice of material enables Dr Prestwich to present a convincing picture of growing resentment on the part of the laity and clergy alike, fuelled by increasingly unrealistic demands for service, money and goods. His introduction contains a clear account of how this opposition took shape, and, indeed, is one of the chief recommendations of this volume, providing as it does a valuable analysis of the often complex events and issues leading up to the Confirmation of the Charters.

CAROLE RAWCLIFFE
History of Parliament

The Crown and Local Communities in England and France in the Fifteenth Century. Edited by J.R.L. Highfield and Robin Jeffs. Gloucester: Alan Sutton. 1981. 192 pp. Hardback £8.95; paperback £4.95.

This book contains ten essays by different authors. J.P. Genet writes on the theorists' view of the relationship between Crown and local community; P.S. Lewis discusses contacts between the French provinces and the central government; M.C.E. Jones analyses the composition and political aspirations of the Breton nobility; Roger Virgoe examines local institutions and authority in East Anglia; Caroline Barron investigates the political allegiances of London in the ten years before 1461; B. Chevalier assesses the connexions between the *bonnes villes* and the council of the French kings; A. Leguai traces the relations between the Burgundian towns and the monarchy; and C.T. Allmand looks at the reaction of Rouen to its 'liberation' by Charles VII. A general discussion by J.R.L. Highfield precedes these specialized papers, and a chronologically displaced article by M. Greengrass on provincial dissension under Henry III of France follows them.

The quality and interest of the contributions vary. The most provocative and original are those of Lewis, Jones and Virgoe, which attempt the broad sweep largely eschewed by the other authors. Lewis shows how both individuals and communities made use of backstairs influence and private deals, rather than institutions, to secure what they wanted from the Crown. Jones, in a piece which bears comparison with the work of K.B. McFarlane, emphasizes the social range comprehended by the Breton nobility and the extent to which its ranks had closed against newcomers by the end of the fifteenth century. Virgoe traces the emergence of the Tudor county communities of East Anglia from those of the later Middle Ages, stressing the growth in the size of the peace commission, the simultaneous decline of the various *ad hoc* commissions which had earlier characterized county administration, and the rise of a less exclusive county society. The remaining pieces are mainly case-studies of a narrower sort. Some are disappointingly negative, like that of J.P. Genet, who demonstrates that political theorists had virtually nothing to say about the local community. As a whole the volume lacks something in balance and coherence. Only two of its ten articles are exclusively concerned with England; there is little attempt to bridge the Channel and to make comparisons; and the 'local communities' of the title, though apparently elastic enough to include London, remain nebulous and undefined. Useful though the book is, it does not quite rise to the interest and importance of its theme.

J.R. MADDICOTT
Exeter College, Oxford

The Public Career of Sir Thomas More. By J.A. Guy. Brighton: Harvester Press. 1980. xii, 220 pp. £20.00.

The problems of politics and government were an abiding preoccupation of Thomas More. His early writings treat them philosophically and historically in a manner characteristic of the Christian humanism which he espoused. The masterpiece of his early middle age, *Utopia*, can claim — like its almost exact contemporary, Machiavelli's *Prince* — the status of an essay in political science, attempting, as it does, to bridge the gap between philosophy and practice, between the ideal and the reality, by the application of rational analysis and planning to the reform of the commonwealth. More's mature years were spent grappling with the problems of politics and government at first hand. Within a year of the completion of *Utopia* he had entered upon a career in public service as a Councillor of Henry VIII (1517), a career that was to culminate in his elevation to the highest office in government, as Lord Chancellor in succession to Cardinal Wolsey, before his opposition to the King's ecclesiastical policy forced him to resign after a brief 31-month tenure in May 1532. It is this final phase of More's career, the period of his active involvement in government and politics, that is the subject of Dr Guy's study. The neglect of the subject hitherto may seem surprising until the formidable problem posed by the sources is called to mind. The disappearance of More's official papers has meant that the evidence for his public career must be gleaned mainly from other surviving public records, themselves extremely patchy and largely formal in character, requiring immense technical expertise for their elucidation. It will be appreciated, therefore, that the appearance of Dr Guy's monograph represents in itself a major contribution to Morean studies and a personal triumph for its author.

What of Guy's findings? These are best reviewed against the background of two seminal essays by Geoffrey Elton to whom the book is appropriately dedicated. For it was Elton's essays in the 1970s that first posed the question of the implications of the public career for what may be called the canonized version of the More phenomenon. Elton used the evidence of the public career as an antidote to the centuries of hagiography that lie between the historiographical perception of More and the historical figure. Here, he argued, we find little to praise and much to criticize or, at best, to excuse. In the first place, More's involvement with politics at all, represents a retreat from the austere Erasmian ideal for the intellectual, a retreat that must be explained in terms of a capitulation to human ambition, financial necessity and an unrealistic aspiration — against More's own better judgment — towards doing good. In *Utopia*, Hythloday, whom Elton takes to represent the Erasmian ideal, withstands these seductions and More's public career was to prove Hythloday right. He failed to advance the interests of the commonwealth by means of his public service; and he failed to prevent the exploitation of his talents for the advancement instead of the selfish interests of the King and his chief minister, Cardinal Wolsey, whom he served as a court ornament and confidential go-between, bereft of any influence over policy. Furthermore, Elton emphasizes, More's public career brings the dark side of his supposedly sunny personality into prominence in the form of a paranoiac campaign against heretics, a campaign which went beyond the bounds not only of common humanity but also, at times, of strict legality. Thus the public career reveals for Elton a substantial strain of lead in the golden wonder of the established historiography.

Guy's interpretation provides general corroboration for this revisionist thesis. However, there are some important modifications. The major one results from Guy's study of the intractable Chancery material. This leads him to conclude that More made a crucial contribution to the development of English law as Lord Chancellor. Wolsey had shown how the failure of the common law to adapt to changing circumstances could be offset by the development of the Crown's judicial prerogative. But his achievement was too personal and too idiosyncratic to be lasting. More's contribution was to systematize and rationalize it, remarkably using his common law expertise to consolidate a development which the ideology of his profession would have urged him to reverse. The significance of his achievement was twofold. Immediately it constituted a measure of social amelioration by providing a remedy against the piratical and intimidatory uses of the law by the powerful and the unscrupulous. Secondly, in the long run it provided the impetus for legal reform '[impelling] the common lawyers on the long course by which their own justice would one day be reformed' (p. 85). Viewed in this light, according to Guy, the judicial activities of Wolsey and More in Chancery can be claimed to have contributed more to the rejuvenation of the realm than the programme of reform by statute initiated in the 1530s by Thomas Cromwell. Guy is less enthusiastic about More's activities in the political domain. He agrees with Elton that More achieved little in directing policy towards the reform of the commonwealth and he elaborates Elton's explanation in greater detail: More's neutralization politically, at first through the machinations of Wolsey, later through his own unwillingness to advance the King's 'great matter'; added to this, the obsession with heresy that increasingly devoured his talents and energies from the mid-1520s. As to the latter, More emerges from Guy's inquisition with his halo less tarnished than Elton left it. Little weight is attached to the insinuations of untoward violence, and Guy concludes that 'More's zeal was objectionable only insofar as it resulted in hysterical polemic and obscured his regard for truth' (p. 174). That, of course, does not go far towards redeeming the reputation of More the politician. And, in fact, the hero of Guy's section on 'More and Politics' — which occupies well over half the book — is not More but Thomas Cromwell. As the discussion develops More is lost from sight for pages on end as Guy pulls together the findings of recent research, including his own, in a fascinating analysis of the superb political coup which Cromwell engineered by hitching the wagon of radical reform to the engine of the royal divorce, using the plentiful commodity of anticlericalism to stoke the boiler. Thus the book concludes with a tribute to Professor Elton no less gratifying surely than the opening dedication.

After Guy's meticulous refinement of Elton's revisionist thesis is there anything more to be said about the public career of Thomas More? I believe that there is; so much indeed that only matters likely to hold special interest for readers of this yearbook can be touched on here. Two such matters have been aired in other contexts and may receive a brief reference first. My own reading of *Utopia* (*Historical Journal*, XXIV [1981], 1–27) persuades me that More's entry into politics is not to be explained in terms of a capitulation to human ambition or to financial need but in terms of his one ineluctable passion — obedience to a conscience highly tuned and highly refined. On the subject of More's continuing commitment to 'Utopian reform' (programmatic reform of the commonwealth) it is perplexing to find Guy struggling so hard to preserve his earlier scepticism intact (*ibid.*, XXIII [1980], 681–7). He is forced to resort to two begging questions to dispose of More's keynote speech to the opening session of the Reformation Parliament (1529) in which considerable prominence is given to commonwealth reform. And he deals with the suggestive fact that one of the early measures passed in that session — provision for compensation in cases of theft — corresponds to a proposal made in *Utopia*, with a coy convolution and insistence upon the limitations of the sources (p. 123). In the light of the evidence that Guy himself adduces with regard to More's continuing commitment to Utopian reform, open-mindedness rather than scepticism seems the least that can be avowed. In these two respects Guy's book constitutes a contribution to a continuing debate rather than a definitive statement. In another respect, peculiarly relevant to the concerns of this yearbook, it must be faulted for failing to provide any discussion at all. That is on the subject of More as a parliamentarian. Clearly the question merits consideration. For one thing, More's achievement in formalizing the privilege of free speech as Speaker of the Commons in 1523 was as fraught with significance for the future as anything he achieved in Chancery. For another thing, More's conception of the role of Parliament was crucial to his response to what Guy calls the radical revolution of the 1530s. A clarification of More's position in the former respect might have saved Guy from the confusion which, as it seems to me, marks his treatment of the latter episode.

Despite admirable succinctness and narrative skill Guy's treatment of the radical revolution is flawed by some fundamental misconceptions. The first relates to the genesis of the imperial ideology on which the claim to royal ecclesiastical supremacy was based. An excessive reliance on G.D. Nicholson's important Cambridge dissertation has led him to account for the emergence of the imperial idea in 1530–1 as a sort of intellectual rabbit conjured up by Edward Foxe and some academic colleagues to whom Thomas Cromwell latched on as impresario. However, as historians of early modern political thought well know, the imperial idea was already in vogue among monarchists on the continent for quite a time before the 1530s; and an important investigation by Walter Ullmann of the intellectual origins of the royal ecclesiastical supremacy reveals that Henry VIII began to ponder the implications for the Crown of England from the moment of his own coronation (*Journal of Ecclesiastical History*, XXX [1979], 175–203). Further corroboratory evidence for Ullmann's thesis is found in the correspondence between the King and the Earl of Sussex in connexion with the latter's Irish expedition of 1520–1 (see D.B. Quinn, 'Henry VIII and Ireland', *Irish Historical Studies*, XII [1960–1], 325–6). All of this serves to throw into sharp relief a second source of Guy's confusion, his Whiggish conception of English constitutional development. Guy affects disbelief that anyone apart from Henry VIII could have taken the imperial ideology seriously; it was the necessary trick to mesmerize the King while Cromwell got on with the radical revolution, i.e. the establishment of the sovereignty of Parliament and of the human positive law which it created. However, there is every reason to believe that Cromwell was as committed to the establishment of an imperial monarchy in England as was the King himself and that Parliament was simply an instrument not the object of his strategy. After all, the legislation which he devised to effect the revolution made no formal claims for Parliament. It was enacted in the name of and for the sake of the imperial Crown. Furthermore it attacked precisely those values which constitutionalists in the late renaissance period perceived to be under threat from consolidating central monarchies: the constitutional restraints upon the ruler and the constitutional liberty of the subject.

Against that background it may be useful finally to draw attention to the cause for which More died, for it throws light on his political values in a way that Guy fails to consider. The crucial matter here is his refusal of the oaths to the Succession and the Supremacy. One point that emerges from a study of that famous episode is that More did not die a victim to the claims of parliamentary sovereignty. Rather he died a victim to the claims of imperial sovereignty; and the defence which he mounted on his own behalf highlights the incompatibility between these two. For More insisted that he was ready to swear loyalty to the succession decreed by statute. However, that is not what the oath required him to do. It required him to swear to the validity of the marriage of Henry VIII and Anne Boleyn and hence to the succession as decreed by legitimate inheritance which statute simply upheld. More's stance implied acceptance of the basic tenet of parliamentary sovereignty, namely that the ruler's mandate derives from the community mediated through their representatives in Parliament. But that is precisely what the doctrine of imperial sovereignty rejected. In that view, as the Act of Succession succinctly declared, the ruler's mandate derives immediately from God and is transferred by inheritance; the monarch rules by divine right and is sovereign even in respect of the community. In the light of this it will be clear that More's death may not be attributed to the onward march of Parliament. Nor may it be attributed to the onward march of the secular state as such. Here his refusal of the Oath of Supremacy deserves special attention. In his explanation of his position on this, both to members of the government and to his own intimate circle, he insisted that the issue for him was not the conflict between the rival jurisdictions of the universal church and the national state. It was rather the question raised by the state's attempt to settle that dispute in its own favour by commanding adherence on oath to its ideology. The issue, therefore, concerned the conflict between the authority of the state and the liberty of the individual. The question was whether the sovereignty of the state in relation to the citizen is such that public law may constrain private conscience. More fell victim, therefore, not to the secular state but to its totalitarian pretensions.

In his treatment of the dramatic struggle of 1529–32 Guy presents More as an ecclesiastical conservative in opposition to the modernizing secularist radicals led by Cromwell. This misconceives the episode and the significance of More's role within it. It is clear that More as much as Cromwell, though in a different way, was both a radical and a pathfinder. His political career as much as Cromwell's constitutes a significant moment in the development of England's political culture. No doubt subscribers to a yearbook such as this will have their own views about which of them left that culture the richer.

BRENDAN BRADSHAW
Queens' College, Cambridge

The House of Lords in the Parliaments of Edward VI and Mary I: An Institutional Study. By Michael A.R. Graves. Cambridge: Cambridge University Press. 1981. ix, 321 pp. £22.50.

With this exhaustively researched book, Dr Michael Graves has made an important contribution to the history of early modern English government. By writing the first systematic study of the Tudor House of Lords, he has not only filled in a big gap in our knowledge of post-Reformation Parliaments, but also demonstrated what questions in future the history of those Parliaments must comprehend.

The received version of the story, set out chiefly in the works of Pollard, Notestein and Neale, described the 'growth' and 'rise' of an institution in the century before the Civil War. This institution was not so much Parliament as a House of Commons whose Members were selectively discovered by 1640 to have wrested the 'initiative' in government away from the Crown. For Neale in particular, the history of Parliament essentially became the history of the progressive 'evolution' of Commons' procedures, a development which was assumed to have been both cause and consequence of the politics of confrontation. Conflict between Crown and Parliament seemed to be inevitable, since (it was assumed) Parliaments functioned as political counterweights to ambitious, wilful sovereigns.

Myopic concentration on action in the lower House alone has given way in recent years to a properly balanced interest in the official activities of all three members of the parliamentary trinity; preoccupation with the politics of parliamentary conflict has given way to an analysis of the legislative function of King, Lords and Commons. The new approach rightly emphasizes what Parliaments actually did, i.e. enact statutes. Individual members occasionally opposed bills, of course, but traditional accounts exaggerated the extent and importance of such opposition, and so obscured the realities of Parliament's law-making function. By concentrating on the business of handling bills and acts, Graves underscores the historically more characteristic co-operation of King, Lords and Commons, co-operation aimed at resolving the problems and meeting the needs, public and private, of both the sovereign and the political nation.

Graves's eight chapters (202 pages of text) essentially constitute a reference work in four parts, each of which may be read independently. Two chapters on the composition and 'quality' of the House cover membership. In a second section (Chapters 4 and 5) Graves examines attendance, absenteeism, proctors and proxies, and what he calls the forces of 'cohesion and division' among the lords. A chapter on procedure and another on the organization and functions of the Lords' clerical and professional staff (principally an advisory corps of judges and lawyers) together form a third distinct section. The eighth chapter stands on its own as a selective discussion of the legislative accomplishments of the upper House during the 11 sessions of seven Parliaments held in the reigns of Edward VI and Mary I. (These sessions are conveniently listed by calendar date and regnal year at the beginning of the book.) Two tables set out the attendance records and dissenting votes of Edward's conservative bishops. Two other tables list by number and percentage the House of origin of all bills and acts; in a separate appendix the author breaks these numbers down by giving the relevant totals for each parliamentary session. In three appendices Graves has supplied more detailed information on the Lords' composition, members' identities and daily records of attendance. The index provides a useful topical and biographical guide to the whole.

Graves has identified 145 men who sat in the Lords between 1547 and 1558: 52 bishops, an abbot, a lay prior and 91 peers. As many as 84 were eligible to sit in a given Parliament; actual membership fluctuated between 65 and 79, including 22–6 bishops and 43–55 peers. Although the Crown possessed the authority to alter these numbers, mid-Tudor regimes rarely attempted to do so for political reasons, and when they did, by summoning heirs apparent, *vita patris*, as in Edward's second Parliament (March 1553), or creating new ones, as in Mary's third (November 1554–January 1555), the results were apparently without benefit to the Crown. Of course the Crown could also regulate attendance through licensed absenteeism, but Graves discovered no evidence that mid-Tudor governments attempted to use the system of proctorial representation to secure a pliant House: the proxies held were never cast. Graves concludes that a proxy apparently represented nothing more than a confirmation of the licensed absentee's right to attend.

In assessing the 'quality' of the House, Graves estimates that 23 of 91 lords temporal had experienced some sort of 'formal and public education' beyond the level of the grammar school. Fully half of all members in Mary's last Parliament had attended university or an inn of court: all of the lords spiritual and almost a third (29%) of the lords temporal, a proportion which (as Graves notes) surpassed that of the much-studied House of Commons in 1584.

This discovery undermines previous assumptions about the allegedly greater 'maturity' or sophistication of the House of Commons. Such assumptions, as already noted, were based in part on some cherished notions about the 'evolution' of Commons' procedures. In fact, Graves's reconstruction of the procedures for handling the Lords' business allows him persuasively to suggest that so far from following the example of a more 'mature' Commons, the Lords had by 1547 taken the lead in developing coherent (if not yet quite formally settled) rules. Similarly, the socially superior, more politically powerful upper House was naturally placed to provide Parliament with legislative leadership. Privy Councillors and non-conciliar courtiers dominated the Lords; the Lords were expected to take the lead in initiating legislation, and they certainly did so: in Edward's reign 65% of the acts passed originated in the Lords, including almost all of the Reformation statutes.

The legislative history of Mary's reign presents an illuminating comparison: only 34% of Mary's acts originated in the upper House. The relative decline of the Lords after 1553 can be measured in other ways — briefer sessions, fewer statutes, inferior standards of record-keeping and increasing absenteeism, much of it politically motivated. In this, members followed the example of some Privy Councillors who deliberately absented themselves in order to avoid the bitter faction-fights which centred on the rivalry of Gardiner and Paget.

Herein lies one of the interesting ironies of Tudor political history: by a variety of means — remodelling of the bench of bishops, creation of four new peers, dispensing of Habsburg patronage (one third of the members were in the pay of Spain) — Mary I attempted to secure an upper House more co-operative than Edward's, where a group of conservative bishops had consistently voiced opposition to the reformation of religion. Edward's conservative bishops, however, had never been able to block legislation, as they stood in a minority; Edward's Privy Councillors, always more united than Mary's, ensured the passage of important bills by their co-ordinated presence in Parliament. The Marian House of Lords, like Edward's, should have provided constructive, unified leadership in Parliament, but the lords of Mary's politically fractured Privy Council carried their divisions into the upper House, and so magnified the government's internal disarray. The Lords' legislative decline thus mirrored court politics. Since this seems to be Graves's conclusion too, I cannot quite agree with his assertion elsewhere (p. 183) that 'the impact [on the House of Lords] . . . of faction politics at Court was limited and ephemeral', even for Edward's reign, the period to which he applies that statement. We simply do not know enough yet about the engines of mid-Tudor court politics; research on this subject is presently going forward. In any case, Graves has unwittingly shown that a satisfactory history of Tudor politics will have to integrate institutionally-based studies of court, Council and Parliament.

Graves's prose occasionally creates needless trouble for him. For example, he cannot quite resist the stylistic convenience of Darwinian metaphors as substitutes for historical explanations. He thinks Parliament once 'evolved' into separate Houses (p. 120) and assigns to the practice of reading bills three times the characteristics of a biological species undergoing 'a tortuous process of procedural evolution' (p. 150). Why did 'evolution' stop at a *third* reading? The 'three-reading procedure . . . evolved simply as the most practical and effective way of making statute law' (p. 151). In discussing the making of law, however, Graves fails to distinguish in other than procedural terms the real differences between 'public' and 'private' bills, a curious omission in a book which describes Parliament as 'a market place for the transaction of an infinite variety of legislative business' (p. 141). Elsewhere Graves's choice of words establishes some hilarious forms of historical unreality. One encounters the 'giddy politicking' of peers in the first Parliament of 1554 (p. 89); Mary I's 'happy-go-lucky attitude' towards proxies (p. 73); the unexpected life of a bill 'agonising its way through the Commons' (p. 197); and some apparently heretofore unnoticed women in 'a parliament hag-ridden by division' (p. 182).

In fact, such irregularities only superficially mar a groundbreaking piece of scholarship which every student of Tudor and early Stuart Parliaments will need to consult.

DALE HOAK
College of William and Mary

Proceedings in the Parliaments of Elizabeth I: Volume I: 1558–1581. Edited by T.E. Hartley. Leicester: Leicester University Press. 1981. xxviii, 564 pp. £38.00.

In the last five years or so the view of Elizabethan Parliaments associated with the writings of Sir John Neale has come under scrutiny and criticism.[1] The process has so far only begun to develop and we may soon expect fuller reinterpretations. The new approaches rest partly upon different assumptions from the old: the prime role of Parliament is considered to be co-operation rather than confrontation with the Crown; political conflict is no longer regarded as the central activity of Parliament by which its vigour should be judged; and the role of the House of Lords is given stronger emphasis. Different sources are coming to be exploited: bills and acts rather than the diaries of debate. It is ironical that just at this moment the 'Neale tradition' should be celebrated with two major projects: the volume under review and *The House of Commons 1558–1603*, ed. P.W. Hasler (3 vols., 1981), the Elizabethan section of *The History of Parliament*. Ironical, but yet appropriate, since we now have available the fullest possible documentation for the older interpretation, at least for the first part of the reign; and against this we can measure the revisionist accounts as they appear. In this work, the first of two volumes, Dr Hartley remarks that he only became aware of 'signs of a vigorous re-examination' after his typescript was complete and expresses his regret that he was unable to refer to them at appropriate points. He need not have worried: readers will be able to find the new work for themselves. His own provides a full record of the sources upon which the 'Neale tradition' rested. Its merits are in no way diminished by the absence of reference to more recent scholarship, for his editorship is commendably unaffected by bias or partisanship. In his general introduction and in his prefaces to the individual sessions Dr Hartley self-effacingly provides a minimum of comment; but he does warn his readers against dogmatic conclusions. He cautiously remarks that the appearance of parliamentary diaries may not necessarily be evidence, as Sir John thought, of increased self-awareness in the Commons; he points out that the speeches printed may not actually have been delivered; and above all he stresses that the materials in his volume depict something more than the flashpoints of confrontation, a matter to which I shall return.

Dr Hartley's editorial method is economical and generally well-judged. He prints the diaries and other items as individual wholes rather than dividing them up into records of each day's proceedings, as some editors of seventeenth-century parliamentary debates have done. This decision was surely right. We are able to follow Cromwell's or Hooker's views of affairs as they wrote them, rather than having to reconstruct their accounts after they have been dismembered by editorial surgery. He has restricted his footnotes to a minimum, for which again we can generally be grateful, though further discussion of the available texts and the reasons for preferring one to another would have been helpful. He abstains from providing biographical information, on the sensible ground that the Elizabethan section of *The History of Parliament* will supply that need, as indeed it now does. (One may however, remark in passing that there seems to have been strangely little co-operation between Dr Hartley and Mr Hasler: the former refers to *The History of Parliament* in a general way; but Mr Hasler appears not to mention Dr Hartley's work at all.) Dr Hartley's transcription from his sources seems, to judge from the samples that I have checked, to be immaculate. His economical approach to his task has been well matched by the Leicester University Press, which has produced a large and handsome volume at what must now be accounted a reasonable price for a work of this kind.

What does Dr Hartley provide for us? What do his documents reveal that we could not already have gleaned from Neale's volumes and such printed sources as were previously available? First, he prints in full the diaries which were the foundation of Neale's work. Second, he brings together other material, much of it available elsewhere, but now very conveniently assembled in a single volume. Third, he presents substantial information on the House of Lords, conspicuously absent or underemphasized in most parliamentary histories until recently: this is a work on *Parliament*, not merely on the Commons. These pages do not in themselves provide any surprising revelations. Major changes of interpretation will probably arise from the study of other parliamentary sources — bills, for instance — and from the application of different assumptions. Nevertheless Dr Hartley's work does — because it prints documents in full rather than in précis — give a somewhat different impression from Neale's, though not a conflicting one. His documents sometimes supply information omitted or abbreviated by Neale; and the diaries provide an invaluable supplement to the sparse entries of the *Commons' Journals*. Neale stated clearly in his work that the diaries were uneven in their coverage. Even so, the extent of this unevenness came as a surprise to this reviewer. There are, as is well known, no surviving diaries for the sessions of 1559, 1563 and 1566. For 1571 there are two: one by Hooker, the other anonymous. For 1572 there are three: a brief one by Fulk Onslow, Clerk to the House, longer ones by another anonymous writer and by Thomas Cromwell, the most prolific diarist of the mid-Elizabethan period. For 1576 there is a further diary by Cromwell — much less full than his first and largely confined to descriptive lists of bills read each day — together with a single anonymous page of notes. For 1581 we have Cromwell alone, in the spare style of his 1576 diary. Thus in only two of the seven sessions covered by this volume do we have adequate accounts of debates and speeches in the House; and we are heavily dependent upon four Members, two of them anonymous.

Despite the absence of diaries the documents printed here do give us some information on the first three sessions additional to Neale's. We have in full the Queen's draft for her closing speech in 1563, which Neale described only briefly. It is worth noting that crucial remarks about her marriage were inserted by her into the first draft: and if anyone thought that she would never marry, 'putt out that heresie, ffor your beliefe is therein awrye'. The striking anonymous speech of 1566 on marriage and succession (pp. 129–39) does not receive any notice in Neale. It may of course never have been delivered, but even so is well worthy of notice. The speaker (or writer) pronounced that anyone revealing to the Queen what was said in the House or bringing to it messages from her was doing an injury to the whole realm. On the question of nominating a successor he produced cogent and powerful arguments to rebut Elizabeth's objections.

The emphases given by Neale in his descriptions of the two best documented sessions, 1571 and 1572, seem broadly right. He reflects the main preoccupation of the diarists, although he omits several matters of lesser concern to them but of some interest to us. If we are to shift our own preoccupations towards a greater concern with the legislative achievements and the day-to-day business of Parliament, we should still bear in mind that four contemporary observers did find the debates on religion, treason and Mary Stuart of more compelling interest and worthy of more detailed description than other matters. If we make a comparison of Neale's account of the 1572 session with the three surviving diaries several points emerge. First, Neale, perfectly understandably, had his personal preferences among the debaters. He preferred the more rhetorical, like Norton and Snagge, to men like Recorder Fleetwood who were concerned with legality. He often dismissed Fleetwood's speeches rather perfunctorily, although their long succession of precedents may have been as telling in argument as more colourful utterances. Second, some of the speeches are more impressive when read in full than in Neale's summaries. Yelverton's speech against Mary Stuart on 6 June 1572 is a case in point. It is long and densely packed, and Neale inevitably had to omit a great deal. Cromwell's report reveals Yelverton's striking gift for sharp critical analysis of the details of a bill. Third, and most significant, the diaries report snatches of debate on topics omitted by Neale: for instance, on bills against vagabonds, on restraining the use of wood for manufacturing iron near London, on dyeing of cloth, and on keeping assizes at Stafford. Of these the first is the most interesting (pp. 366–7). Ralph Segarston (or Sekarston), a Liverpool merchant, complained that whereas London and other great cities were provided for, there was 'no provision for Lirpoole and other smale boroughes'. He complained that bishops, lords and gentlemen spent too much on clothes, too little on employing servants. 'Bishopps and other priestes troble us with their childrine. And as for courteors they care not for us, nor we care not for them.' His was markedly the view of a merchant from an unfavoured port, hostile to landowners, courtiers and clergy; and he was rebuked by Sir Francis Knollys for 'ridiculous jesting'. Serjeant Loveles (or Lovelace) spoke against the bill on the ground that it was impious to give anything to vagabonds: better to follow the example of Worcestershire, where a searcher was appointed to bring them to punishment. Roger Slegge urged a local approach to the problem: 'every country knoweth best his owne estate.' It is apparent that the measures taken in 1572 for relief of the poor were far from receiving universal assent.

Cromwell's diaries for 1576 and 1581 are at first glance disappointing, for they contain very little commentary on the debates. But their author does provide a full descriptive list of the bills read each day. Except when he was away from the House on committee business Cromwell is scrupulous in his record, which tallies very well with the *Commons' Journal*. It is a good deal fuller than the latter, providing welcome information on bills which receive only the most terse description in the official record. This material may not be vivid or dramatic, but it is likely to prove invaluable to students of the legislative process. In this way the work of Dr Hartley creates a bridge between the 'Neale tradition', from which he started, and the new approaches. All students of early modern parliamentary history should be grateful to him for a valuable task scrupulously performed.

PENRY WILLIAMS
New College, Oxford

Notes

[1] See for instance: G.R. Elton, 'Parliament in the Sixteenth Century: Functions and Fortunes', *Historical Journal*, XXII (1979), 255–78; Jennifer Loach, 'Conservatism and Consent in Parliament, 1547–59', *The Mid-Tudor Polity c. 1540–1560*, eds. Jennifer Loach and R. Tittler (1980), pp. 9–28; M.A.R. Graves, 'Thomas Norton the Parliament Man: An Elizabethan M.P.', *Historical Journal*, XXIII (1980), 17–35; N.L. Jones, *Faith by Statute: Parliament and the Settlement of Religion 1559* (1982).

Queen Elizabeth and the Making of Policy 1572–1588. By Wallace T. MacCaffrey. Princeton: Princeton University Press. 1981. 530 pp. Hardback £28.20; paperback £10.80.

In 1968 Professor MacCaffrey published an important book on the Elizabethan regime down to 1572. In the present volume he continues the story to the year of the Armada. A third book is planned to complete the work to the end of the Queen's reign.

This volume, like the first, concentrates on the making of policy. There is no effort to be exhaustive. As MacCaffrey explains, relations between the central government and the localities and government socio-economic policy are omitted. Many will regret the decision to avoid discussion of the regime's financial policy during the early years of Burghley's Treasurership — a large and crucially important area of government policy — but MacCaffrey can justifiably answer that he has already written a large book which concentrates, on the domestic side, on 'the central problem of religious dissidence, both Protestant and Catholic'. A much longer section, the core of the book, is devoted to foreign policy, and there are concluding chapters on 'the two foci of decision-making — the Court and Parliament'.

The Queen dominates the scene. 'There was never', Professor MacCaffrey tells us, 'any weakening in her relentless control over every significant decision of state', and the evidence which he produces throughout the book vindicates his interpretation of a resolutely conservative Queen resisting the demands of the more radical Protestants among her subjects for changes in the Church settlement of 1559 at home and for support for Protestantism abroad. Virtually all of the royal ministers — members of that pivotal Elizabethan institution, the Privy Council — were more sympathetic than their mistress to such demands, but the Queen kept her ministers in line. Individual Councillors were always, in the last resort, prepared to subordinate their personal wishes both to collective Council decisions and, above all, to the royal will, and MacCaffrey argues convincingly that this strong Privy Council, which ensured basic unity at the centre of government, was vital in securing the unity of the realm as a whole.

The leading members of the Council did, of course, have very different views on crucial issues, and we are given fascinating analyses of the ideas of Leicester and Burghley, the two most important Councillors in 1572, and of Walsingham and Hatton, who joined them at the centre of the power structure in 1573 and 1577 respectively. Walsingham was undoubtedly, as MacCaffrey sees him, 'the most single-minded ideologue' of the four, determined to promote the Puritan cause at home and international Protestantism abroad, firmly committed to securing early English intervention in the Netherlands on behalf of the Dutch rebels. Leicester, who shared Walsingham's basic views, tempered them with a watchful eye to his own material interest. He stood at the centre of a great patronage network, which brought him profit as well as prestige, but his career during the 1570s and 1580s, when judged by his more general policy aims, must be reckoned a failure. He was unable to secure, during the late 1570s, the direct English intervention in the Netherlands for which he worked so hard, and when he was appointed commander of the English expedition which was eventually sent to the Low Countries in 1585 he was a disastrous personal failure there. At home, too, his role as the great 'patron-general' of left-wing Protestants, relatively successful up to the 1570s, was under severe challenge during the 1580s when Whitgift, whose personal religious views were so much closer to those of the Queen, began to edge him out of much of his influence in the distribution of ecclesiastical patronage.

Indeed, as Leicester's star declined, that of Sir Christopher Hatton steadily rose, and it is arguable that by the mid-1580s Hatton had more effective influence on policy than Leicester, an influence he secured essentially because he made certain that his views on important issues — especially ecclesiastical issues — coincided closely with those of the Queen herself. Starting life as a royal favourite, he ended it as Lord Chancellor and Whitgift's most powerful ally in the application of discipline to a Church of England which saw the presbyterian movement within it crushed as an organized force during the late 1580s and early 1590s. As for Elizabeth's greatest Councillor, Lord Burghley, MacCaffrey sees him as a somewhat enigmatic figure during this period. The daring Cecil of the 1560s, who inspired, for example, the notable English intervention in Scotland at the beginning of the reign, was now 'a monument of caution', weighing up the pros and cons of alternative policies with meticulous care, but reluctant to come down firmly on one side or the other. Only in his attitude to the Catholic threat — which he opposed with determination — did he retain his former vigour and decision — but MacCaffrey concludes, surely correctly, that the major overall thrust of his policy was the avoidance of war, a determination he shared with the Queen herself. In tandem with his mistress he resisted the demands of Leicester and Walsingham for direct military intervention in the Netherlands until the situation in 1585 made such intervention essential if England's fundamental security, perhaps her very existence, was to be maintained.

The picture which MacCaffrey presents of the Queen as the dominant figure in the making of policy, a thesis in the classic tradition of Neale and Wernham, is a convincing one. More controversial are his judgments on the *wisdom* of the royal policies, very different from the flattering pictures so often presented of Gloriana. He stresses the Queen's errors, both on the domestic and foreign fronts. In her unyielding attitude towards moderate Puritanism, especially in her treatment of Archbishop Grindal, she missed golden opportunities to reconcile moderate evangelicals to the Church of England, and she stored up future trouble for the Church by her firm support for Whitgift's authoritarian regime. Her foreign policy in the late 1570s and early 1580s was 'bold and clearly conceived', but it was also, MacCaffrey argues, 'fundamentally misconceived'. In her quest for a French alliance she grossly overestimated the power of France, which had for so long been subjected to the strains of internal religious strife, and she severely underestimated the domestic difficulties of securing the Anjou marriage, which was the only practicable way of binding France and England together. As a result of these and other misjudgments the plan for the French alliance collapsed, and England, when she was forced to intervene in the Netherlands in 1585, did so in conditions which realized the worst fears of many of Elizabeth's Councillors; she was virtually isolated in face of the mighty Spanish empire.

The Queen, assisted by her Council, determined policy, but Parliament, that occasional institution which was active for only about three years during the entire Elizabethan period, did occupy a central place on the political stage during its relatively brief meetings, and MacCaffrey's picture of Parliament will be of especial interest to readers of this yearbook. Here, it must be said, his views are a somewhat uneasy compromise between the work of Neale, now under such heavy assault, and the ideas of the revisionists. In line with revisionist views, he lays some emphasis on the legislative activities of the Parliaments of the period, but his picture of growing conflict between Crown and Commons, which he attributes partly to what he sees as 'the steady erosion of the Crown's moral authority . . . over the Lower House' and to 'a mysterious loss of charisma' on the part of the Crown, seems highly doubtful. Elizabethan Parliaments during this period generally co-operated with the government, just as early Tudor Parliaments had done, and the contrast which is drawn between 'difficult' Parliaments in the 1570s and 1580s and the 'reasonably biddable parliaments' of Henry VIII's reign seems unconvincing. Moreover, the House of Lords, which is now being so convincingly rehabilitated in the sixteenth-century parliamentary story, is almost entirely missing from the picture. That is a regrettable omission, but the qualifications which can be made about some aspects of the book do not detract from its overall importance. It is the most significant study we have yet had of the making of policy in Elizabethan England during the central years of the reign, and the overall picture which emerges, essentially critical of the Queen, is one which her defenders may find it difficult to answer. Meanwhile, we can eagerly await the final volume of Professor MacCaffrey's trilogy.

A.G.R. SMITH
University of Glasgow

Commonwealth to Protectorate. By Austin Woolrych. Oxford: Oxford University Press. 1982. xii, 446 pp. £22.50.

We have had to wait a long time for this book but the waiting has been well worthwhile. It was originally conceived simply as a study of Barebone's Parliament, but it has become an account and examination of one of the most fascinating years in English history, the year which saw the transition from republic to Protectorate. The story of the inauguration, membership, government and breakdown of Barebone's takes up only just over half the book. Overall this is a formidable and meticulous piece of scholarship, based on massive research and much pondering of sparse and tantalizingly inadequate evidence. One of its great strengths is that the author is immensely knowledgeable about the Interregnum as a whole and particularly about the period when the Rump returned to power in 1659–60. His references to that period often enhance the subtlety of his account. The book's fastidious style is an indication of Professor Woolrych's concern to provide exact description of the flux of day-to-day politics and of the nuances of personal standpoints. Yet he also writes with colour and feeling, allowing us an occasional glimpse of his personal response to the events described as when he admits to 'a pang at the gulf between Milton's vision of the Commonwealth's future and the reality'.

Chapter III, simply entitled 'The Bill', is the most intricate in its argument, the most challenging but in the last resort perhaps the most exciting of the book. With exemplary clarity Woolrych lays before us the hypotheses that can be built on the slender evidence about the Rump's plans for its successor. He acknowledges his debt to Dr Blair Worden, whose investigation of the Bill for a New Representative opened up this subject. His conclusions though are strikingly different. By tracing the relations between the leading officers and the Fifth Monarchist activists over the last months of the Rump and by showing how uncertain Major-General Harrison appears to have been himself about what should replace it, Woolrych, it seems to the present reviewer, has effectively disposed of Worden's claim that the dissolution represented 'the triumph of Harrison and the prophets of imminent millennium'. Whereas Worden located Cromwell's motives for his precipitate action on 20 April 1653 in his relationship with Harrison, Woolrych locates them in Cromwell's own deep anxieties about preserving the cause of the godly while at the same time securing political consent. The crux of the matter in other words, as an official publication put it a few days after the dissolution, was 'that the bill would not answer the thing desired'. Cromwell had not ceased to believe in freely elected Parliaments but he had come to accept that a nominated assembly was a necessary temporary expedient before normal constitutional ways could be restored.

So far as the precise content of the bill, as it stood on 20 April, is concerned Woolrych is open-minded, though he does confess to a liking for the second of three hypotheses he presents. This is that two stages were envisaged: an immediate filling of vacant seats to strengthen the Rump's case for judging the qualifications of the new Parliament and then a handing over of power on 3 November. In opting for this hypothesis, Woolrych is quite candid that the specific evidence that can be adduced in its favour is exceedingly thin. But his hunch, as in the end it must be, deserves to be carefully considered. One great merit of his second hypothesis is that it makes sense of the conflicting statements we have about the bill. Another is that the Rump did actually attempt a scheme along the same lines in 1660.

Before the drama of Barebone's opens we are given, in Chapters VI and VII, a painstaking establishment of the cast list. The first of these chapters, partly a survey and partly pen-portraits of individuals from a heterogeneous collection of M.P.s, is a leisurely exploration of characters and careers. We are introduced, among others, to the scientist Jonathan Goddard, who was 'most curious in his wines' and at last fell dead of apoplexy on his way home from the Crown Tavern in Bloomsbury, and to the political survivalist Bussy Mansell, who lived to be elected to the Parliament of 1698. Woolrych gives us a sense of men whose religious and political views were developing as they lived through years of uncertainty and turmoil and whose standpoint at one moment can never be adduced with confidence from their words or actions at another. The simple generalizations about an assembly run by a clique of Fifth Monarchists fall away as one reads these chapters.

The task of reconstructing a Parliament that lacks private journals and diaries has not been easy. The narrative in the central section is bound at times to seem rather dry. The book is necessarily much fuller on the background to the issues that dominated proceedings than on the debates themselves. The interpretation nevertheless commands assent. Conflict began early and deepened steadily. It was focused on issues — tithes, lay patronage, law reform, foreign policy, finance — which were at the heart of the controversies of the decade. Cromwell could not have imposed effective management on this Parliament if he had tried. As so often in this period the House soon became overburdened with business and pulled in different directions by Members with varying priorities. Exaggerated fears of the intentions of opponents, wild accusations, sheer distrust killed the Parliament in five months. Woolrych properly reminds us that the M.P.s were not isolated from exterior developments such as the royalist insurrection in Scotland and the increasing stridency of millenarian enthusiasts in London. The resignation was above all a plea by men of substance for authority and order.

Woolrych is persuasive in his characterization of the new settlement of December 1653 as an attempt to learn lessons from the recent past. By emphasizing the eclectic nature of the Instrument of Government and by showing how skilfully it wove together constitutional ideas that had been in the air during the 1640s and early 1650s he provides an important new perspective. What appealed to Cromwell about the Instrument, he suggests, was that it was a serious attempt to find a correct balance between the legislative, executive and judicial powers. There is no necessity to think that Oliver was simply dramatizing for effect when he referred later to the anarchy which threatened the nation at the resignation of Barebone's. The fear of further disorder bit at his heart yet he was innocent of ambition. A revision of our thinking about Cromwell's political aims and skills is well overdue. This book points toward it. Cromwell is never here the visionary remote from the exigencies of politics, manipulated by others with more coherent ideas. He is rather the man constantly in the middle, pondering, worrying, seeking a way forward that will take account both of his social assumptions and of his reforming hopes. In 1651 and 1652, home from the battlefields, we see him rallying moderates at Westminster, acting as a go-between among army radicals and the Rump. In April 1653 he stood between the poles represented by Harrison and Lambert. The proposal he offered to the meeting on 19 April for a select body of men to rule until the time was ripe for the election of a new representative — his proposal — was the germ of Barebone's. In December 1653, finally convinced of his responsibility to the nation as a whole but balking at kingship, Cromwell accepted power as the mediator between the army and the gentry. Woolrych puts Cromwell's millenarianism in context. He is sensitive to the disheartenment that the attempt to bring together the cause of the 'people of God' and the concerns of the political nation was to bring. He is also excellent on Cromwell's foreign policy.

It is perhaps churlish after so much to ask for more, but one could wish for a closer attention to provincial responses as Woolrych's story unfolds. 'Government had by 1653 come to be unhealthily cocooned from the feelings and pressures of the regions', he claims at the end of the book, excusing his concentration on Westminster politics. But had it? The point requires demonstration. News certainly travelled as fast as ever into the localities. Brian Duppa assumed on 14 December, two days after the resignation, that Sir Justinian Isham would already have heard in Northamptonshire about 'that vertigo that hath happened to us'. A week later he wrote of new wonders 'which I believe your diurnals are full of'. The flow of opinion in the other direction deserves investigation. More can surely be said, for instance, about local power and the remodelling of many of the benches in 1653. But this analysis of events at the centre, so shrewd, so perceptive, so careful, will undoubtedly stand the test of time.

ANTHONY FLETCHER
University of Sheffield

The Declaration of Rights 1689. By Lois G. Schwoerer. Baltimore and London: The Johns Hopkins University Press. 1981. xvi, 391 pp. £18.50.

For a generation historians have insisted that the Glorious Revolution was a conservative event. Pinkham led the way in 1954 by puncturing the myth of William of Orange's lofty disinterestedness: the Revolution was not the heroic forging of a constitution, but a dynastic coup. Since then, Carswell has underlined the diplomatic and strategic aspects, Frankle has shown how an originally radical draft of the Declaration of Rights was emasculated, and Carter has argued that constitutional change was the accidental outcome of the exigencies of war. Meanwhile, students of political theory (Dunn, Kenyon, Straka, Franklin, Goldie) have stressed the cautiousness of official Whiggery, the unrepresentativeness of Locke's doctrines, and the readiness of Tories to present non-revolutionary justifications for new allegiances.

Recently, the pages of the *Historical Journal* have seen a skirmish against this 'Tory interpretation' of 1688. Thomas Slaughter argues that 'abdication', the Tories' supposed saving clause in the famous declaration of the throne's vacancy of 6 February 1689, carried the connotation of deposition. But John Miller has withstood the attempt. (*Historical Journal*, XXIV [1981], 323–37; XXV [1982], 541–55.)

Schwoerer's book is a bigger battalion on behalf of a radical 1689. Her central claim is that the Revolution was a uniquely daring event because the Declaration was proffered to William *before* the crown was offered (pp. 19, 26, 255, 263). Although the Declaration was not explicitly the condition of kingship, the event was structured to give that impression. It changed the kingship as well as the king. Hence the event was 'the greatest . . . of the revolutions that occurred in early modern European history', and 'its legacy was ongoing' in the Revolution of 1776 (p. 291).

Schwoerer herself poses an obvious difficulty. When William replied, at the ceremony of 13 February, he 'reversed the order of things. . . . Two could play this game! He accepted the crown *first* and then referred to the statement of rights' (p. 258, her emphasis). Worse still, her account is largely circumstantial, and concerned with presumed intended 'impressions', both in wording and procedural panoply. There are no dramatic new documentary finds, except for a new journal of the Convention (printed in *B.I.H.R.*, XLIX [1976], 242–63), which does not settle this question. On her central claim her grounding is self-admittedly impressionistic. The fact is that so long as William III upheld the Protestant cause, he could, and did, get away with murder.

On two points Schwoerer is on surer ground. She argues that the Declaration's language of 'ancient rights' is misleading: it is not true that all the original proposals requiring new legislation were dropped to speed its passage (pp. 38, 100). The Convention marched backwards into reform, blithely announcing new rules to be ancient rights. In particular, the Ecclesiastical Commission, and the suspending and dispensing power, though controversial, had been plausibly grounded in law. Now they were forbidden forever, as if self-evidently unlawful. Schwoerer's fourth chapter, on the legal and historical background to the Declaration's clauses, is the useful one for students.

The second point gives weight to Slaughter. The assertion that James had 'abdicated the government', as it appears in the Declaration, follows directly the 13-point indictment of James, and thus seems to amount to 'constructive abdication', to deposition. It is undeniable that the predominantly Tory Lords fought hard on 4 February to replace the word 'abdicated' with 'deserted' (pp. 214 ff.).

Schwoerer takes aboard the insights of recent years. There is no disinterested William here: his henchman, the dreadful Burnet, is appropriately ubiquitous. None the less, she insists that William took a colossal risk in leaving the dynastic decision to the Convention. Monmouth's mistake dictated this, but the strength of legitimism, and of the belief that William really had come just to set James's affairs to rights, should not be underestimated.

It is certainly time to call a halt to the 'Tory interpretation'. This trend will one day seem an over-extended expiation for the Whiggishness of earlier generations. And, by depicting so anaemic an event, it has allowed other historians to magnify the events of mid-century. But Schwoerer's book is limited by its terms of reference. It is an exhaustive account of a document. If the Revolution is fully to be reappraised, a larger perspective is needed, and one which takes religion seriously. I do not believe the way forward is simply to give the constitutional seesaw a tip back in a Whiggish direction. The powers of the state grew relentlessly, Revolution notwithstanding, and it was not power that provoked opposition, but the uses to which it was put. William's reign brought massive taxation, bureaucratic intrusiveness, a standing army, and the suspension of Habeas Corpus, but it was Protestant power wielded against a French king who seemed set on rolling back the Reformation. It was necessary *not* to delimit William's authority, for this godly prince had a providential task to perform. 1688 was not a modern revolution, but an act of the Reformation, and it was not constitutional reformism, but the ability to be unequivocally the party of the Reformation that guaranteed the Whigs a political future.

What also marks the Revolution as a caesura is the collapse of 'prelacy'. If the Revolution was Whig, it was because it was Erastian. The Act of Toleration is as much the document of 1689 as the Declaration. Sacheverell was to be judged to have impugned the Revolution because he advocated dismantling toleration. James so emasculated the Church that he drove the hierarchy to a deal with the Dissenters, which they had not seriously countenanced before. Toleration was the price for the political security of the Established Church. This was the historic compromise of 1688. William's army was not only a stick to beat James, but a guarantee that the Church would keep its side of the bargain: it had not done so in 1673. The 'prelates' persecuting itch' was now perforce abated. In *A Tale of a Tub*, Swift recounts the Revolution as the story of Peter, Martin and Jack: Catholic, Anglican and Dissenter. Schwoerer upholds the myth of the Revolution as a heroic crusade against Stuart tyranny. But the central fact of Restoration politics was Martin's tyranny, and Jack was never quite sure who he hated most, Peter or Martin.

MARK GOLDIE
Churchill College, Cambridge

London Politics 1713–1717: Minutes of a Whig Club 1714–1717, edited by H. Horwitz; *London Pollbooks 1713*, edited by W.A. Speck and W.A. Gray. London: London Record Society Publications, Volume XVII. 1981. v, 131 pp. £10.00 to non-members.

This is a volume of as much note to those with a general interest in the whole field of the history of early eighteenth-century party as to those with a specialized concern with the politics of the City. The minute-book of a club of prominent London Whigs — a club formed a few months before Queen Anne's death but at its most active in the years 1715–16 — was unearthed by Professor Horwitz among the manuscript collections at the Guildhall Library and is here printed in full with a helpful ten-page introduction and a model index. Published with it, partly for its intrinsic interest and partly as 'the nearest available list [of London voters] to the period during which the minutes were compiled', is a consolidated version of two *Lists of the Poll* for London at the general election of 1713, one of them not hitherto known to scholars. The editors are the old firm of Speck and Gray, pioneers of pollbook analysis, with Mr Gray contributing the computer expertise required in amalgamating and re-ordering the lists and Professor Speck supplying the introduction.

The minute-book for 1714–17 (which Professor Horwitz reveals, from other evidence, was kept by the club's first secretary, David Le Gros) appears to be a unique document, in the context of municipal party organization at this period. It is very probable that party clubs, as such, already existed in a few of the largest provincial cities, as they did in certain county constituencies, such as Hertfordshire. But, so far as we know, none has left a detailed record of its proceedings before 1737; and in any case the sheer complexity of London civic politics had no counterpart elsewhere in England. The only clue to the name of Le Gros's club is the occasional use in his papers of the initials 'H.S.' The editor's suggestion of 'Honourable Society' cannot be discounted, but 'Hanover Society' seems more likely. Although its earliest minuted meeting was on 20 May 1714, the 'settling' of the club took place the previous month, very soon after the safety of the Protestant

Succession had been the subject of grandstand debates at Westminster. Also, one of the club's most important concerns when the Jacobite rebellion threatened in the summer of 1715 was to draw up at the instance of Colonel John Shorey, founder member and common councilman, long lists of 'persons disaffected to the government' in every ward — in effect, search lists for the benefit of the London lieutenancy. No sooner had news arrived that Mar had raised his standard for the Pretender at Braemar than the club's members voted to resume their earlier custom of holding weekly rather than monthly meetings. Possibly, therefore, the 'Society' had originated as the City Whigs' counterpart to the more famous 'Hanover *Club*', with its star-studded Westminster cast, of which Steele and Oldmixon have left us a record.

Although Le Gros's minutes are mostly terse they amply reward careful study: indeed, with the help of an admirable index it is possible to read almost as much between their lines as on them. In this review only four of the most interesting conclusions to be drawn from the document can be mentioned. In the first place, while it has long been known that both the Whigs and Tories in Anne's reign had some kind of organization at ward level in London, we can now observe an attempt, possibly for the first time, to co-ordinate a party's effort in every ward. That this was an *intention* of the (?) Hanover Society from the start — even though it took more than a year to bring it close to realization — can be safely deduced from two of the earliest entries, one looking forward to filling up the membership with at least one representative from every ward, the other commissioning the original members to prepare forthwith not only ward books of liverymen but precinct books listing every householder. Secondly, we can see why the club failed for more than a year to fulfil its potential. Its original 22 members contained a few prominent businessmen, such as Richard Houblon and the former Whig M.P., Robert Baylis, together with a good sprinkling of common councilmen and militia officers, but little in the way of real political heavy-weights. Only two Members of Parliament, John London and John Eyles, and possibly Charles Cooke, the Turkey merchant, could seriously have been described in such terms. Attempts to stiffen the ranks in July 1714 had little success: for example, invitations to the bookseller-politician, Awnsham Churchill, and to John Deacle to represent Castle Baynard ward in the club were not taken up. And it was doubtless because the biggest Whig fish in the City (despite an exclusive membership fee of four guineas a year) had still not nibbled by the end of the year that the club played no recorded part in promoting the successful Whig campaign in London at the general election of January 1715. The turning-point came in the spring of 1715 when the ministry first became awakened to the club's possibilities. Over the next six months or so a squad of great City magnates, several with parliamentary experience, became members. They were led by the formidable Sir Gilbert Heathcote, doyen of the Bank, and included Sir Gregory Page, Samuel Shepheard, Jacob Jacobsen and, interestingly, Sir Theodore Janssen, now seemingly forgiven for his former co-operation with Harley and the Tories. The club which, with a membership of around 80, played such a strenuous part in organizing the London common council elections of December 1715 and December 1716 was thus a very different body from the original creation of 1714.

These minutes can leave no informed reader in any doubt that the Whig government's eventual involvement with the club was a close one. It culminated in the disbursement to it, in stages, of £1,700 of public money to strengthen its bid to overthrow a Tory majority in the common council, a majority which had become deeply embarrassing to the ministry and potentially encouraging to those forces of popular dissidence and disorder in the capital which were so active during 1715–16.

In revealing this involvement the minute-book throws especially interesting new light on the activities of James Craggs, the joint Postmaster-General, the key figure in the mutual relationship. Craggs has sometimes been credited with the role of being 'minister for the City' in the early years of George I's reign: in the minute-book we now have the clearest indication that this role was no myth. Finally, this exciting new source provides impressive indirect evidence of the resilience of Toryism after the divisions and disasters of 1714. Despite the club's galaxy of big names, its funds and its close direction of two municipal campaigns, the dents made in that Tory majority which the early Hanoverian common council had inherited from Anne's reign were in the end remarkably few. It may be, of course, that the Tories had a parallel club of their own. It certainly seems very unlikely that the (?) Hanover Society itself, despite its disappointments, meekly folded up without record at the time this set of minutes ends abruptly on 2 January 1717: it is far more probable, as Henry Horwitz suggests, that when Le Gros ceased to be its secretary at this very time, because of his appointment to a key office in the Bank of England secretariat, the society appointed a new secretary and continued in being, while Le Gros simply took his own minute-book home. Perhaps, one day, further evidence will be uncovered which will resolve both these intriguing matters, along with others of relevance.

By comparison with the minute-book the London pollbooks of 1713 afford more orthodox fare. In one of the heaviest turnouts of liverymen in the first half of the eighteenth century (6,787 out of around 8,200) the number of cross-voters, winnowed out by the editors, total a mere 615. It is plain, moreover, that even of those nine per cent many split their votes three and one between one list of candidates and the other. This is a tribute to the compelling force of the 'party ticket'; and especially so on the Tory-Court side, because in the aftermath of a damaging split among the Tories in the Commons four months earlier which had cost Harley's ministry the ratification of the Franco-British trade treaty, the Whigs deliberately competed for their opponents' votes in the London election by including on their list at least one 'Hanover Tory', the Barbados merchant Robert Heysham. (The party credentials of a second 'Whig' candidate, Peter Godfrey, were also open to some question.)

In editing the pollbooks the editors decided to consolidate the two lists by re-arranging the voters' names in alphabetical order throughout. Although a rational enough decision, it does have one drawback. The document as presented makes it difficult to construct a rough 'social profile' of the London electorate's behaviour in 1713. Professor Horwitz tells us in his introduction, for instance, that in the common council elections of 1715–16 the most Whiggish wards were in the prosperous 'inner city' and the most Tory were those wards 'without the walls' containing a preponderance of the dwellings of the 'poorer sort'. It had not always been so; and it would have been interesting, therefore, to discover whether some of those manual trades segregated by livery in the original printed *Lists* (carpenters, cutlers, plumbers, plasterers, *etc.* — and especially butchers) — trades which, as we know from Professor Speck's own analysis, made in 1970,[1] had declared emphatically for the Tories at the London parliamentary election of 1710 — show any shift of allegiance in 1713, when the four Tory candidates squeezed home more narrowly. It would be nice to think that sometime, somewhere, in the future a manuscript pollbook for the London election of 1715, when the Tories lost two seats, will at last surface. If it does, with the aid of the present publication and of the work done earlier by Speck and Gray on the 1722 as well as the 1710 city contests,[2] it will be possible to subject the behaviour of London's large and idiosyncratic electorate to uniquely close scrutiny over four elections, compressed into 12 years of bitter partisan feuding.

GEOFFREY HOLMES
University of Lancaster

Notes

1 *Tory and Whig: The Struggle in the Constituencies 1701–1715* (1970), p. 118.
2 'Londoners at the Polls under Anne and George I', *Guildhall Studies in London History*, I, No. 4 (1975).

The Dynamics of Change: The Crisis of the 1750s and English Party Systems. By J.C.D. Clark. (Cambridge Studies in the History and Theory of Politics.) Cambridge: Cambridge University Press. 1982. xiii, 615 pp. £37.50.

So much source material is now available for the study of politics in mid-eighteenth century Britain that it was presumably inevitable that a revival of narrative history should lead to monster tomes like this volume. The period under survey, from the death of Henry Pelham in March 1754 to the formation of the Pitt-Newcastle coalition ministry in June 1757, is one of the major political crises of the century. The author's concern is not merely to portray this in infinitely greater detail than has ever been done before, but also to draw general conclusions about the nature of contemporary politics, and to correct what he believes to be misconceptions about what actually happened. The focus is a narrow one, the struggle for power among the top politicians. The important events of the time in North America and Europe are mentioned only if they impinge on this theme, and the reader's familiarity with them is taken for granted. 'The news of Braddock's defeat' (p. 186) is for example the sole reference to that episode on the Ohio in 1755. The author evidently believes that no one unfamiliar with the decade will read his book, and he may well be right!

The traditional picture of the crisis is as follows. That it was caused by the attempt of the Duke of Newcastle to take power himself on the death of his brother Henry Pelham, thereby overturning the political practice of the previous generation, when the Prime Ministership had been established in the Commons by Sir Robert Walpole and Pelham. This move is held to have been checked by his Commons rivals for power, Henry Fox and William Pitt; and after Newcastle had temporarily saved himself by deals with Fox in December 1754 and September 1755, the duke was swept out of office in October 1756 by public indignation at the loss of Minorca and other early disasters of the Seven Years War. He did not dare overthrow the popular but minority Devonshire-Pitt ministry during the ensuing parliamentary session; but Pitt's dismissal by George II in April 1757 caused him to appreciate the value of Newcastle's parliamentary strength, and the two men formed the famous coalition that won the Seven Years War.

Clark seeks to provide new explanations for this course of events. He opens with the contention that in 1754 there was neither a convention nor a need for the Prime Minister to be in the House of Commons, adducing in support of this claim the circumstance that eight out of the next ten first ministers from 1754 were peers (pp. 9, 63, 93–7). But convention is here confused with political reality. All the long ministries of the century were headed by commoners. Those led by peers were short-lived and unsuccessful (except for the special case of the Newcastle-Pitt coalition). This contrast was not coincidence, for it arose out of the practical importance of having as 'the Minister' a man able to lead and persuade the Commons. That Clark should dismiss this situation as 'historians' fictions' (p. 93) casts doubts on his own insight.

More convincing is his detailed rewriting of the story of the crisis. What occurred in 1754–5 was not the defeat of Newcastle's attempts to subordinate the Commons to a minister in the Lords, but a battle for power won by the duke, who outmanoeuvred Fox into accepting poor terms. His eventual fall in the autumn of 1756 was due to Fox's desertion, not to any popular outcry or Pitt's parliamentary onslaughts. Pitt, indeed, is cut down to size. He was not a serious contender for power in 1754. His famous denunciations in 1755 of the European subsidy treaties were not only unsuccessful in the Commons but wrong-headed, being based on the erroneous forecast that Prussia would be driven into the arms of France (p. 225). Pitt failed in Parliament. He was debarred from high office by the veto of George II (pp. 75–6, 165–6). And his traditional path to power, public opinion, is discounted by Clark, who believes that little practical significance need be attached to this phenomenon, in the form of either the press or the mob. Ministerial support and morale were both higher in the autumn of 1756 than in the summer, for Prussian successes had replaced British defeats as the war news. How then does Clark explain Pitt's rise to power?

His central theme (e.g. pp. 284, 380) is that any viable ministry at the time had to be founded on a coalition of any two out of Newcastle, Fox and Pitt. Fox's desertion of Newcastle, and Pitt's refusal to serve with the Duke, made his resignation a matter of political honour. Pitt only perceived his own need of an ally after the Pitt-Devonshire ministry, which lacked both royal support and a parliamentary majority. Newcastle refused to challenge Pitt in the Commons, and also to back Fox's attempts to form a ministry after Fox and his mentor Cumberland, George II's son, had engineered Pitt's dismissal in April 1757. And so the Pitt-Newcastle ministry was born out of political necessity, not military crisis. The whole scenario has obvious similarities to the later political crisis of 1782–3 that led to the Fox-North coalition, not an analogy noted by Clark, but with one important difference. It was not a matter of counting heads in Parliament: Newcastle's papers in 1756–7 are singularly devoid of the parliamentary lists characteristic of the 1760s, for he lacked not a Commons majority but an ally.

All this is a far cry from the study of party politics implicitly promised in the title. Clark is one of the historians who postulate the survival of Whig and Tory parties throughout George II's reign, using phrases like 'either party' (p. 234) and making frequent use of party terminology. The independents in regular opposition are usually labelled Tory, a term applied at the time only by their opponents. Even Sir Roger Newdigate, the High Church M.P. for Oxford University and surely the archetypal Tory, regarded himself as 'of the country interest' (p. 214). Clark's immensely detailed study, which clearly demonstrates the complex, subtle and individualistic nature of politics in the 1750s, is in fact itself convincing evidence that party politics had not survived in any meaningful sense. There was no contest for power between organized parties, and it is perverse to claim that this book refutes a Court-Country analysis of politics and demonstrates 'the survival of the Whig and Tory parties of Queen Anne's reign until the 1750s' (cover synopsis). The story Clark tells is of the manoeuvres of individuals and small groups, with all ambitious men claiming to be Whigs.

Clark's book, therefore, does not significantly change the shape of politics in mid-eighteenth-century Britain as delineated by Sir Lewis Namier. It is the work of a first-class historical technician, immensely industrious in the compilation of his evidence, sensitive in the judicious employment of the mass of detailed knowledge he has acquired. But the importance of Clark's work does not match up to his pretensions, or those of his publisher. He is a superb craftsman, but not a major new historical architect.

PETER D.G. THOMAS
University College of Wales, Aberystwyth

The Parliamentary Agents: A History. By D.L. Rydz. London: Royal Historical Society, Studies in History series No. 17; published for the Royal Historical Society by Swift Printers (Publishers) Ltd. 1979. viii, 234 pp. £15.30 (£9.83 for members of the Society).

Accounts of the development of parliamentary private bill procedure have necessitated some discussion of the role of the parliamentary agents, whose skills have over the centuries eased the passage of private bills through the maze of procedure in both Houses. These shadowy figures have however never received the kind of specialist attention they deserve. The relative informality of their status and the paucity of records of their lives have not encouraged research. D.L. Rydz's *The Parliamentary Agents: A History* is the first comprehensive study of their function. It therefore fills one of the many gaps which remain to be closed if the changing nature of the working parliamentary machine is to be understood. Its main focus is on the agents in the heyday of the private bill, 1830–70, but in addition it surveys their predecessors as far back as the sixteenth century and also their twentieth-century successors. It brings together much scattered material on the agents and on the procedures followed by them and thus provides an indispensable reference tool.

The authoritative histories by F. Clifford and O.C. Williams of private bill procedure and the clerical organization of the Commons[1] provide the essential framework for this account. Against that background, Rydz summarizes the valuable relevant material in Sheila Lambert's *Bills and Acts: Legislative Procedure in Eighteenth-Century England* (Cambridge, 1971) and then describes the way in which the Commons' resolutions of 1751 opened private legislation to 'the widest possible range of legislative proposals' (p. 4) and the developments which followed. Pressures for private legislation for such powers as those of enclosure and the building of canals and railways resulted in the steady growth in the use of private bills, which reached a peak in the late 1840s. This peak coincided with demands for the simplification of procedures and the asking of questions about the public nature of much private legislation. The expansion of public legislation and the appearance of delegated legislation in the second half of the nineteenth century rapidly reduced the need for private bills. By the end of the nineteenth century provisional orders had largely replaced private bills: in the twentieth century the emergence of public utilities in place of independent companies also reduced the demand for private bills. These changes meant that private legislation moved to the periphery of parliamentary activity.

Rydz relates the development of the functions of the parliamentary agents to these changes in private bill procedure and the grossly fluctuating use of private legislation. Originally the agents had been in the main officers of the Lords or Commons: clerks of both Houses were often acting as agents for private bills in the eighteenth century. Rydz explains the way in which standing orders beginning in 1774 introduced complexities which required much greater procedural expertise from agents. The procedural changes together with the great increase in private legislation and the growth in the number of 'outdoor' agents led to the establishment of the Private Bill Office in 1810, which kept a register of parliamentary agents and their activities. In 1830 officers of the Commons were barred from acting as agents and in 1835 the Speaker issued the first rules for parliamentary agents, who were by this time largely members of specialist firms of solicitors. By 1840 an association had been formed of those who saw their work as parliamentary agents as their profession. This association became the Society of Parliamentary Agents in 1846. Although questions were asked from time to time both by outside critics and by some agents about the need for properly recognized qualifications and the desirability of tests for competence, the general desire to maintain parliamentary agency as an 'open profession' successfully prevented the introduction of such controls for members of the Society till 1938.

The burgeoning of private legislation in the 1840s encouraged the publication of various manuals of practice for parliamentary agents. Rydz surveys these and the many reform proposals for simpler procedure and the reduction of costs. Attempts at reform continued despite the steady decline in the use of private legislation and in the number of parliamentary agents. The study ends with the procedural reforms of 1945 which were the fruit of collaboration in an unofficial committee between representatives of the agents and of the officers of the Commons including O.C. Williams himself, then Principal Clerk of the Committee and Private Bill Office. Rydz has managed to present his account unencumbered with a heavy burden of procedural detail and has shown up very clearly the special role of a small group of lawyers, whose very considerable livelihood derived from the demands of highly complex Commons procedure.

Unfortunately the records appear inadequate for a full-scale analysis of fees and the agents' income except at occasional points such as 1883–4 when the Society felt it needed to provide evidence to refute Craig Sellar's attacks in the Commons. Throughout the second half of the nineteenth century it is clear that the agents were often forced to bear the brunt of criticism of the apparently unnecessary delays and cost, which resulted from cumbersome private bill procedure. This study would have gained from the introduction of comparisons of the agents with similar groups whose function depended so directly on legislative developments and administrative procedures in the nineteenth century. A particular example which might have provided useful sidelights is that of the patent agents. Also Rydz seems to be unaware of much of the work of social historians in the last decade on the development of the professions. This is very much a study of the parliamentary agents in isolation. As such it provides an important piece in that jigsaw of the network of professions related to Parliament, administration and the law which built up so rapidly in the nineteenth century.

Parliamentary historians should be grateful for the success of the efforts of a former president of the Royal Historical Society in launching the *Studies in History* series which has made possible the publication of such monographs as this.

VALERIE CROMWELL
University of Sussex

Notes

F. Clifford, *The History of Private Bill Legislation* (2 vols., 1887); O.C. Williams, *The Historical Development of Private Bill Procedure* (2 vols., 1948); *The Clerical Organisation of the House of Commons* (1954).

Holland House. By Leslie Mitchell. London: Duckworth. 1980. 320 pp. £18.00.

Although they were in opposition for nearly 46 out of the 47 years from 1783 to 1830, the Whig followers of Charles James Fox and Earl Grey could never quite shake off an attitude of patrician superiority towards their rivals on the government benches. Whig correspondence in this period reveals perpetual frustration but surprisingly little self-doubt. Four factors mainly contributed to this thoroughly unmerited complacency. In the first place, familial loyalties gave them unrivalled cohesiveness, despite the fact that they differed among themselves over almost very political issue except Catholic emancipation. Secondly, their European connexions and cosmopolitan outlook gave them an *élan* which made the ministries of Pitt and Liverpool seem humdrum and provincial by comparison. In turn, this enabled them to attract much of the aspiring political and intellectual talent of the day, a considerable feat considering their prolonged inability to reward clever young men with official places and favours, or secure preferment for them in their professions. Finally, and most important, they successfully buoyed themselves up with the conviction that their misfortunes, far from being self-inflicted, were all due to the malignity of George III and George IV, both kings operating in the context of a European-wide conspiracy of thrones and altars.

Henry Richard Vassall Fox, third Baron Holland, was an indifferent politician. Despite his seniority, his popularity, and his unrivalled knowledge of foreign affairs, he was not made Foreign Secretary when the Whigs finally came to power in 1830, and Russell was only half joking when he said that this was because Cabinet colleagues would never tolerate Foreign Office despatches being opened by Holland's domineering wife. And yet Leslie Mitchell suggests that Lord and Lady Holland alone gave the Whigs cohesion and purpose through their years in the wilderness, when they were without access to patronage and suffered from weak, often half-hearted leadership. Reference to the four factors cited above will explain why. As his Uncle Charles's nephew, Holland was keeper-in-chief of the Whig conscience, and he performed this function with gusto, organizing Fox birthday dinners, distributing volumes of Fox's speeches as twenty-first presents, and citing the great man's efforts in defence of 'Liberty' whenever possible. Secondly, Holland House was unquestionably the most important literary and academic salon of the day, where men of parts were put through their intellectual paces and, if suitable, recruited to the cause. Then again, the Hollands were ostentatiously cosmopolitan in their interests and tastes, spending long periods of the year abroad, and played host to numerous European ambassadors and *illuminati*. Finally, Holland more than anyone kept alive the Whig 'myths' about George III's treatment of Fox in 1783–4. In leading the cry for a creation of peers during the Reform crisis 50 years later, Holland was almost certainly motivated by his bitter reflections on royal influence over the Lords in December 1783.

Holland House may have helped to sustain Whig vitality, but the price to be paid was that the party remained, in Mitchell's phrase, 'embalmed', locked in its eighteenth-century grievances, and for the most part far less well attuned than many

Tories even to industrialization and the revival of evangelical piety. In the crisis of 1831–2 most Whigs of Holland's persuasion were, as Mitchell demonstrates, more afraid of royal despotism than of the proletariat. This was perhaps a happy misdiagnosis in that it encouraged them to act with uncharacteristic boldness, but for the most part preoccupation with past injustices was enfeebling. Pedantic comparisons between the 1780s and 1830s made many of Holland's judgments appear, as Mitchell says, 'unbalanced' — for example, his interpretation of Mehemet Ali's policies in the light of Fox's pronouncements on Turkey during the 1780s. His aristocratic disdain for political economy spread to many of his colleagues, and contributed to the Whig governments' reputation for impracticality; while much of their lethargy in the later 1830s derived from the fact that for 50 years they had been extolling Catholic emancipation, abolition of slavery, and parliamentary reform as the only things needful for human happiness, and now had to face the fact that the accomplishment of all three had satisfied neither Ireland, nor the West Indies, nor the common people of Britain. If William IV's attempt to sack Melbourne's administration had succeeded, Holland House Whiggery might have secured another lease of artificial life; as it was, Melbourne's reinstatement merely revealed such Whiggery's lack of contemporary relevance.

Over the years there have been many accounts of life at Holland House. Dr Mitchell brings these accounts together elegantly, re-telling most of the best stories in the process, and laces his narrative with appropriate quotations from the voluminous and under-utilized Holland manuscripts in the British Library. Like the party it describes, his book commences in sparkling fashion but becomes somewhat prolix and repetitive; it lacks, for example, the scintillating compactness of William Thomas's essay on Lord Holland in the *festschrift* recently presented to Lord Dacre (reviewed *ante*, p. 223). Nor does Mitchell really solve any outstanding mysteries, of which the most intriguing concerns that 'prejudiced and *very very* sly' librarian, John Allen — 'Jack' to his mistress, and to her only — whose personality, it has been said, was 'so indelibly stamped on the inner life of the Holland family'. However, there is quite enough here to make one see what Greville must have meant in observing that Holland's death in 1840 'eclipsed the gaiety of nations'. Lady Holland, who died five years later, is the dominating figure, of course, and Mitchell brings out very well her imperious hospitality — making her guests swap places and topics of conversation, and generally bossing them about; her own peculiar style of discussion — 'toute assertion', according to Talleyrand; her breathtaking effrontery — seen most notably in her moralistic condemnation of Queen Caroline's antics; her tantrums and her calculated capriciousness. As Mitchell points out, she collected distinction of any kind, even filching Macaulay from the patronage of Lord Lansdowne, and she openly despised mediocrity. Byron and Brougham dared to rebel a little bit, but the greatest non-juror of all was the Hollands' son, a determinedly stolid and common-place, somewhat metaphysical, democratical, and completely apolitical figure, who possessed 'no whig feeling' at all according to the Hollands' surrogate son and political heir, Lord John Russell.

There is an interesting section on Canning, the greatest of the talents that got away. Canning rightly saw that under the Whig dispensation mere talent, unsupported by acres and an aristocratic title, could rise (like Sheridan's) only so far. Lady Holland and many of her set, though not her husband, detested Canning. Mitchell suggests that this was because Canning 'muddied the waters'; by supporting Whig policies (such as Catholic emancipation) and Tory ministries, he destroyed that sense of 'black versus white' with which the Whigs simplistically regarded both domestic and international affairs. There is an important truth here. The age of the first industrial revolution was indeed a time of cultural ambivalence and uncertainty, of opposing truths and intellectual equivocations, and did not suit politicians accustomed to see issues in simple manichaean terms. Mitchell's exposition of Whig principles as they derived from the 1780s and 1790s (Chapter Three) is admirable, but he does not venture far in exploring their engagement with nineteenth-century developments, despite some interesting passages on Jeffrey's literary criticism and an all too brief reference to Millar's and Stewart's 'sociological evolutionism' (pp. 184–5). Perhaps Bowood, about which so much less is known, would have proved a more interesting salon to study than Holland House, for it was there that old Whigs made contact with political economists and even some evangelicals. Within its limits, however, this is a useful and enjoyable contribution to the study of Whig politics during the years of opposition.

BOYD HILTON
Trinity College, Cambridge

Gladstone: Church, State and Tractarianism. A Study of His Religious Ideas and Attitudes 1809–1859. By Perry Butler. (Oxford Historical Monographs.) Oxford: Oxford University Press. 1982. x, 246 pp. £17.50.

So much has been written about Gladstone that it is difficult to suppose that a further study can be truly illuminating. This book, furthermore, has very limited aims: to examine the origin of Gladstone's High Church proclivities, the evolution of his ideas on the relationship of church and state, and his relationship to the Oxford movement. It is restricted to the subject's formative years. Yet within this area Mr Butler has produced a very impressive piece of work, the more important, in fact, for being so carefully circumscribed, since it allows a serious and critical analysis of just that central part of Gladstone's own sense of priorities that the political historians have tended to assume but not to bother to detail. Despite fringe nibblings at the question, furthermore, this is the first proper study of Gladstone's religious ideas since Dr Vidler's *The Orb and the Cross*, published in 1945. Vidler's book ran away into a diverting but unconvincing attempt to represent Gladstone's 1838 study, *The State in its Relations with the Church*, as an enduring work of political science — which it plainly was not. Mr Butler's starting point is precisely there, in effect. His book shows how Gladstone came to compose his ideas in 1838 and how, having shortly afterwards discovered that they were inapplicable to the real world of the nineteenth century, he postponed further theoretical analysis, and any attempt at a coherent position on the relationship of church and state. For this, he has extensively used not only the published volumes of Gladstone's *Diary* — which he helped to edit, with Dr Matthew — but Gladstone family papers, and some letters of Manning which (astonishingly) he was able to persuade the Abbé Alphonse Chapeau to show him. Since the Abbé seems unable to allow most scholars to see the Manning papers, Mr Butler can credit himself with no small success there.

Why did Gladstone not seek ordination to the ministry of the Church of England? The answer is that he wanted to, but in 1832, against the background of the Reform Bill crisis, and his sense that the political fabric was pulling apart, he decided to live out his Christian vocation in politics instead. It is one of the great merits of this book to point to the religious and moral mission which determined Gladstone's entry to public life. He never lost it, and it remains the key to the later Gladstone — the high-principled Liberal of the Midlothian campaign. What changed was the content: Gladstone lost credence in the confessional office of the state, as described in the 1838 book, and replaced it with an unsystematic but moralistic series of Liberal dogmas. Mr Butler does not follow the story through — perhaps he will now do so, in a second book? It would be a very useful contribution to learning if he would. The crisis of Gladstone's religious life, in this sense, and the pivot of his transition, was the Maynooth grant controversy in 1845. Gladstone resigned from Peel's administration, to the great bafflement of most of his colleagues, because he agreed with its policy; but the grant represented the denial of his old Tory, confessional view of the state; and Gladstone was ready to deny it. What this study also shows is how slight, in the end, was the direct influence of the Oxford movement upon him. He claimed (not entirely accurately) never to have read the *Tracts*; but it is certainly true that his general acquisition of High Church principles was independent of the Oxford men, most of whom became influential after he had left Oxford. He welcomed the movement when it occurred, but failed to appreciate its sectarian character. He was at his best in recognizing the bishops as men of straw — prepared to sacrifice their integrity for 'the show of a make-believe unity with men from whom they vitally differ'. That was over the Gorham Judgment in 1850. But it was a short step, really, from that assessment to Gladstone's coldly cynical inducement of the bishops to vote for the Reform Bill of 1884, with the assurance that they would thereby appear to be 'on the side of the people'.

EDWARD NORMAN
Peterhouse, Cambridge

Lord Ripon 1827–1909: A Political Biography. By Anthony Denholm. London: Croom Helm. 1982. [v,] 287 pp. £12.95.

Patrician radicals have long held and still hold a vital place in the political, social, economic, cultural and religious development of England, indeed of the whole British Isles scene. Occasionally they enliven or electrify the foreign scene to the point of genius or disaster in the Tolstoyan or Karolyan mode. Of the domestic strain some have died for their causes like Lord Edward Fitzgerald. Most have flourished and more, using the golden spoons of their birth for the effective furtherance of 'progress'. And the first Marquess of Ripon belonged to this ultra-fortunate majority — not only one of a golden family, but born at a golden address, 10 Downing Street, the second yet sole surviving son of an ephemeral Tory Prime Minister. His brother's death ensured high pampering well beyond the normal degree of solicitude. In some respects at least Studley Royal was one vast 'Intensive Care Unit' — a world in itself. So that all beyond its walls had a certain foreign sameness about it. Just why this particular aristocrat espoused the then 'left', even in a number of its extremer manifestations, has never been clear and Dr Denholm leaves us much as we were and have ever been. What scant indications there are point to a sensitive and secreted soul perceiving the shortcomings of his own vastly privileged surround, and from a great height worrying about the obvious defects of the great world below. When the British 'below' appeared more in hand, then the Indian one became a suitable interest.

The West Riding of Yorkshire made a fitting start as a site for domestic reforms. It was both problem- and wealth-ridden; a vast centre of industrial drive in the world's most affluent nation. From the grandeur of Studley Royal in 1852 came a democratic plea — 'The Duty of the Age' — for extensive political change. That year our subject (currently known as Viscount Goderich) was elected for and unseated from the East Riding borough of Hull. Early in 1853 a by-election at Huddersfield in 'native' territory saw him home — against another Liberal. Thereafter, while not quite true that he always favoured what he himself termed 'the most advanced thing in the Liberal Programme', it was no exaggeration for him to claim in 1908: 'I started at a high level of radicalism and I am a Radical Still.' Alongside or perhaps permeating this marked political questioning of the 'status quo' went a peculiarly active Christian conscience. This led first to Christian socialism in a broad comprehensive sense, and ultimately to a conversion to Rome when deep in the successful pursuit of valued public objects. For between entering Parliament and becoming a Roman Catholic in 1874 the opportunities for legislative influence had multiplied.

Before becoming Earl of Ripon in 1859 Goderich had transferred himself to a wider sphere, choosing to succeed Cobden as Member for the beloved West Riding. Nor had his radicalism been such as to prevent him supporting Palmerston from 1855 until the great Chinese 'crunch' of 1857. One could say he was a radical 'in the round', taking the Under-Secretaryships for War, then India, then War again in the last 'Pam' Ministry — all before 1863, when he was given the full Secretaryship for War. Like many well-heeled men of the left, he took a most prominent role in the Volunteer movement from the outset in 1860, becoming colonel of 'the Prince of Wales Own (West Riding) Regiment'. When the leadership shifted leftwards after Palmerston's death in 1865, Russell appointed him Secretary for India. Upon the formation of the first Gladstone ministry Ripon entered the truly top echelons and took on the Lord Presidency of the Council. Unlike most radicals he had an uncanny capacity for more than survival — for self-advancement no less and in no mean way. The point being, as Lord Granville put it to Gladstone, that Ripon was 'a very persistent man with wealth', and one with a sense of proportion and diplomatic skills of some distinction. He realised that the field of education was central to social change, that one built a reformed world step by step, one block upon another. Hence he was content with the act called after his technical subordinate W.E. Forster and gladly took overall authority for it. He was delighted to chair the joint U.K.–U.S.A. commission entrusted with the settlement of the Alabama dispute. For whatever any individual may think of its outcome, there is no denying that he had and used an immense chance for the implementation of advanced liberal ideas on diplomacy and international arbitration. And Gladstone approved of it all. On 23 June 1871 Ripon was made a marquess.

And then in 1874 he made himself a Roman Catholic and lost all favour with the G.O.M. Yet his doghouse term lasted no longer than the Disraeli ministry. If doghouse term it was. Because the English Roman church had endless Irish Irish privates but few lay English generals. Ripon might have sacrificed his top Liberal Party role for the foreseeable future and have had to cast away the grand mastership of the English freemasons (acquired in 1870), but now the most august recusant family heads found themselves face to face with what Sir Maurice Powicke would have termed 'a man to be reckoned with'. Ripon was wise enough to do in 1874 what Parnell contumaciously rejected in 1890 — to withdraw for a suitable period. With Gladstone back in the Liberal leadership to form a ministry in 1880, Ripon was made Governor-General of India. Another opportunity, and one he took with both hands — once that is peace had been restored on the North-West Frontier. Opinions differ profoundly on the merits of his Afghan policy. Certainly strategic preparation was weak and determination and imagination deployed against Russian machinations outrageously inadequate. Nevertheless, pursuit of internal Indian reforms was undertaken with a zest in excess of that exuded by Roberts before Kandahar. 'Only', wrote Ripon in 1882, 'by removing the presence of direct official interference can the people be brought to take sufficient interest in local matters.' Just as Lord Halifax was later to mistake Hitler for Gandhi, so Ripon mistook the citizenry of Bengal and Calcutta for those of the West Riding and Huddersfield. After all, the height at vice-regal residences and Studley Royal tended towards the Everestian. And height obscures details or indeed basics. Notions of any rapid emergence of responsible and energetic local government; of justice freed from ethnic connotations; or of the creation of a common European mentality among the Indian masses were doomed to ignominious failure. Even so, the mere attempting of such things in the first half of the 1880s had its uses. Error can in many ways only emerge through trial. Such a process offers much to be grateful for.

Again, Irish Home Rule was just the cause for one of Ripon's cast of mind. Back from India in 1884, he became First Lord of the Admiralty in Gladstone's short-lived third ministry and espoused the Irish cause with characteristically unabating zeal. All through the dark and sorrow of the Salisbury second ministry he let no opportunity pass of speaking out for his leader, his party and their causes. During the fourth Gladstone and the only Rosebery ministry he spread his aged wings over the numerous eggs of the Colonial Office. In 1905 he was still there to become Lord Privy Seal and Liberal leader in the House of Lords, and went on in office to outlive his premier Campbell-Bannerman and to enter the Asquith era. He retired, in a manner of speaking, only just in time to die. As for the American founding fathers, so with the noble Marquess, the key political matters were ones of supreme self-evidentness. His career advanced liberally and radically with the mainstream of the left-centre. Radical yet never at the edge of the crotcheteers' spheres, peaceloving yet never anti-imperialist, his mix was that happy brew so rarely attained by 'left' leaders and yet more rarely by their parties. Here in this highly detailed account of his life Ripon appears as a leader but not potential chief, but a leader all the same and not one, like Rosebery, who ever got 'lost'. All too infrequently full attention is given to those just below the line of supreme success. Now it has been directed towards one such person. But Croom should have been more at the Helm (or *vice versa*) — their author meanders too much and digs too little. He should move beyond mere effort and begin to think.

MICHAEL HURST
St John's College, Oxford

Lord Randolph Churchill: A Political Life. By R.F. Foster. Oxford: Oxford University Press. 1981. xi, 431 pp. £16.00.

Roy Foster is an intriguing biographer. In his previous study of Parnell (*Charles Stewart Parnell: The Man and His Family* [1976]) he anchored that exemplar of Irish ambiguity firmly in the context of his bizarre family, the whole as but an eccentric part of the distinctive Anglo-Irish gentry tradition. In this latest study the author approaches his subject — no less a political opportunist — from a high politics point of view. This is a political life and Foster largely eschews the personal, familiar and ideological in what is a devastating *exposé* of what was the banality and ambition of

Randolph Churchill's career. Through the extensive use of private papers and especially those of Churchill himself, Foster sets out to examine the paternal image so carefully constructed by the young Winston Churchill in 1906. The result is a sharply, if at times narrowly, focused act of demolition which leaves the reader wondering why anybody ever thought Randolph Churchill important. The illusions surrounding Randolph as the tribune of Tory Democracy and as the man who put loyalty to party above everything else are ruthlessly exposed, and Churchill is left as a superficial and vain political egoist whose positive qualities were but the elements which explain his total fall from grace and power in 1886. Roy Foster therefore has produced an important and scholarly book.

For a politician who held office for barely ten months Churchill has generated a remarkable amount of biographical interest. Whereas great state servants like Spencer or Hicks Beach have few enthusiasts, Churchill now has three major studies devoted to his career and doubtless more will follow. The thrust of Foster's own argument heightens this paradox. Both as a young man in Ireland and later as Secretary of State for India and Chancellor of the Exchequer Foster demonstrates convincingly how slight was Churchill's grasp of either politics or policy. Influenced powerfully by those with whom he came into contact, Churchill quickly became obsessive about his immediate administrative enthusiasm, using it both as a lever against his ministerial colleagues and as the basis of his continuing attempts at personal self-aggrandizement. In Ireland the links with FitzGibbon and the Howth Circle led Churchill to pursue totally outmoded Irish strategies in 1885 linked to a Catholic reforming unionism despite the evident power of Catholic nationalism as represented in the figures of Parnell and Walsh. At the India Office during 1885 Churchill, having flirted with reform on a private visit, quickly switched to a revived Lyttonism under the influence of Roberts until domestic political circumstance dictated otherwise. Even the annexation of Burma, possibly Churchill's most long lasting administrative achievement, was an unreflected action largely dominated by Birmingham considerations where Churchill was a candidate. At the Exchequer in 1886 Churchill quickly adopted a profile of unimpeachable Gladstonian orthodoxy as the platform from which he was to launch his campaign to secure a personal domination over all government policy, only to be destroyed by the superficiality of his own reading of the political map and a failure to understand how deeply detested he was by both Salisbury and his allies. His was a derisory ministerial achievement and as Bertram Currie commented in 1901, 'I never heard him express any large or statesmanlike views, and in my secret heart I thought him rather deficient in quality' (p. 186).

In the more obviously political aspects of Churchill's career Foster is similarly destructive of illusions. The Fourth Party is shown to be largely an exercise in self-promotion on Churchill's part, with Gorst providing whatever intellectual underpinning it ever possessed. During the debates over the second Irish Land Act Churchill took a vigorously pro-landlord view while toying later in the year with notions of Fair Trade (something which in 1906 Winston Churchill thought it prudent to ignore). The struggle over the National Union emerges not as a Churchillian triumph but as a face-saving climb down which angered provincial Tories as Churchill decided to stay close by Salisbury in the eager anticipation that the Reform crisis might degenerate into a parliamentary dissolution. Tory Democracy is shown to be largely opportunism and the Dartford speech appears to be merely a preparation for the challenge over the estimates in December 1886. Even over the question of Ireland Churchill demonstrates a superficial and unreflecting expediency. Caught in a web of his own making after his foolish attack on the

Spencer administration over the Maamtrasna murders, Churchill in late 1885 is flailing around attempting to find an alternative to both Salisbury and Carnavon. His discovery of Ulster in 1886 was both providential and accidental, Churchill taking almost no part in the debates over Home Rule itself. By the summer of 1886 Foster suggests Churchill's only reputation was that of a man whom no one could trust.

What lay behind such an extraordinary political personality? At one level the answer presented by Foster is simple — an overwhelming egoism and ambition. But this will hardly provide a complete explanation since it was the tone and style of Churchill's ambition which illuminated his meteoric rise and his catastrophic fall from political grace. Here Foster has to move away from a purely political analysis in order to examine the personal and familial background to Churchill's career. It is an aspect of his study that might well have been extended since much of what he has to say is new. Churchill from earliest youth was vain and temperamental and despite an aristocratic pedigree looked in upon the political world as an outsider. The exclusion from society as a result of the Aylesford divorce case forced the Marlboroughs to go to Ireland. Churchill's own family and especially his brother Blandford were unsound financially, politically and morally. Churchill quickly contributed to this reputation by his eclectic range of friends, his biting tongue and his lack of conventional piety. It was a style unlikely to appeal either to Hatfield or Chatsworth and the resulting aloofness merely fuelled Churchill's own demotic desire to break the hold of the old gang. Add to this the fact that the Churchills were high spenders on a low income, that for long periods Churchill's marriage was such that he had virtually no home, and that from mid-1882 Churchill was almost certainly suffering from the degenerative syphilis to which he ultimately succumbed, and it becomes hardly surprising that Churchill's already taut personality should become impossibly arrogant, supercilious and neurotic. Any explanation of Randolph Churchill's extraordinary political career will ultimately have to return to these more personal aspects of his character.

Foster gives us a great deal upon which to base a final judgment but the reader does crave for more. This biography does not attempt to be a comprehensive one. Thus the reader is referred to previous studies for the details of Churchill's early life, the Prince of Wales episode is perhaps too succinctly dealt with, the biographical studies of Dr Quinault laid to one side without discussion and the treatment of the struggle for the National Union too tightly compressed. But it is in the *tone* of the reactions to Churchill that one desires a greater comprehensiveness. Thus this reviewer would have liked to know more about Churchill's relations with Salisbury so as to illuminate the style and language of both. In the same way a more extended treatment of Churchill's relationship with Hartington, something on which Churchill placed so many false hopes, would have helped to explain both the Whig enigma and the Tory failure. Finally the association with the mercurial Hicks Beach, a man who could have made Churchill so much more effective if he had so chosen, would have been interesting to pursue. On the other side many men clearly found Churchill an attractive and irreverent figure, although it must be said that these were mainly to be found outside the tight scrum of immediate political action, in figures such as Rosebery or James or amongst the members of Churchill's rackety private world like Henry Labouchere or Natty Rothschild.

These however are minor cavils about a stimulating and scholarly book and are provoked by the very quality of Foster's analysis itself. In political terms the author has totally dismantled the carefully constructed rescue-job of both Winston Churchill and Rhodes James. Given that Churchill's career seems to show nature imitating art it is unlikely to be the final word about a figure whose image is so much more pervasive than his achievement. As a political analysis however, this study will not be easy to challenge or overturn.

ALLEN WARREN
University of York

Edward Carson. By A.T.Q. Stewart. (Gill's Irish Lives.) Dublin: Gill and Macmillan. 1981. 150 pp. £2.60.

Dr A.T.Q. Stewart's study of Sir Edward Carson is one of 'Gill's Irish Lives', brief biographies directed at the general reader rather than the specialist. Dr Stewart is a professional historian who can write pleasing prose — an increasingly rare specimen these days — and he is particularly well fitted for the task of synthesizing the available work on his subject, as well as adding new material that he has looked up for himself. The result is a well conceived and well planned brief life, which traces the various phases of Carson's career — legal, parliamentary and extra-parliamentary — which places its subject in his proper context of Irish, not Ulster, Unionism, and explains the paradox epitomized by Carson's statue, larger than life, gracing the grounds of a Northern Ireland Parliament that he did not seek to create. But then, as G.M. Trevelyan once remarked in an essay on Cromwell's statue, some of these are 'oddly chosen or curiously placed'.

Carson stands outside a Parliament that is not his; what of his place in the history of the Parliament in whose life he did participate, as an M.P., a minister, and a member of the House of Lords? What interest does his biography hold for the student of British parliamentary institutions? At first sight, it may hardly seem to hold any interest at all. For Carson's name is primarily associated with the Ulster Unionist resistance to the third Home Rule Bill, and that resistance, though it manifested itself in parliamentary opposition, was essentially a popular movement, and one that drew its strength and its political style from open-air meetings, demonstrations and drill parades. But this is surely of importance for the historian of Parliament. For, as Dr Stewart shows, Carson was never an orthodox British M.P.; his Irish temperament drove him to demand that English politicians come clean: that they should say what they mean, and mean what they say. And his resolve to 'take whatever course is best for Ireland' was one that in the end threatened not only the stability of Anglo-Irish relations, but the basis of British parliamentary government.

The Ulster Unionists posed a problem central to the British representative system: what happens if a section of the population opposes bitterly a course of action decreed by the simple weight of a well-drilled parliamentary majority? Must the will of that majority prevail, come what may? This was at the heart of the Irish Nationalist-Liberal alliance formed in 1886 and continued down to Carson's day; and Carson, with his determination to do what he considered best for Ireland, was prepared to place his formidable talents at the disposal of that section of the population that asked the British Parliament a fundamental question about the nature of political obligation.

Dr Stewart's historical skills might have been supplemented by a wider approach of this kind. He describes clearly Carson's role in mainstream British politics between 1914 and 1918, but he perhaps misses the opportunity of explaining its broader constitutional significance. Carson's career illustrates the kind of influence, and indeed power, that a gifted back-bencher could exert in the special circumstances of politics in wartime. As Dr Stewart points out, Carson was more effective as a minister than critics have given him credit for; but in the state of British parliamentary politics in the war, governments feared above all attack in Parliament, attack which, given the nervously patriotic atmosphere, could open cracks in the edifice of government that in normal times would stay closed. Here again is appropriate material for the historian of Parliament-executive relations.

Carson was a British M.P. and an Irish Unionist, roles which, Dr Stewart demonstrates, were not always compatible. His concluding chapter, where he dissects Carson's magnificent, but bitter and destructive, attack on the Anglo-Irish Treaty in the Lords in 1921, provokes further reflection on the place of Carson, and of all Irish politicians, Unionist and Nationalist, in the British parliamentary tradition. In their prime the Irish Members enriched the British Parliament with their oratory and their personalities. But they did so at a price. In 1867 Walter Bagehot's classic study of the English constitution (English/British) noted that the key to the smooth working of British representative institutions lay in party government, but in party government that was, as he called it, non-sectarian: that is, non-partisan, non-ideological, and full of 'studied and illogical moderation'. 'The body is eager', Bagehot declared, 'but the atoms are cool.' This hardly applied to the Irish Members who came to Westminster after 1886. Certainly no one who reads Dr Stewart's thoughtful study of Sir Edward Carson can doubt that the removal of most of the Irish 'atoms' after 1922 rendered the British body politic cooler; but also, surely, poorer. In the wider setting of British constitutional history, therefore, Dr Stewart has written a book about a subject that is, perhaps, even more important than he himself acknowledges.

D.G. BOYCE
University College of Swansea

Property and Politics 1870–1914: Landownership, Law, Ideology and Urban Development in England. By Avner Offer. Cambridge: Cambridge University Press. 1981. xviii, 445 pp. £27.50.

The subject of this book is the historical redistribution of property rights in Victorian and Edwardian England. Property was the key to power and political esteem, but it also involved obligations, most obviously through taxation. As property rights became diversified, strain was put upon the prevailing distribution of political power and financial burdens. Dr Offer admits that this attenuation and emergence of property rights was 'not highly visible', but he contends that it was, and to some extent still is, 'a central mode of internal change'. The 'land question' lay at the heart of English politics between 1870 and the First World War.

The major part of the book consists of a detailed description of the evolution of tenurial politics from the emergence of local taxation as a political issue in the 1840s, through its incorporation into the rival doctrines of Conservatism and Liberalism, to its apogee in the ill-fated land campaign of Lloyd George. The story is a complex one, and is not made any simpler in the telling. The book is divided into five mutually supportive but not always closely interlinked sections. The first deals with solicitors, with their dependence on the property market for the majority of their income, and their opposition to a land registry which, they feared, would undermine their lucrative monopoly of conveyancing. This is an intriguing account of the evolution of a professional pressure group and, like the rest of the book, is meticulously researched and fully supported by a wealth of graphs, diagrams and statistics. In places this wealth takes on the appearance of a glut, with an over-enthusiastic fitting of trend lines, and with seldom a word in the text referring to key statistics like standard deviations and coefficients of determination which are liberally scattered through 22 tables; but other students will find here a full presentation of data for future research.

The second section presents a new survey of the distribution of tenure in the U.K. from 1896 to 1914, derived from the estate duty returns of the Inland Revenue. About one third of all land (by value) was owned by fewer than one per cent of all proprietors, but these great landowners shared a stake in the country with over one million house proprietors. It was this dual aspect of tenure, with the aristocratic whales and bourgeois minnows, that gave a foundation to the Conservative idea of the ramparts of property, 'a protective band of middling and small capitalists, professionals and rentiers huddled together for mutual support and forming a shield for large estates and capitals'.

A shield against whom? The other three sections detail the threats to landowners in town and country, and the political responses to these threats. For the rural landowner, the danger was the propertyless peasantry, a group dangerous because it acquired political power without the responsibility of political and financial obligations. Chamberlain carried his support for Jesse Collings's 'three acres and a cow' from the Liberal to the Unionist benches. Allotments and smallholdings were seen by some Conservatives as the only way to stem the tide of predatory socialism; others followed Lord Salisbury in opposing any politically motivated redistribution of property. The Liberals persisted with their romantically tinged nineteenth-century ideal of rural regeneration, though idealism played second fiddle to the dismal science. Smallholdings had to pay their way, and budgetary retrenchment was not compatible with a rural revolution; only 14,000 holdings were created between 1908 and 1914. The rural land campaign launched by Lloyd George may have frightened some estate owners into disposing of their property, but high interest rates on overseas investments furnished a positive reason for disposal; there was no radical redistribution of rural wealth, property or power in Edwardian England.

A greater threat to property came not from the restless masses but the reforming municipalities. The three decades before the war saw a rapid expansion of municipal capital in the form of sewers, buildings, gas, water and transport systems, and, as a concomitant, a quadrupling of urban debt. This debt had to be funded, someone had to pay for the accretion of property to town corporations. The Conservatives were much taken with Goschen's idea of assigning national taxes in relief of rates, and, having adopted him as their turncoat Chancellor in 1887, they supported his initiation of grants-in-aid. Land, they claimed, bore more than its fair share of tax; although rates were formally a charge upon occupiers, not owners, they were ultimately borne by landowners in the form of reduced rents. The rapid growth of non-landed capital in Britain in the second half of the nineteenth century had not been matched by a redistribution of tax liabilities from 'realty' to 'personalty', and industrialists should now be called upon to bear a fairer share of the costs of industrialization. The Liberals held that rates were seldom shifted to owners; they fell upon urban capitalists and the working class. The remedy was to be the separate rating of ground property, ideally to be based on the capital value of the land, not its realized income. Taxation of land values would claw back from landowners some of the windfall capital gains they acquired through urban and suburban expansion.

In the eight years from 1906 the Liberals failed to accomplish their desired reform of local taxation, for a mixture of economic and political reasons. The collapse of property values in the Edwardian housing slump, itself in part the result of rapid increases in rates, made this an inopportune time to raise tax burdens on property. The proposals for a tax on the artificial concept of 'pure rent' were ill-conceived, the land valuation was maladministered, and it was finally scuppered by Conservative opposition in the courts. Land tax proposals did nothing to help municipal corporations with an onerous and iniquitous rating system, but Liberal dislike of grants-in-aid (held to be a dole for landlords) led to a reduction in the scope of Exchequer support for municipalities at a time when their expenditure was still rising rapidly. The Liberal land campaign had foundered before the lights began to go out around Europe.

The breadth and complexity of the story told makes this a difficult book, and it is not always convincing when it leaves the high road of politics for the byways of the economics of the property market or the ideology of rural romantics. Dr Offer clearly knows his route, but most readers would benefit from better signposting through 400 pages of text, only six of which are devoted to a meagre and discursive conclusion. There is also a feeling that Offer overplays his hand. If the land question was so central to politics, and land reform so important to the Liberal government, why was so little achieved? If L.G. could overcome the resistance of the Inland Revenue to graduation of income tax, of the B.M.A. to health insurance, of the House of Lords to the People's Budget, why not that of solicitors to a land registry, of the Land Defence League to land valuation? Either the radical threat to landed interests was never as menacing as Offer makes out, or the political strength of land was more enduring than Conservative panic suggested.

The book does not answer all the questions that it poses, but this is not surprising in a work that sets out to integrate the many disparate elements of 'property' in late Victorian and Edwardian England. It demands and deserves careful reading.

PAUL JOHNSON
Nuffield College, Oxford

The Nonconformist Conscience: Chapel and Politics 1870–1914. By D.W. Bebbington. London: George Allen and Unwin. 1982. x, 193 pp. £10.00.

The 'Nonconformist conscience' was a force in late Victorian politics which has been often mentioned but has long needed full analysis. Dr Bebbington now offers a careful, even if hardly penetrating discussion of what he calls 'the Nonconformist passion for righteousness' in its political expressions. He rightly devotes a chapter to the Free Church Council, which became the busy mouthpiece of the Nonconformist conscience. A reading of his book does leave one wondering, however, whether the Nonconformists were ever quite so influential within British politics as they pretended (in two senses) to be, either in general or within the Liberal Party in particular. The campaign for disestablishment of the Church of England had obviously faded even before the end of the Victorian period, as had Nonconformist enthusiasm for Irish Home Rule. The Edwardian agitation against aspects of the 1902 Education Act fizzled out, despite a strident campaign of passive resistance and despite the existence of a Liberal government from 1905. Nonconformist interest in peace policies in diplomacy had become overshadowed by the end of the century by enthusiasm for imperialism and even (despite Lloyd George and C.P. Scott of the *Manchester Guardian*) for the Boer War. The Nonconformist conscience was certainly successful in its campaign against the Contagious Diseases Acts (free trade in venereal disease); but official Nonconformity never admitted the need for bold policies of positive social reform to overcome the poverty and deprivation of the new urban masses. Perhaps this was one reason why, quite suddenly, Nonconformist politics seemed to lose momentum during the later Edwardian years, while Lloyd George's social reforms were going through. It may be relevant, too, that after 1906 an absolute decline in Nonconformist numbers began; until then the relative fall in Nonconformist membership in proportion to increasing population had tended to be glossed over. Dr Bebbington ought to have said much more about what he firmly calls 'the end of the conscience'. Perhaps it had always been less solid than it seemed. Perhaps society was simply becoming more secular. Dr Bebbington suggests that the Nonconformist leaders were themselves now eager to withdraw from close involvement in politics. Yet this was the very time when the 1906 Parliament contained more Nonconformist Members than ever before. This important paradox requires much more consideration than it is given here. 'Nonconformity, in making corporate political action bulk so largely upon its programmes, is forsaking its first ideals': so argued one Nonconformist minister in 1909. In other words, ministers were being advised to stay in their pulpits and to stay off political platforms. Yet only seven years earlier another minister, in campaigning against the Education Act, had exclaimed confidently how 'they had no doubt they were on the side of God'. In the new Edwardian world, such a Victorian mixing of religion with politics was ceasing to seem either politically prudent or religiously proper. Perhaps Dr Bebbington will write another book to tell us why.

DONALD READ
University of Kent at Canterbury

Anthony Eden: A Biography. By David Carlton. London: Allen Lane. 1981. 528 pp. £20.00.

Anthony Eden's story seems to be like that of the Buddenbrook family — of a decline from the highest to the lowest of fortunes. But whereas for the Buddenbrooks the decline was one of circumstance, for Eden it was one of reputation, 'political' reputation.

From having begun his political life in 1923, the debonair and high-minded honour which followed Eden from the trenches and the League of Nations, to that which subsequently resulted from his alleged reluctance to join with Chamberlain in 'appeasing the dictators', and which culminated in his committing his country in March 1941 to despatch troops from Egypt to the Balkans, thereafter became increasingly suspect. His evident sympathy towards the Soviet Union during the 1941–4 period which led to his demanding more and more assistance for the Soviets might have redounded to his popularity, were it not for the fate of eastern Europe after the war and the complicity of his own and the American government in the division of spoils. His position, which by 1945 was more 'innocent' than that of Churchill, none the less seemed shabbier on account of his part in repatriating those

Russians who did not want to be repatriated to the punishments they would meet under Stalinist government, by now devoid of any semblance of the benignity attributed to 'Uncle Joe'; indeed this 'deal' compounded the rumours, already circulating, of Eden's previous willingness to cover up the Soviet massacre of Polish officers at Katyn. But even if his pro-Soviet position for the most part of the war could have been attributed to a measured, if adolescent, high-minded radicalism (related to his hatred of what he called the 'old tories'), that radicalism neither served him, nor came to much in the post-war period. Macmillan, and to a lesser degree Butler, rather than Eden, competed with Mr Attlee's governments in promising or promoting measures designed to win popular support for the new and mindless 'social democracy'. Eden had little or no interest in domestic affairs. But even his so-called 'expertise' in foreign matters failed him after his return to the Foreign Office in 1951. He became Prime Minister in 1955, but he failed to retrieve his reputation; and he retired ignominiously from politics in 1957, having presided over what has become a synonym for the greatest *débâcle* in modern British history: Suez.

But to Mr Carlton it is clear that even the high reputation with which Eden's political career began was unwarranted; and he chronicles the way in which Eden's views and interventions in the inter-war years were not what he or his supporters subsequently alleged them to have been. Mr Carlton balances detailed contemporary evidence against those accounts subsequently published by Eden in his memoirs (the first volume, entitled 'Facing the Dictators') to show that, far from being an 'anti-appeaser' or a consistent critic of Neville Chamberlain, Eden did not 'face' the dictators. Instead he advocated the appeasement of Italy, and, at times, Germany, to a greater or lesser degree. This was clear from his desire to 'appease' Italy following the Marseilles incident in 1934, and from his favouring limited recognition of Italy's Abyssinian conquests. Nor did he want a 'sanctionist' League of Nations; and he did not favour retaliation following the German occupation of the Rhineland in 1936, while with Chamberlain, he recognized Germany's Austrian aspirations. Indeed the differences with Chamberlain began only after July 1937; and they were not about principle, but rather arose from Eden's own inconsistencies vis-à-vis Italy. These inconsistencies, combined with a personal moroseness and pique, led to Eden's resignation in February 1938. But neither then, nor later, would he become the acclaimed leader of the anti-appeasers.

The book, therefore, brings forward one important conclusion: Eden's early reputation as an opponent of appeasement was undeserved. Although this has, for some time, been evident to those who know the sources, Mr Carlton's careful and detailed exposition of it is useful.

But the remainder of the book — roughly two thirds — dealing with the 1939–57 period is less valuable.

In part this is due to the author's failure to examine a sufficient number of records; or to treat those records which he does use, with due scepticism. For instance regarding the 'Greek' decision of March 1941, he is unaware of the extent, evident from the contemporary records, of the reservations which Cunningham and Longmore in Cairo entertained with regard to British involvement in Greece: this leads him to conclude, erroneously, that a 'misplaced optimism' in Cairo existed. Moreover the records also suggest that the reasons which led the Cabinet in London, ultimately, to support intervention were far more complex, and in certain respects, more suspect, than Mr Carlton's bland references to the 'weight' of 'neutral opinion' would suggest. In addition, the less than critical use of those records which he has seen, has had its mark. Mr Carlton's reliance, for example, on the Oliver Harvey diary, particularly for the Second World War period, has encouraged him in places to adopt the views of the jealous, radical, and pro-Soviet zealot as if they were at most, an appropriate reflection of some kind of historical truth, or at least, one of Eden's views. In the same way Mr Carlton's reading of the Chamberlain papers has prompted him to a 'new' interpretation of the events surrounding Chamberlain's replacement by Churchill — an interpretation hardly borne out by the document he mentions, and even less so by his references to the views of Beaverbrook and Wood — the first, at any rate, being one of the most notorious and unreliable gossips of the period, and the second anxious to save his skin.

But the book has a more serious underlying deficiency: the author fails to understand or examine the context for Eden of British party politics, or Eden's position in the Conservative Party. Although there are interesting accounts of the differences between Eden and Churchill, these do not help the author to resolve the more profound and complicated political questions. His references to such matters tend to appear without any substantiation. Thus we hear, for example, of Eden at the outset of his political career, being the evident 'heir' to Baldwin, with whom, apparently, he had a special relationship, and for whom he had an equally special 'loyalty' — suggestions which, for the author are designed to 'explain' Eden's successes, but for which not one jot of evidence is provided. Moreover for a good part of the book dealing with the war, Mr Carlton equates those in the Conservative Party who had been pro-Munich, with those who were anti-Soviet or anti-Communist. The author makes much of this theme; but no evidence for its justification is provided (it was, in fact, clear to Halifax, whom the author dubs anti-Communist, that some arrangement should be reached with the Soviet Union, after the outbreak of war). Moreover, Mr Carlton's general lack of historical insight is much evident throughout the book in his resort to meaningless clichés — from the beginning, when he refers to 'policy shaping' and 'policy making elite', to the end when we are given the 'diehard imperialist wing', the 'new pacifist and anti-colonialist set of ethics' and the Prime Minister's foreign policy being conducted 'against a background of growing domestic problems': what Prime Ministers have *not* had 'growing domestic problems'?

This looseness of thought and failure to understand the complexities of politics, also makes the account of Suez unsatisfactory. Mr Carlton describes his verdict as 'interim', since the official records are not yet available for this period. But, in fact, he does provide much detailed documentation. It is his characteristically ponderous interpretation of his sources which makes the account much more interim than it need be: its incompleteness is of a piece with Mr Carlton's superficial view of his subject as a whole. Perhaps, after all, there may still be something of Eden's reputation to be salvaged!

SHEILA LAWLOR
Sidney Sussex College, Cambridge

SOUTHERN HISTORY

Contents for Volume 5, 1983

case edition ISBN 0 86299 059 9
paper edition ISBN 0 86299 060 2

case edition ISBN 0 86299 059 9
paper edition ISBN 0 86299 060 2

Alan Sutton Publishing, 17a Brunswick Road, Gloucester GL1 1HG

Party and Management in Parliament, 1660-1784 *Edited by Clyve Jones*

CONTENTS

0-7185-1199-9
Spring 1984
about £16

LEICESTER UNIVERSITY PRESS

PARLIAMENTS, ESTATES & REPRESENTATION
PARLEMENTS, ÉTATS & REPRÉSENTATION

Volume 3, Part 1, June 1983   ISSN 0260-6755

Rudolfine von Oer   *Quod omnes tangit* as legal and political argument: Germany in the late Sixteenth Century

Stanislaw Russocki   De l'accord commun au vote unanime: les activités de la Diète nobiliaire de Pologne, XVIeme siècles

Jon Roper   Party and Democracy in Nineteenth-century Britain

Michael Bentley   British Parliamentary Institutions and Political Thought 1865–1914

Valerie Cromwell   *Votes for Women* in Britain: a social or political problem?

Marc Szeftel   Le règlement d'ordre intérieur de la Douma russe et sa portée constitutionnelle dans le domaine législatif

Published for the International Commission for the History of Representative and Parliamentary Institutions

Subscription price £20 (US $40.00) including postage

Pageant Publishing, 5 Turners Wood, London NW11, UK

Vol. LVI No. 133   May 1983   £6.00

BULLETIN OF THE INSTITUTE OF HISTORICAL RESEARCH

Edited by F.M.L. Thompson

UNIVERSITY OF LONDON
INSTITUTE OF HISTORICAL RESEARCH
Senate House, London WC1E 7HU